# Political Culture
# and Democracy in
# Developing Countries

# Political Culture and Democracy in Developing Countries

TEXTBOOK EDITION

edited by
## Larry Diamond

LYNNE
RIENNER
PUBLISHERS

BOULDER
LONDON

Published in the United States of America in 1994 by
Lynne Rienner Publishers, Inc.
1800 30th Street, Boulder, Colorado 80301

and in the United Kingdom by
Lynne Rienner Publishers, Inc.
3 Henrietta Street, Covent Garden, London WC2E 8LU

**Library of Congress Cataloging-in-Publication Data**
Diamond, Larry Jay.
    Political culture and democracy in developing countries / Larry Diamond.
    Includes bibliographical references and index.
    ISBN 1-55587-515-7
    1. Political culture—Developing countries. 2. Democracy—Developing countries.
3. Developing countries—Politics and government. I. Title.
JF60.P635 1994
306.2 ' 09172 ' 4  dc20                                            94-2568
                                                                          CIP


**British Cataloguing in Publication Data**
A Cataloguing in Publication record for this book
is available from the British Library.


Printed and bound in the United States of America

The paper used in this publication meets the requirements
of the American National Standard for Permanence of
Paper for Printed Library Materials Z39.48-1984.                    5 4 3 2

*To Gabriel A. Almond*

*From whom we have learned so much about political culture and democracy*

# Contents

# Foreword:
# A Return to Political Culture

*Gabriel A. Almond*

On a quick count, five books, two American Political Science Association presidential addresses, two *American Political Science Review* leading articles, and two *APSR* "controversies," all of them dealing with political culture themes, have appeared in the past several years.[1] From a simple quantitative point of view, it is evident that political culture research and theorizing has had a "return," or as Ronald Inglehart put it, a "renaissance." And the movements that have most actively polemicized against political culture as an explanatory variable (Marxism of various kinds, and rational choice theory) now seem to have run out of steam, appear to be inclined to negotiate settlements, rather than requiring unconditional surrender.

To speak of a return to political culture implies that there was an earlier time when political culture studies were here at hand and prospering, that this was followed by a time in which this approach declined, and that these studies are once again prospering. I want to comment briefly on these three phases in the history of political culture studies.

In the first several decades of the present century a "culture and personality" school emerged out of a synthesis of psychoanalytic ideas and cultural anthropology. This school, which included such luminaries of the past generation as Harold Lasswell, Ruth Benedict, Margaret Mead, Erich Fromm, and many others, sought to explain recruitment to political roles, aggression and warfare, authoritarianism, ethnocentrism, fascism, and the like in terms of the socialization of children—infant nursing and toilet-training patterns, parental disciplinary patterns and family structure, and similar routines and patterns of early childhood.

This school was most influential during World War II, when studies were made of the "national character" of the nations embroiled in the war. But these efforts to account for the political organization and policy tendencies of major nations such as Germany, Japan, Russia, Britain, France, and the United States, by means of hypotheses drawn from observations of child-rearing patterns in the village and tribal community studies of the anthropologists, and the clinical insights of psychiatrists drawn from the treatment of individual patients proved unconvincing to the mainstream social science disciplines as they rapidly expanded and professionalized in the decades after the war.

In reaction against this psychological and anthropological reductionism, the study of political culture developed in the 1950–1970 period, adopting a more rigorous methodological posture, requiring statistical sampling of large populations and of subcultural groups, the sophisticated construction and analysis of interview schedules, content analysis of the media and other materials, and similar quantitative and scientific procedures. Dominating this period of rigorous political culture research were major investigations such as the University of Michigan American election studies (soon replicated in Europe and elsewhere), the Princeton-Stanford Civic Culture Five-Nation study, and the Harvard Becoming Modern study carried on in six developing countries.[2] These major investigations stimulated many other smaller-scale, survey research studies, as well as secondary analyses of the growing collections of public opinion data. The older tradition of culture-personality research continued largely in the form of psychobiographical studies of political leaders.

The radical movements of the 1960s and 1970s challenged the legitimacy of the free and autonomous university, and particularly the objectivity of the social sciences, arguing that universities served as instruments for the exploitation of the working classes, ethnic minorities, and the Third World, and that the claim of objectivity was simply an ideology supporting and concealing this suppression and exploitation. The legitimacy of political culture research was specifically challenged on the grounds that political and social attitudes were reflections of class and/or ethnic status, or else were the "false consciousness" implanted by such institutions as schools, universities, and the media. If "so-called" political culture was simply capitalist ideology, there was no point in researching it, other than to expose it for what it was, and to bring to the surface the true socialist political culture that would lead to and sustain an equitable society and polity.[3] This view received enough support within the university community, and particularly in the social sciences and Third World area studies, to bring into question the validity of research that attributed some autonomous explanatory power to political attitudes and values. And while studies of this kind continued, they were beleaguered and heavily challenged by the neo-Marxists and the "dependency" theorists.

At least as significant in the discrediting of political culture studies was the attack from the discipline of economics, the introduction into political studies of market and bargaining models. The movement began at the end of the 1950s with the publication of Anthony Downs's *Economic Theory of Democracy* in 1957. This was followed by William Riker's *Theory of Political Coalitions*, which appeared in 1962.[4] In the next decades, there was an abundance of "rational choice," "public choice," and "positive political theory" studies of voting behavior, the formation of cabinets, decisionmaking in committees, coalition and decisionmaking in war and diplomacy, and the like, which purported to prove that all these political phenomena could be explained by the simple assumption that voters, politicians, diplomats, and military leaders were rational, short-run-interest maximizers. The practitioners of the rational choice approach asserted that this assumption of short-run interest on the part of political actors came sufficiently close to reality to predict political behavior accurately. Consequently, the study of political culture was largely unnecessary and wasteful of resources, because one could get sufficient explanatory power simply by assuming self-interested short-run rationality. In other words, political culture was not problematic, it was a given. One simply had to plug "rational choice" into any political context, and it would generate the programs and platforms of politicians, the votes of electors and legislators, the decisions of diplomatic bargainers, and the like. In the late 1970s and early 1980s, this "public choice" school in political science became the cutting edge of the discipline, dominating the learned journals and the political science personnel market.

Thus, mainstream political science—both the subjective or the cultural side, and the behavioral or the institutional side—was whipsawed by these reductionisms of the left and the right. But these two movements have in turn been weakened and discredited in the past decade. Social Democratic Marxism was already being questioned in the late 1970s. The increasingly heavy tax, transfer, and regulatory policies of the welfare state were being widely recognized as contributory to inflationary tendencies and serious problems of productivity. The 1980s witnessed a movement to the right in the elections in the advanced democratic nations and a conservative trend in fiscal and regulatory policy, a tendency still in full swing.

The Leninist variety of Marxism began to lose its legitimacy in the 1980s as its failure to bring about a "good society" became increasingly obvious. The incredible then happened: first the collapse of Eastern European communism, and by the mid-1980s the collapse of Marxism-Leninism in the Soviet Union itself. Marxist theorists now began to acknowledge the reality of pluralism, and the autonomy of governmental institutions, recognizing that politics is not simply the reflection of economic structures and process, and that attitudes and values are of importance in the functioning and transformation of economic and governmental institutions.

Similarly, in the 1980s and early 1990s the public choice theorists began to retreat from their intellectually expansive agenda, seeking to escape from the reductionist microrational quandary into which they had dug themselves. This retreat takes the form of a search for "institutions," a recognition that the rational self-interest models must be set in a context of laws, rules, ideas, beliefs, and values in order to contribute to explanation.[5]

Thus the ground has been reopened to a scholarship aspiring to objectivity, methodologically eclectic and ecumenical. Several varieties of "political culture" studies that had been forced underground or marginalized are now back in operation. Though none of them had completely gone out of business, rigorous survey research, historical and descriptive studies, and important theoretical work on political culture are now generally acknowledged to be making contributions to our understanding of economic growth and democratization. These processes are now understood as having significant psychological dimensions for the understanding of which these various methodologies are essential. This volume is an important step in this "return of political culture."

## Notes

1. Lucian W. Pye, *The Mandarin and the Cadre* (Ann Arbor: University of Michigan Press, 1987); Ronald Inglehart, *Culture Shift in Advanced Industrial Society* (Princeton: Princeton University Press, 1990); Michael Thompson, Richard Ellis, and Aaron Wildavsky, *Cultural Theory* (Boulder: Westview Press, 1990); Richard Merelman, *Partial Visions: Culture and Politics in Britain, Canada, and the United States* (Madison: University of Wisconsin Press, 1991); Roland Ebel, Raymond Taras, and James D. Cochrane, *Political Culture and Foreign Policy in Latin America* (Albany: State University of New York Press, 1991); Aaron Wildavsky, "Choosing Preferences by Constructing Institutions: A Cultural Theory of Preference Formation," *American Political Science Review* 84 (March 1990); Harry Eckstein, "A Culturalist Theory of Political Change," *American Political Science Review* 82 (September 1988); Ronald Inglehart, "The Renaissance of Political Culture," *American Political Science Review* 82 (December 1988); Herbert Werlin and Harry Eckstein, "Political Culture and Political Change," *American Political Science Review* 84 (March 1990); David D. Laitin and Aaron Wildavsky, "Political Culture and Political Preferences," *American Political Science Review* 82 (June 1988).

2. Angus Campbell, Philip Converse, Warren Miller, and Donald Stokes, *The American Voter* (New York: Wiley, 1960); Gabriel A. Almond and Sidney Verba, *The Civic Culture; Political Attitudes and Democracy in Five Nations* (Princeton: Princeton University Press, 1963); Alex Inkeles and David Smith, *Becoming Modern: Individual Change in Six Developing Nations* (Cambridge: Cambridge University Press, 1974).

3. See, for example, Fernando Henrique Cardoso and Enzo Faleto, *Dependency and Development in Latin America* (Berkeley: University of California Press, 1979).

4. Anthony Downs, *Economic Theory of Democracy* (New York: Harper and Row, 1957); William Riker, *The Theory of Political Coalitions* (New Haven: Yale University Press, 1962).

5. See, for example, Douglass C. North, *Institutions, Institutional Change, and Economic Performance* (Cambridge: Cambridge University Press, 1990).

# Acknowledgments

Both the substance and title of this book derive from a conference at the Hoover Institution funded by a grant from the Agency for International Development. I am grateful to the Agency for its support, and particularly to Travis Horel, the Agency Coordinator for Human Rights and Democratic Initiatives, whose strong personal interest and enthusiasm for the project was instrumental to its initiation. Later stages of the project, in which additional essays were recruited and all of them revised, updated, and edited, were supported by a three-year grant to the Hoover Institution from the John D. and Catherine T. MacArthur Foundation for a multidimensional program on democracy in developing countries. Throughout the production of this volume, the Hoover Institution provided various additional forms of support. I would particularly like to thank for their consistent personal support Director John Raisian and Associate Director Thomas Henriksen.

Finally, I have been very fortunate to have enjoyed the efficient and talented secretarial and administrative assistance of Nicole Barnes and Susan Hendrick. I thank them not only for their good work but for their calm and cheerful management of a daunting flow of paper over the life of this and several other simultaneous projects.

*Larry Diamond*

# · 1 ·

# Introduction:
# Political Culture and Democracy

## *Larry Diamond*

As Gabriel Almond observes in his foreword to this volume, political culture has "returned" to the study of comparative politics. Yet skepticism persists not only that political culture is a valid concept—that we can identify distinctive and relatively stable distributions of political values, beliefs, and understandings among populations—but also (and even more so) that political culture is a useful concept, that it explains very much.

Within comparative politics, few problems would seem to be more ripe for illumination from the political culture perspective than the sources of democratic emergence and persistence. Prominent theories of democracy, both classical and modern, have asserted that democracy requires a distinctive set of political values and orientations from its citizens: moderation, tolerance, civility, efficacy, knowledge, participation. Beliefs and perceptions about regime legitimacy have long been recognized as a critical factor in regime change, bearing particularly on the persistence or breakdown of democracy.[1] The path-breaking works of Almond and Verba and of Inkeles and Smith showed that countries do differ significantly in their patterns of politically relevant beliefs, values, and attitudes, and that within countries these elements of political culture are clearly shaped by life experiences, education, and social class.[2] As early as the late 1950s, Seymour Martin Lipset presented extensive evidence demonstrating a strong positive relationship between economic development and democracy, and that political beliefs, attitudes, and values were an important intervening variable in this relationship.[3] In 1980 Alex Inkeles and Diamond presented more direct evidence of a relationship between level of economic development and prevalence of democratic attributes within nations. Controlling to some extent for socioeconomic development, they found strong positive rank-order correlations between the average scores of country samples on such measures as tolerance, trust, efficacy, and personal satisfaction, and the per capita GNPs of the countries.[4] Recently, Ronald Inglehart has shown, with comparative survey data from more than twenty mainly European countries, that life sat-

1

isfaction, interpersonal trust, and rejection of revolutionary change are highly correlated not only with economic development but with stable democracy, and that "political culture may be a crucial link between economic development and democracy."[5]

Despite these considerable theoretical and empirical grounds for expecting that political culture plays an important role in the development and maintenance (or failure) of democracy, the post-1960s generation of work on democracy has tended to neglect the phenomenon, particularly at the mass level. In the Foreword, Almond mentions some of the political and intellectual trends in the social sciences during the 1960s and 1970s that challenged or dismissed political culture theory, from both the right and the left. But beyond the systematic assaults by dependency, neo-Marxist, and rational choice theories, much work on democracy from more conventional theoretical perspectives also gave short shrift to the political culture variable.

Incorporation of the political culture variable into analyses of the emergence of democracy has heavily focused (until recently) on the political elite. Two seminal theories on this dynamic, coming at the end of the 1960s, were those of Robert Dahl and Dankwart Rustow. In his classic *Polyarchy*, Dahl argues that stable polyarchy (liberal democracy) is most likely to emerge through a historical sequence wherein the expansion of political competition precedes the expansion of political participation (as in England and Sweden). Historically, this path was most successful because "the rules, the practices, and the culture of competitive politics developed first among a small elite" whose "ties of friendship, family, interest, class, and ideology" restrained the severity of conflict. "Later, as additional social strata were admitted into politics they were more easily socialized into the norms and practices of competitive politics already developed among the elites," reproducing some form of the system of "mutual security" that had developed through previous generations of more restricted conflict. The values, norms, and behavioral orientations underlying this system of mutual security—tolerance, trust, cooperation, restraint, accommodation—"are more likely to develop among a small elite sharing similar perspectives than among a large and heterogeneous collection of leaders representing social strata with widely varying goals, interests, and outlooks."[6] Although later theoretical analyses of democratic transitions would focus heavily on recent cases of democratic reemergence, frequently without explicit treatment of political culture (or of Dahl's contribution), they would owe an important intellectual debt to Dahl's formulation, and to Rustow's.[7]

Rustow's essay on democratic transitions has been particularly influential in directing attention to the elite variable, and to political, structural, and conjunctural factors shaping elite choices, interactions, and ultimately shifts in values. As in Dahl's theory, in Rustow's model democracy begins to emerge when a relatively small circle of elites decide, either in stages over time or in a historical period of fundamental change, "to accept the existence of diversity in unity" and to wage their conflicts peacefully through democratic rules and procedures.[8] In both theories, this critical decision stems initially not from a shift in fundamental values but from strategic considerations—altered perceptions of risk. Elites choose democracy instrumentally because they perceive that the costs of attempting to suppress their political opponents exceed the costs of tolerating them (and engaging them in constitutionally regulated competition).[9] Debilitating political stalemate, or the memory or danger of collective violence, may loom large in this calculation.[10] More principled motives may play a role in the choice of democracy, but "in so far as it is a genuine compromise it will seem second best to all major parties involved. What matters in the decision phase is not what values the leaders hold dear in the abstract, but what concrete steps they are willing to take."[11] Later, in a "habituation phase," contingent and instrumental choices by political leaders acquire a deeper commitment, rooted in values and beliefs, through continuous and successful practice of democracy by elites and the mass citizenry as well.

The emergence of democracy through elite accommodation is also a central theme of Arend Lijphart's work on consociational democracy in deeply divided societies. Although a prior tradition of elite accommodation is a favorable condition for this type of democracy, Lijphart underscores its "voluntary, rational, purposive, and contractual elements," which may lead previously warring political elites to accommodationist (consociational) structures as a way of avoiding the repetition of "tragic events" such as civil war,[12] or warding off "the constant peril of disintegrative tendencies."[13] Because this model features sustained domination and freedom of action by elites of self-contained, segmented groups ("closed camps"), combining mutual isolation at the mass level with overarching cooperation at the elite level, it is not dependent on the diffusion of elite conciliatory culture to the rank and file. Indeed, Lijphart emphasizes that the rules of the accommodationist game in the Netherlands "are part of the 'role culture' developed by and instilled in the elite, and not of the mass culture."[14]

In each of these theories we observe a gradual and incremental emergence of democratic culture, initially or predominantly at the elite level, as a result of the instrumental, strategic choices of a relatively small number of political actors. This was, in fact, the model, based on British historical experience, with which Almond and Verba began in their book *The Civic Culture*:

> The aristocratic Whigs found it possible to enter a coalition with non-conformist merchants and industrialists, to establish securely the principles of parliamentary supremacy and representation. The traditional aristocratic and monarchic forces assimilated enough of this civic culture to compete with the secularist tendencies for popular support and, indeed, to mitigate their rationalism and impart to them a love and respect for the sacredness of the nation and its ancient institutions.
>
> What emerged was a third culture, neither traditional nor modern but partaking of both; a pluralistic culture based on communication and persua-

sion, a culture of consensus and diversity, a culture that permitted change but moderated it. This was the civic culture. With this civic culture already consolidated, the working classes could enter into politics and, in a process of trial and error, find the language in which to couch their demands and the means to make them effective.[15]

In recently revisiting this treatment, and the later literature on transitions, Almond depicts democracy as in a continuous "state of becoming." Stable democracy may approach the "equilibrium version" of the process but is "open to improvement or deterioration" (as conveyed by the choice of Dahl's term, *polyarchy*, instead of *democracy*).[16] Political culture change would figure to be a key variable in determining how and when a political system moves closer to or further from the perfect ideal of "democracy."

The more recent literature on democratic transition articulates in significant (if not always explicit) ways with the earlier writings. The multivolume study of democratic transitions edited by Guillermo O'Donnell, Philippe Schmitter, and Laurence Whitehead similarly pursues a focus on the choices and strategic interactions of contending elites in an authoritarian regime and its democratic opposition. Like Rustow, they explicitly dismiss the importance for transition of prior consensus on democratic values. Regime change begins when a regime splits and some portion of its leadership calculates that its interests are best served (or risks best minimized) by liberalization. Implicit in the O'Donnell-Schmitter model is a shift by key elements of both regime and opposition toward a more flexible, instrumentalist political culture. However, the model emphasizes elite-led political processes of maneuver, mobilization, and negotiation—their analogy is an elaborate, multilayered chess game—in which political culture figures only as an implicit background variable. Although they do treat the resurgent political consciousness and activism of mass-level actors—the decline of fear, the surge in anger, and willingness to undertake risky acts of opposition—they give no systematic attention to how changes in values, norms, and beliefs stimulate, reflect, and advance the transition.[17]

More than many elite-centered approaches, that of Juan Linz does incorporate certain dimensions of elite political culture in its emphasis on the "loyalty" of democratic oppositions as a key variable in determining whether a process of breakdown will be set in motion. Although couched in the language of more specific behavioral imperatives, Linz's ten indicators of "loyalty" heavily involve such generic elements of democratic culture as tolerance, moderation, and above all a commitment to the rules of the democratic game (though they do not specify how deeply these orientations must be rooted in intrinsic values).[18] Other elite-centered approaches also tap implicit dimensions of political culture. Most influential, perhaps, has been the work of Michael Burton, John Higley, and Richard Gunther. Postulating three types of elite structures—"disunified," "ideologically unified," and "consensually unified"—Burton and Higley assert that only a consensually unified national elite "produces a *stable regime* that may evolve into a modern democracy."[19] Two features characterize a consensually unified elite: one is structural, "a more or less comprehensively integrated structure of interaction"; the other is cultural, "a largely tacit consensus about rules and codes of political conduct amounting to a 'restrained partisanship.'"[20] The emphasis on elite accommodation on the rules of the game—"institutionalizing behavioral norms that restrain expressions of conflict"[21]—bears a close kinship with Dahl's theory about the emergence of "mutual security" and Rustow's "decision phase" of the transition, as well as Linz's concept of democratic loyalty and the political and economic pacts that have figured prominently in the recent literature on democratic transitions.[22]

In a more recent formulation of the theory focusing more explicitly on democratic consolidation, Burton, Gunther, and Higley specify that a consensually unified elite can emerge rapidly through a pactlike "elite settlement" or more gradually through a process of "elite convergence." The latter involves the formation of broad electoral coalitions but also the gradual acceptance by "major dissident and hostile elites" of the legitimacy of the democratic system and the moderation of polarized ideological and policy positions. "This moderation gradually bridges the deep ideological chasms that mark elite disunity," and, together with the abandonment of "antisystem or semiloyal stances," breeds political trust.[23] Thus, we observe during democratic consolidation the emergence of an elite political culture featuring moderation, accommodation, restrained partisanship, system loyalty, and trust. These norms enhance the predictability and mitigate the intensity of political conflict.

As we will shortly see, this formulation articulates in important ways with the established literature on political culture and democracy. It differs in two key respects, however. First, it is little concerned with the prior value orientations that impel or motivate elites to forge these mutual understandings but, rather, tends to locate motives in the structural logic of the conflict situation. Second, to the extent that political culture enters into the analysis, it is almost exclusively at the level of the elite. Although their theory incorporates mass democratic participation and broadly shared acknowledgment of the legitimacy of democratic institutions as elements of consolidation, these are not examined. Burton, Gunther, and Higley assert, "What principally distinguishes unconsolidated from consolidated democracies is . . . the absence of elite consensual unity."[24] The neglect of mass-level phenomena can pose serious theoretical problems. As the author of their Mexican case study shows, elite settlements can be exclusionary as well as inclusionary, constituting important *obstacles* to democratic development and vitality.[25] And as John Peeler shows in that same volume, "The effectiveness of elite settlements depends on achieving" a wide inclusiveness among elites and a firm channeling of mass participation into mainstream institutions; where these are not achieved, and if necessary adapted and reproduced with social change, democratic stability can significantly erode.[26] Burton, Gunther, and

Higley concede this point but do not explore the mass-level changes in social structure, politics, and culture that may frustrate or reverse democratic consolidation processes.

Other prominent treatments pose the challenge of democratic consolidation—like that of democratic transition—mainly in terms of "democratic crafting" on the part of key leaders and elites. For Linz and Alfred Stepan, this involves such political challenges as constructing strong procedural commitments to constitutionalism and the rule of law, which will lead people to value democracy even when it does not perform well economically; gradually increasing democratic civilian control over the means of state violence while reining in nonstate violence; and designing new, more appropriate, and viable institutional arrangements such as parliamentary rule.[27] Whitehead's agenda of "critical choices and conjunctures" for consolidation involves an "iterative process of confidence-building" that forges "an unquestionable and overriding commitment" to democracy on the part of five key actors: the military, the propertied classes, the radical left, centrist politicians (inclined to sectarianism), and (in Latin America, at least) the United States.[28] Similarly for Giuseppe Di Palma, political crafting involves wise acts of political institution-building and accommodation on the part of political leaders to guarantee all key groups some stake in the system, such as through "the formation of broad and inclusive constitutional coalitions" and "well-timed tactics and signals" to reassure and sell democracy to strategic groups (such as business and state elites).[29] Each of these theories emphasizes the importance for consolidation of moderation, restraint, compromise, and rigorous commitment to democratic procedures on the part of elites, but none does much to specify the linkage between these types of behaviors and (changing) political values, ideas, and beliefs.

To be sure, there is in each of these treatments some appreciation of the role of cultural change in enhancing popular and elite commitments to democracy. Linz and Stepan refer to "the increased valorization of democracy as an important end that needed to be protected in and for itself," as a result of "the massive and unprecedented abuses of state power" by the bureaucratic-authoritarian regimes in Brazil, Uruguay, and Argentina (one could add Chile as well).[30] Di Palma notes a similar reevaluation by the Spanish left, as well as normative pressure on the right "because of the universal discredit befalling authoritarianism and the high normative standards attached more recently to democracy as a means to recreate a political community."[31] Richard Gunther identifies political learning across the spectrum of Spanish political elites as a key factor inducing pragmatism and moderation.[32] Whitehead concedes theoretically that democratic consolidation involves, in part, gradual enhancement of trust and cooperation between political rivals, and an increasingly "principled" rather than "instrumental" commitment to the democratic rules of the game, as well as broader changes in political perception achieved through mass political socialization.[33] But these auspicious changes in political culture are not systematically evaluated and explored. The overwhelming emphasis remains on elite choices, strategic interactions, and institutional designs. Indeed, it could be argued that no area of theoretical and empirical work on democracy has been more vigorously explored and advanced in the past decade than that of institutional choice and design.[34] In comparison to this massive current, work on the relationship of political culture to democracy has been (until very recently) a rather thin trickle.[35]

Perhaps it is no coincidence that concern with the development of a mass democratic culture, as an important factor in the emergence and consolidation of democracy, has been most evident recently in the writing of democratic citizen activists directly engaged in the tasks of civic education and mobilization.[36] Perhaps they have grasped something that the main currents of academic political science have missed in the past two decades: that political culture does matter to democracy, independently of other variables, and that the development of a democratic culture cannot be taken for granted as a natural by-product of democratic practice or institutional design. One may accept, as I do, that institutions heavily shape choices and behavior, and that the "habitual" practice of those choices and behaviors may eventually become embedded in intrinsic cultural values and norms. But that does not necessarily imply that institutional analysis can satisfy our need to understand the relationship of political culture to democracy, or that institution-building will suffice as an agent of culture change. Almond is surely correct to identify a "return" to political culture in the discipline of political science, but that movement has only begun to inform the contemporary study of democracy. Strangely, there remains a compelling need to address the linkage that inspired so much of the best earlier work on political culture: its relationship to the emergence and maintenance of democracy. This volume, focused on the dynamics of democracy in developing countries, represents one step toward returning the study of political culture to that classic and fundamental theme.

## Approaching the Study of Political Culture

The pioneering political culture work of the 1960s blazed important trails in articulating our understanding of what political culture is and how it is structured. That conceptual foundation has weathered well the test of experience. We have thus largely resisted, in this volume, the temptation of every new generation in the social sciences to reinvent the wheel. This comparative study was initiated with an explicit definition of *political culture* as "a people's predominant beliefs, attitudes, values, ideals, sentiments, and evaluations about the political system of its country, and the role of the self in that system."

The components of political culture—which may be summarized simply as distinctive predispositions or "orientations to action"[37]—have been classified into three types of orientations: a *cognitive* orientation, involving knowledge of and beliefs about the political system; an *affective* orientation, consisting of feelings about the political system; and an *evaluational* orientation, including commitments to political values and judgments (making use of information and feelings) about the performance of the political system relative to those values.[38] Pure evaluations, of course, may change readily with empirical experience, but norms and values represent the most deeply embedded and enduring orientations toward political action and the political system. These elements of political culture—the "subjective dimension" of politics—are, in turn, focused on three objective dimensions of political life: system, process, and policy. The *political system* consists of the regime, that is, the political institutions, both input (political parties, interest groups, mass media) and output (legislatures, executives, bureaucracies, courts); the specific incumbents of those institutions; and the nation. The *political process* is, of course, politics—the actions, conflicts, alliances, and behavioral styles of parties, interest groups, movements, and individuals. The political outputs are the policies and decisions of the system.[39]

As Lucian Pye has written, "The notion of political culture assumes that the attitudes, sentiments and cognitions that inform and govern political behavior in any society are not just random congeries but represent coherent patterns which fit together and are mutually reinforcing."[40] But this does not mean that all social groups share the same political culture, or that values and beliefs are evenly distributed throughout the population. As the elite-centered work cited above suggests, elites typically have distinctive values and norms (and, invariably, more information about the system), and they often lead the way in large-scale value change. Different ethnic and regional groups within a single country often have different value systems and worldviews. In addition, distinctive types of beliefs and norms may prevail in different institutional settings, such as the military, the bureaucracy, and the university. It may even be argued that differences in basic cultural biases are often greater within nations than between them.[41] Thus, we confront another respect in which we need to disaggregate political culture: the existence of *political subcultures*, which are explored in depth in a number of the country studies in this volume. For these reasons, it is at least somewhat misleading to talk of *the* political culture of a nation, except as a distinctive mixture or balance of orientations.[42]

Why are these beliefs, attitudes, and values important for understanding democracy? A crude stereotype of political culture theory sees in it a causal determinism, that political culture more or less predetermines both political structures and political behavior, and that the elements of political culture are relatively impervious to change over time. Such perspectives do not fairly characterize political culture theory, but they can be found in the literature. As John Booth and Mitchell Seligson note in their contribution to this volume, culturalist interpretations of Latin American politics are quite openly deterministic in seeing the authoritarian, hierarchical, monistic cultural heritage of Latin America as greatly diminishing the prospects for liberal democracy.[43] Pye's treatment of Asian political culture, while it recognizes some absorption of world culture, approaches the deterministic model in several basic assumptions: that political culture is "remarkably durable and persistent"; that this is so because of its rootedness both in distinctive national histories and in the personalities of individuals; that the latter are primarily shaped by powerful early socialization experiences in infancy and childhood;[44] and that political culture is essentially causally prior, that "cultural variations are decisive in determining the course of development." [45]

We began this study with a strong skepticism toward cultural determinism, for three reasons. One is theoretical. Almond argues that the cultural determinism stereotype is a distortion of his and other theories about the relationship between political culture and democracy. "The early advocates of political culture explanation . . . recognized that causality worked both ways, that attitudes influenced structure and behavior, and that structure and performance in turn influenced attitudes." Thus, "Political culture affects governmental structure and performance—constrains it, but surely does not determine it."[46] Three decades of research since *The Civic Culture* have shown that the cognitive, attitudinal, and evaluational dimensions of political culture are fairly "plastic" and can change quite dramatically in response to regime performance, historical experience, and political socialization. Deeper value and normative commitments have been shown to be more enduring and to change only slowly, in response to profound historical experiences and institutional changes.[47] "Once established, these orientations have a momentum of their own, and may act as autonomous influences on politics and economics long after the events that gave rise to them."[48]

A second reason for rejecting a deterministic approach to political culture is empirical. Considerable evidence has accumulated—including evidence from a recent twenty-six-country study of democracy in developing countries[49]—that although political culture affects the character and viability of democracy, it is shaped and reshaped by a variety of factors, including not only the types mentioned above—political learning from historical experience, institutional change, political socialization—but also by broad changes in economic and social structure, international factors (including colonialism and cultural diffusion), and, of course, the functioning and habitual practice of the political system itself.[50]

A third reason for avoiding a deterministic approach is normative, involving a "bias for hope." To argue that political culture is not at least somewhat "plastic" and open to evolution and change would be to condemn many countries like the ones examined in this volume—countries in the developing world and the former communist bloc that have not consolidated democracy—to perpetual authoritarianism and praetorianism. This not only offends the sensibilities of democrats, it contradicts the empirical evidence of real and enduring cultural change in countries—such as Germany, Japan, Spain, and Italy—that were once written off as infertile soil for democracy. By understanding how concrete elements of political culture affect democracy, positively and negatively, and establishing their sources of continuity and change, we will be better able to understand the conditions for developing and consolidating democracy in the types of countries considered in this volume.

## Theories of Political Culture and Democracy

Theories about the relationship between political culture and democracy date back at least to the classical Greek political thinkers.[51] From Aristotle in particular, political culture theory has inherited concerns for the importance of moderation and tolerance, and for the dangers of political extremism and unfettered populism that continue to resonate in the contemporary literature. As noted above, the development of a pattern, and ultimately a culture, of *moderation, cooperation, bargaining,* and *accommodation* among political elites has emerged as a major theme of the dynamic, process-oriented theories of democratic transition and consolidation. But well before this generation of work, theorists such as Almond, Verba, Lipset, Dahl, and Inkeles were identifying these orientations in political culture as necessary, or at least highly functional, for the development and maintenance of democracy. These elements of political culture were necessary, they argued, to cope with one of the central dilemmas of democracy: to balance cleavage and conflict with the need for consensus.[52] They further argued that these orientations tend to fit together and cohere. Moderation and accommodation imply *tolerance* for opposing political beliefs and positions, and for social and cultural differences more generally; *pragmatism* and flexibility, as opposed to a rigid and ideological approach to politics; a sense of *trust* in other political actors, and in the social environment more generally; a *willingness to compromise,* springing from an intrinsic belief in the necessity and desirability of compromise; and a certain *civility* of political discourse and respect for other views. To be sure, moderation and accommodation may be induced by structural and institutional incentives and constraints, absent underlying norms—that is a key point of the transitions literature. But these behavioral orientations will be difficult to sustain in the long run unless they become embedded in this deeper, more coherent and encompassing syndrome of beliefs and values, and not only among elites but at the mass level as well.[53]

The interrelationships among these factors are dense and intricate. Pragmatism—one of the qualities Tocqueville first identified as a distinctive property of American democracy—facilitates bargaining and compromise by rendering goals negotiable and opinions and beliefs open to engagement and new information. Such intellectual openness promotes tolerance by accepting "the idea that no one has a monopoly on absolute truth and that there can be no single, correct answer to public policy issues."[54] Thus, pragmatism restrains the role of ideology in politics, and hence the danger of conflict polarization. Moreover, because the goals and beliefs of the pragmatist are implicit and so adaptable to circumstances, they are less likely to be totally abandoned under challenge or stress. From this perspective, the implicit character of democratic commitments is also their strength, rendering them sacred and beyond question or calculation.[55]

Because pragmatism generates flexible goals, it is consistent with a commitment to democratic procedural norms that takes precedence over substantive policy objectives. This overriding commitment to democratic proceduralism is a critical political cultural condition for democracy. In combination with policy pragmatism and political tolerance, it promotes moderate partisanship, and these qualities together are most likely to limit the politicization of social life and the rancor of political intercourse. Similarly, a diffuse sense of political and social trust—what Harold Lasswell called "confidence in the benevolent potentialities of man"[56]—not only facilitates bargaining and compromise but encourages political discussion, makes political conflicts less threatening, and thus helps to transform politics into a non-zero-sum game in which leaders and followers of defeated parties can accept exclusion from state power without having to fear for their basic interests.[57] As elite theorists have argued for the development of "consensually unified elites," so Almond and Verba, Lipset, and others maintained earlier that political moderation and accommodation at the mass level are facilitated by structural patterns of social interaction that bring people together regularly across major social and political cleavages.[58]

Many recent treatments of the transition and consolidation processes have recognized (with varying degrees of explicitness) the importance for democracy of developing this moderate, accommodating style of political behavior. To summarize, I believe their treatment of the political culture variable has suffered from three defects. First, they generally neglect or altogether ignore mass culture. Second, they focus mainly on behavior, and little on the complex processes by which behavior sheds its contingent, instrumental quality and becomes rooted in enduring values.[59] Finally, they ignore completely other elements of political culture—relevant mainly at the mass level—that have been theorized as important for maintaining democracy. Because the mass level has been so much neglected in recent democratic theorizing, it is worth recalling here John Stuart Mill's seemingly self-evident observation:

> The people for whom the form of government is intended must be willing to accept it; or at least not so unwilling as to oppose an insurmountable obstacle to its establishment. They must be willing and able to do what is necessary to keep it standing. And they must be willing and able to do what it requires of them to enable it to fulfil its purposes. The word "do" is to be understood as including forbearances as well as acts.[60]

*Dispositions Toward Authority*

Dispositions toward authority drive to the very heart of what democracy is about. Early in the development of the political culture literature, Inkeles portrayed democratic political culture as the inverse of the authoritarian personality syndrome that makes for political extremism. Inkeles identifies the components of this syndrome as including faith in powerful leaders; hatred of outsiders and deviates; a sense of powerlessness and ineffectiveness; extreme cynicism; suspicion and distrust of others; and dogmatism. To list the components of the inverse syndrome is to comprehend much of what embodies a democratic culture: flexibility, trust, efficacy, openness to new ideas and experiences, tolerance of differences and ambiguities, acceptance of others, and an attitude toward authority that is neither "blindly submissive" nor "hostilely rejecting" but rather "responsible . . . even though always watchful."[61] Or as Sidney Hook phrased it, "A positive requirement of a working democracy is an intelligent distrust of its leadership, a skepticism stubborn but not blind, of all demands for the enlargement of power, and an emphasis upon critical method in every phase of social life."[62] Intimately connected to this is a belief in what Jacques Maritain called the "inalienable rights of the person" and Sidney Hook the "intrinsic worth or dignity" of "every individual."[63]

It is precisely because he believes Asian political cultures are more or less commonly lacking in these orientations of individualism and suspicion of authority that Pye sees the prospects for liberal, competitive democracy as limited in Asia. Treating conceptions of power (and its cognate concepts of authority and legitimacy) as the crucial cultural axis for understanding alternative paths of political development, Pye identifies (within the considerable political cultural variation in Asia) common tendencies to emphasize loyalty to the collectivity over individual freedom and needs; to favor paternalistic authority relations that "answer deep psychological cravings for the security of dependency"; and therefore to personalize political power, shun adversary relations, favor order over conflict, mute criticism of authority, and neglect institutional constraints on the exercise of power.[64] Thus:

> Distaste for open criticism of authority, fear of upsetting the unity of the community, and knowledge that any violation of the community's rules of propriety will lead to ostracism, all combine to limit the appeal of Western democracy. As a result, the development of more open and enlightened politics in Asia is likely to produce a much more contained form of popular participation in public life. At best it is likely to be a form of democracy which is blended with much that Westerners regard as authoritarian.[65]

Although Pye may impute more staying power to political culture orientations than is warranted, he offers a particularly lucid theoretical expression of the compatibility between democracy and core elements of political culture, and of the way institutional forms like democracy may operate differently in different cultural contexts.

Nevertheless, political culture theorists do not assert that democracy is served by unqualified individualism. Common to all these theoretical formulations—and perhaps most prominently that of Almond and Verba, as we will see shortly—is a concern for balance among conflicting values. Authority must be questioned and challenged, but also supported. J. Roland Pennock underscores the importance for democracy of "individuals who are conscious of their rights and willing to stand up and struggle for them against actual or threatened tyranny."[66] Yet he also argues persuasively that radical individualism cannot sustain democracy but must be balanced by a "public spirit" that offers commitment to the welfare of the collectivity, and to a "unifying sentiment," such as nationalism.[67] Similarly for Michael Thompson, Richard Ellis, and Aaron Wildavsky, democracy partly requires "the participatory norms that come with the . . . cultures of individualism and egalitarianism."[68] Individualism legitimates competition and conflict (and thus alternation in office), while egalitarianism "punctures authority's pomposity . . . and prevents governmental power from growing arrogant or domineering."[69] However, democratic governability also requires "hierarchy to inculcate the norm that the parts should sacrifice for the whole."[70]

## Legitimacy, Participation, and the Civic Culture

It is by now a cardinal tenet of empirical democratic theory that stable democracy also requires a belief in the legitimacy of democracy. Ideally, this belief should be held at two levels: as a general principle, that democracy is the best form of government possible, and as an evaluation of the believers' own system, that in spite of its failures and shortcomings, their own democratic regime is better than any other that might be established for their country.[71] This core component of democratic culture derives partly from the performance over time of the democratic regime, but it is also influenced (especially in the early life of a regime) by how specific democratic institutions articulate with traditionally legitimate forms of authority, and later by socialization, expanding education, and other types of social and cultural change. Regime performance is not only assessed in terms of economic growth and social reform but encompasses several crucial political dimensions as well: the capacity to maintain order, to govern with probity and transparency, to maintain a rule of law, and otherwise to respect and preserve the democratic rules of the game.

One factor that would seem to enhance the legitimacy of democracy among citizens is direct experience with it. For this reason, as well as for the quality and authenticity of democracy, *participation* is another central element of the ideal-typical mass democratic culture. This implies both valuing popular participation as a norm of political life and a behavioral disposition actually to participate in politics. Among the features of "participant citizenship," as identified by Inkeles, that might be considered especially important for democracy are an active interest in public affairs, "validated by keeping informed and expressed through participation in civic action," and an orientation toward modern forms of authority and objective rules rather than toward traditional and/or arbitrary forms of authority.[72]

For Almond and Verba, a "participant political culture" involves "an 'activist' role of the self in the polity,"[73] manifested not only through voting but through high levels of political interest, information, knowledge, opinion formation, and organizational membership as well. Underlying a participant orientation is the self-confidence and sense of competence on the part of citizens that their political action may actually produce a change in policy or redress of grievances—what Almond and Verba call *political efficacy* or competence.[74] This may be shaped by many factors, including early socialization and the actual responsiveness of the political system, as well as by the general belief in democratic legitimacy.

However, Almond and Verba argue that the distinctive property of a "civic culture" is not its participant orientation but its mixed quality. In a "civic culture," the participant role is fused with and balanced by the role of political *subject*, embodying passive acceptance of political authority and allegiance to it, and the *parochial* role, which binds the individual to traditional, nonpolitical groups such as family and church and absorbs some of the energy and affect that might otherwise be concentrated entirely on politics. Thus, this mixture of roles moderates the intensity of political participation by giving it (for most citizens) an "intermittent and potential character."[75] At the same time, it provides the system with legitimacy and support, and yet preserves institutions outside the state that might check the abuse or excessive assumption of power by the state. The fusion of participant and subject roles may be seen as one expression of the types of balance articulated above, between vigilance and allegiance toward authority, between individualism and hierarchy or public spirit.[76]

There is as well another sense in which the balanced nature of the civic culture tempers its intensity. Social trust and cooperativeness, and overarching commitments to the system, the nation, and the community moderate the conflicts and bridge the cleavages of politics. Trust also facilitates the vertical ties between elites and their constituencies that keep politics functioning within the institutional boundaries and constraints of democracy. These beliefs and norms keep political conflict from becoming so polarized and intense that it might destabilize the system.[77]

How important are these political cultural "conditions for democracy"? Pennock makes the strong argument that "nearly all the elements of political culture, in significant degree and especially for the political activists in a polity, may be said to be necessary conditions for democracy. Furthermore, this group may well comprise a sufficient condition for democracy."[78]

However, he does not clarify whether there is some necessary temporal sequence by which they must appear. Are these elements of political culture preconditions for the emergence of democracy? Dating back to Rustow, transitions theorists have made a compelling case that there are few preconditions for the emergence of democracy; that in fact "there may be no single *pre*condition for the emergence of a democratic polity," and that "the preconditions for democracy may be better conceived as the outcomes of democracy."[79] With the exception of a commitment among political elites to the legitimacy of democracy and its procedural norms—which may be, initially, quite instrumental and contingent—none of the above elements of political culture seems necessary for the establishment of democracy. Most of them, indeed, appear to be more important among the elite, especially early on. Several theoretical questions still loom large in the literature: How broadly must these beliefs and values be shared across various groups and strata of a nation's citizenry? How soon after the inauguration of democracy must they develop? How important are they to democracy, relative to other types of conditions? Which elements of political culture are most important? What determines the evolution and transformation of political culture over time? What specific consequences for democracy can we attribute to various elements of political culture? These are the sorts of questions on which this volume seeks to advance our understanding.

## Political Culture and Democracy in Developing Countries

Despite the "renaissance" of political culture work, until recently rather little attention has been directed to how political culture affects the possibilities for democracy in the less developed world and the newly transforming polities of the former communist bloc.[80] This volume seeks to fill some of that void. In a sense it may be said to follow in the comparative tradition of Pye and Verba's edited study, *Political Culture and Political Development*, although it is more explicitly focused on democracy and on developing countries. This special paperback edition, specifically intended for classroom use, reproduces from the hardcover edition the five case studies examining political culture and culture change broadly within countries or regions. It also includes, again from the original edition, a study of the political culture of state elites and their impact on democracy in Turkey and a study of religious orientations toward politics in Latin America.

In the first of the five general case studies, Richard Sisson adds to our theoretical understanding by illuminating the dynamic interaction between elite and mass political cultures in India. In line with elitist theories of democratic transition and emergence, he shows how a political culture of bargaining and accommodation began with the early development of the electoral process under British colonial rule during the late nineteenth century. As

Dahl and Rustow, among others, have theorized, the operation of a limited and gradually expanding democracy, dominated by elites, during the final six decades of colonial rule, gave rise to a system of mutual security and tolerance and the increasing internalization of liberal, constitutionalist values among contending elites. But, Sisson demonstrates, there was more to the emergence and institutionalization of democracy than these elite processes of consensus formation and habituation. Traditional cultural mechanisms merged with the emergent democratic processes to emphasize arbitration as a central mechanism for conflict resolution. And elites reached out to mass society during the nationalist movement, raising the Indian masses to new levels of political consciousness, building a wide array of voluntary organizations, and stimulating democratic awareness and participation. Crucial to all of these processes was political leadership, ideology, and choice, particularly in the person of Mahatma Gandhi, who emphasized the importance of liberty, the consensual resolution of conflict, the ever-widening incorporation of excluded social groups, and nonviolent mass mobilization for independence. The result was the considerable diffusion of democratic culture from elite to mass constituencies.

Making extensive use of longitudinal survey data, Sisson demonstrates the emergence "within two decades after independence, if not before," of a mass political culture that "had become knowledgeable about elections, had opinions about governmental performance, and believed in the appropriateness of institutions closely associated with a democratic regime; . . . a public strongly oriented toward government, with the view that government should govern and provide, and that governments should be held accountable." Sensitive to the phenomenon of culture change, Sisson shows how the decline in party institutions and government performance and the growing personalism of politics (changes again initiated by elites) produced changes and elements of erosion in mass democratic culture (including a decline in support for India's political institutions). Nevertheless, despite growing tensions and challenges for India's democracy, its mass political culture continues to manifest impressive levels of knowledge, participation, innovativeness, and belief in such core democratic principles as the efficacy of the vote. This considerable resilience of mass democratic culture must certainly play some part in the persistence of democracy itself.

Naomi Chazan's exposition of African political cultures, in Chapter 3, shows that a crucial difference between the Indian subcontinent and the African continent was time. In contrast to India, colonial rule came relatively late to Africa and afforded little experience with the operation of democratic institutions prior to independence. As Chazan also shows, precolonial Africa also evinced considerable cultural variation and fragmentation (much greater than in precolonial India). But the lack of democratic political experience emerges from her analysis as a particularly fateful variable. As a result, when elite politics and mass political mobilization finally arose, it was almost exclusively in the context of the anticolonial struggle, with self-governance and electoral competition coming only very briefly at the end. Democratic norms were thus expressed primarily in terms of protest, opposition, and "counter-hegemony," rather than in terms of tolerance, liberty, and democratic procedures. Elites formed alliances but lacked real cohesion among themselves or stable mass bases of support; what bound them together was an instrumental concern for power. The democratic constitutional systems left behind by the colonial powers were "alien in derivation and design," with little base of understanding or legitimacy to support them, activated in a political atmosphere that "called for the rejection of imported models." As Chazan concludes, "These circumstances could hardly have been less propitious for the entrenchment of liberal political cultures." Formal democratic institutions quickly collapsed under the weight of corruption and intolerance of dissent, and state power was expanded, centralized, personalized, and corrupted. In the absence of broad political legitimacy, patterns of statism, patrimonial rule, abuse of power, and political repression became entrenched, with governments changing mainly through violence and democracy continuing to manifest itself as protest and resistance. Yet with the growth of associational life, especially during the past decade, civil society has done much to obstruct authoritarian rule and to reintroduce the possibility for democracy from the ground up. This trend, along with a new appreciation for the relational aspects of democracy, involving genuine participation and accountability, offers hope for a more democratic future in Africa.

Hope for democratic development in Latin America is suggested in Chapter 4 by the analysis of John Booth and Mitchell Seligson, who provide the most explicit assessment of mass political cultures in this volume. Comparing survey data from Mexico, Costa Rica, and Nicaragua on two key dimensions of democratic culture—support for extensive political participation and support for civil liberties and rights of dissent—they find some surprising results. Despite Mexico's authoritarian history and politics, their (1978–1979) sample of urban Mexicans manifested high levels of support for democratic civil liberties and rights of participation. And despite Costa Rica's four decades of democratic experience, in contrast to Nicaragua's continuous history of authoritarianism, their (August 1989) Nicaraguan sample manifested support for basic liberties at levels equal to or greater than the Costa Ricans (even when controlling for individual status). Urging from this analysis a rethinking of the relationship between political culture and regime type, they posit multiple possible paths toward democratic culture change: in Costa Rica, reciprocal influence between elite culture, mass culture, and institutional development; in Mexico and Nicaragua, the emergence of democratic commitments partly as a general reaction against authoritarianism and partly as a utilitarian norm for regime opponents who need the protection of civil liberties. While recognizing other sources of culture change (international diffusion, ideology, regime rhetoric), they break new ground in showing how "short-term utilitarian considerations of power rather than long-term historical-cultural factors may determine levels of commitment to civil liberties."

In Chapter 5, we observe a very different path toward democracy and democratic culture, via rapid and broadly experienced socioeconomic development in Taiwan. As Ambrose King shows, this rapid and well-distributed economic progress had contradictory effects. On the one hand, it generated strong public support for the authoritarian system, giving it a broad base of political legitimacy. Yet on the other hand, it also generated pressures and desires for political change. In particular, the dramatic growth in the numbers of people with middle-class status and higher education produced desires for political participation and greater exposure to Western democratic ideas and norms. Some of these cultural changes were evidenced in pathbreaking initiatives of political opposition, but the primary effect of this interplay between support for the system and desire for participation was the growth of popular sentiment for "moderate and gradual democratic reform." And that is what Taiwan got, not only because of the pressures from below but because of the historical vision, determination, and willingness to accommodate change on the part of the top Kuomintang (KMT) leadership, particularly Chiang Ching-kuo. To this mix of causal forces, King also adds the important factor of several decades of mass-level political competition, primarily in local-government elections but also in limited voting for national political bodies as well. This extensive experience with limited electoral competition gradually increased mass political efficacy and consciousness while inclining contending elites in regime and opposition toward greater mutual trust and commitment to democratic procedures (as elite-centered theories argue). Thus, while King sees in the Taiwan experience a "non-paradigmatic search for democracy," Taiwan does powerfully illustrate and support prominent hypotheses in both modernization theory and transitions theory about the relationships among social change, cultural change, political initiative, and regime change.

The role of political experience and practice in shaping political culture and democratic possibilities is richly illustrated in Chapter 6, where Christine Sadowski analyzes the contributions of autonomous groups to democratic change during the final two decades of communism in Eastern Europe. She shows that those communist regimes did not succeed in generating real bases of popular legitimacy for their rule; that there was a sharp contradiction between the overt mass behavior of compliance with authority and a covert culture of opposition and resistance. The "political culture of allegiance" was a cruel illusion. Because compliance was only instrumental,

stemming from widespread repression and fear, these systems were extremely brittle. When the credible threat of repression subsided in the Gorbachev
era, fear eroded, compliance declined, and citizens increasingly organized
against the regime. As they organized and fashioned underground channels
of information, exposing the truth about corruption, repression, and environmental abuse, they destroyed what little legitimacy these regimes may have
had.

Sadowski identifies a number of ways in which autonomous group
activity served to alter political cultures and lay the foundations for democratic change. By showing that individuals could organize independent of the
supposedly monolithic state to achieve concrete objectives (even when these
did not directly challenge the state), autonomous groups both punctured the
psychology of fear and reduced the pervasive feelings of passivity, fatalism,
and demoralization. Providing heroes, symbols, models, and inspiration to
long-inert populations, they produced a new sense of political efficacy and
activism and a "revitalization of social morality." At the same time, they
enabled many citizens to learn through practice essential skills of democratic
strategy and mobilization, while also affording experience in free discourse
and "the art of gathering accurate information." The spread of that information—often shocking even to cynical publics—transformed the cognitive
dimensions of political culture.

In all these respects, Sadowski shows, political culture appeared responsive to political action and structure. Yet her analysis also uncovers enduring
aspects of political culture, with contradictory implications for the future of
democracy in Eastern Europe. On the one hand, democratic prospects in
Poland, Hungary, (the former East) Germany, and Czechoslovakia are to
some extent strengthened by the patterns of "civic-mindedness" derived both
from preexisting political cultures and redeveloped in the waning years of
communist rule. On the other hand, in all of Eastern Europe, negative legacies of communist rule weigh on the political cultures and prospects of the
new democracies. These include a deep-seated aversion to party politics, an
antimarket expectation that government will provide, the absence (ironically) of a healthy subject orientation, and the paucity of trust, tolerance, and a
willingness to compromise (though less so in Hungary than elsewhere).

In Chapter 7, Ergun Özbudun shows the way in which the centralized,
despotic traditions of the Ottoman Empire shaped political culture in Turkey
into the twentieth century. Precluding development of autonomous centers of
power, these imperial structures bred a political culture that exalted political
authority and service to the state, and led the masses to believe in the paternalistic nature of the state. Even with the populist revolution of Kemal
Atatürk early in this century, power remained centralized, while Kemalist ideology stigmatized and suppressed class and other social divisions. Yet despite
the hierarchical structure and culture of this revolutionary transformation, it

also engendered prodemocratic ideas of popular sovereignty and equality before the law that were to blossom later into a competitive democracy.

A recurrent theme in Özbudun's chapter is the role of modernization and social change in creating a more diverse, pluralistic society that undermined the long-standing unity of the nation's elites. Initially, this meant the development of a political elite of businessmen, politicians, and professionals in conflict with state elites. Following the 1960 coup, state elites imposed a constitution checking and constraining the power of elected politicians. This constitution, and that imposed by the military after the 1980 coup, reflected the values and anxieties of state elites who were hostile to competitive party politics. With social and political change after 1960, only the military elites maintained their cohesion, a result of their strong socialization practices. Central to this unity, Özbudun shows, was a belief system that was deeply skeptical of politicians and political conflict, and that viewed as a duty of the military its intervention in politics if necessary to protect the fundamental character of the state. In large part, this meant preserving the Kemalist ideological legacy of a secular, developmentalist state submerging class differences. This powerful sense of mission led to a "half-coup" in 1970, a full coup in 1980, and constitutional changes thereafter, strengthening the presidency and the military role as guardian of the political system.

Given that religion is an important source of basic value orientations, we should expect that it can have a powerful impact on political culture and thus democracy. In Chapter 8, Paul Sigmund traces the rise of new Catholic orientations toward politics in Latin America after World War II, first through the moderate, social welfarist "opening to the left" represented by Christian Democratic parties, and then through the more radical movement of "liberation theology." Both these movements represented sharp departures from the historical posture of the Roman Catholic Church as "conservative, corporatist, and hostile to liberal democracy." Christian democracy emerged alongside and was stimulated by the Second Vatican Council in the early 1960s, which denounced economic inequality and committed the Church to political democracy. Both responded to increasing social ferment and mobilization and a rising threat from revolutionary Marxism. But one effect of these doctrinal shifts, Sigmund shows, was to legitimize an increasingly radical approach within the Latin American Church, influenced by the growing intellectual and political influence of Marxism and the rise of dependency theory during the 1960s. Applying Christian teachings to the needs of the poor, liberation theology sought to raise the political consciousness and participation of the poor by working at the grassroots. In doing so, it challenged (at least implicitly) the hierarchical nature of authority in the Catholic Church and alarmed its higher ranks by its liaisons with Marxist forces. This brought in reaction a new turn in Catholic thinking in the late 1970s, ultimately advanced and sharpened by the Vatican itself, warning against "ideologization" but co-opting important elements of liberation theology such as its grassroots Christian organization and its special concern for (but not class solidarity with) the poor.

Sigmund shows how these shifts in Catholic thinking not only affected or reinforced political trends—toward and away from democracy—but were also in turn shaped by these political changes. It was in good measure the experience with severe repression in Central America and large parts of South America, and the attendant utter collapse of revolutionary fantasies, that discredited liberation theology's contempt for "bourgeois democracy" and blunted its militant, revolutionary overtones. By the mid-1980s, Sigmund writes, "the experience of repression and torture under brutal dictatorship had given the Catholic left a renewed appreciation of the virtues of representative government, however flawed." These changes, he shows, were not just in practice but in the theoretical writings of liberation theologians, and thus more clearly embedded in the political cultural orientations they were generating and modifying. At the same time, pressures from Europe and the United States were effecting cultural shifts toward political democracy on the Christian right as well in Latin America. The cumulative result of these several decades of change in both theory and practice has been a "fundamental change in the political role of Catholicism in Latin America" from "a bulwark of a traditionalist authoritarianism" to a major foundation of ideological pluralism and political freedom. Clearly, theories of the unchanging nature of traditional, Catholic political culture in Latin America cannot be tenable in the face of this historical experience.

## Political Culture and Democracy

The chapters in this volume encompass a wide range of regions, methods, and foci. Yet they all highlight the dense, subtle, reciprocal, and profound linkages between political culture and democracy. As we see in the conclusion, political culture is far from an unchanging phenomenon. Social and economic change, social and civic mobilization, institutional practice, historical experience, and international diffusion can all modify or gradually transform the predominant political values, beliefs, and attitudes of a country. More quickly and decisively, political leadership, strategic calculations, political accommodations, and political learning from dramatic events can all have an impact on political culture. But whether changing or enduring, political culture does shape and constrain the possibilities for democracy. We have seen how it figures significantly, if sometimes subtly, in the very emergence of democracy. The chapters that follow show how central a role it plays in the failure, abortion, erosion, and destruction of democracy as well, and how much it is in turn affected by the presence or absence of democracy. Indeed, it may be asserted that change in the status, strength, or stability of democracy rarely occurs without some visible involvement of a changing—or unchanging—political culture.

## Notes

1. Robert A. Dahl, *Polyarchy: Participation and Opposition* (New Haven: Yale University Press, 1971), pp. 129-140; Juan J. Linz, *The Breakdown of Democratic Regimes* (Baltimore: Johns Hopkins University Press, 1978).

2. Gabriel A. Almond and Sidney Verba, *The Civic Culture: Political Attitudes and Democracy in Five Nations* (Princeton: Princeton University Press, 1963); Alex Inkeles and David Smith, *Becoming Modern: Individual Change in Six Developing Nations* (Cambridge: Harvard University Press, 1974); and Alex Inkeles, "Participant Citizenship in Six Developing Countries," *American Political Science Review* 63 (December 1969): 1120-1141.

3. Seymour Martin Lipset, "Economic Development and Democracy," *Political Man: The Social Bases of Politics* (Baltimore: Johns Hopkins University Press, 1981), pp. 27-63. New supporting evidence for the overall relationship and the intervening role of political culture appears in Larry Diamond, "Economic Development and Democracy Reconsidered," in Gary Marks and Larry Diamond, eds., *Reexamining Democracy: Essays in Honor of Seymour Martin Lipset* (Newbury Park, CA, and London: Sage, 1992), pp. 93-139.

4. Alex Inkeles and Larry Diamond, "Personal Qualities as a Reflection of Level of National Development," in Frank Andrews and Alexander Szalai, eds., *Comparative Studies in the Quality of Life* (London: Sage, 1980), pp. 73-109.

5. Ronald Inglehart, *Culture Shift in Advanced Industrial Countries* (Princeton: Princeton University Press, 1990), p. 45. See also Inglehart, "The Renaissance of Political Culture," *American Political Science Review* 82 (December 1988): 1203-1230.

6. Dahl, *Polyarchy*, pp. 36, 37.

7. Dahl recognizes that the transition path of competition with limited participation (i.e., suffrage) is no longer available but nevertheless cautions that the "risks of failure can be reduced if steps toward liberalization are accompanied by a dedicated and enlightened search for a viable system of mutual guarantees." *Polyarchy*, p. 40. This search is the central preoccupation of the many elite conciliatory processes, such as pacts, elite settlements, and various consociational and semiconsociational arrangements, that have preoccupied subsequent theories of democratic transition (see below).

8. Dankwart A. Rustow, "Transitions to Democracy: Toward a Dynamic Model," *Comparative Politics* 2, (April 1970): 357. For a similar, more recent treatment, see Terry Lynn Karl, "Dilemmas of Democratization in Latin America," in Dankwart A. Rustow and Kenneth Paul Erickson, eds., *Comparative Political Dynamics: Global Research Perspectives* (New York: Harper Collins, 1991), especially pp. 165-172.

9. Dahl, *Polyarchy*, pp. 15-16.

10. Rustow, "Transitions to Democracy," p. 357. Elite political learning from traumatic past experience is a major theme of Nancy Bermeo's superb comparative survey, "Democracy and the Lessons of Dictatorship," *Comparative Politics* 24 (April 1992): 273-291.

11. Rustow, "Transitions to Democracy," p. 357.

12. Arend Lijphart, *Democracy in Plural Societies: A Comparative Exploration* (New Haven: Yale University Press, 1977), p. 103.

13. Arend Lijphart, *The Politics of Accommodation: Pluralism and Democracy in the Netherlands*, 2d ed. (Berkeley: University of California Press, 1968), p. 188.

14. Ibid., p. 122. Rustow also sees this elite-mass cultural divergence at the outset of the transition, "when the leaders search for compromise while their followers

wearily uphold the banners of the old struggle," but argues that it will melt away in the habituation phase. "Transitions to Democracy," p. 360.

15. Almond and Verba, *The Civic Culture*, pp. 7-8.

16. Gabriel A. Almond, "Democratization and 'Crisis, Choice, and Change'" (Paper presented to the annual meeting of the American Political Science Association, Chicago, 3–6 September 1992), p. 6.

17. Guillermo O'Donnell, Philippe Schmitter, and Laurence Whiteheads, eds., *Transitions from Authoritarian Rule* (Baltimore: Johns Hopkins University Press, 1986), multi-volume set. See especially Guillermo O'Donnnell and Philippe Schmitter, *Transitions from Authoritarian Rule: Tentative Conclusions About Uncertain Democracies* (Baltimore: Johns Hopkins University Press, 1986). For a more formal, game-theoretic analysis of this "strategic interaction" approach to democratic transitions, see Gary Marks, "Rational Sources of Chaos in Democratic Transition," in Gary Marks and Larry Diamond, eds., *Reexamining Democracy*, pp. 47-69.

18. Linz, *The Breakdown of Democratic Regimes*, pp. 36-37.

19. John Higley and Michael G. Burton, "The Elite Variable in Democratic Transitions and Breakdowns," *American Sociological Review* 54 (February 1989): 17. See also Michael G. Burton and John Higley, "Elite Settlements," *American Sociological Review* 52 (June 1987): 295-307.

20. Higley and Burton, "The Elite Variable," p. 19.

21. Michael Burton, Richard Gunther, and John Higley, "Elite Transformations and Democratic Regimes," in John Higley and Richard Gunther, eds., *Elites and Democratic Consolidation in Latin America and Southern Europe* (Cambridge: Cambridge University Press, 1992), p. 23.

22. On mutual security, see Dahl, *Polyarchy*, pp. 36-37; on pacts see for example O'Donnell and Schmitter, *Transitions from Authoritarian Rule*, and Terry Lynn Karl, "Petroleum and Political Pacts: The Transition to Democracy in Venezuela," in O'Donnell, Schmitter, and Whitehead, eds., *Transitions from Authoritarian Rule: Latin America* (Baltimore: Johns Hopkins University Press, 1986), pp. 196-220.

23. Burton, Gunther, and Higley, "Elite Transformations and Democratic Regimes," pp. 24-25. They assert that elite settlements differ from pacts in that they are more inclusive of all major elites and deal only (but more comprehensively) with the political system (pp. 33-34).

24. Ibid., p. 5.

25. Alan Knight, "Mexico's Elite Settlement: Conjuncture and Consequences," in Higley and Gunther, *Elites and Democratic Consolidation*, pp. 113-145.

26. John Peeler, "Elite Settlements and Democratic Consolidation: Colombia, Costa Rica, and Venezuela," in Higley and Gunther, *Elites and Democratic Consolidation*, p. 83 and *passim*.

27. Juan Linz and Alfred Stepan, "Political Crafting of Democratic Consolidation or Destruction: European and South American Comparisons," in Robert A. Pastor, ed., *Democracy in the Americas: Stopping the Pendulum* (New York: Holmes and Meier, 1989), pp. 41-61.

28. Laurence Whitehead, "The Consolidation of Fragile Democracies: A Discussion with Illustrations," in Pastor, *Democracy in the Americas*, pp. 81, 94.

29. Giuseppe Di Palma, *To Craft Democracies: An Essay on Democratic Transitions* (Berkeley: University of California Press, 1990), pp. 56, 78, and *passim*.

30. Linz and Stepan, "Political Crafting," p. 47.

31. Di Palma, *To Craft Democracies*, p. 60.

32. Richard Gunther, "Spain: The Very Model of the Modern Elite Settlement," in Higley and Gunther, *Elites and Democratic Consolidation*, pp. 76-77.

33. Whitehead, "The Consolidation of Fragile Democracies," p. 79.

34. See, for example, G. Bingham Powell, *Contemporary Democracies:*

*Participation, Stability, and Violence* (Cambridge: Harvard University Press, 1982);
Arend Lijphart, *Democracies: Patterns of Majoritarian and Consensus Government
in Twenty-One Countries* (New Haven: Yale University Press, 1984); Arend Lijphart
and Bernard Grofman, eds., *Choosing an Electoral System: Issues and Alternatives*
(New York: Praeger, 1984); Bernard Grofman and Arend Lijphart, eds., *Electoral
Laws and Their Political Consequences* (New York: Agathon Press, 1986); Rein
Taagepera and Matthew Soberg Shugart, *Seats and Votes: The Effects and
Determinants of Electoral Systems* (New Haven: Yale University Press, 1989); Arend
Lijphart, "Constitutional Choices for New Democracies," *Journal of Democracy* 2
(Winter 1991): 72-84; Guy Lardyret, Quentin Quade, and Arend Lijphart, "Debate:
Proportional Representation," *Journal of Democracy* 2 (Summer 1991): 30-48; Juan J.
Linz, "The Perils of Presidentialism," *Journal of Democracy* 1 (Winter 1990): 59-69;
Donald Horowitz, Juan J. Linz, and Seymour Martin Lipset, "Debate: Presidents vs.
Parliaments," *Journal of Democracy* 1 (Fall 1990): 73-91; Donald Horowitz, *Ethnic
Groups in Conflict* (Berkeley: University of California Press, 1985), pp. 563-680, and
*A Democratic South Africa: Constitutional Engineering in a Divided Society*
(Berkeley: University of California Press, 1991); and Ehud Sprinzak and Larry
Diamond, eds., *Israeli Democracy Under Stress* (Boulder: Lynne Rienner Publishers,
1993).

35. Some notable exceptions include the work of Peter McDonough and Samuel
Barnes on democratization and political culture change in Spain, as well as previous
work by Booth and Seligson on Central America. See, for example, Peter
McDonough, Samuel H. Barnes, and Antonio López Pina, "The Growth of
Democratic Legitimacy in Spain," *American Political Science Review* 80 (September
1986): 735-760; Peter McDonough, Samuel H. Barnes, and Antonio López Pina,
"Economic Policy and Public Opinion in Spain," *American Journal of Political
Science* 30 (May 1986): 446-479; Peter McDonough and Samuel H. Barnes,
"Democratization and the Culture of Mass Politics: Comparing Spain and Eastern
Europe" (Paper presented to the annual meeting of the American Political Science
Association, Chicago, 3-6 September 1992); Edward N. Muller, Thomas O. Jukam,
and Mitchell A. Seligson, "Diffuse Political Support and Antisystem Political
Behavior: A Comparative Analysis," *American Journal of Political Science* 26 (May
1982): 240-264; and Mitchell A. Seligson and Edward Muller, "Democratic Stability
and Economic Crisis: Costa Rica, 1978-1983," *International Studies Quarterly* 31
(1987): 307-309.

36. See the essays by Maria Rosa S. de Martini, Dette Pascual, Monica Jimenez
de Barros, Xavier Zavala Cuadra, and Chai-Anan Samudavanija in Larry Diamond,
ed., *The Democratic Revolution: Struggles for Freedom and Pluralism in the
Developing World* (New York: Freedom House, 1992).

37. Harry Eckstein, "A Culturalist Theory of Political Change," *American
Political Science Review* 82 (September 1988): 790. The relatively firm and enduring
character of these orientations (for which "early learning conditions later learning")
generates "economy of action and predictability in interaction" in Eckstein's
"culturalist theory" (p. 792).

38. Almond and Verba, *The Civic Culture*, p. 15.

39. This framework is articulated in somewhat differing forms in Almond and
Verba, *The Civic Culture,* p. 15-17; Gabriel Almond and G. Bingham Powell,
*Comparative Politics: System, Process, and Policy* (Boston: Little, Brown, 1978), pp.
26-46; Gabriel Almond, "The Intellectual History of the Civic Culture Concept," in
Gabriel A. Almond and Sidney Verba, eds., *The Civic Culture Revisited* (Boston:
Little, Brown, 1980), pp. 27-28; and Gabriel A. Almond, "The Study of Political
Culture," in Almond, *A Divided Discipline: Schools and Sects in Political Science*
(Newbury Park, CA: Sage, 1990), p. 153.

40. Lucian W. Pye, "Introduction: Political Culture and Political Development," in Lucian W. Pye and Sidney Verba, eds., *Political Culture and Political Development* (Princeton: Princeton University Press, 1965), p. 7. In a more recent consideration, however, Pye has also warned that "logically coherent views do not necessarily prevail and that people, in their collective moods and inclinations, are quite capable of adhering to contradictory positions." *Asian Power and Politics: The Cultural Dimensions of Authority* (Cambridge: Harvard University Press, 1985), p. 29. An especially strong articulation of the coherence of political cultures—as amounting to diffuse "ways of life"—is advanced by Aaron Wildavsky, "Choosing Preferences by Constructing Institutions: A Cultural Theory of Preference Formation," *American Political Science Review* 81 (March 1987): 3-21.

41. For a discussion of this point with reference to the evidence in Almond and Verba's *The Civic Culture*, see Michael Thompson, Richard Ellis, and Aaron Wildavsky, *Cultural Theory* (Boulder: Westview Press, 1990), pp. 247-259. In fact, cultural theory posits as a central premise that none of the basic cultural orientations would be viable in a society without the presence of alternative ones, and hence that differentiation and "conflict among cultures is a precondition of cultural identity" (Wildavsky, "Choosing Preferences," p. 7). The challenge, then, for comparative research on political culture is not to compare different national political cultures but, more precisely, to compare "countries by contrasting their combinations of cultures." (Ibid., p. 18.)

42. The strongest assertion of the existence of distinctive *national* political cultures, reminiscent of the literature on national character, may be found in Pye's *Asian Power and Politics*, which is quite emphatic in identifying shared ways of viewing power and authority relations within Asian nations and even, in some broad respects, across Asia.

43. See, for example, Howard Wiarda, ed., *Politics and Social Change in Latin America: The Distinct Tradition* (Amherst: University of Massachusetts Press, 1974), and other works cited in notes 4, 10, 11, and 12 of the Booth and Seligson chapter.

44. Pye, *Asian Power and Politics*, p. 20; see also pp. 12, 24, 25, 53, and *passim*. Because Pye's is the strongest contemporary view of the durability of political culture over time, it is worth quoting at some length:

> Culture is a remarkably durable and persistent factor in human affairs. It is the dynamic vessel that holds and revitalizes the collective memories of a people by giving emotional life to traditions. Culture has this vital quality because it resides in the personality of everyone who has been socialized to it. People cling to their cultural ways not because of some vague feeling for their historical legacies and traditions, but because their culture is part and parcel of their personalities—and we know from psychoanalysis how hard (and expensive) it is to change a personality. Cultural change therefore involves true trauma. (p. 20)

Although his essay is entitled "A Culturalist Theory of Change," Eckstein shares with Pye an emphasis on the pattern-maintaining qualities of political culture and a profound skepticism about the possibilities for short-term, "revolutionary" transformations of the core (value) features of political culture (no doubt in part because of his shared emphasis on early socialization).

45. Pye, *Asian Power and Politics*, p. vii.

46. Almond, "The Study of Political Culture," p. 144.

47. Ibid., pp. 145-147. For a recent (limited) effort to accommodate political culture theory to the phenomenon of change—in which cultural change emerges as gradual and cumulative, and in the case of response to profound social change,

"prolonged and socially costly"—see Eckstein, "A Culturalist Theory of Political Change," p. 796.

48. Inglehart, *Culture Shift*, p. 17.

49. Larry Diamond, Juan J. Linz, and Seymour Martin Lipset, eds., *Democracy in Developing Countries: Africa, Asia, and Latin America*, 3 vols. (Boulder: Lynne Rienner Publishers, 1988, 1989).

50. On the role of the international system in promoting political culture change within nations, see Samuel P. Huntingtion, *The Third Wave: Democratization in the Late Twentieth Century* (Norman: University of Oklahoma Press, 1991); Lucian W. Pye, "Political Science and the Crisis of Authoritarianism," *American Political Science Review* 84 (March 1990): 8-9; and Diamond, "The Globalization of Democracy: Trends, Types, Causes, and Prospects," in Robert O. Slater, Barry M. Schutz, and Stephen R. Dorr, eds., *Global Transformation and the Third World* (Boulder: Lynne Rienner Publishers, 1993). The role of economic growth and social change in shaping basic value orientations is demonstrated in Inglehart, *Culture Shift*.

51. Other reviews of the relationship between political culture and democracy, framed in terms of the cultural conditions for democracy, may be found in J. Roland Pennock, *Democratic Political Theory* (Princeton: Princeton University Press, 1979), pp. 236-259; and Larry J. Diamond, "The Social Foundations of Democracy" (Ph.D. diss., Stanford University, 1980), pp. 14-28.

52. Lipset, *Political Man*, pp. 78-79; Almond and Verba, *The Civic Culture*, pp. 489-493; and Larry Diamond, "Three Paradoxes of Democracy," *Journal of Democracy* 1 (Summer 1990): 56-58.

53. Lipset, *Political Man*; Alex Inkeles, "National Character and Modern Political Systems," in Francis L. K. Hsu, ed., *Psychological Anthropology: Approaches to Culture and Personality* (Homewood, IL: Dorsey Press, 1961), pp. 193-199; Almond and Verba, *The Civic Culture*; Sidney Verba, "Conclusion: Comparative Political Culture," in Pye and Verba, *Political Culture and Political Development*, pp. 544-550; and Dahl, *Polyarchy*. For an earlier, political psychological treatment that influenced several of the above approaches, see Harold Lasswell, "Democratic Character," in *The Political Writings of Harold Lasswell* (Glencoe, IL: Free Press, 1951), pp. 465-525.

54. Pye, "The Crisis of Authoritarianism," p. 15.

55. Verba, "Conclusion: Comparative Political Culture," p. 546.

56. Lasswell, "Democratic Character," p. 502.

57. Almond and Verba, *The Civic Culture*; Verba, "Comparative Political Culture"; Dahl, *Polyarchy*. Pye also posits trust as a requirement for political development, in the broader sense of increasing mass participation, governmental capacity, and structural differentiation. "Introduction: Political Culture and Political Development," in Pye and Verba, *Political Culture and Political Development*, p. 22.

58. Again, however, consociational theory explicitly challenges the theory of cross-cutting cleavages. See especially Lijphart, *The Politics of Accommodation*, pp. 184-187.

59. An excellent treatment of this process, again, is Bermeo's "Democracy and the Lessons of Dictatorship."

60. Quoted in Pennock, *Democratic Political Theory*, p. 211, from Mill's essay, "On Representative Government."

61. Inkeles, "National Character and Modern Political Systems," pp. 195-198.

62. Sidney Hook, *Reason, Social Myth, and Democracy* (New York: Humanities Press, 1950), cited in Inkeles, "National Character," p. 196

63. Quoted in Inkeles, "National Character," pp. 195-196. See also Pennock, *Democratic Political Theory*, pp. 240-241.

64. Pye, *Asian Power and Politics*, p. vii; see also especially pp. 18-19, 22-29,

326-341.

65. Ibid., p. 341.

66. Pennock, *Democratic Political Theory*, p. 257.

67. Ibid., pp. 245-246, 258-259.

68. Thompson, Ellis, and Wildavsky, *Cultural Theory*, p. 256.

69. Ibid., p. 257.

70. Aaron Wildavsky, "On the Absence of Egalitarianism and Fatalism in Political Theorizing, or What Political Culture Can Contribute to Understanding Democracy" (unpublished manuscript, December 1991), p. 28.

71. Linz, *Breakdown of Democratic Regimes*, p. 16; Lipset, *Political Man,* p. 64.

72. Inkeles, "Participant Citizenship," pp. 1120-1141.

73. Almond and Verba, *The Civic Culture*, p. 19.

74. The inverse of this, fatalism, is not merely the absence of efficacy but a basic cultural bias, a way of life, that "generates (and is generated by) authoritarian political systems. A population that is withdrawn from the political sphere [both deferential and alienated] increases the scope for the exercise of arbitrary governmental power, thus further fueling the citizenry's withdrawal from politics." Thompson, Ellis, and Wildavsky, *Cultural Theory*, p. 256.

75. Almond and Verba, *The Civic Culture*, p. 482.

76. The cultural theory of Thompson, Ellis, and Wildavsky is distinctive in two respects, however. It is more inclined to emphasize differences within nations between basic cultural orientations, and it derives these basic orientations from a two-dimensional grid that essentially reproduces two key variables of *The Civic Culture*, commitment and involvement, as follows:

|  | COMMITMENT | |
| --- | --- | --- |
| INVOLVEMENT | *Allegiant* | *Alienated* |
| *Deferential (passive)* | Hierarchist | Fatalist |
| *Participant (active)* | Individualist | Egalitarian |

The table is mine but the formula derives from *Cultural Theory*, p. 247.

77. Almond and Verba, *The Civic Culture*, p. 490.

78. *Democratic Political Theory*, p. 257.

79. Karl, "Dilemmas of Democratization in Latin America," p. 168. For Rustow's treatment, see "Transitions to Democracy," pp. 342-343. Rustow does posit one background condition: national unity.

80. The latter gap is now being filled with a profusion of new research, much of it involving large-scale attitudinal surveys in Central and Eastern Europe. See, for example, the papers in Frederick D. Weil, ed., *Democratization in Eastern and Western Europe*, vol. 1 of *Research on Democracy and Society* (Greenwich: JAI Press, 1992), and *Political Culture and Political Structure: Theoretical and Empirical Studies,* vol. 2 of *Research on Democracy and Society* (Greenwich, U.K.: JAI Press, 1993, forthcoming).

# • 2 •

# Culture and Democratization in India

*Richard Sisson*

India became an independent state at the midnight hour of 14 August 1947. The powers of government were transferred by the last of the British viceroys, Lord Mountbatten, to a government selected from a constituent assembly elected 18 months before, thus bringing to an end a colonial British presence that had commenced in 1600, became dominant in 1757, and supreme in 1858. The government was formed by the Indian National Congress, the broad and dominant core of the nationalist movement, founded in 1885 some two decades before the British Labour Party, the ruling government in Britain at the time of the transfer of power. In January 1950 a federal constitution was adopted which provided for elections to be held on a universal adult franchise at intervals of no longer than five years, and for a council of ministers headed by a prime minister collectively responsible to the lower house of parliament, the *Lok Sabha*, directly elected from territorially delimited constituencies. The Indian constitution, with over sixty amendments, has been in effect consistently since adoption.

## Is India Democratic?

Before proceeding to examine the cultural context of regime formation and sustenance, it is first necessary to decide whether or not India is democratic, and if so, to what extent. In terms of its ranking according to criteria commonly accepted as constituting the core of democraticness—whether Dahl, Huntington, or Lipset—India is indeed democratic.[1] Ten national elections have been held in India since independence, with an equivalent number having been held in each of the states. A comparatively large proportion of the electorate turns out to vote, showing an upward trend from 46 percent in 1952 to 61 percent in 1989. The vote for anti-regime parties has always been marginal, and with the "domestication" of the Communist parties and their assumption and continuance in power in two states since the early 1970s, the

29

vote for anti-regime parties has all but disappeared.[2]

Elections are competitive. The Congress party, which has enjoyed dominance at the national level, has never secured a majority of the popular vote
in national elections. A large number of parties contest national elections,
vacillating from 76 in 1952 to 24 in 1984. Fifty-seven parties have contested
at least two elections since 1952.

Elections in India are competitive in yet another way; they make a difference in who governs. Four elections (1977, 1980, 1989, and 1991) resulted in the defeat of an incumbent government at the national level. All but
two major states have at one time or another been governed by a party or
party coalitions other than the Congress Party. A competitive two-party system has developed in most of India's 22 states, commencing with the 1967
state elections, after which there were "non-Congress" governments in half
of the 16 major states. All four southern states were governed by regionalist
parties or coalitions throughout the 1980s.

The Indian citizen is surrounded by secular sources of information.
There are over 1,400 daily newspapers and nearly 20,000 other news publications with a circulation of nearly 60 million and published in 91 languages. Nearly 6,000 newspapers are published in Hindi, with nearly 4,000
more being published in English. Thirty-five newspapers have been in print
continuously for more than a century.[3] While the tradition of investigative
reporting is much weaker than in the older democracies, reporting of political news is quite free; and investigative reporting has shown robustness in
the inquiries into governmental corruption in the Bofors arms transfer scandal in the late 1980s. Practically every village is reached by radio, and nearly
70 percent of the country receives television signals.

Table 2.1. Citizen Behavior in Indian National Elections

| Percentage of Respondents Reporting They: | 1971 Election | 1984 Election |
|---|---|---|
| Listen to the radio | 40% | 64% |
| Acquire political information from a newspaper | 20 | 46 |
| Were contacted by a party or candidate representative | 26 | 49 |
| Attended a political meeting | 12 | 44 |
| Watch TV | – | 26 |

*Source:* See footnote 35.

More important, however, is the use that citizens make of these facilities
and the access they have to political campaigns. The data in Table 2.1, drawn
from national election surveys conducted in 1971 and 1984, show that significant and increasing proportions of Indians participate in politics and
make use of the media to acquire political information.

For all but two years since independence the fundamental rights of the citizen, as set forth in the constitution, have been honored and have received judicial protection.[4] Equality before the law is guaranteed by article 14; freedom of speech, assembly, association, movement, settlement, and employment by article 19; the right to life, liberty, and property by articles 2 and 3; the right to follow and to teach the values of one's own culture, religion, and language by articles 25, 29, and 30; and the right to constitutional redress through due process by articles 20, 22, and 32. While the state is enjoined to assure the above rights, it is also obliged by the constitution to assure other conditions of equality including the abolition of untouchability (article 17), free access of all to public places (article 15), and the prohibition of forced labor (article 23).

While we have not measured various indicators of democracy in India with precision, the data are sufficiently robust to establish that India is democratic. This is quite striking given that India is a society with socioeconomic characteristics that are commonly accepted as being inhospitable to democratic regimes. India is poor, uneducated, and linguistically and religiously divided. It is divided vertically by an oft-oppressive caste system; it has been faced at times since independence with conditions that approach internal war; religious conflict, which induced the partition of the subcontinent in 1947, escalated during the decade of the 1980s. Deep societal divisions continue to be reflected in India's politics. Yet during the four and a half decades of independence, the national political community and the constitutional order have been maintained, while incumbent governments unseated through free elections in all cases have voluntarily surrendered power, and in many instances have returned to power by virtue of their success in subsequent elections. How are four and a half decades of democratic performance in India to be explained?

## Historical Precedent and Democratization in India

The symbols, values, and practices of democratic government did not commence in India with independence, but developed gradually over the preceding half century. Elections to representative bodies had been held at both the provincial and national levels for nearly four decades before independence; election to local government bodies had become common two decades before that. Millions of Indians exercised the franchise, and parties had developed electoral organizations for getting out the vote before independence. Popularly elected governments held power in the provinces of British India after the elections of 1937.[5] Furthermore, the creation of a liberal constitutional regime was never a matter of dispute within the dominant nationalist elite, nor was there conflict among those who came to govern independent India over the nature of the Indian political community, though

(Pakistan was created because) the leaders of independent India were unable to convince the dominant political elite of Muslim India of their vision. But there were disputes within India's nationalist elite, concentrated as it was under the "open umbrella" of the Indian National Congress, including Communists, Socialists, Hindu revivalists, Gandhians, liberals, and modernists, who challenged one another in debates and votes within the Congress councils on issues of public policy, national strategy, and political leadership.

Thus, unlike some have contended, colonial polities "arrive" at the moment of achieving autonomy and sovereignty with powerful historical baggage that includes beliefs, institutions, symbols, and other cultural artifacts that have a powerful bearing on subsequent practice and belief.[6] So important are these historical precedents in India that it is essential to review, however briefly, the development of those beliefs and practices that have come to define the culture of Indian democracy in the postindependence period.

A useful way of examining the "origin" and expansion of democratic norms and practices was provided over two decades ago by Stein Rokkan in his insightful analysis of the structuring of mass politics in the smaller European democracies.[7] In that seminal piece, Rokkan argued that there were four "locks," or thresholds, in the process of democratization which, if successfully surmounted in sequence, heightened the probability that stable democracies will result. He conceived these thresholds in terms of *legitimation* (the right of petition, criticism, and demonstration against the regime), *incorporation* (rights of participation in the choice of representation for new groups), *representation* (access of representatives of new groups to legislative institutions), and *executive power* (access of representatives of new groups to the instruments of governance). Inherent in each threshold is the possibility of crisis and reversal, given that dominant elites are threatened by impending change, which would serve to constrain their actions and place limits on their access to public goods. Implicit in the formulation is the necessity for each successive step to be consummated in order to protect the values associated with the previous ones.

By the time the Indian National Congress was founded in 1885, the rights associated with the idea of legitimation had been acknowledged, some by law, others by precedent and practice. Freedom of speech and the press had been formally guaranteed in 1885. Over 690 newspapers and periodicals in the vernacular languages of India were in circulation then.[8] Newspapers reported political conflicts and debates in Britain and Europe as well as within the colonial administration in India. Ultimately, public policies were discussed, laws announced, and activities and matters of public interest in various regions of India reviewed. Newspapers had an educating and unifying impact.

Second, the nineteenth century also witnessed the development of a rich

associational life. These associations ranged from Westernized political discussion groups to reformist organizations that demanded that government
use its resources to engineer social change; it included organizations of landed and commercial interests as well as cultural revivalist organizations and
movements bent upon resisting the encroachments of Western culture.[9]
Particularly after the Mutiny of 1857, numerous political associations were
created for the purpose of petitioning government for reform, in some cases
attempting to develop a mass base in capital cities and provincial towns.
These new "contractual" organizations increasingly took on an institutionalized form with known memberships and constitutionally defined purposes
and rules for deliberation and officer selection. They observed in nascent
form the norms and procedures of internal governance that would subsequently be demanded of public institutions. Organizations submitted petitions for redress and change to the offices of provincial governors, to those
of the governor-general and viceroy, to the secretary of state for India, and to
parliament itself. While closed to Indian representation until 1861, the governor-general's council, when acting in its legislative capacity, was opened
to public view in 1853 with the institution of parliamentary practice: (1) oral
deliberation; (2) debates on public record; and (3) select committees for the
purpose of drafting, securing public comment on, and perfecting legislation.

The crisis of the Great Indian Mutiny ushered in the principle of incorporation. Speaking in anticipation of the Indian Councils Act, and concerned
with how to make governance work, one senior servant of the Raj intelli-
gently observed:

> The addition of the native element has, I think, become necessary owing to
> our diminished opportunities of learning through indirect channels what the
> natives think of our measures, and how the native community will be
> affected by them ... (N)o one will, I think, object to the only obvious
> means of regaining in part the advantages which we have listed, unless he
> is prepared for the perilous experiment of continuing to legislate for mil-
> lions of people, with few means of knowing, except by rebellion, whether
> the laws suit them or not. The *durbar* of a native Prince is nothing more
> than a council very similar to that which I have described. To it under a
> good ruler all have access, very considerable license of speech is permitted,
> and it is in fact the channel from which the ruler learns how his measures
> are likely to affect his subjects, and may hear of discontent before it
> becomes disaffection.[10]

The Indian Councils Act of 1861 expanded the Imperial Legislative
Council to include six "non-official" members, three of whom were to be
Indians. It also created a set of provincial legislative councils and included a
commitment to expand Indian representation in the administrative services.
Thus while this act accepted the principle of representation, it did so not on
the basis of representation as a right extended to or claimed by a community
of citizens; rather it was conceived and exercised as a means of formally

relating representatives from among India's most aristocratic and Westernized classes to the institutions of the Raj. During the next two decades, over half of these appointed "representatives" held princely titles, while the remainder were from aristocratic landlord families. In the decade before the 1892 Reform Act, however, two-thirds of the appointees were "commoners" from landowning families or new professional middle class groups, primarily lawyers, which reflected changes in the structure of Indian elites.[11]

The founding of the Indian National Congress in 1885 as a "native parliament" provided a vehicle for the expression of a nascent political class, "Indian in blood and colour, but English in taste, in opinions in intellect," as Macaulay had envisioned a half century before. It was a class, although supportive of the Raj, which demanded to be heard and ultimately to be represented. Thus within three decades of implementation, the 1861 reforms proved to be inadequate in relating public opinion to the executive bureaucracy. Provision for the formal association with legislative institutions was far removed from the newly educated classes. Because the traditional elites constituted a buffer between the Raj and colonial society, expanded Indian representation in the administrative services, though extended in principle by the Sovereign after the Mutiny, was strongly resisted by the Raj and went unrealized in practice.[12]

The threshold of incorporation was reached in the Acts of 1892 and 1909. The former provided for "selection" of Indian representatives into provincial and national councils through the election of "nominees" by institutions of local government and organizations of important social groups. The latter provided for direct election by constituencies comprised of local governments and functional groups. In the former case, while the principle of election was extended to translocal institutions for the first time, it was not accompanied by the principle of public accountability or by legislative autonomy. These legislative institutions, like those before and those created nearly two decades later, were what we may call "councils of convenience" designed to assist the efficient administration of public affairs.

The Morley-Minto Reforms of 1909 were enacted after a divisive split in the Congress party in 1907. "Moderates" advocated the pursuit of limited political reforms through constitutional means for the benefit of those sufficiently fit by education and property to deserve them. "Extremists" advocated withdrawal of support from the institutions of the Raj, emphasized indigenous symbols and the utility and rightness of mass involvement, and advocated more radical action to force the British to quit India.[13] The moderates emerged the victors in this conflict, assumed control of the Congress organization, and were extended "legitimacy" by the Raj as the latter negotiated with the moderates about the upcoming reforms. The reforms substantially increased the size of legislative councils at both the national and provincial levels, created nonofficial majorities in the provincial legislative councils—although official control was maintained through the power of executive veto and restrictions on the subjects on which councils could take action—and expanded the deliberative powers of the councils to include the right to move resolutions on matters of provincial concern including the budget as well as to move divisions of the house, although such votes were advisory only. The reforms provided parliamentary procedure without parliamentary rule.

The reforms had an important impact on the composition of legislative elites, however, as they had on the development of local political groups. In legislative bodies at both provincial and national levels, lawyers constituted an increasingly large proportion of incumbents, particularly among elected members and strikingly so among those elected by local government institutions, mainly at the expense of landlords.[14] The electoral arrangements placed a premium on political bargaining and negotiation. Since constituencies in many cases were composed of a number of municipalities or district boards under both the 1892 and 1909 Acts, in order to create a winning coalition, candidates had to go beyond their own locality and develop translocal political linkages.[15] Coalitions sometimes extended between rural and urban areas, since factional groups in one arena would support the opponents of their enemies in another. A culture of political bargaining, of course, had commenced with elections to local governmental bodies in the latter part of the nineteenth century, but the creation of larger constituencies for provincial and national legislative bodies required coalitions that transcended local arenas. Smaller towns were connected to larger ones, and rural areas were connected to both. Bonds between center and periphery were established through the newly created necessities of political life in which lawyers were making contracts and landlords and merchants sought advocates.

Translocal coalitions were established in yet another way. The first phase of municipal and district board politics was characterized by vertical linkage systems that could be supplied by local notables who could draw upon traditional fealty or economic dependence. These vertical networks were progressively absorbed into and replaced by translocal coalitions and by caste associations that connected persons of a common social group over far wider areas than had been customary before the age of communication and public election. Political aspirants increasingly saw advantage in encouraging the creation and expanded activity of other forms of voluntary associations, such as cooperative societies, philanthropic organizations, unions, and other advocacy associations, to increase political participation and to mobilize political support.[16] Electoral politics encouraged and built upon extensive communication.[17]

The post–World War I era provided a new context for democratic development in India. Experience with the existing councils had proved wanting to many Indian participants within, as well as to articulate political groups without. In the Lucknow Pact of 1916, the Congress party and the Muslim

League insisted that substantial reform in the Indian constitutional order had to be made and proposed a consensual document that entailed the creation of a more liberal constitutional order. Subsequently, the erstwhile extremists returned to the Congress fold. Thus at the time of the dicennial review of constitutional progress in India, the secretary of state for India announced in the House of Commons that the government was committed to "the increasing association of Indians in every branch of the administration and the gradual development of self-governing institutions with a view to the progressive realization of responsible government in India as an integral part of the British Empire."[18] The reforms enacted in 1919, commonly known as the Montagu-Chelmsford Reforms, constituted the core of the threshold of representation in Rokkan's model of democratic development. They provided for the rudiments of legislative rule by granting provincial legislative councils substantial autonomous powers, and created territorial constituencies and an expanded franchise which enabled a wider range of social interests to enter the electoral and legislative process. Legislative councils were enlarged and all were to have at least 70 percent of their membership elected, with no more than 20 percent being "officials" appointed by the executive and at least 10 percent being "nonofficial" appointees. Elected representatives were to be invited into the ministries to assume administrative responsibility for certain "transferred subjects," while official councillors were to continue to have responsibility for "reserved subjects" in a system known as "dyarchy."

These reforms also devolved power from the central government to the provinces, thus establishing the basis for a federal system of government, which was adopted largely unchanged by the Constituent Assembly after independence. Within these policy subjects, the provincial legislative councils were granted substantial law-making powers. Further, no member of any council could be held liable by reason of any speech or participation in the drafting of any legislation or report in his formal legislative capacity. Councils were afforded the freedom of internal governance, being allowed to elect their own president and vice-president and to decide on their own standing orders and rules of procedure. Under these new rules and with these new powers, legislative councils in many instances vigorously engaged the executive. In the case of the Bombay presidency, for example, during the first four years under the new regime, the council voted down a sizeable number of bills that the government brought before it; had it not been for the "official" members of the council, who tended to vote en bloc for the government, ministries would have faced unusual difficulty in getting their programs through.[19] After their initial period of contestation, government and legislative representatives became more inclined to work things out beforehand or in select committees rather than on the floor of the council.

The threshold of executive power, in Rokkan's terms, was achieved under the Government of India Act of 1935. This act provided for self-governance at the provincial level in the British Provinces and created the framework which, in 1950, became with some modification the constitution of independent India. Under the 1935 Act, the size of the electorate was expanded to encompass 14 percent of the adult male population, a substantial number in a population exceeding 300 million people. Legislative bodies in the provinces were wholly elected, with ministries recruited entirely from the assemblies and collectively responsible to them.[20] Legislative institutions during the first three decades of this century had become transformed from *councils of convenience to councils of consent.*

The reformed legislative institutions in the provinces attracted a new type of political leader. Those entering legislative institutions in the Bombay presidency after 1920, for example, increasingly had bases of political support autonomous from that of the Raj.[21] They had been active in caste and community associations, in cooperative societies, in creating and managing service societies to run secondary schools or medical clinics, had been elected to local government bodies, and after 1930 had been active in a political party. In earlier legislative bodies, elected members, and of course those nominated by government, frequently had been formally associated with the British Raj, whether as an honorary magistrate, Justice of the Peace, or government servant, or had been honored by the colonial administration with awards for meritorious service to the Raj. As electoral politics became more competitive and as the electorate expanded, the proportion of those formally associated with the colonial regime diminished. By a decade before independence, nationalist party elites outside representative institutions as well as elites within them tended to be autonomous from the structures and "bureaucratic culture" of the British Raj.

Thus the transfer of power in India brought to fruition a long process of democratization. This process constituted a series of accommodations between an authoritarian imperial regime and a rising political class that developed from a congress of groups of intelligentsia, social reformers, and propertied interests to a political class with a mass base that claimed to represent the various interests of the Indian political community. The basic structure of the regime of independent India had been advocated and, in a limited way, experienced by that class as it had been conceded by the imperial power before independence was achieved.

## The Cultural Dimensions of Democratization

What cultural elements contributed to the democratization of public authority in preindependence India? First and foremost was the powerful *liberal persuasion of a nationalist political class* that achieved and maintained dominance in the nationalist movement. The first nationalists, the first generation in the India National Congress, were men of property and means who came from all provinces of British India. Most of this group had been educated in

England, where they had come to know one another. This elite, while Westernized, came in the main from families who, as John R. McLane has observed,

> accepted the unifying philosophies and nomenclatures of India's great tra-
> ditions and who in many cases had worked for bureaucracies with an all-
> India pattern; they shared a progressive view of the improving, uniting
> forces of historical development; and most importantly, they had common
> substantial grievances against the colonial power.[22]

This elite, while judging the colonial regime illegitimate, was committed to reforming it, to domesticating it, and to making it more representative of and more responsible to Indian opinion rather than bent on destroying it and replacing it with one or another form of nonliberal regime. At the same time, those most committed to reforming the regime were also committed to reforming their own society; the fight against despotism in one was accompanied by a fight against despotism in the other. This moderate elite was ultimately challenged by a strong radical movement that also enjoyed support from all major regions of the subcontinent, and which was committed to the use of nonconstitutional methods for bringing about the demise of the colonial regime and the achievement of *swaraj* (freedom, self-rule).

It was in this context that the colonial administration started to "recognize" the moderate, constitutionalist wing of the movement as the legitimate representative of nationalist opinion, while isolating and jailing extremists for various forms of provocative activity that allegedly endangered the public interest. The British Raj thus became the "illegitimate legitimator" of what became the dominant core of the nationalist movement. This symbiotic relationship continued between the Raj and the moderates within Congress—each fearing the consequences of uncontrolled social protest—the British ever mindful of the Mutiny of 1857, the moderates fearful of becoming enveloped by social violence released around the margins of even the most carefully calculated and organized civil disobedience campaign. This characterized the pre-Gandhian as well as the Gandhian era (1920–1947).

An important facet of Mahatma Gandhi's genius was his ability to merge the objectives of the moderates with a radical, but controlled, strategy of political action. He referred to Gopal Krishna Gokhale, the eminent moderate leader, as his political *guru*. While he developed his civil disobedience strategy of *satyagraha* to be employed against the British, he emphasized the importance of a consensual resolution of conflict within Indian society in his essentially organic conception of Indian social order. In the Gandhian era, civil disobedience campaigns were terminated when violence occurred, to the dismay of many activists, and when advocates of radical political strategies that risked social conflict achieved prominence within Congress in the mid and late 1930s, they were isolated from power within it.[23]

This liberal constitutionalist ideology found formal expression in the Nehru Report (a draft constitution for a would-be independent India that could just as easily have come from the hand of John Stuart Mill), which was the ultimate outcome of the abortive All-Parties Conference of 1928, as well as in the Karachi Resolution of 1931, which set forth both a declaration of Fundamental Rights of the Citizen and principles of social policy that, in revised form, became enshrined as the moral core of the Indian constitution.[24]

A second dimension of the cultural basis of democratization in the preindependence phase was the pattern of *development of group life*. We have referred to the rise of associational life in the nineteenth century and the creation of constitutional orders within the various public organizations from which many of the first Indian "representatives" selected for legislative bodies came, as well as to the role of these associations as petitioners of the colonial state. The period surrounding the "threshold of representation" witnessed the development of a rich panoply of voluntary associations rooted in particular castes and social groups. They too were organized on a secular model, but unlike the earlier groups were moored in mass society. The development of groups based in traditional corporate collectivities was not unusual. Mobility in traditional society had always been collective; those aspiring to achieve political or social mobility had to bring their caste fellows along with them. This pattern was encouraged by ease of organization. Caste and ethnic groups shared cultural symbols and ceremonies; there was an existent group identity that, in certain areas, was extended to encompass similar groups in other areas.[25] These groups initially organized to petition the colonial state to acknowledge newly claimed status, to acquire educational support, and to acquire employment in government service. The next phase was entry into elected public institutions. As the nationalist movement became mass oriented, it too looked toward traditional social groups as blocks for political support. If mobilized, this was the way groups were organized; if unmobilized, this was the form they would assume. Even peasant movements, both those arising "spontaneously" and those orchestrated under Congress and Gandhian tutelage, tended to be based in a single caste.[26]

Not only were groups numerous and often organized on ascriptive bases (though most had secular ends), the calculus of public elections required bargaining and negotiation to create coalitions with any chance of winning, given that in most instances particular groups comprised a distinct minority in any constituency. Compromise was "accepted" through the institutions of traditional society; it was sought and "expected" in the competitive electoral arenas created in the process of democratization. Bargaining also occurred between groups at different political levels and often with different political interests in the nationalist movement, which was structured more like a political market than a command economy. Electoral and legislative politics created an arena requiring forms of social linkage that had not existed before in India.

A third cultural factor in India's democratization concerns *patterns of conflict resolution.* A common observation of anthropologists studying India is that cooperation and conflict resolution among equals in Indian society is most difficult.[27] Cooperation is easiest in hierarchical situations; the greatest acceptance of conflict resolution is found in mediation and arbitration. Thus in situations of great inequality, conflict is resolved through imposition; in situations of equality or where inequality is problematic, there is an expectation and an acceptance of an arbitrator who will be "fair" and will resolve disputes with non-zero-sum outcomes. In traditional Indian society, this function was served by village and caste *panchayats* (councils of elders) or by a local notable whose authority was commonly accepted. In the qualitatively new political arena created by elections and public contestation and in situations lacking clear social hierarchy, the role of arbiter came to be as much expected as it was necessary. It was this function that the party system, and especially the Indian National Congress, came to provide. The expectation and exercise of arbitration consequently integrated lower or subordinate levels of conflict with superordinate ones. Those in local areas in this fashion became associated with leaders in translocal arenas to form a political marketplace of complex interdependence.

Central to this pattern of conflict resolution was Mahatma Gandhi's ingenious ability to act as both agitator and arbiter during the quarter century before independence. Gandhi acted in an historic tradition of reform movements in India, but he expanded and changed them. There had been a long tradition of movements of religious and social reform in medieval as well as early modern Hindi and Muslim society in India. The change introduced by Gandhi was not only that of raising mass society to new levels of consciousness and collective pride and of encouraging new attitudes toward traditional status groups and social behavior, but of asserting the idea that government must be responsible, that the state must be held accountable for India's myriad social ills, and that it be held accountable as a matter of right. One of the consequences of his public ministry was to establish that government mattered and that publics could do something about it. This confrontational strategy was employed not only by those outside legislative halls, but by those within them as well.

Gandhi also became the "ultimate arbiter" between contending groups in Indian society, within the Indian National Congress (from the mid-1930s onward), and between Congress and the British Raj (as independence approached). The role of arbiter and those who filled it have been extremely important in the postindependence era, the Congress party for the first two postindependence decades being a complex system of group mediation.

Fourth, nationalist elites shared a *conception of a national political community*, of the appropriateness of national unity in the context of regional diversity, during the preindependence period. This vision of Congress was partially eclipsed with the creation of Pakistan to house Muslim majority areas in a sovereign state and avowedly to provide sanctuary for Muslims in Muslim-minority provinces. The conception of a national community, nascent in the early nationalist period but an overt symbol by the end of World War I, was encouraged by the centralization of authority in both the British Raj and through elite participation in the institutions of the Raj, whether educational, bureaucratic, or representative.

Thus, during the nationalist movement the major issues of debate among those who became the citizens and leaders of free India concerned neither the issue of national unity nor the character of the regime for public conflict resolution, but rather how best to achieve *swaraj*, who was to govern, and for what purpose.

## Political Elites and the Culture of Democracy in Independent India

Political elites brought with them to independent India a strong commitment to liberal democracy. Alternative regime forms were not an issue in the Constituent Assembly to which sovereignty and power was "transferred" by the departing imperial power. It is true that Gandhi and a number of his closest associates, in their theory of the Indian state, conceived it to be village-centered, with Congress as an essentially social uplift organization divorced from the conflicts inherent in public affairs. However, such a measure of decentralization was never seriously considered by the Constituent Assembly, nor did Gandhi's vision of a postindependence Congress receive much support. With the coming of independence, Gandhi's historical mission was fulfilled. The time had come—as the Mahatma's "chosen" leader of the Congress party, Jawaharlal Nehru, observed in his eloquent speech on 14 August 1947 to the Constituent Assembly—to assume the responsibility that came with freedom and power: "that responsibility rests with this Assembly, a sovereign body representing the sovereign people of India." It was the Assembly that became the directly elected lower house of parliament (*Lok Sabha*) under the Indian constitution that became effective in January 1950.

The new governing Congress elite honored the principle of free political competition in the postindependence period. Commencing shortly after independence, major groups split from the Indian National Congress to form opposition parties, including the socialist parties and numerous regional parties. After the first general election in 1952, Congress was responsive to the electoral threat posed by regionalist party coalitions—the "linguistic states movements"—that demanded a reorganization of states on the basis of linguistic cultures. This the government commenced to do in a major way in anticipation of the second general elections of 1957. A system of reciprocity developed between Congress and opposition parties during the Nehru era (1947–1964) in which Congress became a party of broad consensus with the opposition as "parties of pressure" working at the margins of the dominant Congress.[28]

Although Congress has fared better in national elections than opposition parties and has usually enjoyed large majorities in parliament, due in substantial measure to the single-member-plurality electoral system and a pervasively divided opposition, party competition has been substantial in all areas of India since independence. While there are few districts in which Congress candidates have not enjoyed at least moderate electoral support, they have been electorally dominant in surprisingly few districts. They won a majority of the vote in four or more of the seven elections held through 1980 in less than 25 percent of the districts of India, and in only 13 percent did they receive majorities in five or more elections.[29]

Congress elites attempted, through incorporation, to assure the unity of the political community in the preindependence years, to create and maintain electoral majorities, and to establish a tradition of prime ministerial and cabinet supremacy over the bureaucracy and military services. Ministerial representation was extended to non-Congress groups, religious and cultural minorities, and representation from the erstwhile princely states. In retrospect, the Nehru era was characterized by relatively long cabinet tenures, with cabinet members holding particular portfolios for the duration of their tenure, and with members drawn from a national political class—those whose political lives before independence had been wholly invested in nationalist politics at the "national" level or, as dominant leaders from major states, in both national-level and state-level politics.[30] The Indian princes, the former rulers of "Indian India" which comprised two-fifths of the territory of the subcontinent, were coopted into the new regime through appointment to constitutional positions in their former territories as those areas were "integrated" into the state structure; they also retained certain of their substantial assets and received a "privy purse" from the state as a form of guaranteed income.[31]

The ideology of social incorporation was also extended toward the grass roots in an effort to mobilize political support. Major social groups that had stayed away from Congress were courted, such as the "landed gentry" and those Muslim groups not inducted into Pakistan. Newly enfranchised castes—e.g., small peasants, tenant farmers, and artisans—were likewise pursued. A major effort was made to attract the support of untouchables and tribals, who were given separate legislative seats and constituencies at both the national and state levels to assure their "representation." Competition existed between factional groups and coalitions within Congress for the support of new groups just as it existed between Congress and opposition parties, and in numerous cases alliances developed between factions in Congress and those in the opposition.[32]

The culture of democracy manifest in elite ideology during the Nehru era also found expression in the creation of *panchayati raj*—a complex of elected rural institutions reaching from the village to the district level designed to bring electoral competition (though not party competition) to the local level, to associate local society with development efforts, and to involve citizens more closely with the state and its policies. During the 1960s and 1970s, those aspiring to political careers often entered politics through elections to these institutions. While elective and designated with secular ends in mind, this system of *panchayats* drew upon ancient institutions of the same name that existed to manage conflict in castes and villages and that had historically enjoyed autonomy from outside interference.

Thus the national political class that assumed power at independence by preparation and choice became transformed from an elite of nationalist protest to an elite of national governance. Its vision of a liberal constitutional order, developed and elaborated by two generations of leaders, was given form and adopted. The traditions of internal competition within the Indian National Congress and the principle of electoral competition for public office developed before independence continued thereafter. Through party competition and constitutional design, elites endeavored to encourage the diffusion of political knowledge and the desire to participate in public life.

## Ideology and Culture of the Indian Electorate

But what of the "mindscape," the feelings, the interests, and the judgments of the Indian citizenry? With independence came a vastly expanded electorate, which grew from approximately 175 million in 1952 to 500 million in 1984; after 1952 anywhere from 40 to 60 million newly eligible voters were introduced in each successive election.[33] Voter turnout over the past two decades has been consistently above 55 percent and at least 60 percent in each of the two elections held in the 1980s.

The common conception of the Indian voter during the first two decades after independence derived from general demographic characteristics of Indian society. The voter was perceived as uneducated, illiterate, rural, isolated physically by virtue of poor communication and emotionally by virtue of caste. The citizen was part of a "vote bank" contracted by those more powerful, clever, better educated and connected, rather than being a free autonomous actor with the knowledge and opinions to register independent preferences in the polling booth. Evidence was provided by the ballot itself—in the mind of the voter, candidates had symbols rather than names.

The 1967 elections challenged these presumptions in a dramatic way and provide a benchmark in the development of the mind of the Indian electorate. Congress governments were defeated in eight states and barely managed to hang on at the national level. The first of a series of national election surveys revealed a citizenry that was knowledgeable, opinionated on a wide range of matters, critical of governmental performance, and that held government accountable.[34] If the independent-mindedness of the Indian electorate was not yet clear in 1967, it was convincingly demonstrated in the 1977 electoral defeat of Indira Gandhi, the incumbent prime minister with a powerful state apparatus at her disposal. The independent spirit of the electorate was again expressed in the 1980 elections, which saw the defeat of the incumbent Janata government after three years of internal bickering and policy indecision and the return of Indira Gandhi as prime minister. It was felt in the ninth national elections of December 1989 in which the Congress lost power and a large proportion of its incumbent MPs and cabinet members went down to defeat. And it was made evident once again in the elections of 1991 when the Congress was returned as a minority government, having garnered 38 percent of the popular vote.

Elections attract the interest of the Indian citizen. One-third of the electorate in 1967 observed that they had at least "some interest" in the election campaign, and approximately two-fifths indicated that the results "mattered to them," while slightly over three-quarters expressed satisfaction with the election results at both the national level and within their state.[35] In a survey of the electorate in 1984, one-third indicated that they were at least "somewhat" interested in politics *between* election campaigns, while nearly half indicated that they had an interest in the campaign of that year with somewhat over half in 1991 evincing an ongoing interest in politics. A marginally smaller proportion in 1984 expressed some level of satisfaction with the election results of that year than did their cohorts in 1967. India's voters are not only in the political marketplace at election time; they tend to be satisfied with electoral outcomes and "accepting" of the victories of those for whom they had not voted.

The level of political knowledge and the incidence of Indians' opinions about public matters are greater than their self-professed levels of interest in political life. In 1967 slightly over half of the electorate could identify the winning candidate from their constituency for the state assembly, and half was also able to identify the runner-up, the corresponding proportions for the *Lok Sabha* being slightly over two-fifths and slightly under one-third, respectively. Interestingly, nearly as many constituents could identify the caste (*jati*) of the winner and runner-up as could identify them by name or party affiliation. In 1971, nearly three-fourths of the electorate knew either the name or the party of the candidate elected from their constituency; nearly three-fifths could identify the prime minister, though less than half, interestingly, knew her party affiliation. Not surprisingly, in the context of the short-lived coalition governments in the states between 1967 and 1971, slightly less than one-third knew either the name or the party of the chief minister of the state. The 1971 national elections mark the rise of the "personality factor" in structuring Indian politics; they also mark the decline of party institutions and the erosion of party identification in the electorate.[36]

The Indian electorate is an electorate with opinions. Citizens hold and express their sentiments (positive or negative) about public figures, public institutions, governmental performance, and themselves as participants in public affairs. In 1971, for example, slightly over 70 percent of the Indian public held some opinion about the leadership of Prime Minister Gandhi, while in 1984 the proportion had increased to 90 percent. (In 1991, 80 percent registered an opinion about the impact of Rajiv Gandhi's assassination on the fortunes of the Congress that year.) Between 80 and 90 percent register opinions about governmental performance. There is a much wider range—60 to 90 percent—in response to such questions as whether "voting by people like me" has an effect on government and whether elections or parties "are necessary" in Indian political life, but the portrait of an involved citizenry remains.

Government is seen as the primary source of assistance in meeting personal as well as community needs—"government minded-ness" or "governmentalization" as Rajni Kothari has proposed to call it. In a 1966 survey, Kothari found that fully half of the public felt assistance would likely be forthcoming from government in a time of serious crisis, with slightly less than one-third feeling confident that it would be forthcoming from relatives outside the household.[37] In rational-actor fashion, over two-thirds indicated that they would prefer that assistance be forthcoming from government.

This strong expectation of government as provider makes the fact that the Indian citizen registers strong opinions about governmental performance and the capacities of political leaders particularly important. The most negative assessments are registered at times of electoral reverses of incumbent governments. In 1967, for example, over half the electorate "strongly agreed" that the Congress governments in nation and state had "failed to keep prices down," "failed to distribute food properly," and "failed to root out corruption," with nearly an additional one quarter of the population registering "agreement" with these judgements. Indeed, 60 percent of the electorate agreed that in at least three of four policy areas Congress had failed, opposition voters not unsurprisingly being more critical than Congress voters.[38] Only 5 percent of opposition and Congress party identifiers judged government performance in at least three areas to have been adequate. This constituted a strong indictment of governmental performance.

Nearly two decades later, however, in 1984—when Congress was returned with the largest proportion of the popular vote it has ever received in a national election (49 percent)—slightly over half the population gave the incumbent government a positive rating while one-third was negative. In terms of party identification, as expected, Congress identifiers (70 percent) were the most positive, opposition identifiers less so by a thirty-point margin, with over 90 percent of party identifiers registering either a positive or a negative judgment. Performance when judged good tends to be rewarded;

when judged poor it tends to be punished.

Just as important as knowledge and judgments of performance in our portrait of belief and effect of the Indian citizen are attitudes and feelings about political institutions and processes. To what extent are they judged right and appropriate; in other words, to what extent have India's "two political cultures" become intermingled; to what extent have the values of elite political culture been transferred to mass political culture?[39] We find change in this regard over the two decades following the critical elections of 1967.

In the national election survey conducted that year and replicated in four major states two years later, the vast majority of the population (some 80 percent) felt that parties and elections were "necessary" to organize public affairs, even though proportions of only slightly lesser magnitude felt that "government was too complicated to understand" by people "like me," and that on the whole "government officials don't care" about public needs. Two-thirds of the 1969 four-state sample felt the existing system of government was right even if it "delayed action" in public matters, with a small minority registering a negative view.[40] This is particularly noteworthy since these four states at the time had experienced two years of unstable and ineffective governments. A large proportion also indicated that they felt parties and elections helped make government more responsive than it would otherwise be. Interestingly, the sentiment was stronger in the case of elections than parties. This latter sentiment was expressed, too, in the election of 1971 when slightly over half of the population registered their feeling that voting was the only way to influence a government, with a sizable proportion being undecided. Approximately half felt that their vote did "make a difference" in political affairs. The very fact of opinion polling and the voter's preparedness to register opinions, of course, are themselves indicators of the value of free expression in the culture of Indian democracy.

The quarter century since 1967, however, has witnessed a decline in the public's affirmation of India's political institutions. While only a small fraction of the population at the time of the 1980 elections felt that parties and elections were "unnecessary," the remainder was evenly divided between those who felt they were "necessary" and those who were "uncertain." The increase in "uncertainty" and decline in "necessity" constitute a noticeable change in the level of support for institutions at the core of the democratic process. Similarly, there was a marked increase in the proportions who felt that parties and elections did not make governments responsive; in 1991 less than one-third of those surveyed felt that elections make governments more responsive to their needs. Similarly, a high proportion of the citizenry in the 1980s, though less than in 1967, continued to feel that government was too complicated for a citizen "like me" to understand and that government officials "do not care" about public needs.

While feelings about the efficacy of parties have consistently declined, a large majority of the electorate has consistently indicated that it feels voting "has an effect" on government. The effectiveness of voting was dramatically demonstrated in the national elections of 1977, 1980, 1989, and 1991, when incumbent governments in New Delhi were unceremoniously turned out of office, and in 1967, as well as on numerous subsequent occasions, in the states. Furthermore, while Indian citizens have tended to express increasing ambivalence about the efficacy of parties and elections in making government "pay attention" to the public, substantial proportions indicate they feel that "people like us" have influence on government, the high points being in elections of high turnout (1967 and 1984), the low point being in 1971 after a four-year period of unstable coalition governments in many of the states. This is an important point: the Indian citizen feels that voting is the most important way of influencing the behavior of government.

The social and political distributions of these sentiments are interesting. The belief that "voting by people like me makes a difference in government" is consistently higher among the educated and the high castes than among the less educated and lower castes. Strength of the sentiment is found in equal measure in rural and urban areas, except in 1971 when there was a noticeable diminution of this belief in the rural electorate. Particularly important is the finding that "party identifiers" have a much stronger belief in the power of voting than do "non-identifiers," with non-Congress voters consistently showing *stronger* sentiment in this regard than their Congress counterparts. A similar distribution in terms of party identification exists with respect to belief in the responsiveness of public institutions.

We find in India a mass political culture that, within two decades after independence, if not before, had become knowledgeable about elections, had opinions about governmental performance, and believed in the appropriateness of institutions closely associated with a democratic regime. We find a public strongly oriented toward government, with the view that government should govern and provide, and that governments should be held accountable. Indian citizens register a rather low sense of political efficacy with the exception of voting, which they feel is consequential in making governments responsive. While opposition party supporters naturally tend to be more critical of governments than supporters of the incumbent party, party identifiers in general tend to register stronger support for public institutions than non-identifiers do. Non-Congress as well as Congress party identifiers evince a strong belief in the power of the vote to make government responsible, but non-Congress identifiers are, interestingly, more sanguine in this regard than those identifying with Congress.

## Tension and Change in India's Democratic Culture

The diffusion of democratic values within mass society in India occurred under circumstances of elite commitment to seeing diffusion succeed, under long periods of governmental stability, and where party institutions attracted and absorbed new groups of political aspirants and effectively mediated between competing interests. While India remained poor compared to other democracies during this period (1947–1967), it experienced economic growth and modest redistribution among middle and lower-middle castes.[41]

The two decades since 1967, however, have witnessed a decline both in party institutions (especially in elite commitment to them) and in party identification among voters. The decline of party and secular "input" institutions has been accompanied by increases in political interest but also in feelings of ambiguity on the part of the Indian public about the effectiveness of public institutions. As successive postindependence generations of citizens become publicly active and start going to the polls, we must ask, what is "replacing" the mediating functions of party institutions and the former positive and supportive sentiments about the effectiveness of (democratic) public institutions?

Three factors have become increasingly critical in the maintenance of political support for governments as well as the regime—primordialism, personalism, and performance. The first is found in the continuation of a strong sense of caste and communal identity, and the expectation on the part of the members of particular castes and communal groups that their fellows should and will act collectively in elections. The same holds true for one's family and one's village. In this regard we find an element of "cultural closure" occurring in India's politics. Second, there has been a pronounced increase in the salience of personalism and "leadership effect" in the mind of the electorate. Political commentators have referred to the "Indira waves" as have political activists themselves. National surveys have not only revealed a public that is more cognizant of political leaders, but a public that tends increasingly to extend them favorable ratings as long as government is stable, ratings that are more favorable than the government of which they are a part. Affinity for political personality, for example, has replaced party identification as the strongest predictor of party vote; the "personal party" has replaced "party organization."[42] And as part of this transformation, Congress at the center has come to rely increasingly on members of the national council of ministers and cabinet secretariat for information and decision making concerning electoral strategy and political support.[43]

This phenomenon is also found in the support extended to leaders of movements committed to liberating a state from what have popularly been perceived as corrupt and iniquitous governments.[44] It has been particularly pronounced in the development of regional political movements organized around film stars, particularly in Andhra Pradesh and Tamil Nadu, where chief ministers and other prominent political leaders have developed mass followings through their portrayal of god-like epic heroes or romantic defenders of public virtue before their entry into politics.[45] It is seen in smaller, though no less dramatic, scale among groups felt to be under threat, such as the popular mass identification with Jarnail Singh Bhindranwale as well as others in the Sikh community of Punjab. The phenomenon is also evident in the activity of various devotional movements and is powerfully demonstrated in contemporary movements of social reform in which religious symbolism is utilized, as it so successfully was in the years immediately preceding the beginning of the Indian nationalist movement over a century ago.

Government performance, including the stability of governing coalitions, remains extremely salient for the Indian voter. What government is doing and how well it is doing it command the attention of citizens, and almost all have opinions that they register. There is a high level of "government-mindedness" on the part of the electorate, not as passive "subjects" being acted upon, but as potentially critical "participants," in Almond and Verba's classic terminology,[46] who are prepared to judge and to act. With the decline in support for public institutions, however, it may be that the factor of governmental performance will become increasingly important in the inculcation of political support, including the continuing renewal of support for democratic institutions among new generations of voters.

A second tension in the culture of Indian democracy is engagement with government through episodic and localized demonstrations of varying populist magnitude such as *hartals* and *bandhs* (business and work stoppages), political fasts, and *gheraoes* (sit-ins). Such modes of engaging government hark back to the nationalist movement and have consistently been perceived as legitimate forms of political behavior by between 25 to 40 percent of the electorate. These constitute strategies of getting government's attention, to force it to be more responsive and less withholding.[47] The electorate makes a distinction between the use of collective pressure with respect to government and the use of collective violence, however, with only a minuscule fraction supporting organized violence as a legitimate political strategy.

A third tension in the culture of democracy in India is the increase in collective violence. This is manifest in communal conflicts between Hindus and Muslims, in movements for greater autonomy among ethnic minorities on the geographical periphery, in "sons of the soil" movements following immigration of "outsiders" into culturally distinct geographically bounded areas, and in conflicts between higher castes and backward castes over the reservation of government jobs, scholarships, and educational admissions for the latter.

Division between Hindu and Muslim communities prompted the British to "divide and quit" their Indian empire in 1947. As they were then, Hindu and Muslim communities continue to be structurally and psychologically separate from one another. Residential areas, while often juxtaposed, are self-contained; intermarriage is minimal, even within castes common to both religious communities; there is minimal interaction in schools, attended by fewer Muslim than Hindu children. Lack of social interaction is mirrored in psychological separateness infused with attitudes of mutual suspicion and depreciation.[48] In the late 1980s, politicization of communal tensions expanded into rural areas where it had been unknown before, and became more pronounced in the south and in Jammu-Kashmir.

The pattern of separation and autonomy within Indian society has been accompanied by a linear increase in communal violence. While initially expressed in isolated incidents between a limited number of combatants, it was transformed by the decade of the 1970s in frequent large-scale clashes between communal groups. Such deadly quarrels also characterized linguistic conflict, and in greater measure, conflict between untouchables and landed upper-castes, and the "Anti-Reservation" riots of upper against backward castes in opposition to the latter's being favored by policies of "compensatory discrimination."[49] In the 1980s, such communal violence has come to characterize relations between Hindus and Sikhs, through terrorist acts on the part of Sikhs and, in the aftermath of Indira Gandhi's assassination, Hindu destruction of Sikh life and property in many northern Indian cities. Political support in Punjab has become polarized among parties and groups on the basis of religion, as central governments have successively shown reluctance to concede Sikh demands for greater autonomy and decentralization of power within the federal system.[50]

Most powerfully, however, violence has visited relations between Muslims and Hindus. Though there was relative calm in the first decade and a half of independence, the year of Nehru's death, 1964, saw a sharp increase in communal incidents, claiming 2,000 lives by government report.[51] Deaths from Muslim-Hindu communal violence increased to an annual average of 111 in the 1970s and 454 in the 1980s. Communal division and conflict is reflected in political alienation among large segments of the Muslim community, especially Muslim elites, two-thirds of whom registered a high level of political dissatisfaction in a 1971 survey.[52] It has been evident most recently and dramatically in the conflict over the presence of an historic mosque in Ayodhya, accepted by Hindus as the birthplace of Lord Rama.[53] The destruction of the mosque in December 1992 by Hindu militants touched off a new wave of religious violence that claimed several thousand lives.

The consequences of communal riots are deep and entail major implications for political organization and behavior. Communal riots confirm feelings of suspicion and distrust within each of the embattled communities, more so among Muslims than Hindus. When riots occur, there has been an expectation that government will intercede to restore order, to save the warring communities from themselves. Riots, however, have drawn an increasingly broad spectrum of Muslims into a ghetto mentality, as Muslims' faith in government to intercede and protect them, particularly in northern India, has eroded. Some observers suggest that a new generation of Muslim political aspirants will find fertile soil in such situations to encourage religious fundamentalism for translation into electoral support—a process that developed with deeply divisive and ultimately devastating consequences in the late 1980s.

## Summary and Discussion

A democratic regime has existed in India in conditions that are not normally hospitable to such a constitutional order. India at the time of independence was largely rural, illiterate, and impoverished. Its densely populated countryside was culturally heterogeneous, divided vertically into mutually exclusive regions and linguistic cultures and horizontally into mutually exclusive primordial collectivities known as castes. Two-fifths of the territory that came to constitute India was under the direct governance of some 550 semi-sovereign princely autocracies before independence. A democratic regime was created at independence and has continued through the four decades since.

The culture of democracy in modern India has historic roots. The principles of free speech, assembly, and movement were established before independence, as were those of popular representation, election, and self-governance. These values were advocated and elaborated by successive generations of a strong nationalist elite, and they assumed institutional form as an authoritarian colonial raj took steps toward decolonization. Practices predicated upon these principles were often violated by the British colonial administration, but after a hiatus there was a return toward the practice of principle. During the preindependence period the convention of responsible government developed in the provinces of India, where electorates continually expanded along with the responsibilities of the elected governments.

The culture of liberal democracy became the ideology of a dominant national political class that transcended the particularistic interests of various social groups that it deemed to represent. This ideology was elaborated during the nationalist movement, and after petition to and confrontation with the British Raj progressively assumed institutional form, not fully as conceived by national elites at the time, but in substantial measure. Demands for constitutional reform focused upon the entirety of the bureaucratic and representative apparatus of the colonial state and emphasized the unity of the political community. Agitational and electoral nationalist politics created an Indian public oriented toward government as an institution, the actions of which did, or could, affect their lives. "Government-mindedness" in India has preindependence roots. Both in parties and legislative bodies there developed a tradition of tolerance for opposition, as well as traditions of mediating conflicting interests and negotiating for political support.

Translocal coalitions developed at various "levels" of politics as political aspirants sought public office or positions of consequence in the Indian National Congress. In one major instance, however, conflict proved intractable and mediation impossible—between the Indian National Congress advocating a united India and the All-India Muslim League advocating division of the subcontinent on communal grounds and the creation of a separate state for undivided India's Muslim peoples. The Indian nationalist elite came to accept partition as a necessary price for sovereignty and freedom.

Independence found in India a national political class committed to the creation of a liberal democratic political order, to a common vision of the political community, and to diffusing its values concerning the purposes and practices of public life to encompass a newly endowed Indian citizenry. Indeed this class served as the functional equivalent of a middle class in other cases of democratization. This class constituted a coalition of urban and rural social segments; while it appealed to all regardless of status or economic holdings, it was composed of merchant and professional groups in the cities and upwardly mobile peasant castes in the villages.

Furthermore, in contrast to many former nationalist movements, that in India focused upon using the legislative institution to control the bureaucracy—a bureaucracy that by the time of independence had been undergoing a process of "Indianization" for a quarter-century. The founding national leadership was from the outset committed to making legislative institutions rather than party the instruments of governmental accountability. This ideological commitment was shared by several generations present at the time of founding.

The measure of success in the expansion of elite ideology has been evident in the development of a public with opinions, that expects governments to govern, and that holds them accountable for the quality of their governance. It is a public that believes in the power that voting by people like themselves can have in public affairs, even though it feels a sense of inefficacy in otherwise keeping governments responsive. The power of the vote received public witness in the defeat of an incumbent prime minister and the government in 1977, which brought an end to the Emergency regime, as well as in the defeat of important leaders of government in nation and state both before and thereafter. The culture of democracy has come to characterize the beliefs and practices of a substantial proportion of India's active and attentive public.

But as the existence and operation of democratic institutions may create the conditions of their own sustenance, so conditions may come about that are disruptive of their operation. Such conditions are perhaps latent in all democratic societies; they have become manifest, however, in India. We find these conditions in the "communalization of politics" in both ethnic and religious terms, in the apparent primacy of performance in maintaining public attachment in the wake of a decline in support for public institutions, and in the transformation from a "politics of mediation" to "politics by plebescite" with the decline of party institutions, the rise of the personality factor, and increased governmental dependence on administrative sources of political intelligence and power.

## Notes

1. Robert Dahl, *Polyarchy: Participation and Opposition* (New Haven: Yale University Press, 1971), Chap. 1; Samuel P. Huntington, "Will More Countries Become Democratic?" *Political Science Quarterly* 99 (Summer 1984): 193–218; Seymour Martin Lipset, *Political Man: The Social Bases of Politics* (Garden City: Doubleday, 1960), pp. 45–96; and Larry Diamond, Juan J. Linz, and Seymour Martin Lipset, eds., *Democracy in Developing Countries: Asia* (Boulder, CO: Lynne Rienner, 1989), pp. xvi-xviii, and Chapter 1. For broader conceptions of "democracy" that embrace and are instructive for the Indian case, see Giovanni Sartori, *The Theory of Democracy Revisited* (Chatham, N.J.: Chatham House, 1987), 2 vols., Chaps. 1, 2, and 9; and Richard L. Sklar, "Developmental Democracy," *Comparative Studies in Society and History* 29 (October 1987): 686–714.

2. Account must be taken of anti-government movements in this regard, however. Several smaller regionalist parties in the northeastern states advocate a decentralization of power as do powerfully visible groups within the Sikh movement in the state of Punjab. For useful surveys see Robert L. Hardgrave, Jr., "The Northeast, the Punjab, and the Reorganization of Indian Politics," *Asian Survey* 23 (October 1983): 1171–1181; and Bhagwan D. Dua, "India: Federal Leadership and the Secessionist Movements on the Periphery," in Ramashray Roy and Richard Sisson, eds., *Diversity and Dominance in Indian Politics: Division, Deprivation and the Congress* (New Delhi: Sage, 1990), pp. 189–218.

3. Government of India, *India 1985: A Reference Annual* (New Delhi: Ministry of Information and Broadcasting, 1986), pp. 200–201.

4. The two years encompass what is customarily referred to as "The Emergency" (1975–1977), during which time India was governed under provisions of Article 352 of the constitution and normal constitutional processes were severely curtailed.

5. See William Vanderbok and Richard Sisson, "Parties and Electorates from *Raj* to *Swaraj*: An Historical Analysis of Electoral Behavior in Late Colonial and Early Independent India," *Social Science History* 12 (Summer 1988): 121–142; and P.D. Reeves, B.D. Graham, and J.M. Goodman, *A Handbook to Elections in Uttar Pradesh, 1920–1951* (Delhi: Manohar, 1975).

6. I here refer to Phillips Cutright's minor classic, "National Political Development: Social and Economic Correlates," in Nelson W. Polsby, et al., eds., *Political and Social Life* (Boston: Houghton Mifflin, 1963), pp. 569–82. In his coding scheme for his dependent variable (viz. democracy), Cutright allows no points for colonial regimes, regardless of their character, before independence. It is possible for a case to go from fully autocratic to fully democratic with the stroke of a pen.

7. Stein Rokkan, "The Structuring of Mass Politics in the Smaller European Democracies: A Developmental Typology," *Comparative Studies in Society and History* 10 (January 1968): 173–210; also in his *Citizens, Elections, Parties: Approaches to the Comparative Study of the Processes of Development* (New York: David McKay, 1970), Chap. 3.

8. Sharad Karkhanis, *Indian Politics and the Role of the Press* (Delhi: Vikas, 1981), Chap. 2; Robert I. Crane, "The Transfer of Western Education to India," in William B. Hamilton, ed., *The Transfer of Institutions* (Durham: Duke University Press, 1964), pp. 108-138; Kalikinkar Datta, "Early Publications," *Bengal Past and Present* 87 (Jan.–June 1968): 92–98; and M.M. Ahluwalia, "Press and India's Struggle for Freedom, 1858 to 1909," *Journal of Indian History* 38 (December 1960): 599–604.

9. See S.R. Mehrotra, *The Emergence of the Indian National Congress* (Delhi: Vikas, 1971); and Bimenbehari Majumdar, *Indian Political Associations and Reform of Legislature, (1818–1917)* (Calcutta: Firma Mukhopadhayay, 1965), Chaps. 1-4; Charles H. Heimsath, *Indian Nationalism and Hindu Social Reform* (Princeton: Princeton University Press, 1964); and Kenneth W. Jones, *Arya Dharm: Hindu Consciousness in Nineteenth Century Punjab* (Berkeley and Los Angeles: University of California Press, 1976).

10. The words are those of Sir Bartle Frere spoken in 1860 and published in *Government of India, Report on Indian Constitutional Reforms, 1918*, and reprinted as *Constitutional and National Development in India* (New Delhi: Ess Ess Publications, 1981), p. 39.

11. Calculated from data presented in Majumdar, *Indian Political Associations*, Chap. 16.

12. Anil Seal, *The Emergence of Indian Nationalism: Competition and Collaboration in the Later Nineteenth Century* (Cambridge: Cambridge University Press, 1968), Chaps. 1, 3, and 4.

13. John R. McLane, *Indian Nationalism and the Early Congress* (Princeton: Princeton University Press, 1977); Bimanbehari Majumdar and Bhakat Prasad Mazumdar, *Congress and Congressmen in the Pre-Gandhian Era (1885-1917)* (Calcutta: Firma Mukopadhayay, 1967); Stanley Wolpert, *Tilak and Gokhale: Revolution and Reform in the Making of Modern India* (Berkeley and Los Angeles: University of California Press, 1962); and Rajat Kanta Ray, "Moderates, Extremists, and Revolutionaries: Bengal 1900–1908," in Richard Sisson and Stanley Wolpert, eds., *Congress and Indian Nationalism* (Berkeley and Los Angeles: University of California Press, 1988), pp. 62–89.

14. *Constitutional and National Development in India*, pp. 54–55; and Hugh Tinker, *The Foundations of Local Self-Government in India, Pakistan, and Burma* (London: Athlone Press, 1954).

15. See Harold A. Gould, "Local Government Roots of Contemporary Indian Politics," *Economic and Political Weekly* (February 13, 1971): 457–464; C.A. Bayly, "Local Control in Indian Towns: The Case of Allahalad, 1880–1920," *Modern Asian Studies* 5 (1971): 289–311; Francis Robinson, "Municipal Government and Muslim Separatism in the United Provinces, 1882-1916," in John Gallagher, Gordon Johnson, and Anil Seal, eds., *Locality, Province, and Nation: Essays on Indian Politics, 1870–1940* (London: Cambridge University Press, 1973), pp. 69–122; and David Washbrook, "The Influence of Government Institutions on Provincial Politics and Leadership in Modiar, c. 1880–1925" (paper presented to the Seminar on Leadership in South Asia, University of London, 25 January 1973).

16. For an insightful treatment of the importance of associations and roles as nodules of autonomy and freedom and their relationship to democratization see Sklar, "Developmental Democracy."

17. Lloyd I. and Susanne Hoeber Rudolph, *The Modernity of Tradition: Political Development in India* (Chicago: University of Chicago Press, 1967), Part I.

18. Constitutional and National Development in India, p. 1. The report upon which the 1919 reforms was based was prepared by Edwin Montagu, Secretary of State for India, and Lord Chelmsford, the Governor General of India.

19. Calculated from data presented in Indian Statutory Commission, *Memorandum Submitted by the Government of Bombay* (London: His Majesty's Stationery Office, 1930), Vol. VII, pp. 504 and 560.

20. The classic review of governmental performance during this period still remains Reginald Coupland, *The Indian Problem: Report on the Constitutional Problem in India* (London: Oxford University Press, 1944).

21. See Richard Sisson and Lawrence L. Shrader, "Legislative Formation in Pre-Independent India: The Issue of Prerequisites for Democratic Regimes," in Paul Wallace, ed., *Region and Nation in India* (New Delhi: Oxford University Press, 1985), pp. 192–218.

22. The most dramatic example of isolation was the "forced" resignation of the charismatic Bengali leader, Subhas Chandra Bose, in 1939. Earlier in a contest over the basis of representation within Congress, the socialist wing, which advocated a class and functional basis of representation, was isolated by a coalition of social conservatives and Gandhians who perceived such a change as conflict-inducing and as a threat to their position of dominance. See D.A. Low, "Congress and 'Mass Contacts,' 1936–1937: Ideology, Interests, and Conflict over the Basis of Party Representation," in Sisson and Wolpert, *Congress and Indian Nationalism*, pp. 134–158.

23. John R. McLane, "The Early Congress, Hindu Populism, and the Wider Society," in Sisson and Wolpert, *Congress and Indian Nationalism*, p. 47.

24. The first has subsequently been published as Motilal Nehru, *The Nehru Report: An Anti-Separatist Manifesto, The Committee Appointed by the All Parties' Conference, 1928* (New Delhi: Michiko and Panjathan, 1975). The latter is examined in V.A. Narain, "The Karachi Resolution and the Development of Nationalist Ideology in India," a paper presented at the Conference on the Indian National Congress and Indian Nationalism, UCLA, March 1984.

25. Rudolph and Rudolph, *The Modernity of Tradition*, Part I; Rajni Kothari, ed., *Caste in Indian Politics* (Delhi: Orient Longman, 1981, fifth printing); and Richard Sisson, "Peasant Movements and Political Mobilization: The Jats of Rajasthan," *Asian Survey*, 9 (December 1969), 946–963. The development of "mini-polities" in the form of voluntary associations is congruent with Harry Eckstein's understanding of the relationship between culture and authority systems. See Appendix B: "A Theory of Stable Democracy," in his *Division and Cohesion in Democracy: A Study of Norway* (Princeton: Princeton University Press, 1966).

26. D. N. Dhanagare, *Peasant Movements in India: 1920-1950* (New Delhi: Oxford University Press, 1983); and Gyan Pandey, "Peasant Revolt and Indian Nationalism: The Peasant Movement in Awadh, 1919–22," in Ranajit Guha, ed., *Subaltern Studies I: Writings on South Asian History and Society* (New Delhi: Oxford University Press, 1982), pp. 143-197.

27. For a summary of this literature see Richard Sisson, *Politics and Culture in India* (Ann Arbor: Center for Political Studies, Monograph Series, 1988).

28. Rajni Kothari, "The Congress 'System' in India," *Asian Survey* 4 (December 1964): 1161–1173. Also W.H. Morris-Jones, "Dominance and Dissent: Their Inter-Relations in the Indian Party System," *Government and Opposition* 1 (September 1966): 451–466.

29. Richard Sisson and William Vanderbok, "Mapping the Indian Electorate: Trends in Party Support in Seven National Elections," *Asian Survey*, 23 (October 1983), 1140–1158.

30. Norman Nicholson, "Integrative Strategies of a National Elite: Career Patterns in the Indian Council of Ministers," *Comparative Politics* 8 (July 1975): 533–557; and Richard Sisson, "Prime Ministerial Power and the Selection of Ministers in India: Three Decades of Change," *International Political Science Review*, 2 (1981): 137–157.

31. V.P. Menon, *The Story of the Integration of the Indian States* (London: Orient Longman, 1956); and his *The Transfer of Power in India* (Princeton: Princeton University Press, 1957). For a study of efforts to bring the princely states closer to the new structure of centralizing authority during the preindependence period, see Urmila Phadnis, *Towards the Integration of Indian States, 1919-1947* (London: Asia Publishing, 1968).

32. In some cases autonomous "party systems" developed at the local level, located primarily within Congress, but instructing opposition groups as well. An illustrative case is provided by B.S. Baviskar's analysis of *gats* (factions) in rural Maharashtra. *Gats* hold "party meetings," have "parliamentary boards" to select candidates for local office, and enforce "party discipline" on their members. See his "Factional Conflict and the Congress Dilemma in Rural Maharashtra (1952–75)," in Richard Sisson and Ramashray Roy, eds., *Diversity and Dominance in Indian Politics: Changing Bases of Congress Support*, vol. 1 (New Delhi: Sage Publications, 1990), pp. 37–54.

33. For these data, see William Vanderbok, "Institutionalization, Alignment, and Realignment in the Indian Electorate," a paper presented at the Conference on Comparative Dimensions of Indian Elections and Party Politics, UCLA, June 1987, Table A.

34. Rajni Kothari, "Continuity and Change in India's Party System," *Asian Survey*, 10 (November 1970): 937–948; Samuel J. Eldersveld and Bashiruddin Ahmed, *Citizens and Politics: Mass Political Behavior in India* (Chicago: University of Chicago Press, 1978).

35. The surveys employed here are for the elections of 1967, 1971, 1980, 1984, and 1991. The first two surveys were conducted by the Centre for the Study of Developing Societies in New Delhi and were conducted immediately after the election had taken place; the subsequent two were conducted by the Indian Institute of Public Opinion, New Delhi, and were conducted immediately before the elections. The 1991 data are preliminary and derive from a survey conducted by the Organisation for Socio-Economic Systems, New Delhi. The sampling frame was somewhat different for each election, but the sample of respondents approximates quite closely, in each instance, the general distribution of the adult population in terms of standard social, cultural, and economic categories, except for 1991 which has an oversampling of males and is unweighted. All items of interest were not included in all surveys. Where appropriate longitudinal data points are available, they are used; when they appear only once or twice they are used illustratively. Copies of interview schedules, codebooks, and descriptions of sampling frames are available in the Statistics Laboratory, Department of Political Science, UCLA.

36. Pradeep K. Chhibber and Richard Sisson, "The Rise of the 'Personal Party:' Evaluations of Congress Dominance in India, 1962-1984," a paper presented at the Annual Meetings of the Western Political Science Association, Salt Lake City, 1989.

37. Kothari, *Politics in India* (Boston: Little Brown, 1970), pp. 284–288.

38. Those who felt Congress failed include all who registered such an opinion on at least three items; supporters included *all* who responded favorably on at least three items. The "ambivalent" include *all* other combinations including "don't knows."

39. For an early examination of these two cultures and their relationships see Myron Weiner, "India: Two Political Cultures" in Lucian W. Pye and Sydney Verba, eds., *Political Culture and Political Development* (Princeton: Princeton University Press, 1965), pp. 199–245. Another slightly different formulation is W.H. Morris-Jones, "India's Political Idioms," in C.H. Philips, ed., *Politics and Society in India* (London: Allen and Unwin, 1963), pp. 133–154.

40. Ramashray Roy, *The Uncertain Verdict: The Study of the 1969 Elections in*

*Four Indian States* (Berkeley and Los Angeles: University of California Press, 1975).

41. Amartya Sen, "How is India Doing?" in Dilip K. Basu and Richard Sisson, eds., *Social and Economic Development in India: A Reassessment* (New Delhi: Sage Publications, 1986), pp. 28-42. For a useful comparative examination of the relationship between political practice and governmental performance in India, see Jyotirindra Das Gupta, "India: Democratic Becoming and Combined Development," in Diamond, et al., *Democracy in Developing Countries: Asia*, pp. 53–104.

42. Chhibber and Sisson, "The Rise of the 'Personal Party.'"

43. See Bhabani Sen Gupta, "Cabinet-Making and Unmaking," *Economic and Political Weekly* 23 (February 6, 1988): 230–233; and Richard Sisson, "Pathways to India's National Governing Elite," in Mattei Dogan, ed., *Pathways to Power: Selecting Rulers in Pluralist Democracies* (Boulder: Westview Press, 1989), pp. 181–198.

44. John R. Wood, "Extra-Parliamentary Opposition in India: An Analysis of Populist Agitation in Gujarat and Bihar," *Pacific Affairs* 48 (Fall 1975): 313–334; and Anand Purushottam Mavalankar, "The Politics of Confrontation in India: A Study of the Bihar Movement," Ph.D. Dissertation, Department of Political Science, UCLA, 1984.

45. Robert L. Hardgrave, Jr., *Essays in the Political Sociology of South India* (New Delhi: Usha, 1979), Chap. 3, "When Stars Displace the Gods: The Folk Culture of Cinema in Tamil Nadu," pp. 92–124.

46. For this formulation see Gabriel A. Almond and Sidney Verba, *The Civic Culture: Political Attitudes and Democracy in Five Nations* (Princeton: Princeton University Press, 1962), Chap. 1.

47. An early elaboration of this idea is found in Myron Weiner, *The Politics of Scarcity: Public Pressure and Political Response in India* (Chicago: University of Chicago Press, 1962); an explanation of this phenomenon in terms of socialization in childhood and early adulthood is found in Sisson, *Politics and Culture in India*, pp. 9-22.

48. These attitudes were early on reflected in Gardner Murphy's inquiry into communal tensions and reported in his *In the Minds of Men: The Study of Human Behavior and Social Tension in India* (New York: Basic Books, 1953). These conditions and sentiments have been more recently reflected in such studies as Bipan Chandra, *Communalism in Modern India* (Delhi: Vikas Publishing, 1987), 2d revised ed.; and in Asghar Ali Engineer, ed., *Communal Riots in Post-Independence India* (Hyderabad: Sangam, 1984).

49. John R. Wood, "Reservations in Doubt: The Backlash Against Affirmative Action in Gujarat," in Roy and Sisson, eds., *Diversity and Dominance*, pp. 146–169. For an illuminating analysis of the broad issues concerning compensatory discrimination, see Marc Galanter, *Competing Equalities: Law and the Backward Classes in India* (New Delhi: Oxford University Press, 1984).

50. For an analysis of electoral and party polarization see M.S. Dhami, "Shifts in the Support Base of Political Parties in the 1985 Punjab Assembly Election," paper presented at the Conference on Comparative Dimensions of Indian Party and Electoral Politics, UCLA, June 1986; and Paul R. Brass, "The Punjab Crisis and the Unity of India," in Atul Kohli, ed., *India's Democracy: An Analysis of Changing State- Society Relations* (Princeton: Princeton University Press, 1988), pp. 169–213.

51. P. R. Rajgopal, *Communal Violence in India* (New Delhi: Uppal, 1987); see also the longitudinal analysis presented in Gopal Krishna, "Communal Violence in India: A Study of Communal Disturbances in Delhi," *Economic and Political Weekly* 20 (1985): 61–74 and 117–131.

52. Gopal Krishna, "The Problems of Integration in the Indian Political Community: Muslims and the Political Process," in Basu and Sisson, *Social and*

*Economic Development in India*, pp. 172–193.

53. For a brief appreciation of the effect of this conflict on the 1991 elections see Walter K. Andersen, "India's 1991 Elections: The Uncertain Verdict," *Asian Survey* 31 (October 1991): 976–989.

# • 3 •

# Between Liberalism and Statism: African Political Cultures and Democracy

## *Naomi Chazan*

### Political Cultures and Democratic Tensions

The African experience with democracy in the postcolonial period has been paradoxical. With the notable exceptions of Botswana, the Gambia, Mauritius, and most recently Senegal, repeated attempts to introduce and sustain democratic government from the 1960s through the 1980s faltered. At the same time, many Africans have conducted an unremitting quest for democratic rule, as evidenced in the new wave of democratic transitions and pressures in the early 1990s. The ambiguity of democratic practice in the vast majority of African states has gone hand in hand with the ongoing search for a democratic order.

What can account for the persistent democratic tensions that have permeated the continent? How have institutions, symbols and power intertwined to maintain distinctive democratic impulses without necessarily promoting democratic processes? What is the connection between political outlooks and the practice of politics in recent African history? What are the implications of these interactions for political transformation and regime change? Seeking answers to these questions, this chapter examines the relationship between political cultures and democracy in contemporary Africa. It reviews, in broad strokes, the historical legacies, contemporary expressions and multiple manifestations of the cultural facets of African politics, attempting to assess their impact on political institutions and their implications for democratic survival and revival on the continent.

Political cultures, those particular combinations of subjective orientations to political objects,[1] are deeply rooted in social relations. The specific contours of political attitudes, beliefs, values, and sentiments are an integral part of the institutional settings in which they emerged and through which they operate. Political cultures are consequently endogenous to political structures; they are to be found within political life.[2] Although political symbols reflect varieties of social constructions, they also possess an instrumental dimension: people do use culture to gain wealth and power.[3] Cultural symbols are articulated and disseminated by carriers who, through coalitions with other elites, seek to entrench their interpretation of group activity and enhance their own position within society.[4]

To understand the contours of African political cultures, it is consequently necessary to study the specific historical, social, and institutional environments in which they were forged and the precise means by which they have been conveyed. To divorce the study of political cultures in Africa from the political structures and concerns of time and place is to obscure the richness of cultural presentations and to overlook their many political ramifications.

African political cultures are marked by their proliferation and fragmentation.[5] Over the years varied traditional institutions and cultural traditions have come to interact with colonially derived structures and beliefs and with the apparatus and concomitant values of independent states. Institutional multiplication has been accompanied by cultural diversification. Despite the salience of authoritarianism in the postcolonial era, hegemonic schema have not been able to achieve symbolic ascendancy. A constant tug-of-war exists between competing institutions and orientations, between alternative explications of consciousness and meaning.[6] In many parts of the continent, different political outlooks and beliefs have yet to coalesce on a countrywide basis into cohesive cultural frameworks.

The main contention of this study is that the extent of consolidation of political cultures in contemporary Africa is directly related to the degree of stateness. "Authoritarianism is not the major issue in contemporary Africa; rather, it is the absence of central state authority and the resulting search for it."[7] States play vital security and economic roles and therefore appear strong, but they are also weak because they have precarious links with domestic social groups and consequently vie with other organizations for legitimacy and dominance.[8] Statism is not always akin to stateness. In statist situations articulators of state power are pitted against carriers of solidarity; all too frequently the state and the values it seeks to uphold are in conflict with civil society.[9] In the absence of adequate political institutions, integrating ideas cannot flourish. The fragility of state-society relations thus accounts for the profusion of political outlooks and worldviews.

The paucity of linkage mechanisms between state and society has an important bearing on the meaning and influence of democratic norms on the continent. Indeed, the "continued quest for democracy [can be seen] as a commentary upon the relationship between state and civil society."[10] Since 1945 democracy in Africa has assumed different meanings, been interpreted in quite heterogeneous manners, and generated distinct political consequences. The history of democracy in independent Africa has, however, been primarily one of response rather than action, of protest as opposed to construction. Various democratic precepts have been asserted as a reaction to the successive curtailment of competition, participation, representation, equality, and, ultimately, freedom and individual well-being. These expressions, however, have not been translated into political practice because they lack an institutional dimension. Democracy has appeared in the African arena most frequently as the political culture of counterhegemony.

Because democracy is first and foremost a relationship between organized power and those for whom it is organized, democratic political norms take on constructive meaning through the elaboration of appropriate interconnecting political structures.[11] The gradual development of interlocking social and economic networks is beginning to alter the nature of state-society interaction. The crystallization of civil society may be the prelude to the formulation of accompanying civic cultures. The potential institutionalization of these patterns holds forth the possibility for the refinement of uniquely African brands of democratic government. The gap between democratic visions of politics and their authoritarian expressions will, in all likelihood, persist in various forms pending the creation of such institutional mediations.

## Sources of African Political Cultures

The preindependence histories of sub-Saharan Africa offer a wealth of examples of both authoritarian and democratic precepts and structures. The daily lives of Africans are informed by three distinct legacies: precolonial traditions and institutions; colonial economic, social, and administrative structures; and frameworks designed during the anticolonial struggle.[12] Each of these inheritances possesses well-defined concepts of the parameters of the political community, attitudes toward authority, and access to leadership; an understanding of societal goals and desiderata, some ranking of important spheres of human activity; and ideas about the functions of government, distributive justice, and terms of exchange.[13] The continuity of many of these cultural premises through the maintenance of a variety of institutional arrangements yielded particularly heterogeneous political culture traditions on the eve of independence.

### Precolonial Origins

Traditional political institutions in Africa were endowed with an elaborate cultural apparatus. At the center of the specific traditions of various political units were well-defined myths of origin that provide the foundation for the investigation of key elements of these societies' political cultures.[14] These myths, despite many substantive variations, highlighted the centrality of human beings in the social order and projected an essentially pragmatic view of political life. They also delineated principles of social differentiation, division of labor, and access to valued resources (which was usually indirect and effected through a series of mediators).

The conveyors of the values of the society (religious leaders, political authority figures, chiefs) were articulators of models who gave meaning to mythical traditions. They interacted in a variety of ways with articulators of solidarity (lineage heads, representatives of age and gender groups) to form different types of political centers and to support many specific varieties of political interaction.[15] In many respects, both politically and culturally, pre-colonial Africa consisted of many little traditions that did not—the growing importance of Islam notwithstanding—generate a great tradition similar to those that flourished in Asia, Europe, and the Near East.

Despite the extraordinary diversity of African polities prior to the imposition of colonial rule, several democratic strands were discernible in most traditional political formations on the continent. The first was the principle of public involvement in decisionmaking.[16] In segmentary societies, such as the Kikuyu of East Africa or the Tiv and Igbo in present-day Nigeria, adults participated directly in the planning and implementation of communal affairs and in the adjudication of disputes. In more complex political entities, notions of representation were deeply embedded. Youth, traders, artisans, religious leaders, and heads of kin groups had their own delegates in ruling councils. Asante and Buganda furnish excellent case studies in this respect. Even in some highly centralized states consultation was the norm, and the great empires of the Western Sudan (Mali and Songhai, for example) practiced a form of indirect rule that allowed for a considerable amount of local autonomy. Values of participation, representation, and involvement were evident in a multiplicity of political settings.

Closely allied to indigenous provisions for popular inclusion were notions of consensus. Decisions in many areas were arrived at through lengthy debate whose purpose was to blur opposites, to find the middle road, and thereby to ensure compliance. The rules of the political game among the Igbo and the Tswana, for instance, put a premium on compromise. At the same time emphasis was placed on discussion (frequently termed palaver), on the public airing of different positions. Debate was an essential feature of the practice of politics in much of precolonial Africa.

Traditional African institutions also tended to highlight the importance of the community above the individual. The value attached to human relationships and communal harmony contained an equally strong rejection of unharnessed individualism and authoritarianism. Many precolonial societies in Africa established machinery to oversee rulers (see the checks and balances entrenched in the Yoruba states), monitor their actions, and call them to account when they failed to fulfill their obligations. Among the diffuse sanctions against the abuse of power were gossip, ridicule, the spread of rumor, and the withdrawal of services. Institutional sanctions included private and public admonitions, provisions for the statement of grievances, and elaborate measures for the removal from office of unwanted leaders.[17]

Inherent in these practices was an effort to balance multiple pressures for popular autonomy with rulers' demand for control. Decentralization, financial independence, and/or large measures of local self-government were integral features of even the most hierarchical political institutions in the precolonial period.[18] In many respects, contemporary Africans draw on well-entrenched notions of accountability, probity, and limited government (often enshrined, as in the Asante case, in constitutional forms).

Certain antidemocratic features were nevertheless also clearly in evidence, especially in the *jihad* states of West Africa (such as Sokoto, Macina, Tukulur) and the militaristic states of Southern Africa (Zulu, for one). Traditional African politics assumed a highly personal aura: power was vested in particular authority figures and, although carefully supervised, these leaders developed paternalistic and even highly authoritarian styles. Filial obligation to leaders was stressed. In organizationally complex systems, such as the Hausa-Fulani emirates, the authority of the state was seen as an extension of personal affiliations and depicted in familial terms. Platonic concepts of good government, based on faith in the wisdom and justice of rulers, overshadowed a belief in laws and procedures.

The idea of deference—of obedience to elders, officeholders, clan heads, village chiefs—was widespread. The mutual responsibility contained in concepts of kinship was often offset by the inequality adhering to ideas of seniority. Human rights could not be neatly dissociated from place in community, and strict hierarchies (based on ascription, age, or achievement) were maintained. The notion of individual liberty was notably absent in societies that valued group affiliation as the basis for social interaction.

In these circumstances the organization of formal oppositions or of competing interests was either circumscribed or considered to be subversive. Indeed, internal conflicts, when left unresolved, led to factionalism and ultimately to fragmentation and secession. The history of Bakongo and of ancient Ghana or Songhai are illustrative of this pervasive pattern.[19]

The institutional codification of these values and practices varied from society to society. In different areas, democratic traditions, principles, and procedures were juxtaposed to authoritarian norms in very specific ways, yielding a rich diversity of cultures ranging from the highly participatory to the heavily autocratic and repressive. By the time of the colonial influx many African political cultures were receptive to the participatory elements of Western democracy, while others were not; most were less amenable to its competitive premises and legalistic accoutrements.

## Colonial Legacies

Colonial rule compounded the democratic ambiguities evident in precolonial Africa. Despite the fact that the main colonial powers in Africa, Britain, and

France were democratic countries, the institutions they created were, first and foremost, instruments of domination. Established to enable control over vast areas containing disparate populations, they stressed functional utility and law and order but not participation and reciprocity. Hierarchical administrative networks buttressed by coercive devices were grafted upon, but usually did not displace, preexisting institutions.

The colonial state exemplified Western concepts of sovereignty and territoriality at the expense of notions of nationality and legitimacy.[20] Within this highly authoritarian structure, connections between rulers and ruled were strictly vertical: the definition of government lacked a popular component. Access to the colonial order was generally blocked and removed from the scrutiny of the people it purported to govern. A remote, bureaucratic image of politics (containing traditional patrimonial strains through heavy reliance on local big-men) emerged. Supraterritorial public administrations were superimposed on local civil communities.[21]

This pattern was reinforced through selective techniques of economic penetration. The encouragement of agricultural and mineral production for export together with the creation of a cash economy and the opening of markets for European goods brought the African continent into close and unequal contact with the global economy. The foundations for autonomous development were not, however, adequately prepared. In colonial Africa the vehicle of capitalism was the colonial state (and not local entrepreneurs or private concerns). The colonial economic inheritance linked accumulation to the externally oriented public sphere. African economic life was bureaucratized and commercialized, although hardly capitalized, at this juncture.[22]

The colonial state apparatus played a crucial role in structuring social relations and delimiting lines of conflict and interchange. Because of the imperatives of administrative efficiency and social control, local communities were designated as the primary units of African social life, frequently balkanizing traditional social networks. In francophone Africa, this pattern took on territorial forms; in anglophone areas, by means of the mechanism of indirect rule, traditional institutions were incorporated into the colonial hierarchy and divested of much of their autonomy. Carriers of power thus ruled over redefined articulators of solidarity. Ethnicity emerged in these institutional circumstances as an acceptable (and instrumentally viable) avenue of social exchange.[23]

To assist in the task of administration and to provide basic services, colonial regimes also encouraged the formation of new horizontal strata. These colonially dependent elites, usually formed through the introduction of Western education and Christianity, relied for their position on privileged access to the new centers and their resources. Social standing within the colonial order was linked to proximity to state power rather than to material resources. This tiny African bureaucratic class was the outward expression of a new norm that placed particular value on the state as the primary source of social mobility.[24] At the same time, however, this Western-educated elite did imbibe some democratic ideals (participation, accountability, popular mobilization) and created urban-based groups through which they could be expressed.[25]

The restructuring of the nature and direction of officially relevant societal relations did not, however, substantially alter the social structures of production, nor did it impinge on associational life in areas not of concern to the colonial powers. The colonial political culture model was hegemonic rather than incorporating and imposed rather than integrating. It was also avowedly partial. Colonial rule left a legacy of bifurcation between public administration and popular involvement and between official institutions and civic structures, while offering precious few suggestions for their interconnection.

The democratic political baggage carried by colonial officials was consequently transformed by the exigencies of colonial government. To be sure, the British, French, and to a lesser extent Belgian attempt to transmit, through ideological rhetoric and the school system, a normative worldview, did highlight the theoretical connections between intellectual enlightenment, economic advancement, and democratic modes of thought. The reality of colonial rule was, however, the antithesis of many of these ideas and conveyed quite different political messages. The values of participation and competition were obviated by the hegemonic statism of colonial structures and the power considerations of its allied political culture.

*Anticolonial Norms*

The dissonance between the proclaimed goals of colonial rule and the structure of alien control prepared the groundwork for the dissolution of colonial systems. The 1939–1945 period was a watershed in the political development of Africa. The recruitment of Africans to colonial armies and of African economies to the war effort in the name of democracy and pluralism highlighted the discrepancy between the political values of the metropole and the actual condition of its subjects. The wartime experiences of African soldiers magnified these contradictions: exposure to new ideas was accompanied by outright discrimination in military units. The myth of the invincibility of the white man was shattered at precisely the same time that the conceptual tools for the struggle against colonialism were widely disseminated.

In the aftermath of the war—with the defeat of Nazism and the decline in power of Britain and France—the international environment was especially receptive to demands for self-determination. Colonial countries began to adjust their dreams of empire in light of the growing costs of continued

administration. The demand for the termination of colonial rule spread rapidly in this political context. Initially raised by educated elites in West and East
Africa in the interwar years, the cry for self-determination assumed mass
dimensions after 1945. Anticolonialism was equated in the eyes of its cham-
pions with the democratic coming of age of the continent. Liberation from
foreign domination through political independence was viewed as the outward expression of the most fundamental human desire to determine one's
own future. And, indeed, "the leaders of the anticolonial struggle constantly
linked the right of self-determination with the right to choose and change
one's government."[26] Political mobilization, organization, and protest were
the means to achieving this universal democratic goal of freedom.

Broadly based political movements emerged throughout the continent in
the immediate postwar era. Based on urban-based civil associations, in virtually every colonial territory these congresses were inclusive in organization
and design.[27] They sought to encompass as many groups as possible in an
effort to give substance to their claims to societal representation. In these circumstances participation was interpreted in terms of demographic compre-
hensiveness rather than individual involvement. Emphasis was placed on the
demand for full citizenship and not on any particular form of rule. Freedom
was integrally linked with notions of peoplehood, nations-in-formation,
inevitably with internal cohesion in the face of external control.

At the head of anticolonial movements stood Western-educated elites,
those who owed their position most directly to the colonial presence, those
most conversant with the operations of the colonial state, and also those
most immediately affected by colonial discrimination. Nnamdi Azikiwe,
Kwame Nkrumah, Ahmed Sekou Touré, Leopold Sedar Senghor, Julius
Nyerere, Kenneth Kaunda, and Jomo Kenyatta—to mention but a few—conducted their campaign against the colonial order on two levels, the first of
which was ideological and symbolic. The struggle for self-rule was justified
in terms familiar to the colonizers: the injustice of foreign domination, the
rights of the governed to shape their own destiny.

The realization of these demands depended on successful mobilization
and negotiation, the second level of anticolonialism. The ranks of anticolonial forces were swelled by appeals to solidarity groups who saw liberation
not only in terms of divestment from foreign control but also in terms of
autonomy from the colonial state. Two quite separate sets of considerations,
expressed by distinct types of articulators, were joined within nationalist
movements. Decolonization, therefore, created alliances between different
elites without, in most instances, fostering elite cohesion.[28]

Political movements developed a variety of strategies and tactics to promote their objectives. Initial requests were presented in private conversations, petitions, and rallies. The intensity of action then escalated as
demonstrations, strikes, open clashes, and—when these means proved inef-

fective—outright violence replaced more legalistic methods. The tenor of decolonization was directly affected not only by the organization and resources of these associations but also by the willingness of the colonial powers to concede the basic demand for independence. In most instances, decolonization in Africa was smooth: militancy was contained and compromise was apparent. Where the process was prolonged—Zimbabwe, Angola, Mozambique, Guinea-Bissau—violent techniques became the norm and ideological radicalization ensued. In all instances stress was placed on employing those means necessary for successful struggle; no explicit ethic of conflict resolution evolved in these circumstances.

Anticolonialism in Africa was marked, quite emphatically, by its protest quality on both the symbolic and operational planes. Liberation was defined in negative rather than positive terms; a premium was put on the redefinition of polities but hardly on integration. Democratic norms were thereby injected into the African political arena under a distinctly protest rubric. They were attached to new concepts of social inclusion and exclusion but were rarely endowed with specific substantive contents. The precise definition of national communities in other than the territorial terms delimited by colonialism was left vague.[29] And the successful termination of colonialism, the takeover of the state, effectively étatisized the civic associations created during the period of foreign rule.[30]

The decision to dismantle the colonial apparatus was the culmination of the call for liberation. But the by-products of democracy seen in terms of freedom were far more uncertain. Emphasis was put on consensus as opposed to tolerance, on loyalty in contrast to self-expression, on identity and not on individual rights, on political boundaries but hardly on procedures. Nationalism in many parts of Africa was not, in any fundamental sense, liberal.[31]

Independence came in the guise of confrontation with the cradle of modern democracies. Indeed, democratic terminology was introduced together with anti-Western sentiments. The more vocal the call for democratic participation, the more prominent the rejection of colonialism, imperialism, and ultimately capitalism. In this situation, the ties with democratic metropoles were strained precisely when opportunities existed for the dissemination of democratic norms. The fact that the articulators of Western democratic precepts were themselves far removed from the bulk of the population further accentuated the ambivalence of the relationship between nationalism and democratic impulses in the African context.

The concept of democracy that developed during the anticolonial phase of decolonization was of an abstract, aggregate sort. Democracy was seen as an ideal writ large, as a macro symbol of grand historical processes. It became the password for the enfranchisement of broad social communities. Notions of democracy first surfaced in the modern African political lexicon as a response to the human indignities of colonialism. Their representation was primarily psychological and rhetorical, future-directed and, above all, outward-oriented.

## Elite Dimensions of African Political Cultures

African political cultures have developed along two discrete lines in the contemporary period. The first, elite, strand of African political cultures has been formed by individuals and groups linked to the formal political apparatus and has revolved around the state. The second, popular, brand of African political cultures has its base in the social order. Although it addresses issues related to the public domain, it focuses more explicitly on questions of economic survival, the maintenance of autonomous social relations, and meaningful participation. Each of these dimensions of African political cultures has developed an institutional, normative, and symbolic structure of its own since the waning years of the colonial era.

The decision to grant independence implied, by definition, a shift in the location of political authority and in the composition of officeholders. The last phase of decolonization was concerned with the transfer of power, with establishing principles of decisionmaking and consolidating institutions for their realization.

The issues raised at this juncture have informed the elite political agenda in Africa during the past thirty years. The first, core, challenge centered on the formation of workable regime principles, the elaboration of provisions for political interaction, and the establishment of an apparatus capable of sustaining these visions. The second concerned problems of ethnic pluralism, the consolidation of new communities from a medley of social groups with differing histories, languages, cultures, and institutions. The third related to questions of economic planning and development, theretofore the exclusive monopoly of colonial officials, and included the need to confront problems of social inequality, social welfare, and strategies for improving human well-being. And the fourth dealt with the delineation of the role of the new sovereign entities in the international arena.[32]

The preindependence debates were conducted by several groups, each of which continues to be actively engaged in the molding of elite political cultures. External actors (initially the colonial powers and subsequently other foreign countries and international agencies) were involved. The central African actors were aspiring politicians: the leaders of anticolonial movements and their main supporters. They were joined, albeit to a lesser extent, by key figures in professional associations. Prominent lawyers, doctors, journalists, and intellectuals were active in the nationalist movements but even then found independent avenues for political expression. Also party to these discussions, albeit to a much lesser extent, were small groups of entrepre-

AFRICA

69

neurs, a tiny minority composed mostly of wealthy traders, who had succeeded in establishing their own economic bases despite colonial restrictions. Chiefs, too, especially in English-speaking countries, continued to make their voices heard on central politics because they owed much of their position to their status within the state network. Finally, civil servants, who had played only a small role in preindependence discussions, emerged in subsequent years as a growing elite force.

These elite groups have been bound to one another by interlocking membership, income, status, and life-styles. They were bred in the colonial context and possessed privileged access to education, the colonial state, and concomitant wealth. In many respects, these groups had begun to develop corporate interests that coalesced around the maintenance of supremacy at the center.[33] Despite internal factionalization and cleavages, they were the key elements of what gradually developed into the dominant class, or the managerial bourgeoisie.[34] The unifying feature linking these groups was concern with power. "The power cult is everywhere embedded in the total culture of elite groups."[35]

*Liberalism*

African elite political perceptions have vacillated over the years, in varying degrees, between liberal and statist visions. The liberal strain emerged most forcefully on the eve of independence. The final act of most colonial powers was to oversee the formation of successor regimes. With the notable exception of the former Belgian Congo (now Zaire), Angola, and to a lesser extent Mozambique, where the colonial authorities abandoned the new countries without determining their replacements, the creation of alternative governments was considered a precondition for the attainment of independence.

However, the colonial experience provided few, if any, precedents for the formation of countrywide political (as opposed to administrative) structures. Legislative councils in some portions of British colonial Africa and the limited franchise granted to the precious few African citizens of France could hardly be used as the basis for the establishment of a comprehensive political apparatus. Inevitably in such circumstances, recourse was made to the regime modes and procedures entrenched in the metropoles. The Westminster model of majoritarian rule and the presidential system of the Fifth French Republic constituted the major blueprints for the design of initial forms of modern African politics.[36]

The precise political institutions for the future were ironed out in a series of negotiations between the presumptive heirs and the departing administrators. The first set of questions addressed at this juncture related to the structure of the political system. The virtues and drawbacks of decentralization were debated at length, with the former British colonies emerging with federal or quasi-federal arrangements (Nigeria, Kenya, to a lesser extent Ghana) and the former French possessions opting for more centralized authority systems.[37] A second group of issues centered on the specification of major political institutions and their spheres of operation. Throughout Africa parliaments were endowed with sovereign decisionmaking powers, with the executive branch subject to the scrutiny of the electorate through its representatives.

The specific organization of political institutions was detailed in a spate of new constitutions, which varied widely in length and scope. These documents were perceived by their drafters as the embodiment of the prevailing political wisdom and as guidelines for future action. They encompassed the Western notion of democracy as government, which emphasized the rule, rather than the right to self-rule so closely associated with democracy as liberation. The essence of government lay, in this view, in the entrenchment of a set of procedures and structures that would subject political leaders to binding laws and make them accountable to citizens who themselves could organize, vote, and compete freely for office.[38] This Western liberal approach stressed individual rights and ruler obligations, and equated political power with limited government. It assumed that institutions built on values of pluralism and tolerance would foster behavior and yield policies that were both reasonable and responsive.

Although in each case special provisions were made to account for local conditions and particular colonial interests, the political legacy bequeathed on the eve of independence was alien in derivation and design. Certain elite groups, most notably professionals and some intellectuals, were strongly committed to these ideas. But many nationalist leaders, all too aware of the fact that acceptance of these designs would hasten the colonial withdrawal, sometimes accepted the suggested political arrangements mainly for the sake of expedience. Liberal conceptions of power at this point were therefore embedded only in portions of the dominant class.

This became apparent in the struggles for control of the system-in-formation just prior to independence. In virtually every territory, the universal congresses established in the anticolonial phase gave way to a multiplicity of parties representing different social, geographic, ethnic, religious, and economic interests. Ethnic and class forces were mobilized to gain support at the polls. And, although in almost every country contending leaders used ethnicity to forward class goals,[39] a variety of parties emerged, each with its own constituency, concerns, and political agenda. These parties tied a growing number of individuals vertically to politicians and aspiring leaders but did not necessarily strengthen horizontal social ties.

Preindependence elections in Africa furnished the opportunity for determining the precise composition of the first sovereign governments. Interest in these elections varied substantially from place to place, as did the volatility of electoral campaigns and participation rates at the ballot box.[40] In almost all cases, however, the victors were the key figures in the anticolonial struggle: Kwame Nkrumah, Jomo Kenyatta, Felix Houphouet-Boigny, and Robert Mugabe. Ironically, the colonial powers in their rush to establish successor regimes frequently aided the largest anticolonial movements, thus indirectly bolstering the trend toward single-party dominance even prior to independence.[41] Hence, the key beneficiaries of the introduction of liberal notions of democracy were precisely those who could attribute their rise to power to their nationalist activities and therefore did not have a vested interest in perpetuating these democratic tenets.

The structures of democratic government were implanted in Africa with very little prior preparation by external elements. By independence, Africans had barely had a chance to familiarize themselves with competitive institutions and the franchise, let alone acquire any experience with their operation. Moreover, these institutions were activated in a political atmosphere which magnified notions of self-determination and called for the rejection of imported models. These circumstances could hardly have been less propitious for the entrenchment of liberal political cultures.

The political arrangements established at independence were at best unformed and uncertain. Beneath the veneer of democracy and the mood of euphoria that accompanied the declaration of independence of dozens of new states, the political arena was in flux. The leaders of the new African states were faced with the question of abiding by pluralist democratic rules of alien origin when the bulk of their political education had been acquired in the highly centralized and authoritarian context of colonialism. More to the point, their support bases were generally fragile, the institutions they headed usually lacked legitimacy, and the resources at their disposal were meager.

Faced with increasingly vociferous demands to make good on the promises of independence, with a variety of sectional pressures, and with growing friction among emergent patrons, many governments in the first years of independence found their weaknesses glaringly exposed. To avoid the specter of loss of authority, they opted to maintain control through domination.[42] With the notable exceptions of the Gambia and Botswana, all African states moved from liberal to authoritarian forms of government.

There were numerous reasons for the rapid abandonment of liberal democratic practices. First, African countries lacked an autonomous middle class; the social foundations for effective political competition and capital accumulation away from the state were not in place, making domination of the official apparatus indispensable for the maintenance and reproduction of ruling coalitions. Second, the complicated provisions of independence constitutions were frequently seen as cumbersome impediments that hampered efficient government and took little, if any, account of the centrifugal tendencies resulting from ethnic and regional cleavages.[43] Third, the view of democracy as government, with its stress on process, required a level of civic competence that had been given little time to mature. Fourth, democratic procedures seemed to offer very few answers to the substantive dilemmas of early independence. Because democracy preceded industrialization in Africa, governments were forced into the difficult position of "revolutioniz-ing the society and the economy while being electorally dependent upon the uprooted."[44] The centralization of power and the curtailment of personal lib-erties were often justified as a way of achieving rapid development. Fifth, some African leaders asserted that by disposing of alien institutions they were promoting the cause of Africanization. Sixth, personal ambitions, par-ticularly in the face of growing opposition, inevitably intruded. And, finally, most rulers still enjoyed the leeway that came with their leadership of the anticolonial struggle. They could afford, politically, to introduce institutional changes with relative ease.

The failure of the first African experiments with democratic government should not, however, be understood as implying the general unsuitability of such constructs to African conditions. The circumstances in which these ventures were undertaken did not bode well for their longevity. Three requi-sites for the flourishing of liberal elite cultures were palpably absent: "a political leadership committed to it; political institutions nurturing it; and a civilization (political culture or tradition) that tolerates and defends it."[45] Democratic institutions and norms require time to take root and thrive, to form liberals determined to uphold them. The impulses and urgency of the transfer of power furnished neither the pause nor the climate for such nurtur-ing.

The fortunes of liberal elite cultures since independence have been inti-mately tied to the political position of the articulators of these precepts. With the exception of the brief liberal civilian regime of the Second Republic in Ghana (1969–1972), for the first twenty years of African independence elite factions advocating liberal concepts were systematically excluded from power. In the late 1970s, however, a series of attempts to revive liberal gov-ernment were launched. These movements for the reinstatement of competi-tive and representative institutions had in common a call for greater public participation in decisionmaking, for popular scrutiny of official actions, and for the protection of human and civil rights. These demands were raised most consistently by professionals, intellectuals, and a growing group of entrepreneurs. The thrust of these initiatives was the eradication of dictatori-al regimes and their replacement with popularly legitimated administrations.

During the 1970s and 1980s, liberalization occurred within already existing governments. Certain single-party systems, such as Côte d'Ivoire and Cameroon, made provisions for greater competition for elected office following on the examples of Kenya and Tanzania, while Senegal revamped its constitution, allowing for multiparty competition in regularly scheduled elections.[46]

The most ambitious experiments with the reinstatement of liberal insti-tutions took place in Ghana and Nigeria in 1979. In these two countries new (presidential) constitutions were drafted by panels of experts and debated in constituent assemblies. The promulgation of these democratic constitutions coincided with the lifting of bans on party activity and free elections. Despite relatively low participation rates, civilian regimes were installed in place of the incumbent military coalitions. In both countries a new phase of liberal democracy commenced.[47]

The multiparty systems of the Third Republic in Ghana and the Second Republic in Nigeria were short-lived. The government of Hilla Limann proved inadequate to the task of dealing with Ghana's thoroughgoing economic deterioration and was ousted by the army barely two years after it had gained office. The Shehu Shagari regime in Nigeria survived one term in office, but could not maintain itself in the wake of the violent elections of 1983. In both instances the demise of these civilian administrations can be attributed to widespread corruption, economic waste and mismanagement, and electoral fraud, which, in conditions of growing economic scarcity, drained these systems of legitimacy.[48]

The sorry experience with democratic revival during this period pressed home the fact that the self-interest of the elites who championed the return to competitive politics undermined the viability of the institutions they supported. Electoral politics became patron politics writ large. Moreover, officially sanctioned contests for public office did not imply limited government. To the contrary, in the Ghana and Nigeria of the 1980s "political centralization *per se* became a democratic and liberal cause."[49] The inability to protect the bureaucracy from politicians and the public, coupled with the close connection between administrative and political elites, cultivated a general intolerance of political opposition scarcely conducive to the entrenchment of democratic norms. Although the social and economic conditions for sustaining liberal political beliefs were less in evidence in the 1980s than in the 1960s, both Ghana and Nigeria sought, at the end of the decade, to experiment yet again with democratic government.[50] In the meantime, the main lesson emanating from the failed attempts of the past was that the battle against unjust and arbitrary regimes was qualitatively different from the struggle for freedom, justice, and democratic government.

The liberal elite orientations at the time of the transition to independence were of a decidedly procedural and rule-oriented sort. The emphasis on equality, accountability, choice, the rule of law, and the separation of powers did attract important proponents who, organized in elite associations, have consistently promoted these political approaches. But this borrowed and individualistic concept of democracy as government has not been based on substantive consensus, nor has it been able to rely on an indigenous tradition of separation between the public and the private realms.

## Statism

The statist strain of elite political cultures in Africa has been more closely linked to ruling coalitions than its liberal counterpart. Statist propensities crystallized into the central pillar of dominant elite cultures with the early and rapid shift to authoritarian government in postindependence Africa.

The transition to authoritarianism involved two distinct processes. The first was the dismantling of competitive institutions. The activities of rival parties and groups were systematically curtailed. Opportunities to voice dissent were sharply reduced. Opposition leaders were harassed, and when not successfully co-opted, either detained or exiled. Methodically and deliberately, ruling coalitions consolidated systems of one-party dominance.

The second process was the expansion and strengthening of the central administration. Bureaucratic structures were augmented. In some cases, such as Kenya, Uganda, and Ghana, intermediate regional political structures were eliminated. Military and paramilitary agencies were fortified, and decisionmaking procedures were heavily centralized. Several years after independence executive constitutions were adopted throughout the continent.[51] Together, these measures increased the consolidation of power around the state while reducing formal avenues for societal and intraelite competition.

This reordering of public structures at independence exacerbated already existing hegemonic proclivities. Political elites, who had rarely succeeded in mobilizing social groups effectively other than on the basis of local solidarity, adopted and adapted to the bureaucratic systems relegated by colonialism.[52] Participatory and representative institutions were downgraded and their decisionmaking functions severely limited. The executive branch was, in turn, elevated and endowed with extensive powers.[53] The postcolonial state assumed neopatrimonial characteristics, including the accentuation of bureaucratic and coercive structures, the reduction of pluralism, the politicization of the public arena, and highly personalistic forms of rule.[54] Institutionalized linkage mechanisms were undermined, avenues of access to decisionmakers circumscribed, and the control of public resources monopolized.

State expansion and centralization served ruling elites in several ways. They provided "the fundamental opportunity both to maintain political control and to achieve remarkable wealth amidst great and growing poverty."[55] Because the state relies on liquid revenues and interacts with transnational economic forces, state power became a prime vehicle for material accumulation,[56] while also enhancing the position of rulers in their competition with other groups.[57] Thus, the state and proximity to its resources emerged as a crucial determinant of class formation and class relations.[58] The ruling class in Africa in most instances is a state class "because its culture, its basic values, its power and its economic base result from its relationship to the state."[59]

The turn toward statism was undertaken in search of a legitimating formula. Curtailment of personal liberties was justified as a necessary sacrifice to fulfill a broader vision of the public good. Governments were portrayed as bearing the brunt of the responsibility for the well-being of their citizens, and the augmentation of their capacities was seen as vital to the achievement of economic progress. Whether the proponents of the single-party state defended their actions by asserting that they were merely sanctioning the unity that existed (Houphouet-Boigny in Côte d'Ivoire), that multipartyism was antithetical to the needs of national integration and social progress (Kwame Nkrumah in Ghana), that the party was the embodiment of the nation (Sekou Toure in Guinea), or that one-party rule was evocative of the indigenous democratic traditions of Africa (Julius Nyerere in Tanzania), they were unanimous in their insistence on the negative implications of dissent.

The new arrangements inevitably highlighted the weakness of formal institutions at this juncture. Consolidation of power did not imply full control. While social groups were excluded from the official realm, they were not easily subordinated to its dictates. At issue was the degree of government rather than its type. Confronted with an absence of agreement on the rules of the political game, centralization became a substitute for consent. The African state was "sometimes excessively authoritarian, in order to disguise the fact that it is inadequately authoritative."[60]

The contents of statist elite cultures have stressed certain common themes. First, state power has been equated with the will of the people, with majority rule, with national unity and even unanimity, inevitably with consensus and some notions of the common good. The public agenda, as defined by the political leadership, took precedence over individual and specific group preferences. Membership in the community has therefore been seen in terms of adherence to common goals, in many instances by highlighting uniformity of thought.

Second, related to this, concepts of authority have stressed acquiescence, thus precluding constructive criticism and preventing active involvement in central politics. Consensus is applauded and risk-taking discouraged.[61] The authority of leaders has been freed from limitations, rationalizing, if not encouraging, ruler privilege. Abuses of office have often been perceived as a necessary evil, and bureaucratic corruption condoned.[62]

Third, statist political cultures have justified the extraction of resources from the populace and fostered a highly instrumental view of politics. A functional rationality evolved that promoted zero-sum norms. But contradictorily, policy initiatives have been rationalized in terms of common interests and joint objectives. To placate potentially disgruntled groups and to sustain a modicum of order, resources have been distributed according to political rather than economic considerations. Highly pragmatic, grossly inequitable, and tremendously costly notions of distributive justice could be upheld in this worldview.[63]

Finally, the centralization of public institutions has accentuated growth at the expense of other goals. Legitimacy has been tied to performance, primarily in the economic sphere. Political leaders could deal with quantitative questions, but not with normative problems of distribution of power or the social consequences of public policy. Statism as a utilitarian ideology became a means of bridging the gap between the reality of authoritarianism and the elite project of development.[64]

Elite orientations of the statist variety have not been devoid of certain democratic components. These ideas do stress a concern for social equity and for achieving agreement on common goals and priorities. Curtailment of the individual will is viewed as a necessary evil in pursuit of the democratic goal of promoting the public good. The more radical notion of democracy underlying these ideas has been consciously contrasted with the liberal precepts purveyed by competing elites.[65] It has also been employed to present authoritarian actions in a more acceptable wrapping.

The statist political culture of African rulers has supported a variety of authoritarian forms of government. The first pattern, patrimonial-bureaucratic, developed in such countries as Cameroon, Côte d'Ivoire, Malawi, and to some extent Kenya during the Kenyatta years. In these cases the public interest was interpreted as overlapping the concerns of ruling patrons. The party was downplayed. It was utilized mostly as a means for dispensing goods and services and as a mechanism for rejuvenating the second rung of leadership at periodic intervals. Political life acquired a highly materialist texture with the creation of elaborate patronage networks that provided rewards in return for support. Participation was not nullified in these countries; its influence was, however, carefully modified through the preservation of social and ethnic cleavages, the amplification of clientage, and the concomitant limitation of direct access to state resources. With the replacement of the founding fathers in the early 1980s, this pattern gave way in some countries to either repressive governments (as in Kenya) or to a bureaucratic-corporatist variant (Cameroon) that permitted limited competition among officially sanctioned social units.

A second, more populist, pattern emerged in countries of a self-proclaimed socialist persuasion (Ghana under Nkrumah, Uganda during Milton Obote's first term in office, more consistently in Tanzania and Zambia). In these cases mobilization and participation in party auxiliaries has been encouraged. Common objectives were determined by the leader and the party executive, which had an uneasy relationship with an increasingly politicized civil service. While opportunities for affecting policy decisions varied widely (in Tanzania participation was promoted, in Ghana the party was used primarily as an instrument of control), concern for social equity and national unity was constantly highlighted.[66]

Following the creation of Afro-Marxist governments in the mid-1970s in Angola, Mozambique, and Ethiopia, a third, vanguard party, pattern took shape.[67] In these countries membership in the ruling party was limited to those committed to a "democratic revolution." Ideological zeal was rewarded through appointments and benefits, and all forms of opposition were deemed subversive. Emphasis consequently shifted from social equality to people's power, and the party was depicted as the only vehicle for promoting the interests of progressive forces (usually comprising workers and peasants).[68] Not only was the party accorded supremacy over other public institutions but the state and party were merged conceptually.

Not all regimes were able to regularize viable authoritarian methods of control. By the mid-1960s military interventions became commonplace, and within two decades over fifty successful coups d'état had taken place in Africa. Most of the military regimes bore a strong resemblance to their civilian counterparts and, in several notable cases, even carried a reformist aura.[69] In some countries, however, a fourth, absolutist and coercive, pattern developed. Uganda under Idi Amin, the Central African Republic under Jean-Bedel Bokassa, Equatorial Guinea under Macias Nguema, Liberia under Samuel Doe, and to a lesser extent Zaire under Mobutu Sese Seko and Togo under Eyadema are cases in point. Here highly personalistic structures of control were refined and repression displaced even the most feeble efforts at consultation. Individual citizens were subjected to the personal whims of frequently erratic leaders. In these countries, few linkage mechanisms survived, and ruling elites were pitted against social groups in a particularly stark fashion.[70]

Despite the diversity of authoritarian arrangements in Africa, hegemonic impulses rarely gained total ascendancy. Cultural heterogeneity, the strong organization of civil society, and some possibilities for autonomous accumulation away from the state combined to place some limitations on state power and on elite cultures.[71] A variety of social, economic, and religious organizations found various ways to make their concerns known and to avoid excessive subjugation to state elites. Mass political cultures and informal activities blossomed precisely where attempts at control were most apparent.[72] Conversely, autonomous popular action was limited where some avenues of participation and representation were maintained or where patron-client linkages had been institutionalized. Nevertheless, in virtually every African country the control exerted by authoritarian governments was at best uncertain and their societal reach contained. Statist elite subcultures did not gain broad social approval.

The political fate of carriers of statist models has been tied, first, to their capacity to regularize some forms of mediation.[73] Stability has been linked to representational accommodation, instability to the failure to provide some mechanisms for state-society interaction.[74] Statist and liberal elite political cultures have thus continuously clashed even in authoritarian settings. The perpetuation of statist elites has also depended on their economic achievements and hence on their administrative capacities. Hegemonic normative and symbolic structures highlighted issues of political economy, and here the choices of ruling groups have been exceedingly narrow.[75]

In most countries, the conflict between various groups at the center encouraged the adoption of exclusionary policies that marginalized increasingly larger portions of the population. In these circumstances it was difficult, if not impossible, to define concepts of citizenship that went beyond the notion of the individual as subject. More to the point, contradictions inevitably abounded. By the end of the third decade of independence it became apparent that clientelistic networks, which had provided a shaky adhesive in the absence of other structures of political interchange, themselves generated substantial competition, often inducing systemic instability. With patronage, it was difficult to retain stability; without it, no government could maintain support.[76]

The shrinkage of the social foundations of elite legitimacy varied in intensity from place to place. Nevertheless, throughout the continent political enfeeblement further strained the capacities of overextended state institutions. Performance levels diminished and economic progress, where it had occurred, ground to a halt. Social cleavages heightened and with them ethnic and class tensions. Statism in its multiple institutional and cultural manifestations proved to be "the graveyard of socialism as well as of democracy."[77]

## Liberalism Versus Statism

During the first three decades of independence elite political cultures focused heavily on alternate liberal versus statist approaches to the definition of state power. Several factors determined the nature of these elite political cultures and their relative salience. First, economic and social conditions played a role. Economic scarcity had the effect of suppressing liberal tendencies.[78] Second, external constraints (particularly of an economic sort), continued to affect elite choices. Third, interelite strife promoted hegemonic beliefs, while greater cohesion may have permitted limited liberalism. Fourth, idiosyncratic variables inevitably had an impact as well. Fifth, the degree of access of elite groups to state resources was important. Where access was skewed, statism gained momentum; where notions of proportionality pertained, elite political stances exhibited some liberal propensities.

Three critical factors, however, had an overriding influence. The first was the relative autonomy of articulators of power models from various communal groups. Where the state decisionmaking apparatus was permeable to particularistic pressures, it tended to evince pronounced hegemonic predispositions. When some autonomy was sustained, the dominant class could afford to allow a degree of (albeit circumscribed) pluralism.[79] Yet heightened autonomy was a prescription for arbitrary rule. Second, the types of connections with solidarity groups were central. If no such ties prevailed, coercion was especially apparent. And finally, the degree of institutionalization of state agencies was critical. Where state structures lacked regularity, hegemonic impulses were accentuated; where some patterns of decisionmaking had been entrenched, a greater degree of elite openness was apparent.

The determinants of elite political cultures in contemporary Africa help to account for the absence of viable integrating visions. These patterns and institutions expressed the nature of elite debates and predilections. They lacked a well-defined popular foundation.

## Popular Dimensions of Political Culture

By the beginning of the 1980s, most states on the continent were in the midst of a multifaceted economic, social, and political crisis. One aspect was the unwieldy character of the state bureaucracy and its propensity to dissipate already scarce resources. A second element was the widespread diversion of public funds for the private use of ruling groups. Official corruption was rampant. A third problem concerned the inability of official organs to carry out even the most essential tasks. Social, medical, and educational services deteriorated. In too many countries food scarcities were recorded and basic commodities were unavailable. A fourth facet of the crisis centered on the palpable diminution of state power as well as elite legitimacy and authority in many African countries.[80] Finally, and perhaps most significantly, state-society relations were frayed. Distrust of officials was commonplace, cooperation with formal agencies was at a low ebb, decrees were ignored, and laws were skirted. The efforts of the state to assert hegemonic control over the social order resulted in the growing rebellion of society against the state.[81] Regime incapacity had led to fundamental problems of governability.

In this tense political and economic environment, popular political impulses, previously obscured by the pervasiveness of organized statism and consequently all too often overlooked, came to the fore, generally outside the formal domain. Full-scale campaigns to protest unbridled state-centrism were launched.

These activities were conducted by a variety of social groups; some dated back to the precolonial and colonial periods, others were relatively new constructs. These organizations proliferated substantially during the third independence decade.[82] Prominent among the groups involved in the molding of popular political cultures have been primary associations, which include households, villages, kinship units, ethnic groups, local development societies, and traditional political systems. In some places, the position of indigenous authority figures has been augmented.[83] These groups are contained geographically, highlight ascriptive affiliation, and possess specific historical or mythical symbols that unite their members.

Other groups have been constructed along horizontal lines. These have included occupational networks, such as professional, farmer, worker, and trader organizations. Voluntary service, recreation, savings, and special interest groups have also flourished.[84] In this category it is also possible to place groups constructed on the basis of age and gender, most notably women's associations and student organizations.[85] In recent years, small crime networks have also emerged. These many different associational groups are usually urban-based, although they may have rural branches.[86] They bring together individuals on a voluntary basis to pursue common interests, and tend to be more achievement-oriented than their vertical counterparts.

In recent years, the importance of religious communities, networks, and organizations has also increased. Participation in church activities has grown significantly, and a variety of spiritualist cults and syncretic churches has sprung up. In Islamic areas, religious orders have gained additional followers, and new militant and reformist movements have been established.[87] Membership in these groups is based on adherence to a common belief system, usually spans rural and urban areas, and may possess strong authoritarian overtones.

What distinguishes associational life in Africa is its diversity, vitality, and centrality in organizing social relations. Each grouping is based on substantive pacts that have real meaning for the daily lives of its members. Associational leaders have often become the carriers of specific mass concerns, interests, and identities. They have emerged as the central articulators of solidarity, often in opposition to the declared objectives of power elites. These formations have served as the vehicles for community self-preservation and sometimes as frameworks for growth away from the state. In many respects, the vibrancy of associational arrangements in Africa has been the most potent obstacle to authoritarianism.[88]

The issues that preoccupy leaders of popular organizations reflect the specific mixtures of interest, affinity, and consciousness that motivate their members and define their roles. Their primary purpose is to cater to the needs of their members, and hence to control or provide access to both material and value resources.[89] A second objective is to secure group maintenance and the continuity of group norms (which usually include well-formed notions of justice, consultative patterns of decisionmaking, some mechanisms of accountability, accepted rules of procedure, and specific concepts of power and authority, although at times informal networks may foster hegemonic norms as well). And a third set of goals delineates the interaction between these associations and the wider social, economic, and political environment. They act not only as channels for the transmission of information and communication and as barometers for popular feeling[90] but also as contenders for power and as framers of the parameters of an alternate, perhaps nonhegemonic, political agenda.

Popular organizations have, in recent years, consistently pressed for some autonomy from the state. Individuals and social groups have joined in a drive to gain control over their own existence and destiny. They have formulated, in word and deed, a spatial notion of power, which puts a premium on the establishment of autonomous niches.[91] The rejection of formalized repression and interference was punctuated by calls for social equality and official probity. Thus, these popular movements have carried a strong protest against the symbolic codification of ruling class dominance.

A generation after the original employment of democratic precepts to bolster demands for liberation from colonialism, similar arguments were used by social groups against independent African leaders. The differences between the two interpretations are nevertheless significant: the call for freedom during decolonization was presented in the most abstract terms on a grand, macroscale; the move to avert official oppression assumed personal and concrete meaning at the microlevel. Thirty years previously the entire colonial system was challenged; in the popular cultures purveyed in the 1980s the issue was not the boundaries of political control but its character. The nationalist search for self-determination was conducted by elites in potential; recent agitations have possessed a mass quality.

Social groups have found multiple methods to assert a measure of autonomy, most notably in the economic sphere.[92] One type of survival strategy has been to suffer and find ways of managing to accommodate to reduced circumstances. Arbitrary laws have been ignored and others flouted. Silent means have been employed to resist perceived exploitation.[93] Consumption habits have been altered as ingenious mechanisms were devised to make do with less.

A second coping technique has revolved around the rapidly expanding informal sector. The second economy burgeoned in the 1980s throughout Africa, frequently accounting for well over 50 percent of productive activity.[94] The elaborate (and often illegal) parallel market became the most important funnel for the distribution of goods and a significant setting for petty manufacturing and small-scale agricultural production.[95] Heavily organized, the informal sector evolved norms of interchange that were carefully enforced by popularly backed arbiters.[96]

A third mechanism for dealing with the economic crisis of the 1980s has involved self-encapsulation. Especially in the rural areas, communities attempted to disengage from state channels, though not always from the market. Peasants shifted from export to food cropping,[97] and in many villages self-provisioning was nurtured.[98] Local communities began to make implements from available materials, to organize their own schools and clinics, to construct substitute marketing networks, and, above all, to enunciate an ethic of self-reliance.[99]

When these methods no longer proved viable, some individuals and groups turned to migration as a fourth, more drastic, means of survival. Africa holds the sorry record of having the highest proportion of refugees in the world. These people have uprooted themselves from their homes to escape civil wars, government repression, and economic impoverishment.

These unofficial economic strategies have enabled capital accumulation away from the state and provided the foundation for the insertion of material (rather than solely political) criteria for social stratification.[100] They have also encouraged the development of lateral transactions between various groups, thereby fostering horizontal channels of communication and perhaps enhancing social cohesion along lines other than those established through vertical political links.

Popular expressions of political attitudes have been conveyed through numerous channels. Political information is frequently transmitted via an informal "bush telegraph" ("radio trottoir" in Zaire, "radio Treichville" in the Côte d'Ivoire). The word-of-mouth technique (which possesses many of the characteristics of a rumor mill) has been supplemented in some countries (Ghana, Kenya) by an underground press or by privately owned newspapers and magazines (Nigeria). These activities point to systematic efforts to bypass state monopolies on information. "Songs, jokes and anecdotes may be the principal channel of communication for people who are denied access to the official media."[101]

Ideas and values are conveyed through music and the arts, through constant debates and discussion, indeed, through the creation of alternative modes of discourse. Religious movements and traditional leaders have, in a more organized way, played a central role in redefining norms of behavior and either nurturing participation in smaller settings or suppressing it in fundamentalist trappings.[102] These articulations have symbolically emancipated individuals and groups from official restraints, recast political norms, and culturally reinforced the economic dimensions of civic restructuring.

Africans of all walks of life exhibit an extraordinarily high level of political knowledge. Their cognitive skills are extremely well honed, especially when illiteracy is still so widespread. A few examples will suffice. Several surveys conducted in the rural areas of Ghana and Sierra Leone have consistently yielded broad and accurate information about national politics and national figures.[103] In Nigeria, it has been demonstrated that "public opinion is informed, pragmatic and rational."[104] Comparative studies of student populations in East and West Africa corroborate these findings. Throughout the continent, very heterogeneous social segments have exhibited familiarity with the workings of formal agencies and with the subtleties of less visible elite behavior patterns.[105]

Since popular political orientations are molded in so many different social-institutional settings, it is virtually impossible to deal with all their substantive permutations. Some common themes nevertheless appear to characterize these popular cultures. First, mass attitudes deal extensively with government policy and performance records, with the uses (and abuses) of state power. On the affective level, dissatisfaction is voiced with economic achievements and the way governments have handled growing problems of scarcity. On the level of evaluation, judgments are almost uniformly critical. Criteria for the assessment of performance include the ability of state agencies to enhance material well-being, administer justice, protect civil rights, and promote equitable distribution.[106] People blame the government for inefficiency, waste, mismanagement, corruption, and exploitation. They also directly attribute their own depressed situation to official actions.[107] These sentiments point to an awareness of the pervasiveness of the state in daily life. They are also couched in highly cynical language, and frequently demonstrate a deep-seated fatalism.

A second major focus of popular concerns is political leaders, the wielders of state power. Once again, mass attitudes evince a discontent with the incumbents of national office that frequently borders on outright contempt. Individual politicians are accused of enriching themselves at the public expense, abandoning responsibility for the welfare of the people, and defying popular interpretations of leadership norms. Governments simply do not command respect. Inherent in these feelings and harsh judgments are fairly well defined notions of authority. Leadership at all levels is perceived in highly personalistic and hierarchical terms.[108] Criticism of leaders is voiced in the language of betrayal, separation, loss, and even suffering.[109] The obligation to obey leaders is offset by the right to call them to account. When the trust upon which the relationship between rulers and ruled is grounded is abrogated, popular demands for retribution increase.[110]

Third, popular cultures address issues of the boundaries of the political community. Political attitude surveys have found that many Africans identify and express loyalties to four types of political organization: town or village, region, ethnic group, and country. In most instances, they sense no conflict or contradiction between these levels.[111] Thus, the political boundaries of postcolonial states have been internalized by their citizens, but not as exclusive frames of reference. Popular cultures exhibit a recognition of incorporation into the state network without a concomitant acceptance of its superiority as an integrating mechanism.[112]

The fourth, and possibly the most commonplace, theme in popular political cultures is one of alienation from the state system as currently constituted. In virtually every conceivable way, social groups have expressed a sense of oppression and a desire to minimize exposure to the exigencies of state intrusion. Assessments of individual efficacy in the state context are remarkably low: people feel helpless and often express these sentiments through studied indifference and apathy. The validity of state power is therefore constantly questioned: while people are willing to exploit the state and its resources to pursue their own ends, they also advocate avoidance and disengagement.[113]

Alternative notions of authority, community, distributive justice, and conflict resolution are then defined in particularistic terms. Each social group has amplified its own set of operative norms and endowed them with symbolic and practical meaning.[114] Thus, although there is broad consensus on the rejection of the authoritarian, exploitative state, there are not many common distinguishing characteristics to the alternate visions propagated by specific social groups.

Several key characteristics of popular political cultures emerge from this analysis. First, nonelite groups value diversity: they keep their options open and try to maximize opportunities by stressing flexibility.[115] Second, fluidity and vacillation beyond the boundaries of familiar social frameworks are seen as given. Patterns of official politics are unpredictable and changeable; sentiments and evaluations of these operations can also fluctuate. Nonstate settings, in contrast, are prized precisely because they offer continuity in the midst of uncertainty.[116] Third, political protest and criticism, though pointed and incisive, greatly outweigh efforts to detail the parameters of acceptable norms. Moderation, compromise, and accommodation are not central to these perceptions. And, finally, an overriding concern is to define the place of individuals and groups vis-à-vis the state. Reformulating the official order is less important than devising means of surviving within its confines.

Grassroots initiatives in a variety of spheres have enabled specific groups to carve out their own social, economic, and political spaces within which they can operate. Informal institutions have had the effect of chipping away at the state from below, of defying statist pretensions by limiting the human reach of state organs.[117] In a very real sense, "Africa's potential for democracy is more convincingly revealed by the creation of [these] small collectives established and controlled by rural or urban groups than by parliaments and parties, instruments of the state, of accumulation and of alienation."[118]

Several factors have determined the ability of popular groups to articulate and pursue their goals. First, contextual conditions such as economic circumstances, external influences, and official power constellations play a role. Second, factors internal to the organization of social groups have been important: historical continuity, access to or control of autonomous resources (especially land or labor), location, size, social organizing principles—and the consequent differences in internal cohesion, autonomy, institutionalization, and normative coherence.[119] And third, the distribution of certain attributes of individual group members, such as income, gender, and access to formal education, have affected group capacities.[120]

The political consequences of the multidimensional dissociation of social groups from the state have not been clear-cut. On the one hand dissent and disaffection have been channeled in ways conducive to individual and small-group sustenance. Frameworks for protection against overexposure to capricious government have been institutionalized. Processes of power accumulation away from monolithic formal structures have consequently been set in motion. On the other hand, these responses have been fragmented and frequently highly particularistic and parochial. They have helped to weaken and in extreme cases to dissipate the formal apparatus but have not fomented a concomitant reordering of the political center. In fact, at least in the short term, local rebellion has invited greater repression.[121]

Distinctly inward looking and present-oriented, these manifestations of diffuse democracy were generally not accompanied, in the first half of the 1980s, by the institutionalization of integrating patterns of state-society interactions. What was palpably missing was a legitimating idea, a new set of organizing principles that could unite civil society. Without such a normative scheme, counterhegemonic activities ran the risk of increasing state dominance, undermining state control, and further eroding the prospects for democracy on a countrywide scale.[122]

## Dynamics of African Political Cultures

The political history of Africa since independence has been marked by cultural variegation and the partial institutionalization of formal structures. In no country has the authority of the state been extended throughout its territory; in no instance have official structures completely disintegrated. In the absence of examples of full state consolidation, political culture patterns have come to reflect differing degrees of stateness and various forms of state-society relations.

The institutional forms of political interaction have varied considerably in different countries since independence. Intricate combinations of autonomy and exchange have emerged that point to the crystallization of distinctive national characteristics in the many countries on the continent.

Burundi, South Africa, and preindependence Rhodesia stand at one pole of the state-society continuum. Until recently, in these countries state elites enjoyed heightened autonomy and possessed few structural linkages with the bulk of the population. Coercion was employed as the prime method of control. Because local communities retained few autonomous resources, they were particularly vulnerable to state intrusions. The other pole on the continuum is illustrated most dramatically by the examples of Chad and Uganda during the 1970s and early 1980s. The political center in these countries was wracked by elite dissension and by the absence of autonomy of state leaders from specific ethnic and regional forces. The reach of the state apparatus was negligible, and social groups mobilized their own resources, devised their own systems of justice, and sought to protect themselves from their neighbors and from the remnants of official agencies. Political life was haphazard and capricious.

In between these two extremes, many dynamic types of institutional and cultural interaction have emerged, each indicative of varying degrees of stateness. One such pattern is that of individual domination (Liberia under Doe, Equatorial Guinea under Nguema), in which personal rulers have used the state to assert their supremacy and social groups have been systematically repressed. A second is one of direct state-society confrontation (most visible in Afro-Marxist regimes). In these countries the state is on a par and actively competes with heavily organized social groups. These areas have experienced ongoing civil wars. In the third pattern, evident in Côte d'Ivoire, Cameroon, and Zaire, among others, some measure of state dominance has been attained and social interactions with the formal apparatus have been structured along vertical lines. In these conditions patronage networks formed around instrumental links.

Nigeria, Zambia, and more recently Kenya exemplify a fourth variant, in which intraelite competition has nurtured systemic official abuses and more radicalized popular responses. A fifth mode of structuring political interchanges developed in Ghana and Sierra Leone. In these two countries strong social groups have intermittently tied themselves with or disconnected from state elites depending on the extent to which association with the center was deemed worthwhile. A sixth pattern has been one of contraction. Tanzania, for one, has experienced a gradual shrinkage of the centrality of state organs as a growing number of social organizations have withdrawn from the formal arena.[123] And finally, Senegal and Botswana have sustained a relatively participatory dynamic on the basis of principles of unequal reciprocity.[124]

Two common features of these heterogeneous patterns stand out: the incomplete institutionalization of the state apparatus in Africa and the inverse relationship between the degree of state consolidation and hegemonic propensities. The political experience of independent Africa has highlighted the risks of expanding administrative devices at the expense of representative mechanisms. The initial frameworks of public life in Africa, with all their increasingly distinctive features, have been too detached from social concerns, economic exigencies, and local processes.

By the mid-1980s renewed efforts were made to tackle these problems. African leaders, faced with endemic economic regression, increased dependence on external props, and growing popular unrest, could no longer avoid confronting the consequences of their rule. They began to investigate ways of fortifying the capacities of state institutions without adversely affecting their already tenuous ties with large segments of their populations. The challenge they have faced is threefold: to devise appropriate methods of reviving failing public agencies; to construct viable political institutions; and to restructure the foundations of the relationship between official organs and social groups. The success of these experiments depended on the ability of rulers to build a mediatory network and thereby resurrect the state as the focus of integration and as the guardian of general interests.[125] The dynamic of statism that prevailed in the first decades of independence began to give way to a quest for greater efficiency through more fruitful interaction.

The process of review and readjustment had become evident first in the near-wholesale adoption of IMF and World Bank structural adjustment measures (devaluations, hikes in producer prices, stringent fiscal austerity) to attract foreign financial support. This has meant increased reliance on market mechanisms and greater economic liberalization.

Related to this have been efforts, also spurred by foreign donor pressure, to reduce government involvement in production. State employment has been frozen and in some instances the ministries have downsized. In certain countries (most notably Nigeria, Tanzania, Kenya, Côte d'Ivoire, Zaire and Ghana) governments have begun to divest themselves of unprofitable public enterprises and have dismantled many of the formidable marketing boards that previously served as vital instruments of state hegemony. The net result has been to pare down the size of the state apparatus.

A third aspect of contemporary reassessments has revolved around decentralization schemes. In Ghana and Zaire, for example, plans have been drawn to restructure official agencies so as to reduce the concentration of decisionmaking powers at the core. Although these projects have yet to be implemented in full, they may point to a move away from past monopolistic dispositions. The concern with decentralization underlines the declared intention (as yet unrealized) of promoting more participatory networks.[126]

The reconsiderations of the mid-1980s have also addressed the issue of regime change more directly. The range of theorizing on forms of government has increased noticeably in recent years. Constitutional questions have been reexamined with a view to placing effective restraints on power holders.[127] Indigenous democratic traditions have been rediscovered in an attempt to align central political institutions with consultative and participatory themes rooted in specific local histories.[128] Plans have been designed for resurrecting liberal modes of rule in coming years. These programs for regime reorientation remain largely on the drawing boards. The problem of institutional remolding still stands as the most pressing issue on the contemporary African political agenda.

In light of past experience, present attempts to revive liberal government in new guises have been met with not inconsiderable skepticism. Indeed, hegemonic rule still persists in most parts of the continent. Many observers assess democratic prospects for the last decade of the century as dim.[129] Yet at least on an empirical level the sober introspection of the mid-1980s diverged in both substance and tenor from the more facile prescriptions suggested ten years earlier.

Central to emerging political approaches to institutional reordering has been a stress on accountability, on defining codes of official conduct and devising methods to monitor government behavior and to make various organizations and agencies responsible to one another.[130] Accountability from this vantage point is closely linked both to increased possibilities for political scrutiny (such as freedom of the press) and greater responsiveness (political skill). Academic attention has therefore been directed to refining concepts of citizenship and to providing adequate channels for representation and participation of the national level. In stark contrast with past political culture constructs, present-day interpretations appear not only more dynamic and functional but also more strongly anchored in the African experience and more cognizant of the nuances of the contemporary predicament.

The concept of democracy that emerges from these considerations differs from its predecessors in that it perceives democracy in relational terms. In this unfolding democratic vision the culture and values of democracy are integrally linked to institutional channels for participation, mechanisms for the limitation of official excesses, provisions for the protection of human rights and social pluralism, and principles of economic rationality and the emergence of vibrant civil societies (which reinforce stateness).

## Political Cultures and Democratic Challenges

The recent history of Africa has nurtured a multiplicity of political forms and sustained a myriad of political cultures. The diversity of political experiences and practices presents an invaluable opportunity to reassess approaches to the study of political culture and democracy and to point to some policy implications.

In the past three decades African state agencies have expanded rapidly but the state itself has not been sufficiently institutionalized, allowing for the coexistence of a variety of social institutions alongside formal bodies. The lack of coherence of state structures has coincided with the absence of vital civil societies. Dynamic patterns of state-society interaction have endowed specific countries with distinctive political cultures. But statism is not a substitute for stateness. These findings suggest that the state is a crucial constituent part of any good theory of political culture.[131]

Many elements of democratic belief and practice have surfaced in Africa in recent years. Notions of democracy as liberation, government, rationale, ideal, counterhegemony, and mediation have been defined and explored. These have not always appeared in the sequence apparent elsewhere in the Third or Western worlds; their repercussions have differed as well. Various African evocations of the democratic ethos persist on the continent even if democratic regimes are scarce, but democratic currents of political culture remain defined at the popular level largely in opposition to formal government.

The fortunes of political regimes and the thrust of political trends have been heavily influenced by these democratic impulses. Problems of governance have continuously hampered the search for a viable political order. Although Africans exhibit a sophisticated familiarity with democracy, they have not yet invented suitable modes of democratic practice because they have been unable to augment the amount of government in order to reconstruct its forms. The construction of new, reliable and trusted frameworks of interaction between state and society has become the prime precondition for democratization in Africa.[132]

The recent history of Africa is replete with manifestations of democratic aspirations and with examples of democratic blockage. Cycles of democratic decline and liberal reinvigoration characterize the ongoing quest for a form of government that will mirror the weblike structure of African social organizations.

If democracy is everywhere under construction, in Africa it has assumed especially imaginative expressions and accumulated particularly strident setbacks. The need for improved design is especially acute in light of the monumental human costs of continuous impoverishment.[133] The problems of democracy in Africa focus on two main issues. First, at the national level, inherited state institutions still have to undergo a process of decolonization and local entrenchment; otherwise no regime stabilization, let alone democratic consolidation, is possible. Second, on the level of civil society, intermediary organizations need to be fortified as a means to linking social groups with one another and with the state. In Africa in recent years, fragments of democracy have flourished.[134] The challenge for Africa's political future rests in putting these democratic segments together in workable ways.

## Notes

The Harry S. Truman Research Institute for the Advancement of Peace at the Hebrew University of Jerusalem provided support and facilities for the preparation of this chapter. Multiple thanks are due to Larry Diamond for his meticulous suggestions for revision of an earlier draft.

1. Gabriel A. Almond and Sidney Verba, *The Civic Culture* (Princeton: Princeton University Press, 1963), pp. 12-13.

2. Aaron Wildavsky, "Choosing Preferences by Constructing Institutions: A Cultural Theory of Preference Formation," *American Political Science Review* 81, no. 1 (1987): 17.

3. See David Laitin, "Political Cultures and Political Preferences," *American Political Science Review* 82, no. 2 (1988): 589-596.

4. The concept of articulators of cultural models is explicated in S.N. Eisenstadt, Michel Abitol, and Naomi Chazan, "The Origins of the State Reconsidered," in S. N. Eisenstadt, Michel Abitol, and Naomi Chazan, eds., *The Early State in African Perspective: Culture, Power and Division of Labor* (Leiden: E. J. Brill, 1988), pp. 1-27.

5. Colin Leys, "Economic Development in Theory and Practice," *Daedalus* 111, no. 2 (1982): 119-120.

6. Joel Migdal, "Strong States, Weak States: Power and Accommodation," in Myron Weiner and Samuel P. Huntington, eds., *Understanding Political Development* (Boston: Little, Brown, 1987), pp. 391-434. The competition between alternative political cultures in African countries is accounted for by the fact that, once formed, values and beliefs created in one setting take on a life of their own and affect understanding of new social settings. See David Laitin, "Religion, Political Culture and the Weberian Tradition," *World Politics* 30, no. 4 (1978): 586.

7. Thomas M. Callaghy, *The State-Society Struggle: Zaire in Comparative Perspective* (New York: Columbia University Press, 1984), p. 32.

8. This point is made in a series of recent studies on the state in Africa. For one formulation see Christopher Clapham, *Third World Politics: An Introduction*

(Madison: University of Wisconsin Press, 1985). For a comparative view, see Lisa Anderson, "The State in the Middle East and North Africa," *Comparative Politics* 20, no. 1 (1987): 12 esp. The most comprehensive analysis may be found in Joel Migdal, *Strong Societies and Weak States: Power and Domination in the Third World* (Princeton: Princeton University Press, 1988).

9. See Jean-Francois Bayart, "Civil Society in Africa," in Patrick Chabal, ed., *Political Domination in Africa: Reflections on the Limits of Power* (London: Cambridge University Press, 1986), p. 112.

10. Ibid., p. 111.

11. For an explanation of the notion of democracy as a relationship, see Joseph-Marie Bipoun-Woum, "Are We Heading for a Cultural Blockage of Democracy in African States?" *Presence Africaine* 97, no. 1 (1976): 12.

12. This triple legacy is generally acknowledged in the literature. An explicit treatment may be found in Maxwell Owusu, "Custom and Coups in Africa: Toward a Juridical Interpretation of Civil Order and Disorder in Ghana," *Journal of Modern African Studies* 23, no. 4 (1985): 5-6, esp.

13. For an explanation of this framework for the analysis of political cultures, see S. N. Eisenstadt, "Cultural Traditions and Political Dynamics," *British Journal of Sociology* 32, no. 2 (1981): 294-314; S.N. Eisenstadt, M. Abitol and N. Chazan, "Cultural Premises, Political Structures and Dynamics," *International Political Science Review* 8, no. 4 (1987): 291-306.

14. For a fuller explanation, see Naomi Chazan, "The Africanization of Political Change: Some Aspects of the Dynamics of Political Cultures in Ghana and Nigeria," *African Studies Review* 21, no. 2 (1978): 16-22; and N. Chazan and M. Abitol, "Myths and Politics in Precolonial Africa," in Eisenstadt, Abitol, and Chazan, *The Early State in African Perspective*, pp. 28-59.

15. For some excellent in-depth studies, see J. F. Ade Ajayi and Bashir Ikara, eds., *Evolution of Political Culture in Nigeria* (Ibadan: University Press, 1985).

16. Richard Hodder-Williams, *An Introduction to the Politics of Tropical Africa* (London: George Allen and Unwin, 1984), pp. 13-14.

17. These points are elaborated in Robert Smith, *Kingdoms of the Yoruba* (London: Methuen, 1976), and Kwame Arhin, *Traditional Rule in Ghana: Past and Present* (Accra: Sedco, 1985), pp. 79-82.

18. For details, see Nehemia Levtzion, *Ancient Ghana and Mali* (London: Methuen, 1973).

19. Pathe Diagne, "De la Democratie Traditionelle," *Presence Africaine* 97, no. 1 (1976): 18-43.

20. An excellent overview may be found in Crawford Young, "The African Colonial State and its Political Legacy," in Donald Rothchild and Naomi Chazan, eds., *The Precarious Balance: State and Society in Africa* (Boulder: Westview Press, 1988), pp. 25-66.

21. Peter Ekeh, "Colonialism and the Two Publics in Africa: A Theoretical Statement," *Comparative Studies in Society and History* 17, no. 1 (1975): 91-112.

22. For an excellent analysis of the introduction of capitalism and its effects on political trends on the continent, see Richard Sandbrook, *The Politics of Africa's Economic Stagnation* (London: Cambridge University Press, 1985), esp. pp. 42-62.

23. See Robert Bates, "Modernization, Ethnic Competition and the Rationality of Politics in Contemporary Africa," in Donald Rothchild and Victor Olorunsola, eds., *State versus Ethnic Claims: African Policy Dilemmas* (Boulder: Westview Press, 1983), pp. 152-171.

24. By far the best analysis of this process may be found in Richard L. Sklar, "The Nature of Class Domination in Africa," *Journal of Modern African Studies* 17, no. 4 (1979): 531-552. Also see Larry Diamond, "Class Formation in the Swollen

African State," *Journal of Modern African Studies,* 25, no. 4 (1987): 567-596.

25. For a fuller discussion of these groups, see Immanuel Wallerstein, *The Road to Independence: Ghana and the Ivory Coast* (Paris and the Hague: Movuton, 1964).

26. Kwame Ninsin, "Citizenship, Participation and Democracy," in K. A. Ninsin and F. K. Drah, eds., *The Search for Democracy in Ghana* (Accra: Asempa, 1987), p. 73.

27. The term *congresses* is taken from the classic work of Thomas Hodgkin, *Nationalism in Colonial Africa* (New York: New York University Press, 1957).

28. Several case studies demonstrate this alliance between articulators of solidarity and emerging state elites. See, for example, Carl Rosberg and John Nottingham, *The Myth of the Mau Mau: Nationalism in Kenya* (New York: Meridien Books, 1970); and James S. Coleman, Nigeria: *Background to Nationalism* (Berkeley: University of California Press, 1958).

29. See Yves Person, "L'Etat Nation et l'Afrique," *Presence Africaine* 190-191 (1981): 27-35.

30. See Naomi Chazan, "Engaging the State: Associational Life in Sub-Saharan Africa" (Paper presented at the Workshop on State Power and Social Forces: Domination and Transformation in the Third World, Austin, University of Texas, February 1990).

31. See Richard L. Sklar, "The Colonial Imprint on African Political Thought," in Gwendolyn M. Carter and Patrick O'Meara, eds., *African Independence: The First Twenty-Five Years* (Bloomington: Indiana University Press, 1985), pp. 1-30.

32. For a discussion of these challenges, see Patrick Chabal, "Introduction: Thinking About Politics in Africa," in Chabal, *Political Domination in Africa,* p. 5; and Irving Leonard Markovitz, *Power and Class in Africa: An Introduction to Change and Conflict in African Politics* (Englewood Cliffs, NJ: Prentice-Hall, 1978), pp. 14-24.

33. Ali A. Mazrui, *Political Values and the Educated Class in Africa* (London: Heinemann, 1978).

34. Naomi Chazan, Robert Mortimer, John Ravenhill, and Donald Rothchild, *Politics and Society in Contemporary Africa* (Boulder: Lynne Rienner Publishers, 1988), pp. 82-83.

35. Abner Cohen, *The Politics of Elite Culture: Explorations in the Dramaturgy of Power in a Modern African Society* (Berkeley: University of California Press, 1981), p. 9.

36. The most comprehensive analysis of these processes may be found in Ruth Berins Collier, *Regimes in Tropical Africa: Changing Forms of Supremacy, 1945-1975* (Berkeley: University of California Press, 1982). It is important to note that the consensual, consociational model of democracy was not referred to at this time. See Robert Jackson and Carl Rosberg, "Democracy in Tropical Africa: Democracy versus Autocracy in African Politics," *Journal of International Affairs* 38, no. 2 (1985): 298.

37. For a discussion of federalism, see John Ayoade, "Federalism in Africa: Some Chequered Fortunes," *Plural Societies* 9, no. 1 (1978): 3-17.

38. This idea of liberal democracy in Africa is expounded in Richard L. Sklar, "Democracy in Africa" (Presidential address to the Twenty-Fifth Annual Meeting of the African Studies Association, Washington, DC, November 1982; Special Publication of the African Studies Center, University of California, Los Angeles, 1982), esp. pp. 2-3.

39. This is a paraphrase of Larry Diamond, "Class, Ethnicity and the Democratic State: Nigeria, 1950-1966," *Comparative Studies in Society and History* 25, no. 3 (1983): 460.

40. For a good review of elections in Africa, see Fred Hayward, "Introduction," in Fred Hayward, ed., *Elections in Independent Africa* (Boulder: Westview Press,

1986), pp. 1-24.

41. This point is made forcefully by Joel D. Barkan, "Legislators, Elections and Political Linkage," in Joel D. Barkan and John J. Okumu, eds., *Politics and Public Policy in Kenya and Tanzania* (New York: Praeger, 1984), p. 65.

42. The following discussion relies heavily on Thomas M. Callaghy, "Politics and Vision in Africa: The Interplay of Domination, Equality and Liberty," in Chabal, *Political Domination in Africa,* pp. 30-51.

43. See the justification provided by Robert Jackson and Carl Rosberg, "Popular Legitimacy in African Multi-Ethnic States," *Journal of Modern African Studies* 22, no. 2 (1984): 198. See also Dov Ronen, "The Challenges of Democracy in Africa: Some Introductory Observations," in Ronen, ed., *Democracy and Pluralism in Africa* (Boulder: Lynne Rienner Publishers, 1986), pp. 1-6.

44. Hodder-Williams, *An Introduction to the Politics of Tropical Africa,* p. 64.

45. Peter Anyang' Nyong'o, "The Decline of Democracy and the Rise of Authoritarian and Factionalist Politics in Kenya," *Horn of Africa* 6, no. 3 (1983/84): 25. For a more general treatment, see Juan Linz, *The Breakdown of Democratic Regimes: Crisis, Breakdown and Reequilibrium* (Baltimore: Johns Hopkins University Press, 1978).

46. On Senegal, see Robert Fatton, Jr., *The Making of a Liberal Democracy: Senegal's Passive Revolution,* 1975-1985 (Boulder: Lynne Rienner Publishers, 1987); and Dominique Gauthiex-Riecau, "La Democratie au Senegal," *Afrique Contemporaine* 133 (1985): 12-32.

47. For information on these elections, see Naomi Chazan, "The Anomalies of Continuity: Perspectives on Ghanian Elections Since Independence," and Paul Beckett, "Elections and Democracy in Nigeria," in Hayward, *Elections in Independent Africa,* pp. 61-86, and pp. 87-120.

48. Larry Diamond, "Nigeria in Search of Democracy," *Foreign Affairs* 62, no. 4 (1984): 905 and *passim*; and Naomi Chazan, "Ghana: Problems of Governance and the Emergence of Civil Society," in Larry Diamond, Juan Linz, and Seymour Martin Lipset, eds., *Democracy in Developing Countries: Africa* (Boulder: Lynne Rienner Publishers, 1988), pp. 112-115.

49. Richard L. Sklar, "Democracy for the Second Republic," *Issue* 11 (1981): 15.

50. See Naomi Chazan, "Planning Democracy in Africa: A Comparative Perspective on Nigeria and Ghana," *Policy Sciences* 22 (1989): 325-357; and Larry Diamond, "Nigeria's Search for a New Political Order," *Journal of Democracy* 2, no. 2 (Spring 1991): 54-69.

51. Aristide Zolberg, *Creating Political Order: The Party States of West Africa* (Chicago: Rand McNally, 1967), remains the classic exposition of these processes.

52. This point is made elegantly by Richard Crook, "Bureaucracy and Politics in Ghana: A Comparative Perspective," in P. Lyon and J. Manor, eds., *Transfer and Transformation: Political Institutions in the New Commonwealth* (Leicester: Leicester University Press, 1983), p. 185.

53. For an early analysis, see Michael Lofchie, "Representative Government, Bureaucracy and Political Development: The African Case," in Marion Doro and Newell Stultz, eds., *Governing in Black Africa* (Englewood Cliffs, NJ: Prentice-Hall, 1970), pp. 278-294. For an analysis rooted in political culture traditions, see Ali A. Mazrui, "The Cultural Fate of African Legislatures: Rise, Decline and Prospects for Revival," *Presence Africaine* 112 (1979): 26-47.

54. On the relationship between personalization and lack of political institutionalization, see Robert Jackson and Carl Rosberg, *Personal Rule in Black Africa: Prince, Autocrat, Prophet, Tyrant* (Berkeley: University of California Press, 1982).

One of the most sophisticated analyses of the neopatrimonial state is Callaghy, *The State-Society Struggle.*

55. Nelson Kasfir, "Class, Political Domination and the African State" (Paper presented at the Twenty-Eighth Annual Meeting of the African Studies Association, New Orleans, November 1985).

56. Keith Hart, *The Political Economy of West African Agriculture* (London: Cambridge University Press, 1982), p. 90 and *passim.* For a more general discussion, see Theda Skocpol, "Bringing the State Back In: Strategies of Analysis in Current Research," in Peter Evans, Dietrich Rueschmeyer, and Theda Skocpol, eds., *Bringing the State Back In* (London: Cambridge University Press, 1985), esp. pp. 8-11.

57. Nelson Kasfir, "Introduction: Relating Class to State in Africa," *Journal of Commonwealth and Comparative Politics* 21, no. 3 (1983): 4.

58. For details, see Diamond, "Class Formation in the Swollen African State."

59. Thomas H. Callaghy, "Culture and Politics in Zaire" (Washington, DC: Department of State, Bureau of Intelligence and Research, 1987), p. 68.

60. Ali A. Mazrui, "Political Engineering in Africa," *International Social Science Journal* 35, no. 2 (1983): 293.

61. For a fascinating case study, see Jan Kees van Donge and Athumani J. Liviga, "Tanzanian Political Culture and the Cabinet," *Journal of Modern African Studies* 24, no. 4 (1986): 619-639.

62. One of the first and most skillful analyses of corruption as a cultural system of government is Stanislav Andreski, *The African Predicament: A Study in the Pathology of Modernization* (London: Michael Joseph, 1968), esp. pp. 92-109. See also Monday V. Ekpo, ed., *Bureaucratic Corruption in Sub-Saharan Africa: Toward a Search for Causes and Consequences* (Washington, DC: University Press of America, 1979).

63. Martin O. Heisler and B. Guy Peters, "Scarcity and the Management of Political Conflict in Multicultural Polities," *International Political Science Review* 4, no. 3 (1983): 327-344. The notion of a political logic at odds with economic logic was first skillfully examined in Robert Bates, *Markets and States in Tropical Africa: The Political Basis of Agricultural Policies* (Berkeley: University of California Press, 1981).

64. For further discussion of this point, see Harvey Glickman, "Reflections on State-Centrism as Ideology in Africa" (Paper presented at the Twenty-Eighth Annual Meeting of the African Studies Association, New Orleans, November 1985).

65. See Jackson and Rosberg, "Democracy in Tropical Africa." For some concrete examples, see Claude Riviere, "Rites de la Democratie et de l'Autocracie en Afrique," *Cultures et Developpement* 17, no. 3 (1985): 453-471.

66. Several case studies deal with this process in depth. See, for example, Deborah Pellow and Naomi Chazan, *Ghana: Coping with Uncertainty* (Boulder: Westview Press, 1986), and S. R. Karugire, *A Political History of Uganda* (London: Heinemann, 1980).

67. David and Marina Ottaway, *Afro-Communism* (New York: Africana, 1981); see also P. F. Gonidec, "La Conception de la Democratie dans les Etats a l'Orientation Socialiste," *Le Mois en Afrique* 243-244 (1986): 34-45.

68. Edmond J. Keller and Donald Rothchild, eds., *Afro-Marxist Regimes: Ideology and Public Policy* (Boulder: Lynne Rienner Publishers, 1987).

69. Owusu, "Customs and Coups," *passim.*

70. The best treatment of this model may be found in Thomas Callaghy, "The State as Lame Leviathan: The Patrimonial Administrative State in Africa," in Zaki Ergas, ed., *The African State in Transition* (London: Macmillan, 1987), pp. 87-116.

71. Bayart, "Civil Society in Africa," pp. 114-115. Also see Jean-Francois

Bayart, *L'Etat en Afrique: La Politique du Ventre* (Paris, Fayard, 1989).

72. Naomi Chazan, "The New Politics of Participation in Tropical Africa," *Comparative Politics* 14, no. 2 (1982): 169-189.

73. Guillermo O'Donnell, "Tensions in the Bureaucratic-Authoritarian State and the Question of Democracy," in David Collier, ed., *The New Authoritarianism in Latin America* (Princeton: Princeton University Press, 1979), pp. 285-318.

74. See Larry Diamond, Juan Linz and Seymour Martin Lipset, "Democracy in Developing Countries: Facilitating and Obstructing Factors," in Raymond Gastil, ed., *Freedom in the World: Political Rights and Civil Liberties* (New York: Freedom House, 1988), pp. 229-258.

75. Crawford Young, *Ideology and Development in Africa* (New Haven: Yale University Press, 1982), p. 293 and *passim.*

76. Chris Allen, "Staying Put: Handy Hints for Heads of State" (Paper presented at the Symposium on Authority and Legitimacy in Africa organized by the African Studies Association of the United Kingdom and the Center for Commonwealth Studies, University of Stirling, May 1986), esp. p. 9.

77. Sklar, "Democracy in Africa," p. 13.

78. Peter Anyang' Nyong'o, "Introduction," in Peter Anyang' Nyong'o, *Popular Struggles for Democracy in Africa* (London: Zed Press, 1987), p. 19 and *passim.*

79. See Robert Price, "Neo-Colonialism and Ghana's Economic Decline: A Critical Assessment," *Canadian Journal of African Studies* 18, no. 1 (1984): 163-193.

80. See Sandbrook, *The Politics of Africa's Economic Stagnation*, esp. pp. 112-113.

81. Robert Jackson and Carl Rosberg, "Why Africa's Weak States Persist: The Empirical and the Juridical in Statehood," *World Politics* 35, no. 1 (1982): 1-24, describes the weakness of the African state but does not relate this weakness to domestic social processes.

82. For an overview of social groups in historical perspective, see Chris Allen and Gavin Williams, eds., *Sociology of "Developing Societies": Sub-Saharan Africa* (New York: Monthly Review Press, 1982). Also see Michael Bratton, "Beyond the State: Civil Society and Associational Life in Africa," *World Politics* 41, no. 3 (1989): 407-430.

83. For one example, see Henry Silver, "Going for Brokers: Political Innovation and Structural Integration in a Changing Ashanti Community," *Comparative Political Studies* 14, no. 2 (1981): 233-263.

84. For a general discussion, see Margaret Peil, *Consensus and Conflict in African States: An Introduction to Sociology* (London: Longman, 1977). Specific case studies are rare. For two excellent examples, see Sandra T. Barnes and Margaret Peil, "Voluntary Association Membership in Five West African Cities," *Urban Anthropology* 6, no. 1 (1977): 83-106; and Sandra T. Barnes, "Voluntary Associations in a Metropolis: The Case of Lagos, Nigeria," *African Studies Review* 18, no. 2 (1975): 75-88. The most updated case study is Aili Marie Tripp, "Tanzania," in Michael Bratton and Goran Hyden, eds., *Governance and Politics in Africa* (Boulder: Lynne Rienner Publishers, 1991).

85. Chazan et al., *Politics and Society in Contemporary Africa.* Chapter 2 provides a detailed analysis of these groups.

86. See Richard Stren, "L'Etat au Risque de la Ville," *Politique Africaine* 17 (1985): 74-85, for a discussion of the blurring of some of these distinctions.

87. Christian Coulon, "Le Reseau Islamique," *Politique Africaine* 9 (1983): 68-83.

88. Jean-Francois Bayart, "Les Societes Africaines Face a l'Etat," *Pouvoirs* 25

(1983): 23-39; "La Politique par le Bas en Afrique Noire," *Politique Africaine* 1 (1980): 53-82; and "Le Revanche des Societies Africaines," *Politique Africaine* 11 (1983): 95-127.

89. M. K. Schutz, "Observations on the Functions of Voluntary Associations with Special Reference to West African Cities," *Human Relations* 30, no. 9 (1977): 803-816.

90. Hodder-Williams, *An Introduction to the Politics of Tropical Africa*, p. 164.

91. See Frank Holmquist, "Defending Peasant Political Space in Independent Africa," *Canadian Journal of African Studies* 14, no. 1 (1980): 157-167. Also see Naomi Chazan, "Liberalization, Governance and Political Space in Ghana" (Paper presented at the American Political Science Association meetings, Atlanta, September 1989).

92. The ensuing analysis is based on Victor Azarya and Naomi Chazan, "Disengagement from the State in Africa: Reflections on the Experience of Ghana and Guinea," *Comparative Studies in Society and History* 19, no. 1 (1987): 106-131. See also Catherine Newbury, "Survival Strategies in Rural Zaire: Realities of Coping with Crisis," in Nzongola-Ntalaja, ed., *The Zaire Crisis: Myths and Realities* (Trenton: Third World Press, 1986), pp. 99-112.

93. Robin Cohen, "Resistance and Hidden Forms of Consciousness Amongst African Workers," *Review of African Political Economy* 19 (1980): 8-22.

94. See Pierre Mettelin, "Activities Informelles et Economies Urbaine: Le Cas de l'Afrique Noire," *Le Mois en Afrique* 223-224 (1984): 57-71.

95. One of the best case studies is Sara Berry, *Fathers Work for their Sons: Accumulation, Mobility and Class Formation in an Extended Yoruba Community* (Berkeley: University of California Press, 1985).

96. Claire Robertson, "The Death of Makola and Other Tragedies," *Canadian Journal of African Studies* 17, no. 3 (1983): 469-495.

97. For one example, see Stephen G. Bunker, "Bagisu Agricultural Innovation and Political Organization in the Ugandan Crisis" (Paper presented at the Twenty-Fourth Annual Meeting of the African Studies Association, Boston, December 1983).

98. See Goran Hyden, *No Shortcuts to Progress: African Development Management in Perspective* (Berkeley: University of California Press, 1983). The debate over Hyden's identification of an exit option in the rural areas has been conducted in the pages of *Development and Change*. See Nelson Kasfir, "Are African Peasants Self-Sufficient?" *Development and Change* 17 (1986): 335-367; Goran Hyden's response, "The Anomaly of the African Peasantry," in the same volume, pp. 677-705; and the exchange between Lionel Cliffe, Gavin Williams, and Goran Hyden in *Development and Change* 18 (1987). For an analysis of this literature, see Naomi Chazan, "State and Society in Africa: Images and Challenges," in Rothchild and Chazan, *The Precarious Balance*, pp. 325-341.

99. Roy Preiswerk, "Self-Reliance in Unexpected Places," *Geneve-Afrique* 20, no. 2 (1982): 56-64.

100. Janet MacGaffey, "Economic Disengagement and Class Formation in Zaire," in Rothchild and Chazan, *The Precarious Balance*, pp. 171-188. See also Nelson Kasfir, "State, *Magendo*, and Class Formation in Uganda," *Journal of Commonwealth and Comparative Politics* 21, no. 3 (1983): 99, 101.

101. Karin Barber, "Popular Arts in Africa," *African Studies Review* 30, no. 3 (1987): 4.

102. Terence O. Ranger, "Religious Movements and Politics in Sub-Saharan Africa" (ACLS/SSRC Joint Committee on African Studies Paper presented at the Twenty-Eighth Annual Meeting of the African Studies Association, New Orleans, November 1985).

103. Fred M. Hayward, "A Reassessment of Conventional Wisdom About the

Informed Public: National Political Information in Ghana," *American Political Science Review* 70, no. 2 (1976): 433-451.

104. Margaret Peil, *Nigerian Politics: The People's View* (London: Cassel, 1976), p. 185.

105. For some early examples, see Otto Klineberg and Marissa Zavalloni, *Nationalism and Tribalism Among African Students* (Paris: UNESCO, 1969); and Kenneth Prewitt, ed., *Education and Political Values: An East African Case Study* (Nairobi: East African Publishing House, 1971). For a more recent analysis, see Dirk Berg-Schlosser, "Modes and Meaning of Political Participation in Kenya," *Comparative Politics* 14, no. 4 (1982): 397-416.

106. Naomi Chazan, *An Anatomy of Ghanian Politics: Managing Political Recession, 1969-1982* (Boulder: Westview Press, 1983), pp. 139-145.

107. Again, drawing on Ghanian data, see Donald Rothchild, "Comparative Public Demand and Expectation Patterns: The Ghanian Experience," *African Studies Review* 22, no. 1 (1979): 127-147.

108. Robert Price, "Politics and Culture in Contemporary Ghana: The Big-Man Small-Boy Syndrome," *Journal of African Studies* 1, no. 1 (1974): 173-204.

109. See Callaghy, "Culture and Politics in Zaire," pp. 50-51, 76-77.

110. Sandra T. Barnes, *Patrons and Power: Creating a Political Community in Metropolitan Lagos* (Bloomington: Indiana University Press, 1986), esp. pp. 201-219.

111. Fred M. Hayward, "Correlates of National Political Integration: The Case of Ghana," *Comparative Political Studies* 7, no. 2 (1974): 165-192; and "Rural Attitudes and Expectations About National Government: Experiences in Selected Ghanian Communities," *Rural Africana* 18 (1978): 40-59.

112. For data corroborating these points, see Naomi Chazan, "Political Culture and Socialization in Politics: A Ghanian Case," *Review of Politics* 40, no. 1 (1978): 12-17.

113. Pauline H. Baker, "Seeds of Radicalism Among an Aspirant Elite," in Ukandi K. Damachi and Hans Dieter Seibel, eds., *Social Change and Economic Development in Nigeria* (New York: Praeger, 1973), pp. 194-196. See also Margaret Peil, "The Common Man's Reaction to Nigerian Urban Government," *African Affairs* 74, no. 296 (1974): 300-313.

114. For one extensive case study, see John Paden, *Religion and Political Culture in Kano* (Berkeley: University of California Press, 1973).

115. Berry, *Fathers Work for Their Sons*, p. 83, suggests that this attitude fosters nonproductive investments.

116. David Laitin, *Hegemony and Culture: Politics and Religious Change Among the Yoruba* (Chicago: University of Chicago Press, 1986), pp. 181-182.

117. Karen Hansen, "The Black Market in Lusaka, Zambia" (Paper presented at the meetings of the American Anthropological Association, December 1986) demonstrates persuasively the limits of state intrusiveness.

118. Bayart, "Civil Society in Africa," p. 125.

119. Chazan et al., *Politics and Society in Contemporary Africa*, p. 74.

120. Edmond J. Keller, "Education, Ethnicity and Political Socialization in Kenya," *Comparative Political Studies* 12, no. 4 (1980): 442-469. See also Edward N. Muller, Mitchell A. Seligson, and Ilter Turan, "Education, Participation and Support for Democratic Norms," *Comparative Politics* 20, no. 1 (1987): 19-33.

121. John Dunn, "The Politics of Representation and Good Government in Africa," in Chabal, *Political Domination in Africa*, pp. 158-174.

122. Martin Kilson, "Anatomy of African Class Consciousness," in I. L. Markovitz, ed., *Studies in Power and Class in Africa* (London: Oxford University Press, 1987), pp. 50-66.

123. See Dean McHenry, "A Measure of Harmony/Disharmony in a One-Party State," *Journal of Developing Areas* 17 (1983): 337-348.

124. Jonathan Barker, "Local-Central Relations: A Perspective on the Politics of Development in Africa," *Canadian Journal of African Studies* 4, no. 1 (1970): 3-16.

125. See Metin Heper, "Extremely 'Strong State' and Democracy: The Turkish Case in Comparative and Historical Perspective" (Paper presented at the Workshop on Conditions for Democratization, Jerusalem, December 1985).

126. For a particularly harsh critique of Zaire's decentralization policies, see Newbury, "Survival Strategies in Rural Zaire."

127. Harvey Glickman, "Reconstituting Political Ideology in Africa" (Paper presented at the Twenty-Ninth Annual Meeting of the African Studies Association, Madison, October 1986), *passim.* For one specific example, see Larry Diamond, "Issues in the Design of a Third Nigerian Republic," *African Affairs* 86, no. 343 (April 1987): 209-226.

128. Republic of Ghana, "The Search for True Democracy in Ghana" (Accra: Information Service Department, 1985), provides one example. See also Jibrin Ibrahim, "The Political Debate and the Struggle for Democracy in Nigeria," *Review of African Political Economy* 37 (1986): 38-48.

129. Larry Diamond and Dennis Galvan, "Sub-Saharan Africa," in Robert Wesson, ed., *Democracy World Survey, 1987* (Boulder: Lynne Rienner Publishers, 1988).

130. John Lonsdale, "Political Accountability in African History," in Chabal, *Political Domination in Africa*, pp. 126-157.

131. This is a play on David Laitin's contention that "a good theory of political culture should be a constituent part of any theory of the state," *Hegemony and Culture*, p. 174.

132. The contributors to Larry Diamond, Juan Linz, and Seymour Martin Lipset, eds., *Democracy in Developing Countries: Africa* (Boulder: Lynne Rienner Publishers, 1988) emphasize this point.

133. Richard Sklar, "Developmental Democracy," *Comparative Studies in Society and History* 29, no. 4 (1987): 686-714.

134. See Naomi Chazan, "Democratic Fragments: Africa's Quest for Democracy," in S. N. Eisenstadt, ed., *Democratization and Change* (The Hague: E. J. Brill, 1990).

# • 4 •

# Paths to Democracy and the Political Culture of Costa Rica, Mexico, and Nicaragua

## *John A. Booth & Mitchell A. Seligson*

> The social and cultural matrix within which Latin America's leaders oper-
> ate at present is such that effective and representative popular democracy
> is, with really few exceptions, not a feasible alternative.
> —*Frank Tannenbaum*[1]

Authoritarianism is now on the wane and democracy on the rise across the
globe in spite of widespread midcentury pessimism about the prospects for
democratic governance.[2] Indeed, the decline of authoritarian rule in
Southern Europe and Latin America in the 1970s and 1980s, followed by the
collapse of communism in Eastern Europe and the former Soviet Union, may
constitute one of the most significant and encouraging historical trends of the
turbulent and often tragic twentieth century. Yet even though the extensive
decline of military authoritarianism and the rise of civilian, constitutional
rule in Latin America have become the region's hallmark in the past
decade,[3] predictions about democratization in Latin America have long been
gloomy and to some extent remain so.[4]

Efforts to account for major world political patterns and for historic
changes in the world's political landscape have often turned to political culture as an explanatory factor. Social scientists have long viewed political
culture as an important determinant of regime type, or vice versa.[5]
Phenomena such as the rise of European fascism,[6] the supposed authoritarianism, irrationality, and intolerance of mass publics,[7] the degree of democracy in regimes,[8] authoritarian coalitions in developing nations,[9] and general
economic and political traits of Latin American nations[10] have attracted the
attention of social scientists.

Of particular interest here are culturalist interpretations of Latin
American politics that argue against the likelihood of constitutional, repre-
sentative democracy in the region. Dealy, for example, asserts that Latin
Americans do not understand the very term *democracy* in the conventional
Western sense of political pluralism, representation, and competing interests
but as "political monism or *monistic* democracy: that is, the centralization

and control of potentially competing interests ... an attempt to eliminate
competition among groups."[11] Wiarda argues that U.S.-style democracy is
"probably ill suited to the nations of Iberia and Latin America,"[12] because
they are

> Catholic, corporate, stratified, authoritarian, hierarchical, patrimonialist,
> and semifeudal to [the] core. Largely untouched by the great revolutionary
> movements . . . the Iberic and Latin American nations remain locked in
> this traditional pattern of values and institutions. . . . [T]he hold of these
> traditional patterns and institutions has remained continuous, modified to
> be sure by the newer currents of modernity but not submerged and replaced
> by them.[13]

Members of this school, then, would certainly have concurred with
Fitzgibbon and Fernandez in 1981 that "analysis . . . would lead one to conclude that the countries of Latin America are probably not developing along
a democratic-participant cultural path."[14]

A distinct approach to the problem of political culture and democracy
provides a different reason for pessimism about Latin American prospects
for democratization. This approach has been articulated by a number of
authors[15] but is especially prominent in the work of Inglehart.[16] Inglehart
asserts that the beliefs of mass publics heavily influence regime type.[17]
"Cultural patterns, once established, possess considerable autonomy and can
influence subsequent political and economic events." He views political culture as an essential link between democracy and economic development,
arguing that the widely observed correlation between development and
democracy stems largely from "its linkages with social structure and political culture," the latter more important than the former.[18] Inglehart argues,
based on a study of twenty-four nations, that the path to democracy in
Europe and the Anglo-American nations has involved a series of sociocultur-
al changes over a long period. He believes that the rise of Protestantism
increased popular receptivity to capitalism, which as it developed eventually
brought about higher levels of economic development. The resulting widespread prosperity permitted increases in interpersonal trust among citizens
and, ultimately, the development of a "durable set of orientations that roughly corresponds to the 'civic culture' discussed by Almond and Verba."[19] This
civic culture led to the development and stabilization of democratic governments. Inglehart notes that the Protestant tradition may no longer be central
today and that there may be alternative roads to democratization, including
an Asian path involving Confucianism in a role rather analogous to
Protestantism in the Anglo-European path he examines in detail.[20]

Given these arguments about known and conjectured paths toward
democracy (and the received wisdom about Latin American political culture), one would hardly expect to find either democratic cultures or stable

representative, liberal, constitutional regimes in Latin America. Latin American nations historically have not had widespread experience with Protestantism and remain predominantly Catholic. Nor have their experiences with capitalism brought prosperity in comparison with the Anglo-European countries.

The recent nearly universal adoption of the *forms* of representative democracy in Latin America may well have produced regimes that are insufficiently undergirded by a civic culture, and that are therefore likely to be unstable or perhaps ephemeral. There may well be a serious problem of culture-structure incongruity in Latin America today, of democratic governmental structures ungrounded in an appropriately supportive cultural matrix.[21]

This possibility of culture-structure incongruence raises two critical questions. First, can these new Latin American democracies survive, or will they soon succumb to a new wave of authoritarianism? There is much historical evidence for a cyclical alternation between representative constitutional rule and authoritarian rule in Latin America,[22] with major shifts in regime styles being triggered by major economic crises. The onset of the Great Depression of the 1930s ushered in many military regimes, and the more recent trend away from militarism has followed new regional economic crises in the 1970s and 1980s. To the extent that political culture does indeed shape regime type, the absence of a civic culture in Latin America would make a return to authoritarianism more likely.

The second critical question is, might there be other paths toward democratic political culture and stable democratic governance than the Anglo-European and Asian ones discussed by Inglehart? In Latin America, economic crisis rather than gradual social evolution may well be the engine of major political change, but crisis in itself lacks a teleological compass. Extreme economic difficulties or political crises may so discredit and weaken authoritarian regimes that they may crumble, but hard times of themselves constitute no road map for subsequent political transformation. The specific nature of crisis-driven political change must, therefore, be shaped by other factors. Latin America today cannot democratize as the industrial West has or as Asian nations may be doing, it is clear, but might there be other paths? Can the political culture of particular Latin American countries lead them toward democracy? Or will Latin American political culture indefinitely bar democracy from the region?

## Measurement of Political Culture

Considerable prior research from two schools has identified two main elements of democratic political culture. One, from the "civic culture" tradition, emphasizes a mixture of participation in politics with more passive subject

and parochial roles.[23] The civic culture approach to democratic norms, ultimately, held that such cultures supported and encouraged a wide variety of
political participation.[24] The key tests have come to involve the degree to
which citizens express support for the right to organize civic groups, work
for political parties, protest, and vote.

The second approach to democratic culture, based on the work of
Stouffer and McClosky,[25] involves citizens' tolerance—the willingness to
extend civil rights to proponents of unpopular causes. It is argued that tolerance is a critical element of democratic political culture because intolerant
attitudes may lead to intolerant behavior toward the targets of intolerance.[26]
The early studies during the 1950s and early 1960s focused on tolerance
toward communists, but later methodological refinements centered on
groups defined by respondents themselves as being disliked (that is, one's
"least-liked group").[27]

We employ both approaches—support for the right to participate and for
the right of minority dissent—in evaluating democratic political culture. In
*Polyarchy*, Dahl argues that both elements are essential to a culture that supports liberal, representative institutions: citizen support for widespread or
*extensive* political participation (EP—approval of taking part in civic groups,
political parties, protests, and voting), and support for the right of minority
dissent, or *inclusive* values (IP—approval of civil liberties for unpopular
groups or regime critics).[28]

## Testing the Theory: Mexico, Costa Rica, and Nicaragua

We propose to explore further the linkages of mass political culture to
regime type using three Latin American cases, Mexico, Costa Rica, and
Nicaragua. Recently collected data on political values in these nations provide a test for theories about democratic culture and regime type, as well as a
chance to examine possible alternative paths by which nations might develop
stable democratic practice.

### Mexico

We first examined popular political culture in a study of urban Mexicans.[29]
In our 1984 study of Mexico, we reviewed a substantial literature that characterized Mexico as an authoritarian political system.[30] Despite liberal constitutional trappings, Mexico was then ruled (as it is today and as it has been
for decades) by the dominant and authoritarian Institutional Revolutionary
Party (PRI). Moreover, most experts concluded that Mexicans shared an
authoritarian political culture.[31] Attempting to evaluate this received wisdom
empirically, we interpreted political authoritarianism as opposition to democratic liberties and extensive citizen participation—the inverse of the democ-

ratic values discussed above.

Given the impressionistic historical evidence and extant theories about culture and regime type, we expected Mexicans to be authoritarian in political orientation, whether regime type were either the cause or the effect of political culture.[32] First, should culture shape structure, Mexico's inherited authoritarianism (from both its Iberian and indigenous cultural matrices) should never have permitted the development of a civic culture; authoritarian popular values would have persisted and undergirded the nation's authoritarian regimes. Second, to the extent that regime type shapes political culture, one would expect that seven decades of PRI rule following upon two decades of revolutionary authoritarianism and the thirty-five-year dictatorship of Porfirio Díaz (1876-1911) would have certainly nurtured antidemocratic norms among Mexicans, no matter what their original political culture. Third, there could well have been reciprocal causation between political culture and regime type. Mexican institutional authoritarianism might have contributed to authoritarian popular values, which in turn would have reinforced authoritarian rule. In short, each variant of the structure-culture causality argument suggests that Mexican culture and regime type should have been congruent with each other.[33]

The study reported on interviews of 430 urban Mexicans, working-class and middle-class citizens of voting age distributed among six northern industrial cities and Guadalajara, Mexico's second largest city. The sample, not a national probability sample, was purposefully concentrated on working- and middle-class urban dwellers in order to measure the impact of class membership on democratic/authoritarian values.[34]

Our analysis showed that despite the undisputedly authoritarian nature of the polity and despite the general pessimism about democratic inclinations of Latin Americans in general and Mexicans in particular, these urban Mexicans manifested high levels of support for a system of extensive participation (EP) and for inclusive political rights (IP) for regime critics (see Table 4.1). Indeed, our sample of urban Mexicans generally compared quite favorably to a 1978 sample of New Yorkers, with average intensity of support for democratic liberties scores at levels similar to or only slightly below the New York City respondents.

Attempts to account for these surprising findings revealed that despite a modest significant positive correlation between higher social class and support for democratic liberties, urban, working-class Mexicans were still strongly supportive of democratic norms. We also found modest, significant correlations between these values and both level of education and gender, with the more educated and males being somewhat more supportive of democratic liberties than the less educated and females.[35] It should be emphasized, however, that Mexican women and the less educated, despite their slightly lower levels of commitment to both IP and EP, were still notably in the prodemocratic end of the scales.

Table 4.1  Support for Democratic Liberties, Mexico (Mean Scores)

| Question | Score |
|---|---|
| A. *Extensive Participation (EP)* | |
| To what extent would you approve or disapprove of: | |
| 1. Participating in a new group or organization to try to solve community problems? | 8.8 |
| 2. Working for a political party, candidate, or election campaign? | 7.3 |
| 3. Participating in a legal demonstration? | 8.2 |
| B. *Intensive Participation—Opposition to the Suppression of Civil Liberties (IP–OSDL)* | |
| To what extent would you approve or disapprove of the government passing a law that would prohibit critics of the Mexican form of government from: | |
| 4. Holding public demonstrations? | 6.3 |
| 5. Holding meetings? | 6.4 |
| 6. Expressing their point of view? | 6.4 |
| 7. To what extent would you approve of the government censoring radio, TV, or newspaper ads that criticize the government? | 6.4 |
| C. *Intensive Participation—Right to Dissent (IP–RD)* | |
| To what extent would you approve or disapprove of people who say bad things about the Mexican form of government having the right to: | |
| 8. Vote? | 6.3 |
| 9. Hold peaceful demonstrations to express their point of view? | 7.6 |
| 10. Run for public office? | 4.7 |
| | (n=430)[a] |

Note: Mean scores are based on a scale of 1 to 10, with 10 indicating highest support for civil liberties.  Note that for presentation purposes here, the scale on the OSDL items has been reversed in conformity with the other indices, so that on all three sets a high score means support for democratic liberties.

[a]Varies slightly due to nonresponse.


## Costa Rica and Nicaragua

Attempting to examine further the intriguing possibilities concerning political culture and regime structure raised by these data from urban Mexico in the late 1970s, we collected data on the political beliefs of Costa Ricans and Nicaraguans. We wished to consider more carefully how mass culture might be linked to regime type and possible paths toward democratization. Unlike Mexico, which is one of Latin America's largest, most populous, and most industrialized nations, Costa Rica and Nicaragua are both small. Like Mexico, they are both poor and predominantly Catholic, but they have a number of common traits that make them a particularly valuable pair of countries for this study.

Costa Rica and Nicaragua are neighboring nations that were both on the southern end of the Kingdom of Guatemala (part of the Viceroyalty of New Spain) during their colonial epoch. Guanacaste, once part of Nicaragua, is now a Costa Rican province. With relatively few Indians, both nations developed predominantly mestizo cultures. From 1823 to 1838 both were part of the five-province Central American Republic; since 1838 both have been independent. Their economic development patterns have had many similarities, until fairly recently, with both developing dependent, agro-export-oriented commodity production. During the nineteenth century both nations had many subsistence smallholding farmers, and both have seen expansion of succession of new export crops that have displaced many small farmers from their land and caused considerable urbanward migration. Costa Rica and Nicaragua both joined the Central American Common Market (CACM) in the 1960s and both experienced considerable industrialization and rapid GNP growth from 1960 through 1975. The mid-1970s oil shock and collapse of the CACM brought severe recessions to both countries.[36]

Despite their numerous similarities of history, location, population, language, ethnicity, and economy, the two countries have long been virtually opposite in regime types. Costa Rica's democratic institutions began to develop in the late nineteenth century. Latin America's longest-standing and most stable democratic regime, Costa Rica has an unbroken record since 1950 of constitutional rule, electoral honesty, and peaceful transfers of executive power.[37] In contrast, Nicaragua's political tradition has been one of Latin America's most violent and turbulent; its regimes have typically been authoritarian if not dictatorial. The Somoza dynasty ruled Nicaragua from 1936 to 1979, when it was overthrown by a coalition headed by the Marxist-led Sandinista National Liberation Front (FSLN). The resulting FSLN-dominated government implemented revolutionary policies and struggled against the U.S.-backed contra insurgency. Although the 1984 election, won by the FSLN, was characterized by most experts and international observers as fair, prior to 1990 Nicaragua had never had a peaceful transfer of power to a victorious opposition party following a free election.[38]

Given these many similarities and the key differences in regime type, we may use Nicaragua and Costa Rica for a "most-similar-systems" study to seek the source of the great difference between their regimes. Specifically, this study should reveal whether the political cultures of Nicaragua and Costa Rica are congruent with their distinctive patterns of rule. Political culture theory would suggest that Costa Ricans have political values far more supportive of democratic liberties than Nicaraguans, a hypothesis consonant with impressionistic studies.[39]

Given the historical evidence available, Costa Ricans should be more democratically inclined than Nicaraguans because regime type should be either a cause or an effect of political culture. If culture shapes structure, Costa Rica sometime well prior to 1950 must have developed a civic culture that would have eventually supplanted its putative Iberian cultural authoritarianism and helped shape contemporary democratic institutions. Nicaragua presumably would never have developed a civic culture, and mass authoritarianism would have undergirded its authoritarian regimes.

Reversing the logic, one might conclude that the emergence of democratic institutions in Costa Rica may have gradually helped transform the political culture into a civic, democratic one. Culture and regime type would have been incongruent for some time until authoritarian Iberian cultural legacies were supplanted. But because Costa Rica has had a stable democratic regime for several decades, its popular political culture should by now have become congruent with national institutions—that is, both regime and political culture should be democratic. Applied to Nicaragua, the logic that regime type shapes culture would militate in favor of an authoritarian political culture. The Sandinista revolution has been criticized for authoritarianism and for restricting civil liberties, yet for the prior forty-three years the Somozas embodied capricious dictatorship, and before them there was authoritarian *caudillo* rule punctuated by frequent civil war and foreign intervention. No matter what the original political culture, this national experience should have left a legacy of authoritarianism in the political culture despite recent steps toward formal democratization.

A third possibility is that of reciprocal causation between political culture and regime type. Given the stability of regime types, culture and structure should have reinforced each other in both countries. Nicaraguan institutional authoritarianism should have contributed to authoritarian popular values, which in turn should have reinforced authoritarian rule. Costa Rican democratic institutions should have reinforced a popular civic culture, and vice versa.

In short, all logical paths suggest congruence between political culture and structure in Nicaragua and Costa Rica, manifested in popular support for democratic liberties in Costa Rica and in authoritarian values in Nicaragua.

*The data.* The Nicaraguan sample totaled 1,150, and was based on face-to-face interviews in respondents' dwellings conducted in August 1989 by the Fundación Manolo Morales of Managua. The poll, the foundation's third for the Nicaraguan newspaper *La Crónica*, was conducted by an experienced interview team technically advised on sampling, questionnaire design, training, and fieldwork by a team of two U.S. academics (including coauthor Booth) and one Spanish academic with extensive field experience in survey research. The sample was drawn from four major cities: Managua, Masaya, León, and Estelí, with sample size proportional to city population. Sampling substrata within each city were based upon neighborhoods, stratified for economic status. Individual respondents age 16 or older, the legal voting age in Nicaragua, were selected by quotas based upon gender and age.

Questions have been raised about the accuracy of the preelection sur-

veys conducted in Nicaragua because several failed to predict the defeat of
the Sandinistas. (A number of other surveys did correctly predict the outcome.) Central to the difficulty was that many of the survey organizations
were closely associated with one side of the political spectrum or the other
and revealed this bias to the respondents in some way. There may also have
been considerable volatility in voter preferences during the final month of
the campaign, when no polling was done. In contrast to these problems, the
survey we use was conducted several months prior to these problematical
polls (and so early in the campaign that candidates had not yet been named)
by an organization without partisan identification and virtually unknown to
the public at large. Analysis of the survey shows highly consistent
responses.[40]

The Costa Rican data, from face-to-face, in-home interviews, were collected in May and June 1987 and consist of a national probability sample of
927 respondents. The multistage stratified survey was conducted by our col-
laborator at the University of Costa Rica, Miguel Gómez B. The sampling
frame was the 1984 national population census and produced eighty-five primary sampling units stratified into nine strata and distributed throughout all
of Costa Rica's seven provinces. Because the Costa Rican sample included
both urban and rural areas, whereas the Nicaraguan included only major
cities, we have taken care do all analyses first with the entire Costa Rica
sample and then once again with only the urban area respondents to assure
comparability.[41] For the items discussed, the urban Costa Rican sample has
generally similar responses to the national sample. In several of our tables,
where our purpose is to contrast overall levels of support for democracy, we
compare the entire Costa Rican national sample with the urban Nicaragua
sample. One subset of items on support for the right to dissent was not
included in the 1987 Costa Rican national sample, but was included in a
1985 urban sample (n=506). The 1985 sample used the same sampling frame
as did the 1987 sample and was conducted by the same group in Costa Rica.

*Findings.* We look first at the three Extensive Participation items (Table
4.2).[42] The Costa Rican results present no surprises. Overwhelming majorities, exceeding 90 percent, approve of conventional forms of participation
such as working with community groups or working for a political party in
an election campaign. Support declines for participation in protest marches,
but even so more than three-fourths of the population approves of the activity.

The Nicaraguan results do surprise us, however, because on each item
significantly fewer Nicaraguans than Costa Ricans support extensive participation, but Nicaraguans still overwhelmingly support EP. These items, however, might be regarded as "easy." That is, although support for a system of
extensive participation is vital in a democratic political culture, these forms
of participation are conventional and uncontroversial in modern, mass-based

electoral systems. Costa Rica has long had such a system, but Nicaragua has not; hence, the lower levels of support for these forms of participation in Nicaragua are not surprising. What does come as a surprise is that Nicaraguans have values so similar to those of Costa Ricans.

Table 4.2  Extensive Participation, Costa Rica and Nicaragua

| | Country | | | | |
|---|---|---|---|---|---|
| | Costa Rica | | Nicaragua | | |
| Question | % | (n) | % | (n) | Sig.[b] |
| I am going to read you a list of actions people can take to accomplish their political objectives. Do you approve or disapprove of: | | | | | |
| Participation in an organization or group in order to try to resolve a community problem? | | | | | |
| Approve | 98.0 | (908) | 84.9 | (976) | |
| Disapprove | 2.0 | (19) | 7.0 | (81) | |
| DK[a] | .0 | (0) | 8.1 | (93) | |
| TOTAL | 100.0 | (927) | 100.0 | (1,150) | <.001 |
| Working in election campaigns for a political party or candidate? | | | | | |
| Approve | 93.5 | (866) | 74.7 | (859) | |
| Disapprove | 6.5 | (60) | 9.7 | (112) | |
| DK[a] | .3 | (3) | 15.6 | (179) | |
| TOTAL | 100.0 | (927) | 100.0 | (1,150) | <.001 |
| Participating in protest marches? | | | | | |
| Approve | 76.8 | (712) | 60.3 | (693) | |
| Disapprove | 23.2 | (215) | 25.0( | 288) | |
| DK[a] | .0 | (0) | 14.7 | (169) | |
| TOTAL | 100.0 | (927) | 100.0 | (1,150) | <.001 |

[a]Includes "don't know," "no response," and "indifferent" responses.
[b]Chi-square significance.

The more stringent test of depth of commitment to democratic norms comes in an examination of Inclusive Participation. We include two dimensions of IP for both countries. The first of them includes three items measuring Opposition to the Suppression of Democratic Liberties (OSDL) —opinions regarding government suppression of protests and meetings of regime critics, and government censorship of the media. The second IP

dimension includes four Right to Dissent items that tap respondents' willingness to grant key civil liberties to those who "only say bad things" about the
government. We would expect significantly higher levels of support for the
RD items in Costa Rica than in Nicaragua.

In Costa Rica, where two main parties have alternated in power for the
past two decades, political criticism tends to be opposition to specific policies of the incumbent party or *ad hominem* attacks on the president and his
cabinet. More extreme views, in which "only bad things" are said about the
government, would most likely come from leaders of various extreme leftist
and rightist parties with no reasonable chance of taking power in an election.
Costa Rican respondents to the survey would likely have such extremists in
mind when they discuss their willingness to grant the right to vote, demonstrate, run for public office, and speak out against the government. These
would be rights enjoyed by extremist parties, which since 1948 have shown
only feeble or waning electoral strength.[43]

In Nicaragua at the time of our survey, the opposition was very large
and, although diverse ideologically, strongly in favor of ousting the
Sandinistas. When our survey was being conducted, the dominant political
issue was the formation of the opposition coalition and the upcoming
February 1990 elections. Clear lines were drawn between the supporters of
the revolutionaries who had ruled since 1979 and their opponents. Hence,
when Nicaraguans were asked about their support for the civil rights of critics of their government, it could not have seemed to them a hypothetical
question. At stake were the rights of the opponents of Sandinista rule to run
for office and possibly unseat the revolutionary leaders.

The data for the IP items tapping OSDL are presented in Table 4.3. Note
that for this table, we used the 1985 urban Costa Rica sample because the
1987 Costa Rican national sample did not contain them. The Nicaraguan
sample remains the same. Once again, the Costa Rican results present no
surprise. Strong opposition to the suppression of democratic liberties is
expressed by urban Costa Ricans, with approximately three-fourths of the
sample opposing restrictions on demonstrations, meetings, and censorship of
the mass media. What does surprise us are the high levels of OSDL of the
Nicaraguan respondents. Consistently more than three-fourths of urban
Nicaraguans oppose restrictions on civil liberties. Indeed, on two of the three
variables, a statistically significant higher proportion of Nicaraguans oppose
restrictions on civil liberties than do Costa Ricans. With samples as large as
the ones we are analyzing, small differences in proportions can produce statistically significant results and therefore we do not wish to exaggerate the
differences between the two countries. Far more important is that,
Nicaragua's long history of authoritarian rule notwithstanding, opposition to
suppressing civil liberties in Nicaragua is higher, not lower, than in Costa
Rica with its long tradition of democratic rule. One must begin to wonder

what factors operated in the socialization process of authoritarian Nicaragua
to produce such results, but we leave consideration of that question until
later.

Table 4.3 Inclusive Participation:  Opposition to the Suppression of
Democratic Liberties, Costa Rica and Nicaragua

|  | Country | | | | |
|---|---|---|---|---|---|
|  | Costa Rica (1985)[b] | | Nicaragua | | |
| Question | % | (n) | % | (n) | Sig.[c] |
| Do you think that the government ought to take the following actions: | | | | | |
| Prohibit demonstrations? | | | | | |
| Yes | 24.3 | (123) | 15.0 | (172) | |
| No | 72.9 | (369) | 78.3 | (900) | |
| DK[a] | 2.8 | (14) | 6.6 | (78) | |
| TOTAL | 100.0 | (506) | 100.0 | (1,150) | <.001 |
| Prohibit meetings of groups that criticize the government? | | | | | |
| Yes | 20.2 | (102) | 17.8 | (205) | |
| No | 77.1 | (390) | 76.8 | (883) | |
| DK[a] | 2.8 | (14) | 5.4 | (62) | |
| TOTAL | 100.0 | (506) | 100.0 | (1,150) | NS |
| Censor newspapers, radio, and TV? | | | | | |
| Yes | 19.4 | (98) | 12.7 | (146) | |
| No | 78.3 | (396) | 80.1 | (921) | |
| DK[a] | 2.4 | (12) | 7.2 | (83) | |
| TOTAL | 100.0 | (506) | 100.0 | (1,150) | .002 |

[a]Includes "don't know" and "no response" responses.
[b]As explained in the section on data, for these items, only a 1985 urban Costa Rica sample
was available.
[c]Chi-square significance.

Support for civil liberties in the abstract, as measured by OSDL, may
not be the strongest test of commitment to democracy—it may be too easy to
agree to support the right to demonstrate, hold meetings, and be free of censorship. Let us examine the more stringent test of commitment to a system of
Inclusive Participation, the four variable series measuring the Right to
Dissent—RD (Table 4.4). The first item deals with support for the right of
people who say only bad things about the government (regime critics) to
organize demonstrations. Although the level of support in Costa Rica for this

key democratic norm is lower than it was for any of the previous items examined, nearly two-thirds of the sample express democratic sentiments. As expected, Nicaraguans express lower levels of support for RD compared to their attitudes on the previous items, but well over half of them still express democratic views. More interesting is that the difference between Costa Ricans and Nicaraguans is not statistically significant. Moreover, fewer Nicaraguans than Costa Ricans oppose the right to demonstrate by government critics.

The second item in Table 4.4 presents some real surprises. We would expect that granting the right to vote to regime critics could imply a higher level of political tolerance than allowing such individuals to hold a demonstration. After all, a demonstration indicates potential power, but casting a vote is an exercise of real political power, albeit in diluted form. Viewed from another perspective, the right to vote should receive greater support in Costa Rica because of that country's recent political history. The civil war of 1948 was fought largely over the issue of the integrity of the electoral process.[44] Perhaps the results of this survey on this item reflect contradictory opinions, with some stressing the danger of allowing the extremist opposition to vote and others emphasizing the importance of the integrity of the election system.

Nicaraguans not only were more supportive of the right of regime critics to vote than they were of any of the other six IP items (and indeed higher than all but one of the Extensive Participation items), they also supported the vote for regime critics more than did Costa Ricans. Table 4.4 shows that nearly 85 percent of Nicaraguans compared to only 60 percent of Costa Ricans support the right to vote of critics.

Although it might be thought that this finding is merely idiosyncratic, it is consistent with the two remaining variables in the series. About 40 percent of Costa Ricans support the right of people who say only bad things about their government to speak out against it; 70 percent of Nicaraguans defend this right. Similarly, about one-third of Costa Ricans support the right to run for office; over half of Nicaraguans do so. In each case, Nicaraguans manifest significantly greater support for IP-RD democratic norms than do Costa Ricans.

*Testing the Standard Explanations:*
*Socioeconomic and Demographic Factors*

The findings presented above are surprising enough to raise the possibility that they may be spurious. Indeed, as was noted in the data section above, there are differences between the two samples that might explain the findings. We noted there that the Costa Rican sample was national, whereas the Nicaraguan was confined to the major cities of the country. If rural Costa Ricans turn out to have much lower support levels for democratic norms,

their inclusion in the Costa Rican sample could well have affected the overall sample results. Because education is associated with levels of urbanization and is also associated with support for democratic norms, especially
those related to political tolerance, one would expect democratic support to
be lower in the countryside.[45] Finally, age and gender distributions could
influence the results. If, for example, rural areas of Costa Rica contain a larger proportion of females and older individuals, we might find lower levels of
support for democratic norms in the Costa Rican sample because of a correlation between age, sex, and support for democratic norms. We examine
each of these possibilities in the analyses that follow.

**Table 4.4 Inclusive Participation:  Right to Dissent, Costa Rica and Nicaragua**

|  | Country | | | | |
|  | Costa Rica | | Nicaragua | | |
| Question | % | (n) | % | (n) | Sig.[b] |
|---|---|---|---|---|---|
| There are people who say only bad things about the government. Do you support or oppose their: | | | | | |
| Organizing a demonstration? | | | | | |
| Support | 63.4 | (588) | 58.0 | (667) | |
| Oppose | 36.0 | (334) | 30.6 | (352) | |
| DK[a] | .5 | (5) | 11.4 | (131) | |
| TOTAL | 100.0 | (927) | 100.0 | (1,150) | NS |
| Right to vote? | | | | | |
| Support | 60.1 | (557) | 84.7 | (974) | |
| Oppose | 39.6 | (367) | 9.9 | (114) | |
| DK[a] | .3 | (3) | 5.4 | (62) | |
| TOTAL | 100.0 | (927) | 100.0 | (1,150) | <.001 |
| Speaking out against the government? | | | | | |
| Support | 43.6 | (404) | 70.3 | (808) | |
| Oppose | 56.1 | (520) | 19.7 | (226) | |
| DK[a] | .3 | (3) | 10.1 | (116) | |
| TOTAL | 100.0 | (927) | 100.0 | (1,150) | <.001 |
| Running for office? | | | | | |
| Support | 34.4 | (319) | 52.0 | (598) | |
| Oppose | 65.0 | (603) | 30.9 | (355) | |
| DK[a] | .5 | (5) | 17.1 | (197) | |
| TOTAL | 100.0 | (927) | 100.0 | (1,150) | <.001 |

[a]Includes "don't know," "no response," and "indifferent" responses.
[b]Chi-square significance.

Because the inclusion of rural populations in the Costa Rican case is the major difference between the two samples, we will examine the possible impact of that factor first. As noted, on one of the three dimensions, Opposition to the Suppression of Democratic Liberties, we utilized an urban sample for Costa Rica, so differences observed there between the two countries cannot stem from urban-rural differences. For the other two dimensions (EP and RD), however, we used the Costa Rican national sample, with 55 percent rural dwellers.[46] We therefore crosstabulated EP and OSDL items from the Costa Rican national sample with urban/rural residence. Urban-rural differences on all three EP items proved to be statistically insignificant (Chi-square criterion), indicating that rural Costa Ricans were no less likely than urbanites to support widespread participation.

We also crosstabulated urban/rural residence with the Right to Dissent variables. On two of four there was no statistically significant difference. On the remaining two, the right of regime critics to run for office or speak out against the government, there were significant differences. As expected, support for the right to dissent is lower in rural Costa Rica than in the urban areas: support for the right of regime critics to speak out against the government was 39.5 percent among rural dwellers, 48.6 percent among urbanites. Support for the right of dissenters to run for office was 38.7 percent among the urban sample, only 30.9 percent among the rural sample. Yet, when compared even to the more tolerant urban Costa Ricans, urban Nicaraguans still manifested markedly greater support for the right to dissent. In sum, urban-rural residence difference cannot account for lower support for dissent among Costa Ricans compared to Nicaraguans.

We turned to a second set of conventional explanations—age, gender, and education. The literature is replete with associations between these variables and support for democratic liberties. Women have been found to be less tolerant of democratic liberties than men, younger people more tolerant than the older, and educated respondents more tolerant than the less educated.[47] Seeking a possible explanation of the differences between the two countries' samples, we first compared the distributions of these variables within the two samples. Gender and age distributions are very similar in the two samples and therefore do not promise to explain differences in support for democratic norms. Education, often a key predictor of tolerance, does show some differences. A higher proportion of the Nicaraguan urban sample than the national Costa Rican sample had achieved a secondary education (49 percent vs. 38 percent), whereas the proportions of the two samples with University education are almost identical (13 percent each). Because educational achievement is in fact higher in Costa Rica than Nicaragua,[48] we dropped the Costa Rican rural dwellers and found that educational achievement of our urban Costa Ricans exceeds that of the Nicaraguans, with 19 percent of the former having some university education. Thus, differences in the composition of the samples based on gender, age, or education seem far too small to account for the differences we have encountered in the opinion data.

It is possible, however, that the within-sample impact of such variables differs, so we crosstabulated gender, age, and education with each of the democratic norms variables (data not presented). Age proved to have no statistically significant monotonic association with any of the IP or EP items.[49] Gender, however, produced some significant differences, but the results do not help explain differences between the two countries. We found that within the Extensive Participation series, Nicaraguan women were significantly more supportive (at a .05 level of significance) of participating in a group to try to resolve community problems than were Nicaraguan men. Nicaraguan men, however, were significantly (probability <.001) more supportive of participation in protest marches than women. Costa Rican sample males also expressed more support than women for protest marches (probability <.03). The OSDL series also revealed several significant differences, but consistently showed that for both countries women were somewhat less supportive of this measure of democratic political culture than were men.[50] On the Right to Dissent series, the most stringent test of democratic political culture, we found no gender-based differences. We conclude, then, that differential gender effects are not responsible for the results we have observed.

Finally, education showed no significant monotonic relationship to OSDL. It did correlate significantly with some of the Extensive Participation items, but in no way that would help explain the national-level results. Education was more strongly and significantly associated with the RD items. This was markedly true in Costa Rica, with university-educated respondents expressing far higher support for democratic liberties than those with primary education. Nonetheless, on the key items regarding the right to vote and the right to run for office, Nicaraguan university-educated respondents were still more supportive than Costa Rican university-educated respondents. We conclude from this exercise that neither gender, age, nor education can explain the high levels of support for democratic norms we have encountered in Nicaragua.

These analyses confirm our initial impressions from the data and allay our suspicions that major differences in key demographic or socioeconomic effects between within the two samples are responsible for the surprising results we have presented here. We need to move, then, from this unsuccessful attempt to employ conventional explanations to a deeper analysis of the data.

## The Impact of Ideology on Democratic Norms

We turn to the possibility that ideology might help explain these findings. In several studies of democratic norms conducted in Canada, Israel, New

Zealand, and the United States, respondents on the political left have exhibited higher levels of tolerance for democratic liberties than those on the right.[51] A systematic difference in the distribution of ideological preferences between Costa Rica and Nicaragua could help explain the surprisingly high levels of support for democratic norms in the latter country. That is, if Costa Ricans are ideologically further to the right than Nicaraguans and if the political right is indeed less supportive of democratic norms, then Nicaragua's greater support for democratic norms might be explained by having more left-oriented citizens.

To test this proposition we first must show that ideology and democratic norms are associated in both countries, and in the predicted direction. In the Costa Rica survey we used the conventional "left-right scale" question to tap the ideological orientation of the respondents on an eight-point scale. All but 12 percent of respondents answered; we found a far larger proportion of the sample on the right (46.1 percent) than on the left (6.0 percent); the remainder of the sample clustered in the center. That such a large proportion of the respondents located themselves on the ideological right suggested that the ideology might indeed help explain differences between Costa Rica and Nicaragua.

We correlated ideological self-identification with the ten variables that constitute the three sets of democratic support variables.[52] We found, however, that ideology was consistently related only to the IP items measuring Right to Dissent.[53] Because RD is the most stringent test of support for democratic norms, it is particularly revealing that ideology did indeed emerge as a predictor of these attitudes among Costa Ricans. Table 4.5 reveals that, as expected, Costa Ricans on the right consistently are more likely to oppose the granting of key civil liberties than those on the left.[54] Indeed, with the exception of the last item, the right to run for office, the left and center of the ideological continuum in Costa Rica are virtually indistinguishable in their support for these liberties.

To test the ideological explanation for democratic norms in Nicaragua, we would have preferred a similar left-right scale, but none was included in the survey. However, a reasonable surrogate, one that may be even more sensitive to meaningful ideological differences in Nicaragua, may be based on party identification. We counted persons identifying with the FSLN as on the left, and those identifying with the UNO opposition coalition of parties as on the right, with those not choosing in the center.[55] Because the survey was conducted while the UNO coalition was forming, it is not surprising that approximately two-fifths of the respondents did not indicate any party preference. The proportion of the sample indicating support for the well-established FSLN, however, was very close to the proportion of votes the party eventually received in the election.

Ideology correlates significantly with all of the democratic norms variables, but the differences were most marked in the Inclusive Participation series as shown in Tables 4.6 and 4.7. The tables also contain the Costa Rican data (entire national sample) for comparative reference.

We had expected the left, that is, FSLN supporters, to be more supportive of democratic norms. Table 4.6 intriguingly reveals that it is citizens on the right (UNO supporters) who were clearly more supportive of the IP-OSDL items—favorable toward the freedom of regime critics to protest and to hold meetings, and opposed to censorship—by margins of from 17 to 23 percent. The differences are statistically significant. Table 4.7 presents the IP-RD items and reveals a strikingly similar pattern. Respondents who identified with the Nicaraguan right are from 14 to 26 percent more likely to oppose restrictions on civil liberties than the Nicaraguan left (FSLN supporters). Sandinistas also support these rights more than they oppose them, but on two items—support for the rights to organize demonstrations and to run for office—their approval falls below 50 percent.[56]

Ideology indeed makes a difference in both Costa Rica and Nicaragua, but the impact is reversed in the two countries, leaving us with an apparent paradox. We divided the Nicaraguan data into left and right (using party as a surrogate), seeking to show that greater leftism there could explain why Nicaraguans were more supportive of key civil liberties than Costa Ricans. In fact, we accounted for some of the cross-national differences (see Table 4.6), but on a number of key questions, especially on the critical Right to Dissent items (Table 4.7), Nicaraguans of all ideological stripes remained more libertarian than Costa Ricans. Paradoxically, we had expected the left to be more supportive of civil liberties than the right, yet we found precisely the opposite in Nicaragua.

Why might the Nicaraguan right support civil liberties more than the left? Traditional theory argues that the left supports civil liberties more because doing so is consistent with its overall political philosophy. These data, however, suggest that political context and utilitarian considerations may have more to do with support for democratic liberties than does political philosophy. In Nicaragua, at the time of the study, the left (FSLN) was in power and the right (UNO) was preparing to challenge its control. The stronger support for civil liberties expressed by the right was, we believe, a function of its momentarily greater need to exercise such liberties in order to compete successfully for office and political power. Some sympathizers of the left, on the other hand, with their party in power may well have viewed such civil liberties as a threat to their own power. Thus, for Nicaraguans, at least, citizen support of civil liberties may be contingent upon where one sits in the political process; more of the "outs" favor democratic civil liberties than do the "ins." (Indeed, we expect that similar patterns—that is, the right more supportive of civil liberties—will appear in surveys of populations of the declining communist regimes of the Eastern bloc.) Although we do not have space to report fully on the results here, a new survey we conducted in

Table 4.5. Left–Right Ideology and Support for the Right to Dissent, Costa Rica

| | Left–Right Ideology | | | | | | | |
|---|---|---|---|---|---|---|---|---|
| | Left | | Middle | | Right | | No Opinion | |
| | % | (n) | % | (n) | % | (n) | % | (n) |
| Organizing a demonstration?[a] | | | | | | | | |
| Support | 73.2 | (41) | 72.3 | (243) | 57.4 | (245) | 54.6 | (59) |
| Oppose | 26.8 | (15) | 27.7 | (93) | 41.9 | (179) | 43.5 | (47) |
| DK | .0 | (0) | .0 | (0) | .7 | (3) | 1.9 | (2) |
| TOTAL | 100.0 | (56) | 100.0 | (336) | 100.0 | (427) | 100.0 | (108) |
| Right to Vote?[a] | | | | | | | | |
| Support | 64.3 | (36) | 68.8 | (231) | 54.1 | (231) | 54.6 | (59) |
| Oppose | 35.7 | (20) | 31.0 | (104) | 45.7 | (195) | 44.4 | (48) |
| DK | .0 | (0) | .3 | (1) | .2 | (1) | .9 | (1) |
| TOTAL | 100.0 | (56) | 100.0 | (336) | 100.0 | (427) | 100.0 | (108) |
| Speaking out against the government?[a] | | | | | | | | |
| Support | 51.8 | (29) | 53.0 | (178) | 36.5 | (156) | 38.0 | (41) |
| Oppose | 48.2 | (27) | 46.7 | (157) | 63.0 | (269) | 62.0 | (67) |
| DK | .0 | (0) | .3 | (1) | .5 | (2) | .0 | (0) |
| TOTAL | 100.0 | (56) | 100.0 | (336) | 100.0 | (427) | 100.0 | (108) |
| Running for office?[b] | | | | | | | | |
| Support | 50.0 | (28) | 36.6 | (123) | 32.1 | (137) | 28.7 | (31) |
| Oppose | 50.0 | (28) | 63.1 | (212) | 67.2 | (287) | 70.4 | (76) |
| DK | .0 | (0) | .3 | (1) | .7 | (3) | .9 | (1) |
| TOTAL | 100.0 | (56) | 100.0 | (336) | 100.0 | (427) | 100.0 | (108) |

[a]Sig. <.001 ($x^2$).
[b]Sig. at .03 ($x^2$).

**Table 4.6　Ideology and Inclusive Participation: Opposition to the Suppression of Democratic Liberties, Nicaragua and Costa Rica**

| Question | Party Orientation in Nicaragua[a] | | | | | | Costa Rica | |
| | Opposition | | No vote/NR | | FSLN | | | |
| | % | (n) | % | (n) | % | (n) | % | (n) |
|---|---|---|---|---|---|---|---|---|
| **Prohibit demonstrations?** | | | | | | | | |
| Yes | 9.2 | (22) | 12.2 | (57) | 21.1 | (93) | 24.3 | (123) |
| No | 89.2 | (214) | 78.0 | (366) | 72.6 | (320) | 72.9 | (369) |
| DK[b] | 1.7 | (4) | 9.8 | (46) | 6.3 | (28) | 2.8 | (14) |
| TOTAL | 100.0 | (240) | 100.0 | (469) | 100.0 | (441) | 100.0 | (506) |
| **Prohibit meetings of groups that criticize the government?** | | | | | | | | |
| Yes | 8.8 | (21) | 13.2 | (62) | 27.7 | (122) | 20.2 | (102) |
| No | 89.2 | (214) | 77.6 | (364) | 69.2 | (305) | 77.1 | (390) |
| DK[b] | 2.1 | (5) | 9.2 | (43) | 3.2 | (14) | 2.8 | (14) |
| TOTAL | 100.0 | (240) | 100.0 | (469) | 100.0 | (441) | 100.0 | (506) |
| **Censor newspapers, radio, and TV?** | | | | | | | | |
| Yes | 4.2 | (10) | 8.7 | (41) | 21.5 | (95) | 19.4 | (98) |
| No | 94.2 | (226) | 81.2 | (381) | 71.2 | (314) | 78.3 | (396) |
| DK[b] | 1.7 | (4) | 10.0 | (47) | 7.3 | (32) | 2.4 | (12) |
| TOTAL | 100.0 | (240) | 100.0 | (469) | 100.0 | (441) | 100.0 | (506) |

[a]Sig. < .001 ($x^2$)
[b]This category includes "don't know," and "no response."

Table 4.7 Ideology and Inclusive Participation: Right to Dissent, Nicaragua and Costa Rica

| | Party Orientation in Nicaragua[a] | | | | | | Costa Rica | |
| | Opposition | | No vote/NR | | FSLN | | | |
| Question | % | (n) | % | (n) | % | (n) | % | (n) |
|---|---|---|---|---|---|---|---|---|
| **Organizing a demonstration?** | | | | | | | | |
| Support | 75.0 | (180) | 57.4 | (269) | 49.4 | (218) | 63.4 | (588) |
| Oppose | 20.4 | (49) | 24.9 | (117) | 42.2 | (186) | 36.0 | (334) |
| DK[b] | 4.6 | (10) | 17.7 | (83) | 8.4 | (37) | .5 | (5) |
| TOTAL | 100.0 | (240) | 100.0 | (469) | 100.0 | (441) | 100.0 | (927) |
| **Right to vote?** | | | | | | | | |
| Approve | 94.6 | (227) | 84.0 | (394) | 80.0 | (353) | 60.1 | (557) |
| Disapprove | 3.8 | (9) | 6.8 | (32) | 16.6 | (73) | 39.6 | (367) |
| DK[b] | 1.7 | (4) | 9.2 | (43) | 3.4 | (15) | .3 | (3) |
| TOTAL | 100.0 | (240) | 100.0 | (469) | 100.0 | (441) | 100.0 | (927) |
| **Speaking out against the government?** | | | | | | | | |
| Approve | 82.5 | (198) | 68.7 | (322) | 65.3 | (288) | 43.6 | (404) |
| Disapprove | 12.1 | (29) | 15.4 | (72) | 28.3 | (125) | 56.1 | (520) |
| DK[b] | 5.5 | (13) | 16.0 | (75) | 6.3 | (28) | .3 | (3) |
| TOTAL | 100.0 | (240) | 100.0 | (469) | 100.0 | (441) | 100.0 | (927) |
| **Running for office?** | | | | | | | | |
| Approve | 68.3 | (164) | 50.7 | (238) | 44.4 | (196) | 34.4 | (319) |
| Disapprove | 19.6 | (47) | 23.7 | (111) | 44.7 | (197) | 65.0 | (603) |
| DK[b] | 12.1 | (29) | 25.6 | (120) | 10.9 | (48) | .5 | (5) |
| TOTAL | 100.0 | (240) | 100.0 | (469) | 100.0 | (441) | 100.0 | (927) |

[a]Sig. < .001 ($x^2$).
[b]Includes "don't know," "no response," and "undecided."

the summer of 1991 in urban Nicaragua revealed a dramatic reversal of support for civil liberties consistent with the evidence uncovered in this study. We found UNO supporters, whose party was now in power, expressing much lower support for civil liberties than FSLN supporters, whose party was now out of power.

Support for this positional, rather than philosophical, interpretation of the effect of ideology upon support for democratic liberties appears in Table 4.8. In it, we show the results of two items that measure respondents' support for their political system; they are drawn from a scale called "Political Support-Alienation" that has been shown to be reliable and valid in the United States, Germany, Mexico, and Costa Rica.[57] The first item taps pride in the system and reveals dramatic differences between the FSLN supporters and the opposition. Whereas over 90 percent of the FSLN supporters expressed pride in Nicaragua's political system, a proportion exceeding Costa Rica's, less than 40 percent of UNO supporters expressed such pride. The second item taps evaluations of the protection granted to citizens by the system of laws. Here again the differences are dramatic, with four-fifths of the FSLN supporters replying affirmatively compared with only one-fifth of the opposition. With such comparatively low levels of support for the system among UNO supporters, it seems natural that they would favor the rights that might give them the opportunity to change that system.

The types of participation that UNO supporters favored in the months prior to the elections were not always conventional. In response to another query, nearly half of those who both supported UNO and expressed low support for the system of government would approve of citizens who take over factories, churches, and public buildings to achieve their political objectives.[58] In marked contrast, less than one-fifth of FSLN supporters who expressed high support for the system of government approved of such actions. In Costa Rica, by comparison, only 6 percent of the 1987 respondents expressed approval of takeovers of public buildings or factories, far lower than either the UNO or FSLN supporters in Nicaragua.

## Conclusions

Our earlier discovery that urban Mexicans strongly supported democratic liberties in spite of their long-standing authoritarian system led us to delve deeper into the notion that regime type is determined by mass political culture, or vice versa. Costa Rica and Nicaragua presented fascinating further venues to explore the influence of mass culture upon regime type. Costa Rica was immediately intriguing because it has developed a stable democratic regime despite not sharing a historical experience with either of the two models Inglehart specifies for the emergence of democracy. Moreover, Costa Rica has developed a strong mass culture of support for fundamental civil

**Table 4.8  System Support, Nicaragua and Costa Rica**

| | Party Orientation in Nicaragua | | | | | | | | |
| | Opposition | | No vote/NR | | FSLN | | Costa Rica | |
| Statement | % | (n) | % | (n) | % | (n) | % | (n) |
|---|---|---|---|---|---|---|---|---|
| One can feel pride in Costa Rica/ Nicaragua | | | | | | | | |
| Agree | 38.3 | (92) | 62.3 | (292) | 94.3 | (416) | 91.7 | (850) |
| Neutral | 8.8 | (21) | 7.7 | (36) | 3.6 | (16) | 4.9 | (45) |
| Disagree | 51.7 | (124) | 26.9 | (126) | 1.6 | (7) | 3.3 | (31) |
| DK/NR | 1.3 | (3) | 3.2 | (15) | .5 | (2) | .1 | (1) |
| TOTAL | 100.0 | (240) | 100.0 | (469) | 100.0 | (441) | 100.0 | (927) |
| Laws protect the basic rights of Costa Ricans/Nicaraguans | | | | | | | | |
| Agree | 20.0 | (48) | 36.2 | (170) | 82.5 | (364) | 64.3 | (596) |
| Neutral | 12.1 | (29) | 16.6 | (78) | 8.6 | (38) | 19.0 | (176) |
| Disagree | 63.3 | (152) | 35.8 | (168) | 6.8 | (30) | 16.5 | (153) |
| DK/NR | 4.6 | (11) | 11.3 | (53) | 2.0 | (9) | .2 | (2) |
| TOTAL | 100.0 | (240) | 100.0 | (469) | 100.0 | (441) | 100.0 | (927) |

liberties in spite of its Catholicism, poverty, and Iberian cultural legacy. Obviously, then, Costa Rica demonstrates that there must be at least one additional path to the development of democratic political culture and to democratization than those posited by Inglehart.

Nicaragua presents an even more intriguing test of the influence of mass culture upon regime type because not only is it poor and Catholic but its political tradition has been so undemocratic, turbulent, violent, and marked with repression of civil liberties. But astonishingly, we have discovered that urban Nicaraguans in 1989 manifested support for basic political liberties at levels equal to or greater than their Costa Rican neighbors. Clearly, Nicaraguans cannot have arrived at their civic culture either by the conjectured Anglo-European or Asian paths or by the path that was followed by Costa Ricans. Indeed, by culturist arguments Nicaraguans should not have developed these democratic values at all because of the weight of history and because of systemic barriers to such popular values. Neither, given Mexican history and regimes, should Mexicans have developed such democratic values. These stunning incongruities between theoretical predictions and the revealed cultural reality in urban Nicaragua and urban Mexico raise fascinating questions about the linkage between culture and regime type.

Do mass belief systems determine regime types? Perhaps, but at least not always nor in the ways envisioned by Inglehart. In one sense, Costa Rica provides an example in which the data may be read as supporting cultural determination of regime type because it has a stable democracy undergirded by a relatively widespread commitment of citizens to civil liberties. In sharp contrast, however, if mass political culture were consistently determinant of regime types, Mexico and Nicaragua should be stable democracies because of the high levels of support for democratic liberties that we have discovered among their urban citizens.

There still exists the possibility, of course, that Mexico and Nicaragua are in or are entering the process of democratizing their regimes because of mass values that are temporarily incongruent with regime structures. That, however, raises the reciprocal question of whether regime type determines mass values. Again, Costa Rica might exemplify a case in point because one might argue that despite the historico-cultural factors militating against a mass culture of democracy, the development of democratic rules of the game led to the evolution of a mass civic culture. If the system-to-culture influence were universal, however, neither Mexicans nor Nicaraguans should manifest anywhere near the strong allegiance to democratic norms that they do. We therefore submit that the culture-regime type relationship is far more complex than the recent literature suggests. Very important factors yet to be considered—the roles, decisions, and values of political elites, the possibility of cultural diffusion of democratic norms, and utilitarian considerations—may also play critical roles in the emergence of democratic values and democracy.

The importance of these factors may be most constructively explored by returning to the question: What are alternative paths toward democratic values and democratization suggested by our three Latin American cases? We see at least two and possibly three divergent paths.

*The Costa Rican path.* In this relatively poor, Catholic country a democratic regime and democratic political culture may well have emerged simultaneously over the course of more than a century due the isolation of its colonists, the lack of racial exploitation, lower levels of inequality than in other parts of Latin America for significant periods of the nation's history, and a historical need for economic elites to co-opt workers with favorable social policies and democratic rules of the game. Also critically important have been the actions of political elites in building reciprocal trust and mutual accommodation at key moments in the nation's political history, especially the early twentieth century and the period following the 1948 civil war.[59] These factors suggest that in Costa Rica, through a system of reciprocal influence, elite culture, mass culture, and institutional development contributed to both the stabilization of democratic institutions and widespread allegiance to democratic norms.

*The Mexican path* to a democratic urban culture diverges significantly from the Costa Rican and Anglo-European paths. Mexico's 1910–1917 revolution over liberal democratic forms and the economic demands of the working classes eventually led to the establishment of the PRI-dominated regime. Despite their authoritarian political practice, Mexican regimes have traditionally employed the democratic forms of constitutionalism and elections and have emphasized democratic values in public education. Moreover, both Mexico's proximity to the United States and the tradition of heavy migration of Mexicans to their northern neighbor have widely exposed Mexicans to liberal democratic norms and practices. These factors in combination may well account for the emergence of democratic values among urban Mexicans in spite of their authoritarian polity. Support for democratic liberties may also have grown among Mexicans increasingly disillusioned with the PRI-dominated system for the very practical reason that freedom to protest, dissent, and work for change would benefit those dissatisfied and bent upon reforming the polity. Indeed, the emergence of a significant opposition challenge to and a large vote against the PRI in the 1988 Mexican presidential election could well constitute steps toward democratization that were presaged by the popular support for democratic norms revealed in our 1978–1979 survey.

*The Nicaraguan path* to a democratic urban culture must differ significantly from the Anglo-European and Costa Rican paths but may have some common elements with the Mexican case. First, as suggested for Mexicans, Nicaraguans may have developed democratic norms over time in part by means of cultural diffusion through the media. Second, diffusion of democratic norms could also come from the Nicaraguans' experiences in neighboring Costa Rica and the United States, where many have lived and traveled, or have relatives. Third, Nicaraguan authoritarianism itself and the struggle to defeat it over the past fifteen years may well have bred democratic values. As in Mexico, utilitarian considerations could have developed a widespread appreciation of democratic liberties in a society that has struggled against repression for many years. In the 1970s the Sandinistas and their broad-front allies fought against the Somozas. In the 1980s the emergent opposition to the revolution worked to defeat the Sandinistas at the polls—and eventually did. All Nicaraguans who worked for or wanted political freedom would have benefited from democratic liberties in their political struggles, and many suffered for their absence. Such experiences could easily have raised Nicaraguans' utilitarian commitment to such rights. Fourth, the Sandinista revolution itself encouraged citizen participation in a wide variety of forms and venues. Despite periodic curtailment of the participatory rights of some opponents, the political values inculcated by the revolution itself included democratic norms.

Although Nicaraguan supporters of the leftist Sandinista National Liberation Front overall supported democratic liberties in 1989, we have seen that they were somewhat less prone to do so than other Nicaraguans, especially the citizens who identified with the emerging United Nicaraguan Opposition coalition. This surprised us because previous research has generally found those on the left to be more tolerant of democratic liberties than those on the right.[60] This additional anomaly suggests that commitment to civil liberties may be less a function of ideological orientation than of position with respect to power. That some Sandinista supporters were less committed to democratic liberties than other citizens suggests that they may have (correctly) perceived their critics' rights to organize, protest, and run for office as a threat to the survival of the revolution.

This argument is the obverse of the utilitarian explanation for the emergence of support for democratic norms among people living in repressive regimes, irrespective of ideology. Because civil liberties could help the opposition, they might well weaken the incumbents and thus in practice seem less attractive to regime supporters. Here, then, short-term utilitarian considerations of power rather than long-term historical-cultural factors may determine levels of commitment to civil liberties. We therefore suspect that during the final years of communist rule in Eastern Europe, the politically centrist and conservative opponents of communist regimes manifested, for utilitarian reasons, markedly higher commitment to civil liberties than supporters of the ruling Communist parties. Indeed, we may find that Nicaragua and Mexico constitute examples of nations following another path toward democratic culture and democracy—an authoritarian breakdown path.

In summary, we have found the culturist propositions that mass culture determines regime type (or perhaps vice versa) to be substantially lacking in the cases of Mexico and Nicaragua. Although we by no means rule out reciprocal influence between mass culture and regime type, it is evident that other factors including elite culture and interactions,[61] institutional evolution, diffusion of democratic values by the media and migration, and utilitarian considerations must also influence the evolution of democratic culture and the emergence of democratic regimes. Political culture thus appears to be much more changeable and responsive to short-term forces than the culturist approach assumes.

Ultimately, high levels of commitment to democratic values among Mexicans and Nicaraguans should be a source of qualified optimism to those who value political liberty and democracy. Their unexpected existence in authoritarian settings heralds prospects for mass support for the development of democracy in the region and for other authoritarian regimes. Although we do not believe that the emergence of mass democratic values will necessarily assure the development of democratic institutions in either country, they could well encourage national elites to choose democratic rules and practices as they confront national crises. In the middle run such tolerance of others' rights could well be a harbinger of moderation among populations striving to transform their systems, a factor that might reduce the propensity to violence in the struggle for change. In the long run, mass support for democratic liberties could, as in Costa Rica, reinforce elite commitment to democratic regimes and, by thus enhancing the stability of new democracies, break the tragic Latin American tendency to cycle back to authoritarian rule.

## Notes

This chapter is drawn from our previous analyses of Mexico in the *Latin American Research Review* and of Costa Rica and Nicaragua in the *Journal of Politics* (cited below).

1. From *Ten Keys to Latin America*, New York: Vintage, 1966, p. 144.

2. Dankwart A. Rustow, "Democracy: A Global Revolution?" *Foreign Affairs* 69 (Fall 1990): 75-91.

3. Larry Diamond, Juan Linz, and Seymour Martin Lipset, eds., *Democracy in Developing Countries: Latin America* (Boulder: Lynne Rienner Publishers, 1989); John A. Booth and Mitchell A. Seligson, eds., *Elections and Democracy in Central America* (Chapel Hill: University of North Carolina Press, 1989); John Peeler, *Latin American Democracies* (Chapel Hill: University of North Carolina Press, 1985); James M. Malloy and Mitchell A. Seligson, eds., *Authoritarians and Democrats: Regime Transition in Latin America* (Pittsburgh: University of Pittsburgh Press, 1987); Guillermo A. O'Donnell, Philippe C. Schmitter, and Laurence Whitehead, eds., *Transitions from Authoritarian Rule*, (Baltimore: Johns Hopkins University Press, 1986); and Paul W. Drake and Eduardo Silva, eds., *Elections and Democratization in Latin America: 1980-1985* (La Jolla, CA: Center for Iberian and Latin American Studies-Center for U.S.-Mexican Studies, Institute of the Americas,

University of California, San Diego, 1986).

   4. Russell Fitzgibbon and Julio A. Fernandez *Latin America: Political Culture and Development* (Englewood Cliffs, NJ: Prentice-Hall, 1981), chaps. 1, 17; Emilio Willems, *Latin American Culture: An Anthropological Synthesis* (New York: Harper and Row, 1975), chaps. 5, 14; Frank Tannenbaum, *Ten Keys to Latin America* (New York: Vintage, 1966), pp. 138-145; John P. Gillin, "The Middle Segments and Their Values," in Robert B. Tomasek, ed., *Latin American Politics: 24 Studies of the Contemporary Scene* (New York: Anchor Books, 1966), pp. 23-40; Howard J. Wiarda, *The Democratic Revolution in Latin America: History, Politics, and U.S. Policy* (New York: Holmes and Meier, 1990).

   5. Larry Diamond and Juan Linz, "Politics, Society, and Democracy in Latin America," in Larry Diamond, Juan Linz, and Seymour Martin Lipset, eds., *Democracy in Developing Countries: Latin America*, p. 10.

   6. The work of Theodore Adorno et al., *The Authoritarian Personality, New York: Harper and Brothers* (1950), was later discredited by Bob Altemeyer, *Right Wing Authoritarianism* (Winnipeg: University of Manitoba Press, 1981), pp. 13-116.

   7. Arguments for redefining democracy based on the irrationality and intolerance of mass culture may be found in Joseph A. Schumpeter, *Capitalism, Socialism, and Democracy* (London: Allen and Unwin, 1943); Lester Milbrath, *Political Participation* (Chicago: Rand McNally, 1965); and Robert A. Dahl, *A Preface to Democratic Theory* (Chicago, University of Chicago Press, 1956). Studies debunking such arguments include V. O. Key, *The Responsible Electorate* (Cambridge: Harvard University Press, Belknap Press, 1966), Clyde A. Nunn, Harry J. Crockett, Jr., and Allen J. Williams, Jr., *Tolerance for Nonconformity: A National Survey of Changing Commitment to Civil Liberties* (San Francisco: Jossey-Bass, 1978); and Herbert McClosky and Alida Brill, *Dimensions of Tolerance* (New York: Russell Sage Foundation, 1983).

   8. Gabriel Almond and Sidney Verba, *The Civic Culture* (Boston: Little, Brown, 1963).

   9. Guillermo A. O'Donnell, *Modernization and Bureaucratic Authoritarianism* (Berkeley: Institute of International Studies, University of California, 1973), predicted that authoritarian coalitions rising from modernization would block democratization in Latin America.

   10. Lawrence E. Harrison attributes the lack of development and democracy in Latin America to social and political culture, in *Underdevelopment Is a State of Mind: The Latin American Case* (Lanham, MD: Madison Books; Cambridge: Center for International Affairs, Harvard University, 1985). A similar argument is made by Fitzgibbon and Fernandez in *Latin America*.

   11. Glen Dealy, "The Tradition of Monistic Democracy in Latin America," in Howard J. Wiarda, ed., *Politics and Social Change in Latin America: The Distinct Tradition* (Amherst: University of Massachusetts Press, 1974), p. 73.

   12. Howard J. Wiarda, "Social Change and Political Development in Latin America: Summary," in Wiarda, ed., *Politics and Social Change in Latin America* (Amherst, Mass: University of Massachusetts Press, 1974), p. 274.

   13. Ibid., pp. 269-270. Wiarda, in his latest work on the subject, *The Democratic Revolution in Latin America*, pp. 3-57, recognizes that some changes in support for democracy in Latin America are occurring but essentially reaffirms his earlier pessimism about the democratic potential of the region's culture.

   14. Fitzgibbon and Fernandez, *Latin America*, p. 350.

   15. See, for instance, Harry Eckstein, "A Culturalist Theory of Political Change," *American Political Science Review* 82 (September 1988): 789-804; Lucian Pye, *Asian Power and Politics: The Cultural Dimensions of Authority* (Cambridge: Harvard University Press, 1985).

16. Ronald Inglehart, *Culture Shift in Advanced Industrial Society* (Princeton: Princeton University Press, 1990); and "The Renaissance of Political Culture," *American Political Science Review* 82 (November 1988): 1203-1230.

17. Inglehart, "The Renaissance of Political Culture," p. 1205.

18. Ibid., p. 1219.

19. Ibid., p. 1221.

20. Inglehart, *Culture Shift*, pp. 61-63.

21. See Wiarda, *The Democratic Revolution in Latin America*, pp. 31-57.

22. Mikael Bostrom, "Political Waves in Latin America," *Ibero-Americana, Nordic Journal of Latin American Studies* 19, no. 1 (1989): 3-19.

23. Almond and Verba, *The Civic Culture*, pp. 31-32. Almond and Verba also stressed high levels of national pride and perception of civic competence as elements of the civic culture, but these have been found to be problematical elements. See Enrique Baloyra, "Criticism, Cynicism, and Political Evaluation: A Venezuelan Example," *American Political Science Review* 73 (December 1979): 987-1002; and Gabriel Almond and Sidney Verba, eds., *The Civic Culture Revisited* (Newbury Park, CA: Sage, 1989).

24. Indeed, in subsequent work by Verba, political participation became the dominant focus. See, for instance, Sidney Verba and Norman H. Nie, *Participation in America: Political Democracy and Social Equality* (New York: Harper and Row, 1972); Sidney Verba, Norman H. Nie, and Jae-On Kim, *Participation and Political Equality: A Seven-Nation Study* (New York: Cambridge University Press, 1978).

25. Samuel A. Stouffer, *Communism, Conformity, and Civil Liberties* (New York: Doubleday, 1955); Herbert McClosky, "Consensus and Ideology in American Politics," *American Political Science Review* 58 (1964): 361-382.

26. John L. Sullivan, James Pierson, and George E. Marcus, *Political Tolerance and American Democracy* (Chicago: University of Chicago Press, 1982), p. 51.

27. Nunn, Crockett, Jr., and Williams, Jr., *Tolerance for Nonconformity*; John L. Sullivan, Michal Shamir, Patrick Walsh, and Nigel S. Roberts, *Political Tolerance in Context: Support for Unpopular Minorities in Israel, New Zealand, and the United States* (Boulder: Westview Press, 1985).

28. Robert A. Dahl, *Polyarchy* (New Haven: Yale University Press, 1971).

29. John A. Booth and Mitchell A. Seligson, "The Political Culture of Authoritarianism in Mexico: A Reexamination," *Latin American Research Review* 19, no. 1 (1984): 106-124.

30. See, for instance, Judith Adler Hellman, *Mexico in Crisis* (New York: Holmes and Meier, 1978); Pablo González Casanova, *Democracy in Mexico* (New York: Oxford University Press, 1970); Susan Eckstein, *The Poverty of Revolution: The State and the Urban Poor of Mexico* (Princeton: Princeton University Press, 1977); Roger D. Hansen, *The Politics of Mexican Development* (Baltimore: Johns Hopkins University Press, 1971); and L. Vincent Padgett, *The Mexican Political System* (Boston: Houghton Mifflin, 1966).

31. See, for instance, Eric R. Wolf, *Sons of the Shaking Earth* (Chicago: University of Chicago Press, 1959); Rafael Segovia, *La politización del niño mexicano* (Mexico, D.F.: El Colegio de Mexico, 1975); Samuel Ramos, *Profiles of Man and Culture in Mexico* (Austin: University of Texas Press, 1962); Octavio Paz, *Labyrinth of Solitude: Life and Thought in Mexico* (New York: Grove Press, 1961); Erich Fromm and Michael Maccoby, *Social Character in a Mexican Village: A Sociopsychoanalytic Study* (Englewood Cliffs, NY: Prentice Hall, 1970).

32. Inglehart acknowledges that determining the direction of causality historically is virtually impossible, but he believes that culture shapes structure, in particular, that a "civic culture" contributes to democracy. See Inglehart, "Renaissance," pp. 1212, 1215.

33. Almond and Verba predict that culture and regime type will normally be congruent, i.e., converge to resemble and support each other, or move toward congruence. Periods of incongruence between culture and regime type might occur during periods of rapid change. *The Civic Culture*, pp. 21-23.

34. See Booth and Seligson, "The Political Culture of Authoritarianism," p. 110, for additional methodological details and further data..

35. Ibid., pp. 116-117.

36. See John A. Booth and Thomas W. Walker, *Understanding Central America* (Boulder: Westview Press, 1993), pp. 17-27, for further material on their histories. See also James L. Busey, "Foundations of Political Contrast: Costa Rica and Nicaragua," *Western Political Quarterly* 8 (September 1958): 627-659.

37. Charles Ameringer, *Democracy in Costa Rica* (New York: Praeger, 1982); Mitchell A. Seligson, "Costa Rica and Jamaica," in Myron Weiner and Ergun Ozbudun, eds., *Competitive Elections in Developing Countries* (Durham, NC: Duke University Press, 1987); and John A. Booth, "Costa Rica: The Roots of Democratic Stability," in Diamond, Ling, and Lipset, *Democracy in Developing Countries*.

38. Thomas W. Walker, *Nicaragua: Land of Sandino* (Boulder: Westview Press, 1981); Richard L. Millett, *Guardians of the Dynasty* (Maryknoll, NY: Orbis, 1977); John A. Booth, *The End and the Beginning: The Nicaraguan Revolution* (Boulder: Westview Press, 1985); Latin American Studies Association (LASA), *The Electoral Process in Nicaragua: Domestic and International Influences* (Austin: LASA, 1984); and *Electoral Democracy Under International Pressure* (Pittsburgh: LASA, March 15, 1990).

39. Diamond and Linz, "Politics, Society and Democracy," p. 11; Busey, "Foundations of Political Contrast."

40. Daniel M. Lund, "Polling Failure in Nicaragua Assessed," *Interamerican Public Opinion Report*, Spring 1990, pp. 1, 4-5; Katherine Bischoping and Howard Schuman, "Pens and Polls in Nicaragua: An Analysis of the 1990 Preelection Surveys," *American Journal of Political Science* 36 (May 1992), pp. 331-350; William Barnes, "Rereading the Nicaraguan Preelection Polls, Vanessa Castro and Gary Prevost, eds., *The 1990 Elections in Nicaragua and Their Aftermath* (Lanham: Rowman & Littlefield, 1992).

41. For these analyses, this meant limiting the sample to the metropolitan area of San José, the nation's capital, and the provincial capitals on the meseta central. This limitation reduced the Costa Rican sample to an $N$ of 388.

42. The Nicaraguan sample consistently has more nonresponse than the Costa Rican sample, no doubt because of the turbulent political climate and the newness of public opinion surveying in Nicaragua, compared to stable Costa Rica, where such polls are commonplace. To be cautious, we report nonresponse and calculate percentages based upon all replies rather than on only those who responded. All data reported on Nicaragua and Costa Rica in Tables 4.2 through 4.8 have been reported in Mitchell A. Seligson and John A. Booth, "Political Culture and Regime Type: Evidence from Nicaragua and Costa Rica," *Journal of Politics* 55 (Nov. 1993).

43. The extreme right is represented by the Movimiento de Costa Rica Libre, which actively publishes anticommunist advertisements but has not been active as an electoral force. The extreme left, represented by various parties and coalitions of parties in the 1970s and 1980s, has been steadily losing strength since 1982 and has now lost several of its historical maximum of five seats in the fifty-seven-seat unicameral Legislative Assembly.

44. When the incumbent regime invalidated the 1948 presidential election, there was widespread outrage. A guerrilla force coalesced and toppled the government. Although other issues stimulated individuals to rebel, including opposition to communists in government, anger over tampering with the outcome of the election was a

unifying theme. To prevent the recurrence of corruption of the election process, the 1949 constitution established an independent body, the Supreme Electoral Tribunal, with the power to exercise total control over elections. The system builds in numerous safeguards including the transfer of police power to the tribunal in the months preceding elections.

45. Edward N. Muller, Mitchell A. Seligson, and Ilter Turan, "Education, Participation, and Support for Democratic Norms," *Comparative Politics* 20 (October 1987): 19-33.

46. We coded as urban all respondents in the metropolitan area of San José, the national capital, and in the provincial capitals of Alajuela, Cartago, Heredia, Limón, and Puntarenas.

47. Stouffer, *Communism, Conformity, and Civil Liberties.* In their methodologically more sophisticated study, *Political Tolerance and American Democracy*, however, Sullivan, Pierson and Marcus found these variables were found to be very weakly related to tolerance (pp. 110–144).

48. Inter-American Development Bank, *1989 Report*, pp. 308, 388.

49. In two of the ten crosstabulations on age significant differences were found, but the results were nonmonotonic, i.e., respondents in the oldest and youngest age categories both had lower or higher support for democratic norms than those in the middle category.

50. Females were significantly less tolerant of democratic liberties in four of the six crosstabulations.

51. Bob Altemeyer, *Enemies of Freedom: Understanding Right-wing Authoritarianism* (San Francisco: Jossey-Bass, 1988), pp. 239-252; McClosky and Brill, *Dimensions of Tolerance*, pp. 260-265, 338-340; Mitchell A. Seligson and Dan Caspi, "Arabs in Israel: Political Tolerance and Ethnic Conflict," *Journal of Applied Behavioral Science* 19 (February 1983): 55-66; Stouffer, *Communism, Conformity, and Civil Liberties*; and Sullivan, et al., *Political Tolerance in Context*, pp. 197-199.

52. The original democratic norms items in the Costa Rica surveys were administered using a scale of 1 to 10, but these were recoded as dichotomies to match the Nicaragua survey. For linear correlation purposes, when analyzing the Costa Rica sample alone, it is more appropriate to use the unrecoded ten-point items when using such predictors as the eight-point ideology scale. In the tables presented, the items are recoded for consistency of presentation with the other tables in the chapter.

53. On only one other variable, participation in protest marches in the series of Extensive Participation did we find any significant correlation (r = −.11; sig. <.001). On all other items, the correlations were insignificant.

54. Ideology is recoded as follows (1,2,3 = left; 4,5 = center; 6,7,8 = right).

55. Though UNO included a small number of tiny left-wing elements within its umbrella coalition, it was firmly identified with an anti-FSLN position and on balance much to the ideological right of the FSLN. We found, for example, only 6 respondents among the 240 who identified with UNO but who supported left-wing parties. This included 3 respondents who supported the Partido Comunista de Nicaragua, 2 who supported the Partido Marxista Leninista and 1 who supported the Partido Socialista Nicaraguense.

56. Finally, in both Tables 4.6 and 4.7, the Nicaraguans who refused to identify themselves with a particular party position scored in the intermediate range between UNO and FSLN identifiers. This supports our view that those who did not identify with one political bloc or the other were more likely to be ambivalent in their feelings about politics than party identifiers, and constituted a true ideological center.

57. See Edward N. Muller, Thomas O. Jukam, and Mitchell A. Seligson, "Diffuse Political Support and Antisystem Political Behavior: A Comparative Analysis," *American Journal of Political Science* 26 (May 1982): 240-264; and

Mitchell A. Seligson, "On the Measurement of Diffuse Support: Some Evidence from Mexico," *Social Indicators Research* 12 (January 1983): 1-24. In Costa Rica, the items were administered using a seven-point scale, whereas in Nicaragua an agree/disagree format was used. To make the two formats compatible, the Costa Rican responses were dichotomized, with the middle category being classified in the "neutral" category.

58. These were the UNO supporters who disagreed with the statement that the laws protect the basic rights of Nicaraguans. Use of the other diffuse support item, pride in the system, produces similar results.

59. Peeler, *Latin American Democracies*; and Booth, "Costa Rica."

60. Note that this research and expectation referred to citizens of countries in which Marxists did not hold power. Critics of Marxist regimes and the historical record have amply demonstrated the capacity of Marxist regimes to curtail civil liberties.

61. See, for instance, John A. Booth, "Prospects for Democracy in Nicaragua: Elites, Political Culture, and the 1990 Election" (Paper presented at the American Political Science Association meetings in San Francisco, 2 September 1990; and John Higley and Michael G. Burton, "The Elite Variable in Democratic Transitions and Breakdowns," *American Sociological Review* 54 (1989): 17-32; John Peeler, "Elite Settlements and Democratic Consolidation in Latin America: Colombia, Costa Rica, and Venezuela," in John Higley and Richard Gunther, eds., *Elites and Democratic Consolidation in Latin America and Southern Europe* (Cambridge and New York: Cambridge University Press, 1992), pp. 81-112; and Seligson and Booth, "Political Culture and Regime Type."

# • 5 •

# A Nonparadigmatic Search for Democracy in a Post-Confucian Culture: The Case of Taiwan, R.O.C.

*Ambrose Y.C. King*

## Taiwan's Democratic Transition

In the past three decades, the phenomenal development of Taiwan's economy has caught the attention of the world.[1] Taiwan, or the Republic of China, has successfully become one of the so-called newly industrialized countries. It is praiseworthily called one of the Four Little Dragons together with South Korea, Hong Kong, and Singapore.

The rapid socioeconomic development of Taiwan is amply demonstrated in the following statistics:[2]

- From 1953 to 1982, GNP growth rates averaged 8.7 percent; the 1982 GNP was 12 times that of 1952, and by 1990 Taiwan ranked 25th in the world with a per capita GNP of US$7,997.
- Industry grew at an average annual rate of 13.3 percent from 1953 to 1982, increasing to 42 times its 1953 value.
- The economic structure underwent noticeable structural change. In 1952 industry accounted for only 19.7 percent of the GNP; in 1990, 42.3 percent. Agriculture's contribution to GNP dropped from 32.2 percent to 4.2 percent over the same period. The share of the service sector increased to 53.5 percent in 1990.
- A trade surplus has occurred every year since 1970. Taiwan achieved a trade surplus of US$15.6 billion in 1986, when its two-way trade totaled US$64 billion, and by 1990 held foreign exchange reserves of over US$80 billion, one of the highest in the world.
- There have been nine years of free compulsory education since 1968, and the illiteracy rate fell to 9.2 percent in 1986 from 27.6 percent in 1966. In 1986, about 25 percent of all persons between 18 and 21 years of age attended junior colleges or universities.
- Other social indicators of living standards showed a remarkable

131

improvement between 1952 and 1986: the percentage of households
with electricity rose from 45.2 percent to 99.7 percent; telephones per
1,000 persons from 3.9 to 311.9; television sets per 1,000 persons from
1.4 (in 1962) to 106.2; automobiles per 1,000 persons from 1.0 to 77.
- Between 1952 and 1990 the percentage of the population living in
cities with more than 5,000 inhabitants increased from 30 to 90 percent.

Not surprisingly, Taiwan's success story in economic development has
generated a good number of plausible explanations by economists and other
social scientists, varying in degree of theoretical sophistication and empirical
richness. Broadly speaking, there are two competing intellectual camps, the
institutionalist and the culturalist, that try to make an issue of the relative
importance of structure as against culture.[3] What is most fascinating is the
culturalists'argument crystallized in the form of a post-Confucian thesis. In a
nutshell, it argues that it is the Confucian ethic that has been the driving
force behind the economic miracle of Japan and the Four Little Dragons.[4]
The post-Confucian thesis is in sharp contradiction to Weber's analysis of
Confucianism. For Weber, Confucian rationalism was a "rationalism of
order," incapable of initiating profound social or economic change. The crux
of Weber's analysis is as follows:

> Completely absent in the Confucian ethic was any tension between nature
> and deity, between ethical demand and human shortcomings, consciousness
> of aim and need for salvation, conduct on earth and compensation in the
> beyond, religious duty and socio-political reality. Hence, there was no
> leverage for influencing conduct through inner forces freed of tradition and
> convention.[5]

Weber's view has long been taken by students of Chinese studies as the
authoritative basis for explaining the "nondevelopment" of capitalism in
China. Now the empirical fact of Taiwan's profound economic development
should naturally evoke scholars of Confucian persuasion to question the
validity of Weber's verdict on Confucianism as a negative cultural system.
Thomas Metzger writes:

> He [Weber] concluded that China's failure was due largely to the effects of
> the Confucian ethos, and his conclusion still carries weight today, even
> though his early analysis of this ethos was erroneous. We however live in a
> world where the development of the major societies is based on a mixture
> of indigenous factors and cosmopolitan influences. We consequently are
> led to ask: Why in this kind of world are some societies more effective than
> others in coping with their problems and rising to the challenges of mod-
> ernization? While Weber had to explain China's failure, we have to explain
> its success, but paradoxically our answer, like Weber's, emphasizes the role
> of the indigenous ethos.[6]

It is not the purpose of this paper to settle the issue of the role of Confucianism in the economic development of Taiwan.[7] What concerns us here is the role of Confucianism, as a political cultural system, in Taiwan's democratic development. For some time Confucianism has been seen by most scholars, Western and Chinese alike, as a value system most congruent with Oriental authoritarianism and providing legitimacy for the centuries-old monarchical system. Despite Taiwan's miraculous economic development, its political system was generally considered as authoritarian, and students of Taiwan's modernization almost without exception took the view that its political development has lagged behind its economic development. Nevertheless, since the late 1970s, and particularly in the past few years, Taiwan has clearly moved toward democratization.[8] Taiwan now has meaningful and extensive competition for government power through regular elections; an opposition party of real significance has come into existence; and considerable civil and political liberties, including freedom of expression, freedom of the press, freedom to form organizations, freedom to demonstrate and strike, and so on have become common features of political life. Moreover, the smooth leadership succession following the death of the charismatic leader Chiang Ching-kuo on 13 January 1988 showed a marked maturity of constitutionality in the Republic. All these factors indicate unequivocally that Taiwan has forever bid farewell to dynastic politics and is clearly in the process of transition to democracy. Admittedly, Taiwan's destiny, especially with regard to democracy, is not without uncertainty. However, its democratic transformation is a significant phenomenon that calls for an interpretation.

## Modernization Theories and Democracy

Modernization theories, which emerged as the dominant social-scientific paradigm in the 1950s and 1960s, were no longer in fashion, if not discredited, in the 1970s and 1980s. In recent years, dependency theory and world system theory have attracted a large number of theorists who are concerned with the problem of the capitalist development of "underdevelopment."[9] However, contrary to the argument of dependency theory, Asia has experienced one of the most profound records of development, not "underdevelopment," in human history over recent decades; Asian leaders and intellectuals are vigorously, purposefully striving for modernization. After the downfall of the "Gang of Four," the People's Republic of China has since 1978 pledged to pursue "Four Modernizations" in order to move the country out of backwardness and underdevelopment. Pye is not wide of the mark in saying that "the earlier modernization theories had a close empirical fit with the experience of Asia but not with those of either Africa or Latin America."[10]

Earlier modernization theories that imply the triumph of reason, a legacy of enlightenment, do carry an optimistic tone. However, sophisticated modernization theorists were never naive about the inevitability of democratic development. In fact, democracy is not necessarily implied in the definition of modernization.[11] Almond cautioned us, "The movement of modernization might be in a liberal democratic direction, but it might with equal probability be in an authoritarian direction." And he argues explicitly against the simple diffusionist notion of unilaterality.[12] Max Weber, the first great theorist of modernization, who was fully aware of the paradox of rationalization, is ambivalent toward, if not downright pessimistic about, the prospect of democracy and capitalism.[13]

Modernization theories, like Weber's thesis of the Protestant Ethic, address primarily the problem of economic development. Peter Berger writes, "Modernization must be seen in close relation to economic growth—more specially, to the particular growth processes released by recent technology."[14] Immediately after World War II, as perceptively observed by Parsons, "there was an apparently world-wide consensus on the valuation of economic productivity."[15] Indeed, there was a preoccupation with economic development in the minds of modernizing elites in the "underdeveloped" countries. True enough, the students of modernization have more often than not an inclination to embrace liberal, democratic ideas, and view democracy and pluralism as something inherently good and desirable. A normative theory of political development would most probably include democracy in the definition of modernization. And more important, modernization theories, though not arguing the causal directionality of liberal democratic development, do assert an empirical correlation between economic development and political democracy. Lipset writes: "It seems clear that the factors of industrialization, urbanization, wealth and education are so closely interrelated as to form one common factor. And the factors subsumed under economic development carry with it the political correlate of democracy."[16] However, as Dankwart Rustow points out, empirical correlation between socioeconomic factors and political democracy does not imply a causal relationship, nor can the functional explanation be taken as a genetic explanation. In short, they do not tell "how a democratic system comes into being."[17]

In the case of Taiwan, the profound change brought about by economic development has produced structural forces that seem to have affected Taiwan's democratization. Moreover, as a result of industrialization, and particularly the dramatic expansion of education, the Confucian political culture seems to have undergone significant change. A newly emerging political culture, which, as demonstrated later in the paper, shows clearly some characteristics of what Almond and Verba term "the civic culture," is definitely conducive to the process of Taiwan's transition to democracy. But Taiwan's democratization is not just an automatic outcome of socioeconomic development. Like Spain's, Taiwan's transition to democracy requires an analysis concentrating on the transition process itself.[18]

## The Party-State and Its Legitimacy

The most salient characteristic of Taiwan's political system has been its one-party rule. The Kuomintang (National People's Party or Nationalist Party) has enjoyed dominance since it moved to Taiwan in 1949, after suffering defeat at the hands of Chinese Communists on mainland China. Despite the legal existence of two small parties, the China Youth Party and the China Democratic Socialist Party, the government of the Republic of China (ROC) was run exclusively by the Kuomintang (KMT). Under the KMT, both the structure and the operation of the government were basically the same in the ROC as they had been on the mainland. The Nationalists brought along their formal, national-level party and government structures and superimposed these on one small province, with only .37 percent of China's total land mass and only 1 percent of its population. There were parallel party and state structures at all levels—national, provincial, county, municipal, and district—to ensure firm party control.[19]

The KMT was reorganized with the aid of Soviet advisers in 1924 as a Leninist-style party. However, the KMT is Leninist only in structure. It has its own ideology, Dr. Sun Yat-sen's San Min Chu I (Three Principles of the People), which is rendered as Nationalism, Democracy, and People's Livelihood. There is no room for democracy in Leninism. But in the KMT's ideological system, Sun Yat-sen has a three-stage development theory of state-building: military rule, democratic tutelage, and constitutional democracy. The basic difference between the KMT and a Leninist party lies in the fact that, unlike a Leninist party, the KMT never intended in theory or in practice to have total control over society. The party-state in Taiwan was, to use Metzger's concept, an "inhibited" political center.[20] The ultimate aim of the KMT's state-building was to create a democratic political system. This is at least the theoretical position of the San Min Chu I, which had an abiding effect on the practice of the ruling party in Taiwan.

In keeping with Sun's ideas of tutelary democracy, a new constitution was promulgated by the KMT in 1946. However, the promulgation of a constitution did not bring China into the era of constitutionalism. The civil war between the ROC government and the Chinese Communists then accelerated to an unprecedented level. Amid the war, the first session of the first term of the National Assembly convened in Nanking in 1948 and elected Chiang Kai-shek as the president of the ROC. It also adopted "temporary provisions for the Duration of Mobilization to suppress the Rebellion" through the procedure for constitutional amendment. Upon establishing its rule over Taiwan, the KMT government declared martial law in 1949, and justified its restriction of political and other rights—including the right to organize new political parties—as a necessary measure arising from the subversive threat from the Communists.

The KMT government in the 1950s was preoccupied with the issue of national security since a military invasion by Communist China seemed obvious and imminent. In 1949, 1954, and 1958 there were several military confrontations between these two regimes. From the mid-1950s on, the ROC began to receive economic and military aid from the United States. Moreover, the U.S. commitment to prevent a Communist attack gave the government a breathing spell to create an effective economic and political system. Although the Nationalists under President Chiang never lost hope of returning to the mainland, they shifted their strategy decisively to develop Taiwan into a model province for the whole of China in the early 1950s.

The KMT began its development program with land reform. The motivation was probably more political than economic.[21] The process of implementing land reform was bloodless, and its success was far-reaching, economically and politically. On the one hand, Taiwan created the most equitable rural scene in all of Asia; on the other it definitely enhanced the sociopolitical stability of the island. The former Taiwanese landlords who had been compensated for their land with government bonds became an entrepreneurial class, using their bonds as capital for the first stages of Taiwan's industrialization. In the ensuing years, the KMT government wasted no time in establishing, outside the conservative bureaucratic system, new institutions for guided capitalist development. President Chiang Kai-shek and the premier, the late vice president Chen Cheng, attributing their debacle on the mainland in large part to the collapse of the economy, gave greater scope over Taiwan's economy to Western-trained technocrats. Indeed, persons like K. Y. Yin, a U.S.-trained electrical engineer, and K. T. Li were virtually given a free hand to design and implement Taiwan's economic plan.[22]

Understandably, the United States, through the Agency for International Development (AID), had a deep influence over Taiwan's economy, and Americans supported the modernizing technocrats, who were mainly U.S.-educated, in their pursuit of economic development. It probably is no exaggeration to say that Taiwan's economic modernization was to a large extent the creation of these technocrats, who enjoyed the unflagging support of the top leaders. The more the economy developed, the more the technocrats became involved in the state's affairs. The result was the ever-increasing vitality of the economy and society, though this by no means developed at the expense of the power of the party-state. Moreover, the distinguishing characteristics of Taiwan's development was, to use Gold's expression, "the bifurcation of the economy from the polity."[23] Deliberately intended or not, the KMT's legitimacy has increasingly been based upon its capacity to deliver economic growth. Vidich writes:

> In the contemporary world, both in Third World nations and in the industrialized countries, legitimacy processes include production and economic performance as a critical dimension on which legitimacy is made. The economic performance of a regime may constitute a major prop for legitimacy in the eyes of groups and classes which have accepted life style enhancement as a life goal.[24]

Vidich's observation seems to be confirmed in Taiwan. According to the results of six elections held in the 1970s and 1980s, the KMT consistently won about 70 percent of the votes, and the KMT voters tended to be better educated, higher in occupational status, and more often middle high in income than non-KMT voters. Furthermore, concerning the attitude of voters toward government policies, 78.7 percent expressed their satisfaction with the quality of life.[25] The positive response from the people to the KMT's rule reinforced the party's development-oriented policies. One point worth mentioning is that Taiwan's industrialization has not only brought about wealth but also successfully skipped the so-called Kuznets Trap, according to which inequality tends to increase in the first stage of industrial growth. Taiwan has achieved a remarkable record of equitable income distribution. The Gini coefficient of income inequality fell from 0.6206 in 1953 to 0.2955 in 1972, and further decreased to 0.2806 in 1979.[26]

## Bifurcation of Polity and Economy

The bifurcation of the economy from the polity created a mixed image of the ROC. On the one hand, the ROC was widely acclaimed as a progressive state that produced one of the most dynamic economies in world history. On the other hand, the ROC was seen to be a regime that was ossified, its leaders resistant to change.[27] Neil Jacoby wrote, for example, "In contrast to its rapid social and economic development, Taiwan experienced little basic change in its political structure during 1951–65."[28] In terms of the ROC's formal structure, Jacoby's observation in 1966 was not to be disputed. However, the political change taking place below the surface was not insignificant, especially in the years after the 1960s. Nevertheless, the ossified image of Taiwan's political system persisted even up to the 1970s.

The image of nondevelopment in Taiwan's political system can be attributed to several main reasons. First, as mentioned above, there has been little change in the structure and operation of the government. Its basic framework has not been altered since the move to Taiwan in 1949. Second, the ROC's political ideology and its official claims to be the custodian of Chinese culture, as well as its adamant anti-Communist stand remained unchanged throughout the years. Third, the death of Chiang Kai-shek (1975) produced no visible political change as he was succeeded by his son, Chiang Ching-kuo, after the fashion of succession in Imperial China.[29]

This image was too superficial to reflect the substantial changes in politics taking place in the 1960s and 1970s. Nevertheless, there was no denying the fact that the Nationalists had not yet loosened their restrictions on freedom of political activities, including freedom of speech, freedom of the press, and freedom of association. In 1960 Lei Chen, editor of the influential political journal *Free China*, who attempted to organize an opposition party, was charged with harboring a Communist agent on his staff and sentenced to ten years in prison.[30] In the 1960s several arrests were made on charges of advocating Taiwan's independence. Among them, the arrest of Dr. Pen Ming-min, a well known legal scholar, was the most publicized.[31] In Taiwan, opposition to leadership, attempts to organize new opposition parties, or any attempt to advocate separatist ideologies were severely repressed. Taiwan's political system was indeed correctly called authoritarian in these respects. The KMT's determination to suppress challenges to its political authority could be matched only by its determination to promote economic development.

By this juncture, the bifurcation of the economy from the polity had produced an extraordinary distribution of power between the so-called mainlanders and the Taiwanese. Of Taiwan's population of twenty million, 15 percent, or about three million, are "mainlanders" who came over from the Chinese mainland since 1945 and their descendants. Though mainlanders and Taiwanese are both of Chinese origin, there are marked differences of dialect and customs between the two groups. For a long time the primary source of tension was the dominant position of mainlanders on the island. At the national level, all the higher positions in the government, the party, and the army were initially occupied by mainlanders. In the three elective bodies in the central government—the National Assembly, the Legislation Yuan, and the Control Yuan—the mainlanders constituted the great majority because they had been elected in 1946 on the mainland to represent all the provinces of China. Because the ROC persistently asserted that it was the sole representative government for all China, and because it never officially gave up the goal of recovering the mainland, it justified its perpetuation of a national government that represented all China and therefore one that must not be dominated and staffed by Taiwanese. Being denied the road to national political power, the Taiwanese were, however, encouraged by the KMT's policies to engage in business ventures. Throughout the years, increasingly larger numbers of Taiwanese established successful business careers. For example, the 1974 edition of *Taiwan 500 Kung-shen jen-min lu* listed five-hundred prominent businessmen in Taiwan, of whom 68 percent were Taiwanese. A 1973 statistical abstract of Taipei City showed that 73 percent of those who moved between 1968 and 1973 into the relatively affluent suburbs of Shih-lin, Pai-ton, and others were Taiwanese. In a real sense, the society that was represented overwhelmingly by the economic power of the Taiwanese stood strong vis-à-vis the party-state.

By the 1970s a division of power was evident between the mainlanders and Taiwanese: the former controlled the political sector, and the latter dominated the economic sector. The great beneficiaries of Taiwan's economic development were Taiwanese economic elites who were more than willing to give tacit support to the government's authoritarian way of achieving the national goal of growth and stability. The newly emerging capitalist classes showed no interest or inclination to translate economic muscle into political activity. This is probably one of the reasons that the ethnic difference between mainlanders and Taiwanese was not transformed into class-based conflict, which was conspicuously absent in the political arena. It was not accidental that Taiwan could enjoy continuous political tranquility from 1947 to the Chung-li incident of 1977.

## Society and State in Tension

The KMT's modernization program, although placing high priority on economic development, was not entirely reluctant about democratization. Although the people were virtually denied access to the three elective bodies at the national level until the end of the 1960s, the KMT, pledging to build Taiwan into a model province in conformity with the state-building goals set forth in Sun's writings, began as early as 1950 to implement local self-rule at provincial and lower levels. As with land reform, the development of local representative institutions was geared to gain the support of the local populace, thus ensuring the political stability of the island.[32]

As expected, the KMT dominated the provincial and local elections. With the exception of the elections at village and township assembly level, the KMT candidates have consistently won overwhelming majority votes, ranging from 60 percent to 85 percent at provincial, municipal, and county levels. However, the provincial and local elections showed a high degree of political competition and participation. For example, in 1984 more than 1,500 candidates (including 230 women) filed for 907 seats. Voter turnout was high: in 1964, more than 76 percent voted, and in 1977, 80 percent. A student of Taiwan's politics has the following to say on Taiwan's local democracy:

> Clearly, democracy at the grass roots is seriously limited by the authoritarian and bureaucratic political structure. But it is remarkable that vigorous competition has occurred and some legislative control of executive power has appeared in city and county governments. However, local political competition does not mean lessening Nationalist domination. This is clear in light of the relative power of political parties.[33]

The provincial and local elections brought a number of non-KMT politicians, running independently, into the political arena, and some of them emerged as prominent political figures. A point that should be emphatically made here is that since the 1950s, elections at the local and provincial levels have become a mode of political participation of both the people and the politicians in Taiwan. From 1969 onward, important new avenues for political participation have been opened up at the national level as well. Because a sizable proportion of the members of the three national elective bodies—the National Assembly, the Legislative Yuan, and the Control Yuan—who had been elected in 1949 on mainland China had died by 1969, the government felt that new members had to be added. Consequently, supplementary elections were held in 1969, 1972, 1973, 1976, 1980, 1983, 1985, and 1989. The KMT were consistently able to get about 70 percent of the vote, but 30 percent went to the independent or opposition politicians. (This percentage continued to hold in the December 1991 elections for an entirely new National Assembly, which was characterized by formal party competition and followed sweeping institutional reforms initiated by President Lee Teng-hui.) The KMT's one-party hegemony was being seriously challenged, and it was indeed appropriate to characterize the ROC's political system from the 1970s onward as a "one-party-plus-independents" system.[34] At the same time, however, the KMT's long string of election victories, one after another, gave its elites sufficient confidence to see that the KMT's legitimacy would be built most effectively through popular elections. Equally important was the growing realization throughout these years on the part of non-KMT politicians and independents that electoral competition was a safe and viable road to political eminence and power sharing.

The so-called independents were sometimes called *Dang Wai* ("outside the party") figures. Because the KMT did not allow any new political parties, the opposition politicians had to become "independents." The Dang Wai (DW) was a heterogeneous group consisting of two main factions. The "Mainstream Faction" advocated gradual political reform and favored the Western model of a free market economy and pluralistic politics. The second faction, sometimes referred to as the "Action Faction," was more radical and advocated the use of mass-movement tactics. They were in favor of unqualified "Taiwanization" in the institutional life of the country and in cutting any emotional ties with the mainland.[35]

The emergence of the DW is usually traced to the 1977 Chung-li Incident, a violent demonstration against alleged election tampering in Chung-li City. This was the first open challenge of the opposition forces to the KMT's political authority in thirty years. Symbolically, it can be seen as the resistance of an increasingly autonomous society against the powerful party-state. Politically and psychologically, the Chung-li incident was a watershed event in Taiwan's postwar political development. Thomas Gold writes:

> In retrospect, the Chung-li Incident offers a unique key to understanding both the success and the shortcomings of Taiwan's development strategy wherein a strong authoritarian state guides and participates in rapid economic growth while suppressing the political activities of the social forces it has generated in the process.[36]

Indeed, it can well be argued, from a social and economic viewpoint, that "the Chung-li Incident was inevitable as Taiwan's dynamic social forces, desirous of political participation and a say in the nation's destiny, continued to clash with an ossified political regime."[37] After the Chung-li incident, the Dang Wai, through magazines (*Formosa Magazine* was the main one), campaigns, and demonstrations, began aggressively to press their interests and claims against the party-state. On 10 December 1979, Human Rights Day, the Dang Wai staged a mass demonstration in Kaohsiung, Taiwan's second-largest city. During what became known as the Kaohsiung incident, violence broke out and 183 policemen were injured (only a few demonstrators were hurt, because the police had been instructed not to react with force). The government arrested and tried the leaders of the Dang Wai and more than sixty others, of whom eight received severe sentences, and closed the offices of *Formosa Magazine*, which was the organization— behaving like a political party—behind the demonstrations. Public opinion surveys showed a large majority of the population supported the government's action; the dissidents had to be viewed as a source of political instability that constituted a threat to public order and to the economy.[38]

However, though the KMT's role had the support of the majority of the population, "some Taiwanese voters have deep-seated feelings of having been colonized, and they respond emotionally to the martyr symbolism around such jailed leaders as the Kaohsiung Eight. In this political culture mass allies, emotional rhetoric, and confrontational demonstrations are tools of electoral survival for political moderates."[39] Pye has perceptively observed the unique character of the ethnic division between mainlanders and Taiwanese. He writes:

> Whereas in most ethnically divided societies the social differences are basic and politics often serves as the main avenue for bridging differences, in Taiwan it is the other way around. There is little social distance between the Taiwanese and the mainlanders ... the only area of tension is politics. Hence measures taken to reduce political strains in the political realm have had dramatic payoffs in integrating the society.[40]

In this respect, the KMT government, far from ossified as critics often alleged, was in fact sensitive and responsive to the rapidly changing political reality. The KMT was prepared to take an accommodative approach toward social forces yet was determined to ensure that change took place within the existing constitutional framework. As Myers writes, "Offering more pluralism but determined to control the parameters of political competition, the KMT faces both an implacable minority and a supportive majority."[41]

## Democratic Engineering from Above

Clearly, any major decision in Taiwan's politics has to come from the leader of the Nationalist party-state. Here the late president and party chairman

Chiang Ching-kuo became crucial in Taiwan's transition to democratization. Chiang Ching-kuo, like his father Chiang Kai-shek, enjoyed supreme authority in the Taiwan political system and made himself popular among the people after becoming the premier in 1972. Chiang Ching-kuo never lost touch with the changing spirit of the society. While vigorously pushing the modernization program in the economic realm, including the ambitious Ten Major Projects, he quietly engaged in political reform by initiating a process of "Taiwanization." Taiwanese were not only appointed to the cabinet but also elected to the powerful Standing Committee of the party. As of 1983, Taiwanese representation in the policymaking bodies at cabinet, provincial, and county-city levels was 40 percent, 75 percent, and 100 percent, respectively. Thus, except at the national level, where the mainlanders still enjoyed a majority, Taiwanese had a great majority at the provincial level and monopolized the county-city level. Moreover, since the party has become more electorally oriented, its nominated candidates for elective bodies at all levels have been overwhelmingly Taiwanese. As of today, the KMT has a membership of two million, 75 percent of whom are Taiwanese. The most conspicuous cases of Chiang Ching-kuo's Taiwanization were his vice-presidential appointments of Chieh Tung-min in 1978 and Lee Teng-hui in 1984. (Lee succeeded to the presidency following Chiang's death in 1988 and was reelected in 1990.) Indeed, the party-state of Taiwan has become substantially "Taiwanized."

Chiang Ching-kuo's Taiwanization was inseparable from his policies of liberalization and democratization. He was fully cognizant of the changing times. He said in early November 1986, "The time is changing and so are the environment and the trend. To fit in with these changes, the KMT must adopt new concepts and new forms according with the basic spirit of the democratic and constitutional system. Only by doing so can the KMT be in line with current trends and forever be together with the public."[42] In fact, as early as May 1986, the party-state, obviously with Chiang's blessing, agreed to enter a dialogue (*kuo-t'ung*) with DW members. This symbolized nothing short of the KMT's de facto recognition of the DW as a legitimate competitor. In fact, President Chiang's determination to democratize Taiwan's political system was fully manifested at the third plenum of the KMT's 12th Central Committee in March 1986. He single-handedly persuaded the group of senior party conservatives to accept his view that the time had come to implement further the party's long-standing goal of constitutional democracy. On 9 April he appointed a twelve-man task force of Standing Committee members to suggest reform measures. On 15 October, Chiang, using his enormous personal power and prestige, was able to push resolutions through the KMT Central Standing Committee adopting two key reform proposals prepared by the task force. The first called for abolition of martial law. The second called for the revision of the law on civic organization to reverse the ban on the formation of new political parties. These steps signified a breakthrough in the history of Chinese democratic development. Admittedly, Chiang's democratic reform was no guarantee of full-fledged democracy in Taiwan, but it was a giant step in that direction.

At this juncture the Dang Wai, despite a warning from the KMT, went ahead to found the Democratic Progressive Party on 28 September, less than a month before the KMT's reform resolutions were passed. Again it was Chiang who decided to tolerate the newly formed opposition party. A new era was born. For the first time in modern Chinese history, one-party politics came to an end. The strong personal leadership Chiang exercised toward this eventuality is a striking instance of Larry Diamond's argument that "the most favorable development for democratization is a firm and forceful commitment to the process on the part of a country's leadership."[43] The argument is particularly relevant in Taiwan's case.

In the process of Taiwan's democratic transition, there were many personal and impersonal forces operating at different levels, and in different directions. Among them, the Dang Wai's determination and aggressiveness in challenging political authority and in demanding the right to form an opposition party certainly created great pressure on the KMT, but no one could dispute the fact that it was the charismatic Chiang Ching-kuo who was the real architect of Taiwan's democratic engineering. He was not only pragmatic and confident enough to accommodate and respond to opposition views and demands in a conciliatory way, but was also realistic and powerful enough to overcome the resistance of the conservative forces within the party-state. Ironically, it was the leader of an authoritarian party who used nothing less than his authoritarian power to engineer and legitimize a democratic breakthrough.

Yet, despite the central importance of the role Chiang Ching-kuo played in the party-state, it would be a mistake to neglect the substantial presence in the KMT leadership stratum of reform-minded liberals, especially the young and Western-educated liberals who emerged prominently in the 1970s and 1980s. The reform-minded party elites, young and old, seemed to believe that to recognize the existence of the oppositional party was not only politically inevitable but also ideologically desirable. Chiang did not stand alone; his decisions for democratic opening had considerable support.

## The Political Culture: Continuity and Change

In Taiwan the KMT consciously saw itself as the custodian of Chinese culture, in contrast to the Chinese Communists on the mainland, who have tried systematically to replace Confucianism with Marxism-Leninism. The San Min Chu I, a creative and adaptive amalgam of both Chinese and Western values and concepts, was the official ideology of the party-state and has become a part of the education and life of the people since the Nationalists moved to the island. Studies of the educational process showed that schools in Taiwan were authority-group-centered and paternalistic in their methods of operation. According to Richard Wilson, there was an apparent effort to shift the children's loyalty from the family to the nation and its leaders. Submission to authority and group norms were two basic values of the Chinese children.[44] "Norms of conformity and deviance are among the most heavily sanctioned in the society ... There is no concept of a loyal opposition."[45] Although the degree of success in this socialization at school, except in the elementary grades, was somewhat questionable,[46] one survey conducted in the early 1970s recorded that 93 percent of the students responded that respect for elders was a "most important virtue," while only 13 percent agreed that majority rule, periodic elections, the protection of dissent, and more than one political party were important characteristics of democracy.[47]

The above findings indicate that although Confucianism has been under serious attack by various intellectual forces since the late Ching period, especially during and after the May Fourth New Cultural Movement in 1918, people's attitudes and values in Taiwan still bear a strong mark of Confucian influence.[48] These political attitudes and values can hardly be seen as democratic in nature. However, Confucianism is not totally lacking in semidemocratic or prodemocratic ideas. As is well known, Mencius flatly asserted that "the people are the most important element in a state, whereas the sovereign is the least."[49] This stream of Confucian thought was a firmly accepted part of Confucian political doctrine, which was labeled "people-centered" thought (min-pen-ssu-hsiang).

Further evidence of the shallowness of democratic culture in Taiwan comes from John Lee's study of political change in Taiwan from 1949 to 1974. He concluded that Taiwan's democratization has largely involved "substantive" democracy in the sense that people-oriented government policies have benefited the population. "People in Taiwan do not have a firm belief in democracy so as to act democratically on all occasions. They believe that policies should be in the interest of the people but they seem to prefer authoritarian and informal ways of decision-making to rules of law called for by open process of political competition."[50] It was clear that the political attitudes and values of the people in Taiwan up to the early 1970s were still influenced by Confucian persuasion. To the extent these findings were valid, they imply that political values and attitudes were more congenial to and supportive of the people-oriented authoritarian power of the KMT government, at least until then.

Resistant as culture is to change, twentieth-century Taiwan no longer lives under the Confucianism that Weber analyzed. Weber's Confucianism can probably be labeled "Imperial Confucianism," which was a complex and sophisticated combination of state ideology and a set of strategic institutions, including literati, the examination system, and above all, the Imperial bureaucracy. In the post-Confucian era, the strategic Imperial institutions of

Confucianism are all deconstructed. Clearly, the most important new political institution was the constitution promulgated in 1946, the guiding principles of which were derived from western democratic ideas rather than from Confucianism. In the constitution, the concept of "popular sovereignty" was unequivocally adopted and was written into the textbooks of civic education.

Taiwan's class structure has also undergone rapid change especially since the 1970s. From 1970 to 1980, the middle class (both the new and the old) increased from 21.9 percent to 31.5 percent.[51] The number of people belonging to this class is now around six million. More significantly, several studies show consistently that more than 50 percent of the electorate in Taiwan identify themselves as "middle class." Apart from rapid industrialization, the most important reason for the emergence of the fast-growing middle class was the dramatic expansion of higher education. In 1970 there were 203,473 students enrolled in colleges and universities; by 1988 there were 442,648 students. By 1987 Taiwan had in total 1.4 million graduates of institutions of higher education. Universities and colleges are entirely different in methods of operation from primary and secondary schools. Students at the tertiary level are exposed more to liberal-democratic views than to Confucian values, because many teaching personnel at universities and colleges are Western trained. As elsewhere, the political attitudes of the middle class ranged from moderately conservative to liberal, favoring gradual and stable change. However, a newly developed middle class shows a much higher expectation for political reform and social progress. Not surprisingly, the rise of the middle class is empirically shown to be closely related to the rise of political pluralism in Taiwan.[52]

The change in the political realm over the past ten years was quite significant. In 1978, 57.1 percent of the electorate never talked about politics; in 1985 the percentage had dropped to 32.1 percent.[53] The people have become increasingly interested in and concerned with public and political affairs since the Chung-li incident in 1977. A citywide survey on the voting motives of the Taipei electorate, conducted by Hu Fu and You Ying-long in February 1981, was exceedingly revealing of the changing political attitudes and values.[54]

As Table 5.1 indicates, the reason "to exercise civil rights" or "to perform civic duties" were each mentioned by two-thirds of the voters. More significant, "to exercise civil rights" was cited by 47.4 percent and "to perform civic duties" was cited by 43.9 percent as the most important reason for taking part in the election. From these figures, it is reasonable to assume that the people in Taiwan have formed a role concept of the citizen and a participant orientation toward the political system. This probably can partially explain the relatively high turnout in elections (about 65 to 70 percent) in recent years. The survey also showed that one-fourth of the voters felt they were capable of influencing government policies, and nearly 12 percent said this was a most important reason for exercising the vote. That one perceives oneself as able to affect government policies means that one has a sense of political efficacy. In the present case, 24 percent of the voters have what Almond and Verba would label "citizen competence."[55] Admittedly this percentage is rather low in comparison with what Almond and Verba found in the United States (66 percent) and the United Kingdom (56 percent), but it is comparable to what they found in Italy (27 percent).[56]

Table 5.1  Reasons for Voting, Tapei Elecorate, 1981

| Reason for Voting | n | Mentioned % | Most Important % |
|---|---|---|---|
| To exercise civil rights | 519 | 68.8 | 47.3 |
| To perform civic duties | 498 | 66.0 | 43.9 |
| To express own views | 247 | 32.8 | 15.5 |
| To support the candidate he (she) likes | 228 | 32.8 | 12.2 |
| To influence government policies | 181 | 24.0 | 11.9 |
| Instructed by or advised by parties or other political groups | 98 | 13.0 | 5.6 |
| Urged by family members or relatives | 79 | 10.5 | 5.6 |
| Urged by neighborhood associations | 49 | 6.5 | 2.7 |
| Urged by organization he (she) belongs to | 38 | 5.0 | 2.3 |
| Candidates he (she) has acquaintance with | 28 | 3.7 | .9 |
| Urged by colleagues of the organization he (she) works for | 14 | 1.9 | .5 |
| Other | 15 | 2.0 | 1.7 |

Source: Hu Fu and YouYing-Long , "The Voting Motives of the Electorate," Journal of Social Science (Taipei, R.O.C.) 33 (October 1985): 6.

Note: Each survey respondent could cite one or more reasons for voting, and one or more reasons as most important. Total n = 747.

According to an islandwide survey conducted in 1985 by Hu Fu,[57] people in Taiwan have a high "subject competence" but relatively low "citizen competence."[58] As many as 85 percent of the persons 20 to 70 years of age said that they had the right to appeal to the government about its officials; that they expect officials to be responsive to the needs of the people; that they would express dissenting views on government policies, and so on. But only 13 percent of the people surveyed felt that they had the right to demand and to influence government policies. These findings indicate that the political culture of Taiwan in the early 1980s was a mixture of high "subject competence" and low "citizen competence." Nevertheless, it is interesting that a sizable percentage of respondents (42.8 percent) felt that they had the right to influence the assembly in the making of the rules. Hu explains that this was probably due to the fact that assemblymen, unlike bureaucrats, were elected, and concludes that elections in Taiwan have served well as a mechanism for political socialization. Hu's observation gives additional support to Rustow's argument that there is reciprocal influence between belief and action, democratic values and democratic practice. In the case under study, the forty-year-long practice of elections in Taiwan first at the local and provincial levels, then at national level, have developed gradually and deeply among the politicians and citizens a "habitual vision" of democratic participation and democratic competition. It can well be argued that this kind of democratic "habituation" has become an important source of changes in political values and attitudes.[59]

Table 5.1 shows that the electorate's reasons for voting, apart from fulfilling their rights or duties, were mainly for some explicit purpose, that is, to express one's own views (32.8 percent), to support particular candidates he (she) likes (30.2 percent), and especially to influence government policies (24 percent). In other word, voting has been seen as an instrument to achieve political purposes. Thus, it can be said that a considerable number of the voters have an instrumental-rational orientation towards voting. Some people's voting behavior was also affected by social and environmental forces, such as pressures from parties and other political groups (13 percent), from family members and relatives (10.5 percent), and so on. Yet the latter percentages were relatively low, suggesting that in the emerging political culture of Taiwan, what Huntington and Nelson call "mobilized participation"—participation that is not "self-motivated" but pressured from other sources—is declining. Put another way, political participation in Taiwan is becoming more mature and "autonomous."[60]

Also of note is the finding of Hu and You that the instrumental-rational orientation toward voting was positively correlated with the index of socioeconomic status and level of education. We argue that this is a rather promising phenomenon because education and industrialization have continuously been upgraded and developed in Taiwan.

Based on the survey data cited above, Hu Fu has given another analysis of the voters' orientation toward political issues, that further illuminates the emerging political culture in Taiwan. The pattern of voting showed that 58.9 percent of the voters were candidate-oriented; 38.7 percent political issues–oriented; 21 percent political organizations–oriented; 17.1 percent personal relations–oriented; 10 percent social relations–oriented; and 9.8 percent were based on other factors.[61] Of all types of voters, the political-issues-oriented are the most important because their attitudes inform us more about the changing political culture. It was found that about 42 percent of these voters gave their support to issues with an emphasis on national identity and national prestige; another 33.5 percent supported issues with an emphasis on political stability. Only 18 percent supported issues with an emphasis on political reform and democratization. Judging from the statistics, the great majority of the electorate in Taiwan had a strong psychological inclination to identify with the political system and to see the status quo maintained. They were not in favor of radical sociopolitical change of any kind. This observation is corroborated by Wei's study, which characterized Taiwan's opinion structure as a "moderate-supportive type."[62]

In light of the above analysis, we can say that the evolution of Taiwan's political culture shows a marked departure from Confucianism, but the influence of the latter is far from dead. Some characteristics of a civic culture are taking root. It probably is not too presumptuous to say that a kind of democratic culture is in the making.

## A Non-Paradigmatic Search

The relationship between modernization and democracy has long been one of the central interests for students of development. In the case of Taiwan, it seems that in the earlier phases of modernization, roughly up to the mid-1970s, the development-oriented, authoritarian power of the KMT did not face any serious societywide or structurally based political protests and challenges. Its legitimacy was, in large measure, justified by its capability in producing a very successful and equitable economy. And the political values and attitudes of that period seemed to be compatible with the people-oriented authoritarianism. However, in the later phase the very success of economic development produced a number of structural forces, including especially a growing middle class, that began to affect Taiwan's liberalization and democratization. As a result of the industrialization—but not caused by it—a new political culture that is more congenial to democracy has been evolving. Indeed, as Lucian Pye writes, "Taiwan is possibly the best working example of the theory that economic progress should bring in its wake democratic inclinations and a healthy surge of pluralism, which in time will undercut the foundations of the authoritarian rule common to developing countries."[63] In this connection, an empirical correlation does seem to exist between economic development and democracy in Taiwan, as was argued by Lipset. But Taiwan's transition to democracy would not be likely without the democratic engineering from above, particularly that of the charismatic leader President Chiang Ching-kuo. True enough, Chiang Ching-kuo himself was not immune to the structurally based democratic forces generated by the modernization he had helped to foster. It was not accidental that in December 1986, in a now-famous speech, he announced in no uncertain terms that the Chiang family members "cannot and will not" be his successors.

In his excellent study *State and Society in the Taiwan Miracle*, Thomas B. Gold concluded that "too many unique elements shaped Taiwan's experience to make it a viable model."[64] This is true insofar as Taiwan's modernization is concerned, and is particularly true with regard to Taiwan's democratization. There is no paradigm of democratic transition in the social science literature, and Taiwan's democratization, which took place in a unique social-historical context, had no paradigm to follow. It was a heroic, nonparadigmatic search for democracy. And Taiwan's case is not likely to be made a paradigm of democratic transition.[65] This of course does not mean that Taiwan's case is of no relevance to other countries in transition from authoritarianism/totalitarianism to democracy. The study of modernization is, after all, the study of both generalities and particularities.

The unique and nonduplicable elements of Taiwan's case apart, its generalizable features are of great value for the construction of a much-needed paradigm of democratic transition. To begin with, politics and the economy were intricately interrelated and interactive. The party-state, which was an "inhibited" political center, played a "big-push" role in the people-oriented economic development. The continuous success of economic development, with an equitable income distribution, generated powerful structural forces, including a sizable middle class. The newly emergent and expanding middle class had a strong identification with the political system, yet a desire for moderate and gradual democratic reform. In short, Taiwan's successful economic development fostered the emergence and development of a pluralistic society that, while harboring no animosity against the party-state, was strong enough to exert pressures upon the latter to be more responsible. And the continuing support of the people for the party-state in various elections, especially in the 1970s and 1980s, made the KMT leaders willing to commit themselves to electoral competition. In the same vein, the political challengers also found that electoral competition was a viable and effective route to power-sharing. In a significant way, the political contenders have consciously and unconsciously come to the realization of the necessity of a settled respect for the rules of games, what Robert Dahl called a "system of mutual security."[66]

In Taiwan, politics was never a mere epiphenomenon. The political system, though it was demonstratively influenced by economic development, has always been an autonomous force. The steady effort toward political development in the 1970s and 1980s, especially the giant step taken in 1986, were engineered from the very political center in which President Chiang played a decisive role. The importance of the top leadership should not be theoretically submerged in the sociologistic argument of structural determinism. To fully understand Taiwan's transition to democracy, the *politics* of development must be autonomously assessed parallel to and together with the *economics* of development.

True enough, economic development did produce significant changes of political attitudes and values. These attitudes and values show some characteristics of "civic culture" that depart markedly from Confucianism. Our study shows unambiguously that there was an empirical correlation between economic development and the emergence of political democracy. But what should not be overlooked is the fact that parallel to and independent of economic development, the nearly half-century-long practice of elections at local and provincial levels have institutionalized the values and "rules of the game" of democratic participation and competition. This attests forcefully Rustow's concept of "habituation" as an important source of democratic cultural change.

## Notes

1. This revised essay has benefited greatly from the comments of Dr. Ramon Myers and Dr. Larry Diamond. I am particularly indebted to the latter for his ingenious suggestions.

2. *Economic Development: Taiwan, Republic of China* (Taipei: Council for Planning and Development, 1987); and Ramon Myers, "The Republic of China on Taiwan: The Political Center, Economic Development and Democracy" (Paper presented to the Hoover Institution conference, Economy, Society and Democracy, 7-10 May 1992, Washington, DC), pp. 11-13.

3. Peter Berger, "Secularity—West and East" (Paper prepared for the Kakagakuiv University Centennial Symposium on Culture Identity and Modernization in Asian Countries, 11-13 September 1983).

4. Herman Kahn, *World Economic Development: 1979 and Beyond* (London: Croom Helm, 1979).

5. Max Weber, *The Religion of China,* trans. and ed. H. H. Gerth (New York: Free Press, 1964).

6. Thomas A. Metzger, *Escape from Predicament: Neo-Confucianism and China's Evolving Political Culture* (New York: Columbia University Press, 1977), pp. 234-235.

7. I have discussed this topic in "The Transformation of Confucianism in the Post-Confucian Era: The Emergence of Rationalistic Traditionalism in Hong Kong" (Paper prepared for the Conference on Confucian Ethics and the Modernization of Industrial Asia, The Institute of East-Asia Philosophies, Singapore, 5-9 January 1987).

8. Alexander Lu and Ya-li Lu, "Future Domestic Developments in the Republic of China on Taiwan," *Asian Survey* 25 (October 1985): 1075, 1095; Yangsun Chou and Andrew J. Nathan, "Democratizing Transition in Taiwan," *Asian Survey* 27 (March 1987): 277-299.

9. Ronald H. Chilcote, *Theories of Development and Underdevelopment* (Boulder: Westview Press, 1984), pp. 79-109.

10. Lucian W. Pye, *Asian Power and Politics: The Cultural Dimension of Authority* (Cambridge: Harvard University Press, 1985), p. 3.

11. Robert E. Ward and Dankwart Rustow, eds., *Political Development in Japan and Turkey* (Princeton: Princeton University Press, 1964), p. 5.

12. Gabriel L. Almond, *Political Development: Essays in Heuristic Theory* (Boston: Little, Brown, 1970), chaps. 5, 6. See also Almond, "The Development of Political Development," in M. Weiner and S.P. Huntington, eds., *Understanding Political Development* (Boston: Little, Brown, 1987), p. 449.

13. Wolfgang J. Mommsen, *The Age of Bureaucracy: Perspectives on the Political Sociology of Max Weber* (Oxford: Basil Blackwell, 1974), chap. 5. The pessimistic view of Weber on modernization is particularly discussed and criticized in Richard J. Bernstein, ed., *Habermas and Modernity* (Cambridge: Polity Press, 1985), pp. 1-66.

14. Peter Berger, Brigitte Berger, and Hansfried Kellner, *The Homeless Mind* (New York: Penguin Books, 1973), p. 15.

15. Talcott Parsons, *Structure and Process in Modern Societies* (New York: Free Press, 1960), p. 116.

16. Seymour M. Lipset, "Some Social Requisites of Democracy: Economic Development and Political Legitimacy," *American Political Science Review* 53 (March 1959): 80.

17. Dankwart E. Rustow, "Transition to Democracy: Toward a Dynamic Model," *Comparative Politics* 2 (April 1970): 337-364.

18. José Casanova, "Modernization and Democratization: Reflections on Spain's Transition to Democracy," *Social Research* 50 (Winter 1983): 929-973.

19. Thomas B. Gold, *State and Society in the Taiwan Miracle* (New York: M .E. Sharpe, 1986), p. 59.

20. The concept of "inhibited political center," which was originally developed by Thomas Metzger and later jointly elaborated by him and Ramon Myers, refers to a form of state-society relationship in which a highly differentiated, privatized society checks that center's power. The "inhibited" political center stands in contrast to the fully "subordinated" political center on the one hand and the "uninhibited" political center on the other. See Ramon A. Myers, "Political Theory and Recent Political Development in the Republic of China," *Asian Survey* 27 (September 1987): 1003-1022.

21. Michael Hsiao Hsin-huang, *Government Agricultural Strategies in Taiwan and South Korea* (Taipei: Institute of Ethnology, Academia Sincia, 1981), pp. 101-164.

22. Gold, *State and Society*, pp. 67-68.

23. Ibid., p. 90.

24. Arthur J. Vidich, "Legitimation of Regimes in World Perspective," in A .J. Vidich and R. M. Glassman, eds., *Conflict and Control* (London: Sage, 1979), p. 299.

25. Wei Yong, "March Towards a Stable, Harmonious and Innovative Society: An Analysis of the Trend of Political Development Based on the Results of Six Public Opinion Surveys" (Taiwan: R. O. C. publication 5 May 1986; in Chinese)

26. Michael Hsin-huang Hsiao, "The Development Experience of Taiwan Society: From Colonialism to Capitalism" (Paper prepared for the Conference on the Development Experience of Modern Chinese Areas and the Future of China, Taipei, National Chengchi University, 24-26 December 1987; in Chinese), pp. 11-12. For countries with highly unequal income distributions, the Gini coefficient typically lies between 0.50 and 0.70. A coefficient between 0.20 and 0.35 indicates a relatively equitable distribution. (Zero is perfect equality and one perfect inequality.)

27. John F. Cooper, "Political Development in Taiwan," in Hungdah Chiun, ed., *China and the Taiwan Issue* (New York: Praeger, 1979), pp. 37-73.

28. Neil H. Jacoby, *Aid to Taiwan: A Study of Foreign Aid, Self-Help and Development* (New York: Praeger, 1966), p. 11.

29. Cooper, "Political Development."

30. Douglas Mendel, *The Politics of Formosan Nationalism* (Berkeley: University of California Press, 1970), pp. 114-217.

31. Ming-min Peng, *A Taste of Freedom* (New York: Holt, Rinehart & Winston, 1972).

32. Mingsien Lee, "Political Change in Taiwan, 1949-1974: A Study of the Processes of Democratic and Integrative Change with Focus on the Role of Government" (Ph.D. diss., University of Tennessee, 1975), pp. 87-92.

33. Ibid., p. 112.

34. Cooper, "Political Development," pp. 37-73.

35. Lu, "Future Domestic Developments," pp. 1089-1091.

36. Gold, *State and Society*, p. 3.

37. Ibid., p. 130, Gold's characterization of Taiwan's political system as "ossified" is not quite accurate from my viewpoint, which will be made clear later in this paper.

38. John F. Cooper, "Taiwan's Recent Election: Progress Toward a Democratic System," *Asian Survey* 21 (October 1981).

39. Chou and Nathan, "Democratizing Transition in Taiwan," p. 278.

40. Pye, *Asian Power*, p. 223.

41. Myers, "Political Theory and Recent Political Development," p. 1018.

42. *Chung-yang jik-pao*, 12 November 1986, p. 2. The translation is by Myers, ibid., p. 1007.

43. Larry Diamond, "Beyond Authoritarianism and Totalitarianism: Strategies for Democratization," *Washington Quarterly* (Winter 1989): 151.

44. R. W. Wilson, *Learning to Be Chinese: The Political Socialization of Children in Taiwan* (Cambridge: MIT Press, 1970), p. 106.

45. R. W. Wilson, "A Comparison of Political Attitudes of Taiwanese Children and Mainlander Children in Taiwan," *Asian Survey* 8 (December 1968): 992-998.

46. Sheldon Appleton, "The Social and Political Impact of Education in Taiwan," *Asian Survey* 16 (August 1976): 704-716.

47. Cooper, "Political Development."

48. Consul Tu Wei-ming, "Confucianism: Symbols and Substance in Recent Time," in R. W. Wilson, A. A. Wilson, and S. L. Greenblatt, eds., *Values Change in Chinese Society* (New York: Praeger, 1979), pp. 21-51.

49. *Mencius* VIIb. 14.

50. Lee, "Political Change in Taiwan," pp. 148, 211.

51. Yow-suen Sun, "A Preliminary Analysis of the Class Structure in Taiwan" (Research paper, Sociology Department, University of Hawaii, 1986). Quoted in Hsiao, "The Development Experience of Taiwan," p. 5. *Middle class* refers to self-employed entrepreneurs and managers as well as professionals in the industrial and commercial sectors.

52. Lang-li Wen, "Structural Correlates of Emerging Political Pluralism in Taiwan" (Paper prepared for the International Conference on Taiwan, R.O.C.; A Newly Industrialized Society, 3-5 September 1987).

53. Wei, "March Towards a Stable . . . Society."

54. F. Hu and Ying-long You, "The Voting Motives of the Electorate" (in Chinese) *Journal of Social Science* (National Taiwan University, Taipei) 33 (October 1985): 34. My analysis of the changing political culture in Taiwan is mainly based on their study. I am grateful to Professor Hu Fu for his generosity in providing me with many of his works.

55. Gabriel A. Almond and Sidney Verba, *The Civic Culture* (Boston: Little, Brown, 1965), pp. 168-185.

56. Ibid., p. 173.

57. F. Hu, "The People's Attitudes Towards Political Participation" (in Chinese) (Paper prepared for Symposium on Basic Research on Taiwan's Social Change, National Taiwan University, Academia Sincia, 28-30 August 1987).

58. Almond and Verba define *subject competence* as follows: "The competence of the subject is more a matter of being aware of his rights under the rules than of participating the making of the rules," *The Civic Culture*, p. 169.

59. Rustow, "Transitions to Democracy," pp. 344-345, 358-361.

60. S. P. Huntington and J. M. Nelson, *No Easy Choice: Political Participation in Developing Countries* (Cambridge: Harvard University Press, 1976).

61. The sum of these figures exceeds 100 percent because voters could give more than one answer to the question, "Why did you vote for him (her)?" See Hu Fu, "Voters' Orientation Towards Political Issues: An Analysis of Structure, Type and Practice" (in Chinese), *Journal of Social Science* (National Taiwan University, Taipei) 34 (June 1986).

62. Wei, "March Towards a Stable . . . Society."

63. Pye, *Asian Power*, p. 233.

64. Gold, *State and Society*, p. 132.

65. Samuel Huntington suggested that the particular conjunctions of circumstances that created the world's democracies are not likely to be repeated. See his "Will More Countries Become Democratic?" *Political Science Quarterly* 99

(September 1984): 193-218.

66. Robert Dahl, *Polyarchy: Participation and Opposition* (New Haven: Yale University Press, 1971), p. 36.

# • 6 •

# Autonomous Groups as Agents of Democratic Change in Communist and Post-Communist Eastern Europe

## *Christine M. Sadowski*

For more than forty years, one of the major goals of communism in Eastern Europe was the creation of an "ideal socialist citizenry," obedient to state directives and to centrally formulated policy. Communism attempted to impose, from above, a political culture of allegiance among citizens to programs determined by a narrowly defined ruling elite. In doing so, it prohibited the expression of independent initiatives and punished deviations from the centrally determined "grand plan." Yet the decade of the 1980s proved that autonomous groups, independent of state sponsorship and thus technically illegal under the Marxist-Leninist order, could and did emerge; pursued goals independent of state directives, and hence contrary to the wishes of the ruling elite; and in some cases achieved those goals in East European communist systems. The decade was a period of confrontation between an imposed communist political culture that was never fully integrated into the societies at large, and an indigenous, anticommunist political culture that found its fullest expression in the ranks of the grassroots opposition in some of these countries.

This chapter examines the sociopolitical impact of this seemingly oxymoronic phenomenon of autonomous groups, as an emerging (or reemerging) expression of political culture, in Marxist-Leninist systems. It treats autonomous groups not as anomalies within communist systems nor as mere "dissent" from the enforced status quo but, rather, as strains or remnants of earlier political cultures in East European societies that promoted self-initiative and grassroots efforts. Moreover, autonomous groups in communist Eastern Europe are viewed as the paradoxical result of citizens' attempts to circumvent the rigid structures of totalitarianism and authoritarianism. Finally, note is taken of the manner in which communism left an unmistakable mark on the political cultures of this region during the early stages of postcommunism.

Autonomous groups refer to a form of voluntary association in that they were created by their memberships and functioned outside the sponsorship of the state. They differed from many voluntary associations in the West in that their members formed more of a "community" (with respect to personal bonds) than an "organization" (where ties are more impersonal). They had identifiable memberships, clearly defined goals, and some measure of organizational cohesion. It is precisely these characteristics that distinguished them from other forms of opposition, such as letter-writing campaigns or petitions and resolutions signed and sponsored by an ad hoc gathering of individuals.

Only the groups whose purpose was to initiate change in society are examined here, thus excluding clubs whose sole purpose was social or hobby-oriented.[1] Many of the autonomous groups discussed in this analysis existed illegally and operated at various levels of the underground, while others, though illegal, operated aboveground. In addition, the Gorbachev phenomenon broadened the scope of the types of organizations some states, namely Poland and Hungary, were willing to accommodate (even prior to the changes that swept the region in late 1989) either through legal registration or through tacit approval that lacked any official recognition. Such autonomous groups, incorporated into the official and semiofficial sociopolitical landscape, were also a major component of the push for change from below in Eastern Europe.

Six countries are examined here: Poland, Hungary, Czechoslovakia, the German Democratic Republic (GDR), Bulgaria and Romania. The analysis begins by considering the barriers built into Marxist-Leninist systems to prevent the emergence of autonomous groups, to suppress self-initiated participation in the political process, and to enforce the role of citizen as "political subject." I then explore how, by the late 1970s, these barriers to grass-roots organization were circumvented or destroyed in some East European societies. How did previously "atomized" individuals manage to come together to pursue a common cause? What role did the precommunist political cultures of these societies play?

The second section describes the functions these autonomous groups served, and analyzes the extent to which they laid the foundation for the dramatic changes of 1989 and reasserted a more democratic, pluralistic political culture. The third section shows how autonomous groups altered the structure of power and the nature of legitimacy in some East European countries, and how their introduction of the notion of accountability changed the equation. It also describes the extent to which these groups were able to construct their own institutions and invoke a precommunist political culture to serve their organizational goals. The fourth section examines the role played by autonomous groups in the tumultuous changes that swept Eastern Europe in 1989, both in mobilizing mass protests and in helping to establish new, more democratic systems of government. Finally, the conclusion evaluates the legacy of communist political cultures in contemporary Eastern Europe and considers the prospects and challenges for democracy.

## The Barriers to Democratic Political Culture
## in Communist Systems

Although no sociopolitical system can completely fulfill its own "ideal-type" requirements, it is important to consider its ultimate goals when evaluating the real and potential impact it has on society as a whole. In Marxist-Leninist systems, the barriers to democratic political culture are constructed through a comprehensive ideology and elaborate state policies aimed at atomizing citizens, destroying communities, and controlling the resources necessary for independent action. Punishment for taking part in independent activities—outside the direct sponsorship of the state and therefore "contrary" to its interests—include expulsion from the country, internal exile, lengthy prison sentences, expulsion from one's profession, or payment of exorbitant fines aimed at ruining a person's life financially. Such punishments were enforced to varying degrees in all Marxist-Leninist countries in Eastern Europe.

In addition, in "ideal-type" Marxist-Leninist systems, the state exercises complete control over all forms of activity in society: political, economic, and social. Mass voluntary associations are created and sponsored by the state, which, in turn, uses the organizations to communicate its directives and to implement its policies. If approved by an enforced system of registration, other voluntary associations can be established, but only if their goals do not conflict or overlap with those of the mass organizations sponsored by the state. Thus, competition among groups is prevented.[2]

Through the system of registration, the state controls the resources necessary for the establishment and functioning of voluntary associations. Meeting places and the ability to publicize association goals or to collect membership dues are all part of the package of benefits given to those organizations that register. Unregistered organizations are, of course, denied all rights and privileges.[3]

### Resisting and Navigating the Barriers

For decades these barriers were effective in preventing the establishment of organized, cohesive groups with well-thought-out demands, strategies, and goals, as is evidenced in particular by the common pattern of blue-collar opposition in Eastern Europe, spanning the entire period from 1953 through 1987. Repeatedly, the scenario began with workers calling a wildcat strike at an enterprise. From there they marched to the town square, where they were joined by well-wishing onlookers, and then to the local party headquarters to shout anticommunist slogans and wage-related demands. As the crowd became enraged at the lack of any response, it stormed the headquarters, destroying the symbols of communism and looting the premises.[4] The security forces or military then broke up the crowds with clubs, water cannon, or

guns. Each incident varied somewhat, but the sequence of events was strikingly similar in Berlin and Pilsen in 1953, Poznan in 1956, Novocherkassk
in 1962, Gdansk and Szczecin in 1970, Radom in 1976, and Brasov in
1987.[5] In some cases where workers attempted on their own to establish permanent representation through workers' councils or ongoing strike committees, their efforts were dismantled by the security apparatus.[6]

Barriers to independent action also had an impact on patterns of opposition among the intelligentsia. In contrast to the "bread-and-butter" issues of
the working class, the primary concern of the intelligentsia had always been
freedom of expression. Not surprisingly, its members used the written word
as their principal weapon, confronting elites directly through petitions signed
by *ad hoc* gatherings of individuals wishing to participate in a specific
action, or through publication of open letters in émigré journals. In each
case, petitions and letters addressed well-defined issues, often of limited
scope, focusing by and large on a particular injustice or grievance, or an
unfair aspect of the system, or offering advice on how a certain situation
should be handled. Rarely was there an official response. Oftentimes, participants were blacklisted and the publication of their professional work was
banned. Some, of course, suffered more direct reprisals ranging from outright harassment and physical intimidation to expulsion from the country.
But rarely were intellectuals punished for their activities with the type of
brutality reserved for blue-collar workers and farmers.

When intellectuals formed an organization, it primarily took the form of
a discussion club that established limited opportunities for freedom of
speech within well-defined circles. The primacy of this organizational form
was particularly evident during the period of "the thaw" following the death
of Stalin. Beginning in 1955, forums for free discussion, calling themselves
the "Crooked Circle Clubs," sprang up throughout Poland. Within a matter
of months, 120 such circles came into existence. By 1962 they were officially banned.[7]

Similarly in Hungary in 1956, discussion clubs called the "Petofi
Circles" became extremely popular among the intelligentsia, although their
expansion and development came to an abrupt halt with the Soviet invasion
in October of that year.[8] In the cases of both the "Crooked Circle Clubs" and
the "Petofi Circles," the goals of these informal groups did not go beyond
discussions of topics not normally open for debate in the wider society —
particularly subjects of current political and economic concern. Finally, both
in Poland and Hungary, these groups included party members of high rank
who were prominent participants in the discussions.

Dissension within the writers' unions was also a characteristic feature of
movements for reform in Poland and Hungary in 1956 and Czechoslovakia
in 1968. During union congresses, writers spoke up vehemently for an end to
censorship and the rehabilitation of colleagues who had been blacklisted.
Many union members who were prominent as both writers and communists

led the campaign for freedom of speech.[9]

By the late 1980s identical phenomena were occurring in the German Democratic Republic and in Bulgaria. Members of the East German Writers' Union were demanding greater freedom of expression and publication of the works of previously banned authors.[10] In Bulgaria, at the March 1989 Congress of the Writers' Union, some of the members severely criticized the union leadership for its failure to support *glasnost*. Principal proponents of the movement for freedom of speech, many of whom were members of the Communist Party and some of whom were members of new autonomous groups in Bulgaria, were elected to the union leadership.[11]

Although the patterns of opposition that had workers storming local Communist Party headquarters and intellectuals initiating letter-writing campaigns and establishing discussion clubs continued through the 1980s, by the 1970s these were no longer the only patterns of organized opposition in Eastern Europe. During the 1970–1971 strikes in Gdansk and Szczecin, Polish workers had returned to their shipyards to stage a sitdown strike and to formulate a specific set of demands, including official recognition of their strike committees as permanent representatives.[12] It was also during those strikes that the idea of free trade unions was first articulated. By the late 1970s, free trade union cells arose in Poland with the goal of creating a permanent representative body for the working class that was independent of state sponsorship and control. Intellectuals in Poland and Czechoslovakia established action-oriented autonomous groups with defined memberships and clearly stated goals of an ongoing nature. In the German Democratic Republic, small groups began to form under the aegis of the Protestant churches, pursuing goals of peace and demilitarization. In Hungary, a small group of intellectuals set out to create a permanent forum for free expression through creation of an underground press.

The formation of such autonomous groups in communist systems raises two major questions. First, how did previously "atomized" individuals manage to come together to pursue a common cause in opposition to the dictates of the state; and, second, how did they establish the bases of their operations and find the resources necessary to build their structures? In answer to the first question, each of these societies had been a breeding ground for opposition since the illegitimate establishment of communist rule. Never were these citizens fully "atomized." In his famous essay, "The Power of the Powerless," Vaclav Havel emphasized that disillusionment was constant in East European societies and that at the lowest "prepolitical" levels of society, "opposition," in its broadest sense, occurred on a daily basis. It was manifested in the private lives of individuals long before it emerged on the visible surface of society.[13] Moreover, in addition to the regular "prepolitical" expression of dissent at the grassroots, informal networks developed to help citizens circumvent state barriers in meeting their daily needs. Because "highly valued and needed resources [were] constantly in scarce supply, informal channels and social networks [became] absolutely *vital* for the day to day existence of virtually *all* East Europeans."[14] This combination of widespread personal opposition and well-established informal networks provided citizens with a certain readiness for other types of collective behavior. Paradoxically, it was precisely the overly restrictive measures meant to control individuals that in fact encouraged them to seek out and practice means of circumventing state control.

Finally, and perhaps most important, East Europeans, while adapting to the realities of communism, never fully internalized its values. Societies remained committed to their precommunist political cultures at least in their private, if not their public, lives. Prior to the World War II, the northern tier countries (Poland, Czechoslovakia, and Hungary) had a brief experience with some measure of democratic rule; the southern tier countries (Romania and Bulgaria) did not. By and large, citizens in all of these countries viewed their communist governments as *illegitimate*; grudgingly took part in various forms of *enforced political participation* (such as mandatory voting, mass demonstrations of support for the system, and participation in communist-sponsored social organizations); and found communism to be a *politically inefficacious* system when it came to bringing about necessary change. The general instability of the region, therefore, should come as less of a surprise than its periods of relative stability. During the stable periods, citizens employed certain mechanisms of accommodation, such as the informal networks described above, that helped them cope with what most considered to be an illegitimate political system.

To be sure, state and party controls over autonomous activities varied in intensity throughout the region. For example, leaders in Hungary and Poland exercised something of a grudging tolerance toward such activities, while the leaders of Romania and Czechoslovakia were far more determined to prevent or eradicate independent grassroots activities through systematic repression. In the late 1970s in Bulgaria, there were no attempts at establishing permanent autonomous groups, although individual actors continued to emerge as independent voices in society. Attempts to form independent movements in Romania in the late 1970s failed. In the GDR, those groups that emerged under the protection of the churches were more successful in establishing a permanency than were groups that emerged "unprotected." In Czechoslovakia, Charter 77 and VONS were the only independent groups that emerged in the late 1970s and, despite severe repression against them by the security apparatus, continued to exist through the 1980s.[15] Finally, in Poland and Hungary, the reluctant and partial tolerance of the political leadership evolved as new autonomous groups encountered less official repression than similar groups elsewhere in the region. It was particularly in Poland that the phenomenon of autonomous groups began to flourish, culminating first in the establishment of the Solidarity trade union in 1980 and later in the virtual explosion of smaller underground independent movements during the period of martial law and normalization.

In each of these countries, however, the establishment of autonomous groups was a violation of the law. It was thus a rejection of the existing rules—an act of civil disobedience—and represented a decision among the independent actors to distance themselves from the existing system. In each country, this required that daring individuals test the waters to determine how successful they might be in establishing themselves as a group and then pursuing their stated goals. At first, none of these groups was registered with the Ministry of Interior as mandated by law; many espoused goals that overlapped with existing state-sponsored mass organizations, thus challenging the state's monopoly on group activity; and others pursued activities that could clearly be deemed contrary to the official interests of the state (such as the goal of demilitarization held by the semiautonomous groups in the GDR).

## Mobilizing Resources and Overcoming Constraints

How did these groups establish their operations and find the resources to build their structures? Here, circumvention of the existing barriers required that autonomous groups seek their own material resources independent of the state—and, in some cases, create their own separate institutions and communication networks to facilitate their activities. The acquisition of some material resources was rather straightforward. For example, groups could hold meetings in private apartments (albeit clandestinely) rather than in public meeting rooms officially designated by the state. Laws prohibiting the collection of dues by organizations not registered with the state could be ignored outright, as they were through various fund-raising activities initiated by these illegal groups. What was more problematic (to vastly differing degrees in the various countries of Eastern Europe) was the acquisition of resources that were needed to develop a means of communication through *samizdat* publication. Poland was a special case in this regard; autonomous group activists employed techniques of underground publication that had been used during World War II resistance efforts,[16] clandestinely accessed state printing presses during non-working hours, and received modern copy, offset, and printing equipment from Western organizations via underground networks. Such resources provided the infrastructure for the largest, most extensive underground publishing endeavor in the region.

By contrast, in Czechoslovakia, autonomous group activists, facing far more restrictive barriers against self-publication, continued to employ the more primitive technique of typing multiple copies on regular typewriters. Entire books were duplicated and circulated in this form.[17] In the GDR, autonomous groups existing around the churches were able to use church resources for their publicity needs.[18] In Hungary, independent publishing endeavors often secretly used official printing presses.

Strategies were also devised to counteract government barriers against autonomous group activity. For example, in both Poland and Hungary, independent insurance funds were established among underground publishers to protect them against the losses incurred when their equipment was confiscated by security forces. Funds were set up in Poland, from private donations, to reimburse activists for fines levied against them in the course of their independent pursuits or for wages lost during strikes. Such strategies attempted to guarantee the success of autonomous group activity by alleviating the financial burden imposed by the government as a penalty for "opposition." Obviously, when governments imprisoned or expelled activists, counterstrategies were more difficult to devise. Still, opportunities were created at the grassroots level, in some countries, to enhance autonomous group activity.

Organizational skills were likewise tapped as a resource. In some cases, individuals participating in the formation of autonomous groups were veteran opposition activists who had become known to a wider audience for positions of dissent they had held since the early to mid-1950s. Their strategies of opposition to the status quo had been developed and practiced during the decades of communist rule. In other cases, older individuals were able to access organizational know-how developed and practiced either prior to or during World War II. Such skills had been gained through participation in a very wide variety of organizations, from free trade unions and democratic political parties to clandestine resistance movements operating under conditions of war. Thus, inadequate organizational skills were not the barrier they were once thought to be in Poland, Czechoslovakia, or Hungary—countries that had enjoyed a short though very important period of democracy in the interwar period. By contrast, in Romania and Bulgaria, countries that had virtually no experience with democracy, the lack of organizational skills and civic-mindedness necessary for the formation of autonomous groups proved a rather insurmountable barrier to grass-roots endeavors for change.

There was one other major barrier to independent action, more subjective in nature and far more difficult to measure. Indeed, its collapse could be seen only in the change in behavior among groups in society. This was the barrier of fear used to control, direct, encourage, or prevent certain forms of public activity among East European citizens. Exactly when that fear began to erode is impossible to specify; but it became increasingly evident, at different points in time in different countries, that fear was indeed on the wane.[19]

The most important factor that contributed to the breakdown of barriers to independent action, and perhaps to the erosion of fear as a mechanism of control, was Mikhail Gorbachev's program of reform in the Soviet Union. First, it raised hopes and expectations among East Europeans that a similar course of political and economic reform would be adopted in their countries, thus placing pressure on those party leaders most resistant to change.[20]

Second, the Soviet program of reform signaled, to an originally incredulous Eastern Europe, that individual countries were on their own, expected to solve their own problems, and free to do so without the ominous threat of the Brezhnev Doctrine. Because the Brezhnev Doctrine had long served as the ultimate linchpin guaranteeing conformity among Soviet bloc nations, its demise as a plausible policy marked the onset of new opportunities for independent action never before possible in post–World War II Eastern Europe. It was, indeed, at this point that pressures for change from below increased precipitously.

Nevertheless, it is important to keep in mind that Gorbachev's reform programs and the concomitant loosening of the Soviet Union's political stranglehold over Eastern Europe was the catalyst for very rapid changes that had begun years earlier in Poland and Hungary and, to a lesser extent, in the GDR and Czechoslovakia. Let us turn, now, to examine the nature of some of those changes.

## The Functions of Autonomous Groups in Communist Eastern Europe

Despite official barriers to autonomous group activity, these groups emerged and served a number of important functions in East European societies, both on a daily basis and in preparation for events to come. The manifest functions, of course, were reflected in the stated goals of these autonomous groups: for example, compelling domestic leaderships to observe the international covenants they had signed on human and civil rights, demanding the observance of old policies and the adoption of new ones to protect the natural environment, promoting peace and demilitarization, and defending the rights of ethnic minority groups. There were many cases in which such goals were actually achieved. Poland's autonomous Workers' Defense Committee (KOR), for one, achieved all of its goals within a year, at which point the group adopted broader objectives and changed its name to reflect the expansion of its goals.[21] The Solidarity trade union achieved its goal of obtaining legal status and formal registration not once but twice under communist rule.[22] The Freedom and Peace Movement (WiP) in Poland won the provision it sought for alternative military service and it did so in 1988, while the country was still under communist rule. Ecological groups in Hungary managed to persuade the government, in May 1989, to abandon plans for construction of a dam deemed threatening to the natural environment.[23]

In addition to their stated goals, these autonomous groups were also involved in publicizing the problems of society. This was a particularly important function in the communist setting because restrictions on freedom of speech precluded open discussion of such issues, and especially exposure of the shortcomings of the political and socioeconomic order. Thus, human rights groups not only pressured governments to observe international law but also monitored government activities, collecting information on specific human rights violations and publicizing it both domestically (through an underground press or through organized public demonstrations) and internationally (through direct communication with Western human rights organizations).

One of the best examples of publicity-seeking activities organized by autonomous groups in Eastern Europe was the staging, in November 1988, of "Romania Action Day." Since Romanians themselves had been unable to organize protests in their own behalf to denounce Ceausescu's abominable human rights record, they became a major rallying point for demonstrations among numerous opposition groups in the GDR, Poland, Czechoslovakia, and especially Hungary, with similar demonstrations occurring simultaneously in several Western European countries.[24] The protests in Eastern Europe were met with varying degrees of repression by security forces, they did call attention to the plight of Romanians living under the Ceausescu regime.

Even where the specific goals of autonomous groups were not directly achieved, their pursuit oftentimes resulted in a "reaction" on the part of the government that in some way reflected those goals. For example, the 1988 decision on the part of the government of Czechoslovakia to sponsor an official human rights forum came in response to pressures from autonomous human rights groups. Likewise, the East German government's declaration that it was itself a "peace movement" was a response to mounting pressures from independent peace movements within that society. Although such "reactions" by the state can certainly be viewed as self-serving propaganda aimed at co-opting truly independent movements, they would not have been taken had it not been for the threat posed by the activities of autonomous groups.

There were, finally, many examples of governments in communist Eastern Europe offering "concessions without conceding" in response to mounting pressures from autonomous groups. General Jaruzelski had worked out a scheme for a Consultative Council that was to appease the demands of Solidarity activists and other opposition groups for direct citizen input into the decisionmaking process. This was viewed by the Polish government as a "compromise," but in no way did it meet Solidarity's demand to be relegalized, which would have guaranteed it a regular, institutionalized voice in decisions regarding union matters.[25] In Czechoslovakia, the government decided in 1988 to allow Alexander Dubcek to travel to Italy to accept personally his honorary doctorate at the University of Bologna. Although decision was not undertaken in direct response to specific group demands, it no doubt sought to mollify increasing popular unrest in the society. Such "concessions without conceding" were in fact changes brought about by the pressures of autonomous groups.

Often unstated by the groups was the fact that pursuit of their specific goals in a communist state required systemic change incompatible with the tenets of the existing ideology and structure of power. Strict adherence to international covenants on human and civil rights and to domestic constitutions that reflected those rights (at least in theory) would inevitably shake the foundations of the existing totalitarian or authoritarian order. Freedom of expression, assembly, and conscience and the right to free elections with secret ballots pave the way to political pluralism.[26] This is all the more true if one accepts the argument that although political pluralism may be suppressed, it does in fact exist in all modern societies.[27] Independent ecological movements challenged, on the one hand, state policy to increase material output at all costs and, on the other, linked pollution to the issue of citizen rights to a clean and healthy environment.[28] Thus, autonomous groups called into question the entire communist system.

In addition to their manifest functions, autonomous groups had a profound impact through their latent functions, at both the macrolevel and microlevel of society. At the macrolevel, by virtue of their existence and ability to function, these groups signaled to others that such activity was at least possible. In providing such a signal, they encouraged others to become active. The degree of repression against opposition voices in Eastern Europe had long served as a barometer of the general political climate. Thus, the very ability of these groups to organize indicated to others in society that something had changed—whether that change was in fact real or perceived. It marked in some of these societies (notably East Germany, Poland, Czechoslovakia, and Hungary) the emergence of an alternative political culture that was developing in response to communist repression.

As mentioned earlier, fear, the major mechanism of control in communist systems, began to diminish for some individuals, thereby further encouraging activism in others. To the extent that members of such groups represented a revitalization of social morality, they served "as a 'gauge' of honesty and courage against which people judge[d] their own and others' behavior."[29] They often provided heroes to larger circles of passive supporters who had been greatly demoralized by decades of communist rule. It is true that most activists in these autonomous groups were completely unknown to individuals outside their tightly knit circles, but the autonomous group phenomenon in communist Eastern Europe did produce popular heroes such as Lech Walesa, who was very much a symbol of honesty and courage and an inspiration to millions of people in Poland and abroad.

Autonomous groups pursuing self-proclaimed goals altered the structure of power and eroded the legitimacy and authority of the East European political elite. Such groups introduced noncommunist elements into communist systems where the incompatibility of elements could not be tolerated by the existing structures. In assuming goals akin to those of the state-sponsored mass organizations, they introduced an element of pluralism and competition into these systems for the first time in decades. In Poland and Hungary, even prior to the massive changes that swept the region in 1989, some autonomous groups whose goals overlapped with those of the state-sponsored organizations and agencies had actually been allowed to register legally. The very fact that autonomous groups adopted goals that had previously fallen within the exclusive jurisdiction of state-controlled organizations made a clear statement about the ineffectiveness of the officially created, government-sanctioned, mass voluntary associations, and the extent of unmet national needs. After all, each country had an officially sponsored mass organization whose purpose was to preserve nature. Why, then, the need for a grassroots ecological movement? Each had a state-sponsored voluntary or professional agency assigned the task of providing care to the needy. Why, then, the emergence of self-help organizations, particularly in a system that boasted about its commitment to the social and economic rights of its citizens? Each country had official trade unions that claimed to represent the interests of the working class. Why, then, the need for independent unions?[30]

The emergence of multiple *illegal* autonomous groups, established with their own sense of permanency and long-term objectives, created instability in a political system that prohibited their existence. Whether the state had tried and failed to break the back of the autonomous groups or whether it had chosen to tolerate and ignore them, its monolithic power was undermined. In Poland and Hungary, where the autonomous group phenomenon was most developed throughout the 1980s, the laws on voluntary associations in those countries became obsolete; they no longer reflected the reality of the situation at hand. This contradiction strained the sociopolitical order as well as the judicial system. In fact, one of the first orders of business undertaken by the reform-minded party leaders of Hungary following the ouster of Janos Kadar was the redrafting of the existing laws on voluntary associations to reflect the new reality.

Finally, as a latent function on the macrolevel of society, autonomous groups undermined communist policies aimed at atomizing citizens and breaking apart communities. This was especially true because of the close bonds that were created between group members acting together in defiance of the state and oftentimes at great personal risk. In many respects, the repression these group members faced in the course of their activities was a "rite of passage" that served to underline their shared commitment to the cause.

There were still other latent functions served by these autonomous groups at the microlevel of society. For one, members of autonomous groups got practice in the art of self-organization and in the strategy of confronting political elites. The development of both organizational skills and strategy was problematic on two counts. First, despite the fact that some older activists were able to tap organizational skills developed during the precommunist period, decades of communist political restrictions left most would-be activists in a position of having to learn the rules of self-initiated organizational behavior.[31] Second, the phenomenon of grassroots organizations systematically pressing for change in communist systems was new in these societies, and thus the strategy for confronting elites was uncharted. Participation in autonomous groups offered members the opportunity to learn skills and strategies and to develop new ones. As a consequence, autonomous groups, whether involved specifically in peace initiatives or ecological matters, were able to provide their acquired organizational expertise, in turn, to the disorganized masses demanding change from below. This was the case during the mobilization of the Solidarity movement in August 1980, when striking workers provided the power for change, while autonomous groups, including KOR, the Free Trade Union Movement, and Young Poland, provided the organizational expertise, as well as the local, national, and international communications network.[32] By 1989 (as I describe below) autonomous groups throughout the region lent their expertise to the increasingly restive masses. In 1981 Vilem Precan, reporting on the progress of Charter 77, wrote that "the quality of . . . future changes will be in part determined by the results of the preparatory work in that period of immobility and lifelessness that appeared to be a vacuum, but that in reality was filled with strivings to preserve, regenerate and re-cultivate."[33] Throughout Eastern Europe, early autonomous group activity served the function of accumulating experience and know-how that could later be tapped by others seeking change.

The community of autonomous group activists provided a steady forum for the open discussion of ideas. The individuals who regularly contributed their writings to the Hungarian underground publication *Beszelo* are a case in point. Although they themselves did not constitute a group with the expressed purpose of achieving a specific goal, their contributions to the journal did reflect the common purpose of free discourse. It was in this publication that many of the possibilities for future change in Hungarian society were first formulated. Likewise, it was in the Polish underground publication *Robotnik*, in the late 1970s, that the initial set of demands, later put forth by Polish workers in their August 1980 strikes, was first discussed. It is doubtful that the ideas and formulations of single individuals, acting in isolation or outside the parameters of an established group, however informal, could have had the same impact on the Polish events of that summer.

Oftentimes, members of autonomous groups gained practice in the art of gathering accurate information in societies where strict censorship was enforced. They needed the information in order to strengthen their arguments, formulate their demands, and be perceived as credible actors in the eyes of the broader public, or the ruling elite, or the West. Because access to information is itself a form of power, communist elites had long withheld accurate or complete data and news coverage from nonelites in society.

Thus, the ability of autonomous groups to obtain correct information provided them if not with power *per se* then with a weapon they could use against the rulers.

Accurate and truthful information, in turn, served other functions for the autonomous groups. It substantially contributed to their legitimacy among the broader masses; it opened up avenues for genuine discourse, real debate, and the expression of ideas and demands; and it increased the efficacy and the authority of the actors involved. In short, it provided a basis for the establishment of an alternative political culture.

Moreover, all of these microlevel latent functions taken together—practice in the art of self-organization and in the strategy of confronting elites, access to forums for open discussion of ideas and programs, experience in collecting accurate information—formed the basis for cultivation of an alternative political leadership. Most activists in the autonomous groups had not been known to the wider public. Their work in these organizations, especially considering the personal risks involved, demonstrated their commitment to a set of political ideals and provided them with political credentials that could later be presented to wider groups within society. Such credentials came in handy long before the dramatic changes of late 1989. It was during Solidarity's heyday in 1980–1981 that Adam Michnik arrived at a scene in Otwock where an angry crowd was threatening to lynch a police officer. He intervened in the corporal's behalf, introducing himself to the crowd by saying, "I am Adam Michnik. I am an anti-socialist force," referring to the label given KOR members by the official Communist Party daily. This evidence of his credentials as an opposition activist was met with applause by the group who had gathered.[34] By 1989, in each of the six countries, those credentials proved not only useful but crucial in the hurried establishment of new leaderships.

## The Power of Autonomous Groups in Communist Eastern Europe

Initially, the autonomous groups that emerged under communism were thought to be of only limited significance, given their impotence in a context lacking meaningful channels for the articulation of interests and other institutions to accommodate and implement change. However, the power of autonomous groups to initiate change was demonstrated through the numerous functions they performed, as shown in the previous section. In some cases, autonomous groups were able to achieve their specific goals; in other cases, they provoked a reaction on the part of leaders, who made public overtures in the direction of those goals; and in others, groups were able to win concessions from the ruling elite. All three types of outcomes indicate that the autonomous groups wielded at least some power in getting the ruling elite to take certain actions that it otherwise would not have taken.

With the single exception of the nationwide mass Solidarity movement that swept Poland in 1980–1981, autonomous groups throughout the region (as well as in Poland itself before and after Solidarity's heyday) were characteristically small in size, most often comprising only handfuls of individuals who, in turn, enjoyed the active support of a larger circle of nonelites and the passive support of still larger groups within society. No matter how broadly we draw the concentric circles of active and passive support, the autonomous groups in the late 1970s and early to mid-1980s remained exceptions in these societies, engaging only tiny minorities of the population in their pursuits. Except for the activist leaders who received negative publicity in the official press, most autonomous group members were not known to the vast majority of their fellow citizens. Yet, despite their small size, these movements were able to accumulate real power both domestically and internationally. One reason for this was their credibility. When the general societal consensus is that the ruling establishment is lying, individuals willing to speak the truth— or what is perceived as the truth—can quickly gain authority, which, at some level, can later translate into power. The power of truth and hard evidence is difficult to combat, and especially so when those put on the defensive (in this case, the ruling elite) lack credibility to begin with.

The autonomous group phenomenon in Eastern Europe was characterized by the pursuit of truth.[35] It was the principal weapon of attack against the ruling elite. Groups went about conscientiously collecting evidence in support of their specific goals, documenting environmental pollution, human rights violations, and so on. The accuracy of this information established their credibility not only with other nonelites in the society but also with some members of the ruling elite, interested parties, corresponding organizations in the West, and the Western press. In many cases, these groups became information centers that could be counted on by Western journalists for their accuracy and for their access to information that was officially unavailable. Thus, credibility became an important basis of power.

Having established some credibility themselves, these groups insisted on the same from their rulers by demanding accountability and adherence to the rule of law. Originally disavowing any intention to challenge the political system or the ultimate authority of the communist party,[36] citizens organized efforts merely to ensure that the ruling elite abide by its own laws, apply those laws equally and faithfully in the administration of justice, and make the laws consistent with the international agreements the rulers had entered. Authorities were held accountable by the grassroots organizations, in an increasingly assertive and systematic way, for the economic, social, and environmental failures of the system. In the 1980s Western governments and institutions also began to demand political and especially economic accountability from East European leaders, with financial institutions seeking some guarantees against the risks of future investments.

Not all East European leaders, of course, responded to pressures for accountability. Nicolae Ceausescu, in particular, proved impervious to international outcries against his shameful human rights record. Nonetheless, demands for accountability became increasingly persistent from the late 1970s through the late 1980s, further eroding the authority, legitimacy, and power of the communist ruling elite.

But how could autonomous groups in Eastern Europe bring about change in their societies if they lacked the institutionalized means to do so? This disadvantage had been used in the past to explain why grassroots efforts in communist systems would be unable to achieve their goals. In fact, the concept itself was misapplied. It imposed a democratic model on a system that was its opposite. Autonomous groups in Eastern Europe instead used unconventional mechanisms to articulate their interests, present their demands, and pressure the ruling elite to institute change.

The use of an underground press has already been mentioned. The method was particularly widespread in Poland and also used in Hungary and Czechoslovakia, where circulation, titles, and readerships were more limited. This could be seen as a positive means of gaining a constituency or support for certain goals. Autonomous groups, however, were also able to benefit from negative publicity in the official press, which, in its scathing indictments, inadvertently promoted the groups and their leaders. By publicizing their works and deeds—however inaccurately—the official press made these independent activists known entities to larger groups within society. In a similar vein, public trials were used by autonomous group activists, such as Karel Srp, head of the "Jazz Section" of the Musicians' Union in Czechoslovakia, to gain public recognition. Adam Michnik even refused to be "pardoned" during an amnesty of prisoners following the martial law period in Poland, preferring to stand trial in order to present his views and make them a part of an official record.[37]

In still other cases, autonomous groups in Eastern Europe appealed to Western governments, institutions, and organizations to articulate their interests and goals in their behalf, thereby circumventing the domestic barriers to grassroots influence on state policy. The international human rights movement is a case in point. Following the signing of the Helsinki Accords in 1975 and the introduction of Jimmy Carter's human rights policies in 1977, the United States and other democratic countries took serious heed for the first time, in an institutional way, of protests against human rights violations made by Soviet and East European citizens themselves. Human rights matters became a bargaining chip for the United States in its dealings with East European governments seeking loans, credits, or MFN status. Moreover, unofficial human rights groups throughout Eastern Europe monitored and reported government abuses toward citizens to the appropriate international agencies and organizations. Access to this information varied with each country, and the difficulty in obtaining updated reports was a direct function of the magnitude of human rights violations occurring in each country. Still, the channels had been established, and information presented by autonomous groups in Eastern Europe to Western human rights institutions was used in the negotiation of loans and credits. This was an institutionalized channel for the articulation of interests by nonelites in Eastern Europe, via the West.

Western organizational counterparts to East European autonomous groups served the same purpose. Free labor organizations in the West gathered information from East European groups on the violation of worker rights and free trade union concerns. They assisted the free trade union cause in Eastern Europe both politically and financially. Likewise, environmental groups, civil liberties groups, peace associations, autonomous PEN clubs, and groups seeking religious freedom communicated with their Western counterparts or with other organizations willing to support and promote their efforts.

In addition, East European autonomous group leaders were communicating their concerns directly to Western political leaders on their visits to the West. They became increasingly adept at such Western arts as lobbying, using the broadcast media to promote their cause, and fund-raising. Solidarity spokesman Janusz Onyszkiewicz, for example, met with members of the British Parliament and appeared on a telecast interview with the BBC in 1988 before coming to the United States to testify before Congress on the situation in Poland (an act for which he was severely condemned by Polish authorities and the official Polish media). Such exercises must have contributed to the cultural diffusion of democracy as a political process. Hungarian opposition leaders cultivated extensive contacts in the West, likewise promoting the cause of institutional change in Hungary. In fact, making initial contact with high-level Western political or public figures seemed to become a regular strategy for East European autonomous groups. Even newly formed autonomous groups in Bulgaria—where virtually no tradition of activeness had been established—placed a priority on initiating such contacts. In 1988, only months after its establishment, the Bulgarian Independent Discussion Club in Support of *Glasnost* and *Perestroika* managed to meet with Francois Mitterand during an unofficial visit to the West.

Fund-raising by East European opposition activists, especially though not exclusively from Poland, became a major reason for travel to the West. Some of the money was raised clandestinely from private sources; other sums, such as that given by the U.S. Congress to Solidarity, were raised publicly. In fact, Solidarity had been so successful at getting the funds for its operational costs and its charitable aid programs that the Polish government proposed making the relegalization of the independent trade union conditional upon its agreement to refuse additional money from Western sources. Some concern had been expressed by the Polish authorities that Solidarity was getting money from the same Western institutions the government had planned to approach for assistance, thus disrupting potential avenues of help for the state.[38]

We have seen that the Western media relied on the credible and otherwise inaccessible information collected by autonomous groups in Eastern Europe. But these groups, in turn, relied on the Western media to promote their causes both internationally and domestically. The most important role, in publicizing the issues, activities, and goals of autonomous groups to the citizens of Eastern Europe, was played by the foreign radio broadcasts, particularly Radio Free Europe and the BBC. Action programs were presented, arguments were made, and evidence of wrongdoing by East European governments was publicized through broadcasts into Eastern Europe.

Internationally, Western reporters and news agencies publicized the goals, programs and activities of East European autonomous groups to a world audience. This was, of course, particularly true for countries in which Western journalists had relatively easy access to such information, thus excluding the tiny but relevant opposition activities in Romania. As a consequence, Romanians were unaware of the names of opposition activists in their own country—an ignorance that became particularly important during the December revolution and its immediate aftermath, as we will see.

## The Changing Balance of Power

Faced with the resilience of autonomous groups in their respective societies, East European ruling elites were faced with two undesirable options: (1) rid the society of independent organizations through systematic repression, which, by then, had to be proportional in its strength to the resilience of the groups themselves; or (2) dilute their own power by accommodating autonomous groups institutionally in an effort to reestablish stability. Nicolae Ceausescu continued to employ the first option very effectively, ridding the society of independent voices (largely through internal exile or expulsion from the country) long before they had the chance to establish an organizational base. However, the long-term success of his strategy seemed dubious, at best, given the rising tension in the society. Todor Zhivkov, Erich Honecker, and, to a lesser extent, Milos Jakes, likewise continued to exercise the first option, although the persistence of existing and newly created autonomous groups was continually forcing them to reevaluate just how much force it would take to put an end to independent activities. Fierce repression against the Bulgarian Independent Discussion Club in Support of *Glasnost* and *Perestroika* in 1988, for example, ironically resulted in an increase in its membership rolls. In the GDR, Honecker had been inconsistent in his suppression of the activities of the semiautonomous peace groups, while indecision on the part of the leaders of Czechoslovakia in 1988 was evidenced in the irregularity with which civil disobedience was being quelled and punished. By the latter years of the 1980s, only the leaders of

Poland and Hungary were employing the second option by legally accommodating many autonomous groups already in existence in an attempt to
reestablish a measure of domestic political stability.

Still, the question of the reversibility of changes initiated by
autonomous groups in Eastern Europe was constantly being raised in light of
the fact that real power in these societies was said to remain in the hands of
those who controlled the military and the security apparatus. Thus, even
changes brought about by a very powerful national movement, such as that
of the 1980–1981 Solidarity trade union, could presumably be reversed
through the imposition of military rule. But in drawing such a mistaken conclusion, three important factors were overlooked. First, there was never any
evidence that coercive suppression of movements for change in Eastern
Europe accomplished anything more than to postpone the ultimate resolution
of conflict inherent in those societies. The Hungarian Revolution of 1956
and the Polish national movement for reform of that same year, as well as
the 1968 Prague Spring, all carried their legacies with them into the 1980s.
Moreover, martial law in Poland did not succeed in breaking the spirit of the
Solidarity movement. Second, the amount of power held by authorities
through their control of the armed forces and the security apparatus was in
direct proportion to their willingness to use that power. In 1981 General
Jaruzelski had argued that the decision to declare martial law was made to
prevent a Soviet military solution to the Polish political and economic crisis.
Even in declaring a state of war, Jaruzelski proved unwilling to order Polish
soldiers to shoot Polish civilians in the round-up of Solidarity activists. The
*threat* of the use of military force may be seen as a powerful control over
society, but the fact that Jaruzelski was unwilling to employ that option
already spoke of a change in the power equation in that country. Third, nothing altered the equation of power between rulers and ruled in East European
societies more than Gorbachev's decision not to invoke the Brezhnev
Doctrine. East European communist leaders were left on their own to face
increasingly restive and assertive populations demanding freedom and
democracy in the latter years of the 1980s. While they retained firm control
over their own military and security establishments, these leaders—with the
sorry exception of Ceausescu—proved unwilling or unable to use such force
without the guaranteed backing of Soviet military force.[39]

Throughout the 1980s, autonomous groups in Eastern Europe were laying the groundwork for events to come in the final year of the decade. They
built up their credibility among larger circles within their own society and
recruited international support for their causes. They persistently demanded
that the ruling elite in their countries be held accountable. They used unconventional avenues to publicize their causes and goals and to gain support
both at home and abroad. Finally, when the time came for domestic rulers to
decide whether to begin to accommodate some of these grassroots changes
or to eradicate them forcibly, the ultimate effectiveness of repression

seemed, at best, unclear in all but Romania and possibly the GDR. This change in the balance of power paved the way for the rapid downfall of communist leaders throughout the region in the last months of 1989.


## Autonomous Groups and the Revolutions of 1989


### Prior Country Developments

By the late 1980s the spontaneous emergence of a variety of autonomous groups had become a regional phenomenon in communist Eastern Europe. It demonstrated that the region's precommunist political cultures had not been so thoroughly decimated or stripped of democratic potential and initiative as had been imagined earlier. Moreover, it indicated that opposition to communism had been a breeding ground for yet other dimensions of civic-mindedness. Throughout this analysis, reference has been made to the different stages of development of autonomous group activity in the specific countries of the region. Before examining the role played by these groups in the revolutionary changes that swept the region in 1989, a brief summary of those developments in each of the countries is in order.

Poland had the longest, most continuous, and extensive network of autonomous groups of any nation in the region. This must be attributed, at least in part, to the Polish mentality that thrives on conspiracy, clandestine operations, and strategies to overcome seemingly impossible obstacles. Poland's political culture was born of centuries of foreign occupation and hence of being the underdog in one's own country, as well as location at the crossroads of both World Wars.

Beginning in the late 1970s with small pockets of opposition, autonomous groups by 1980 served to facilitate the mobilization of the nationally based Solidarity trade union movement. With the imposition of martial law in late 1981, the movement moved underground and became factionalized while still operating largely under the unifying banner of *Solidarność*. The 1980s had been characterized by a standoff between a military-political establishment and an angry population that basically held to a position of non-cooperation with the ruling elite. Finally forced to negotiate with Solidarity in order to begin a sorely needed program of economic reform, the Polish government agreed to relegalize the trade union in return for Solidarity's participation in partially free elections that were aimed ultimately at the union's sharing responsibility with the ruling elite for the economic reform program while bearing the bad tidings of financial sacrifice to the population.

What made Poland's autonomous group phenomenon unique was that it operated under the protective umbrella of Solidarity. Countless non-Solidarity groups were thus able to come into existence. Some were offshoots of the trade union movement and consistent with its aim. Others were formed independent of the union and pursued goals in conflict with it. Still, the fact that so powerful a movement as Solidarity had blossomed in 1980–1981 and continued to operate underground provided something of a protective shield behind which other groups could function. Nowhere else in Eastern Europe was this the case.[40] The situation gave way to a virtual explosion of autonomous group activity, both underground and later increasingly aboveground, with an expansive and ever more institutionalized underground press.

Hungary likewise had a rich, though far less extensive, history of autonomous group activity. From the late 1970s through the early 1980s, that activity was centered mainly in Budapest and largely involved Hungarian intellectuals engaging in political and economic discussions through the underground press, with no real ties to the working class. By the mid to late 1980s, and particularly following the ouster of János Kádár in May 1988, various new groups emerged with specific, action-oriented goals including environmental protection and the defense of the rights of the Hungarian minority in Romania. But Hungary's autonomous group movement was never so entrenched in the society as that of Poland's. Part of the reason for this was that, compared to Poles, Hungarians were not suffering from the same persistent economic crisis, and politically they were better off than most other East Europeans, particularly with respect to human rights. Thus, activists had difficulty mobilizing larger groups within Hungary to join the cause of seeking greater freedoms and, at the same time, were much less successful than Poles in gaining the interest of Western audiences. In short, Hungarians had learned to coexist with their communist leaders and the division between rulers and ruled was neither so severe nor so confrontational as that in Poland.

By the later years of the 1980s, political leaders in Hungary were increasingly tolerant of, and in Poland increasingly resigned to, autonomous group activity. Generally speaking, such involvement in autonomous groups was no longer being treated as a criminal offense. In Hungary, many years had passed since "dissidents" had been sentenced to lengthy prison terms, while in Poland, independent activism had been reduced by 1987 to a misdemeanor, although very heavy fines were being levied against "offenders."[41]

In Czechoslovakia, during the decade between 1977 and 1987, only two major autonomous groups existed in the country: Charter 77 and VONS. Over time, Charter 77 had become a virtual clearinghouse for a vast array of problems in Czechoslovak society, including issues of human rights, environmental pollution, and religious freedom, as well as economic concerns;[42] VONS dealt more specifically with the concerns of individual citizens whose rights had been violated. By the late 1980s, Charter 77 had been endorsed by some twelve hundred mostly Czech citizens, only a minority of whom were actively involved in the day-to-day activities of the organization. In this respect, the decision to sign the charter was more a matter of being counted as one of its supporters than of pledging oneself to a life of active involvement. Still, this was a visible and concrete demonstration of support and a means of distinguishing oneself in Czechoslovak society as a person committed to change. As such, the signatory "qualified" for direct and persistent harassment by the security apparatus. In Slovakia, the major form of independent activism was in the growing religious movement. Linked with Slovak nationalism, it had collected as many as three-quarters of a million signatures on a petition demanding religious freedom, and had involved tens of thousands of believers in spiritual pilgrimages with an underlying political agenda.

It was not until 1988 that the number of autonomous groups in Czechoslovakia began to multiply and focus in on narrower and more clearly defined concerns. Most of the new groups emerged through the direct sponsorship of Charter 77 activists, who began employing a conscious strategy of activating diversification.[43] The size of popular protests was growing to proportions reminiscent of the Prague Spring some twenty years earlier. Czechoslovak citizens began to awaken to a renewed life of activism and reform through engaging in grassroots efforts. The communist leaders reacted ambivalently; certain popular demonstrations for change were largely ignored by security forces while others were handled with uncommon brutality. It was, in fact, the brutality used against a relatively small demonstration of students in Prague in the autumn of 1989 that led to ever-larger demonstrations within a matter of days and eventually brought down the communist regime.

In the GDR, there were basically two strands of autonomous group development.[44] The first consisted of a number of independent urban intellectual groups concerned with issues of peace and demilitarization, human rights and civil liberties, ecology, and women's issues. They occupied a far more tenuous position in society and were systematically repressed by security forces, with their leaders often expelled to West Germany. Thus, they were unable to establish a strong constituency in East German society. The second strand was composed of more than two hundred small groups working through the Protestant churches on issues of peace, demilitarization, and human rights. By and large, their activities were ignored by the East German authorities except when they ventured to stage a public protest, in which case they oftentimes suffered the same fate as the leaders of the independent urban intellectual groups. But their quiet meetings and discussions continued in East German society from 1979 through 1989.[45] They were not viewed as a disruptive force and rarely posed a direct threat to the East German leadership.[46] Thus, they enjoyed a lengthy period of gestation prior to the events in October 1989 that toppled the Honecker regime.

Bulgarians were latecomers to the autonomous-group phenomenon in Eastern Europe. In fact, the Independent Association for the Defense of

Human Rights, established in January 1988, was the first autonomous group to emerge in Bulgaria since the 1940s.[47] In March of that year, another group, the Independent Committee for the Defense of Ruse, was founded to protect the city of Ruse from chlorine pollution emitted by a Soviet-built plant on the Romanian banks of the Danube. Finally, the Independent Discussion Club in Support of *Glasnost* and *Perestroika* was established, and the fact that many of its members were also prominent members of the Communist Party foretold troubles for the ruling elite of Bulgaria and the thirty-five-year leadership of Todor Zhivkov.[48] Members of these groups, while systematically harassed and repressed, demonstrated a resilience that was indeed uncommon, especially given their newness to the "opposition" scene and lack of any experience in the workings of civil society from earlier periods in Bulgarian history.

Romania was the single exception to the autonomous-group phenomenon that swept Eastern Europe in the late 1980s. Not only did it lack a history of civic-mindedness and self-initiated grassroots political organization but the barriers to independent activity set in place by Ceausescu simply could not be broken or circumvented. In the 1980s only in Romania were there laws requiring that all typewriters be registered with the state as a means of exercising control over even the most personal correspondence between citizens. The security apparatus was the most extensive in the region, with estimates of the number of paid informants running as high as one in five citizens, forcing Romanians to use extreme caution in even their private conversations. Although communiques were reaching the West in the late 1980s from a group calling itself Romania Democratic Action, those communiques were signed pseudonymously[49]—in stark contrast to the ever more public nature of autonomous group activity elsewhere in Eastern Europe—and thus the actors in that group were known neither to the West nor to wider circles within Romanian society. They were therefore unable to distinguish themselves domestically as the individuals who stood up in opposition to the policies of the regime. There were a few known "dissidents" in the country who acted as individuals, but often their names were better known to Western observers than to a Romanian public that was kept in the dark about domestic opposition activities.

## The Revolutionary Changes of 1989

Nowhere was the new role to be played by the once-illegal autonomous groups of communist Eastern Europe in the transition toward democracy more graphically displayed than in Poland in the first half of 1989. Although there were many strains of opposition in Polish society, Solidarity had remained the unifying movement, symbolic of the only viable alternative to communist rule. Having been cajoled by the ruling elite to campaign in the region's first partially free elections, for one-third of the seats in the parliament and for one hundred seats in a newly created Senate, Solidarity candidates swept the elections, winning all but one of the seats they contested. Individuals whose activities just weeks prior to the June 1989 election were still technically illegal, who had served lengthy prison sentences during martial law and the early years of normalization, and who in every respect had been the nemesis of the current political leadership walked into the offices of government as parliamentary deputies, senators, ministers, and prime minister.

Having been given only six weeks to field hundreds of candidates in the nation's first experience with free elections in more than forty years, the sweeping nature of Solidarity's victory made clear how profound a role was played by these autonomous group activists over the years. Unlike autonomous group structures elsewhere in Eastern Europe, the single Solidarity logo linked intellectuals, workers, and farmers alike. The extensive networks and widespread involvement of groups within society enabled Solidarity to identify scores of trusted individuals to run in opposition to the established ruling elite. Moreover, the movement was well connected to networks of advisers both at home and abroad for consultation on campaign techniques, as well as to sources of immediate funding to launch the political campaign. Although an argument could certainly be made that Polish voters were casting ballots *against* the Communist party rather than for Solidarity, they elected a new set of incumbents, who were enormously skilled and practiced in the arts of political strategy and confronting difficult issues head-on, against nearly impossible odds. Most of these newcomers to the ranks of government and diplomacy were well connected either domestically or internationally, or both. This eased the initial transition away from a communist monopoly of power toward laying the foundations for pluralism and democracy in Poland.

The situation in Hungary was very different for two major reasons. First, the autonomous group phenomenon developed in Hungary in a far more disparate way than in Poland. There was no unifying logo under which Hungarian citizens would join forces, nor a protective umbrella such as Solidarity to encourage the general expansion of autonomous group activity. Second, following the fall of János Kádár as head of the Hungarian Socialist Workers' Party in May 1988, reform-minded party leaders provided much of the impetus for change in that society, thereby diluting the potential power of existing autonomous groups.

In November 1988 a number of seasoned opposition figures, active since the late 1970s in Hungary's autonomous group movement, founded the Alliance of Free Democrats. This was a political party of the urban intelligentsia, running on a platform linking a liberal sociopolitical outlook with a program for radical change to a market economy in Hungary.[50] Representing the largest single consolidation of Hungary's seasoned opposition forces,[51] it successfully led the November 1989 campaign to postpone the election of the president (originally scheduled for January 1990) until after the March National Assembly elections, arguing that incumbent (communist) political leaders would otherwise have an unfair advantage.[52] But, lacking political links with Hungarian workers or farmers, the Alliance of Free Democrats was less successful in the March National Assembly elections, winning only 92 seats; 164 seats were won by the more traditionalist Hungarian Democratic Forum. Still, the fact that actors from earlier groups in Hungary were able to form a strong, viable, alternative political party contributed to a smooth transition to political pluralism in Hungary.

The German Democratic Republic, Czechoslovakia, Bulgaria, and Romania underwent a far more sudden and dramatic change when, in the final months of 1989, their Communist Party leaderships were toppled by popular pressure (real or anticipated) from the society at large. In the first three countries, public outcries demanded that the ruling elite agree to negotiate with representatives of the opposition. Hence, in each of these cases, there was a clear sense among some segments of the general public that political alternatives did in fact exist within their societies. Only in Romania was there a violent uprising singularly targeted at toppling the leadership, with no immediate public sense that a viable alternative leadership was already available in that society.

These four countries had far more rigid political leaderships than Poland or Hungary, and autonomous group activities had met with much greater repression. Until the political avalanche began in the early autumn of 1989, real change seemed unlikely. Autonomous groups were thus left unprepared for the opportunities that suddenly became available to them. In each case, new structures of opposition representatives emerged, gathering together many of the old actors under new organization names in an attempt to form *ad hoc* umbrella groups linking a variety of opposition causes.

In the GDR, autonomous groups played a very uneven role in the sudden changes that occurred in 1989. The events that led to the downfall of Erich Honecker began with the great exodus of East German citizens to West Germany. Despite the lengthy history of autonomous group activity in the GDR, emigration to the West had long been the principal form of opposition in that society.[53] This, together with Honecker's policy of forced expulsion of independent activists, undoubtedly depleted the ranks of those East Germans who might have formed a powerful and extensive network of autonomous groups.[54] Instead, the independent groups (as opposed to the semiautonomous groups that existed around the churches) in East Germany were never able to establish themselves effectively as viable political alternatives. While they were gaining in strength and assertiveness in the late 1980s, the sudden collapse of the Berlin Wall and the subsequent immediate focus on reunification profoundly altered the power equation within the GDR, taking the wind out of the sails of its autonomous groups.

On the other hand, the Evangelical Church in East Germany did come to play a major organizational role in the massive changes that occurred in that society in late 1989 and early 1990. For example, during the initial period of mobilization and mass public demonstrations that immediately preceded Honecker's downfall, specific Protestant churches in Leipzig, known to the public for their sponsorship of the peace and human rights movement, were called upon to assist in the organization of the protests themselves. Throughout the country, churches provided meeting places for the mobilization of the opposition.[55] In addition, the free parliamentary elections of March 1990 resulted in the election of fourteen pastors (to a four-hundred-member body),[56] and four other pastors or former pastors were appointed to Prime Minister Lothar de Maiziere's government.

In Czechoslovakia, the trigger event that led to the mass mobilization of hundreds of thousands of protesters began with the brutal beating by security officers of students demonstrating in Wenceslaus Square in Prague for freedom and democracy. As the crowds multiplied, reaching the half-million mark in a matter of days, members of Charter 77 and other autonomous groups came together to form an *ad hoc* team of opposition representatives and the organizing force behind the crowds calling for the ouster of the communist leadership. The ease with which this new group, calling itself Civic Forum, came together during the very sudden and unexpected changes in that society and the manner in which it quickly proceeded to publicize its existence, hold press conferences, and set forth a solid list of demands were testimony to the vast amount of groundwork that had been laid years in advance by autonomous groups, without any knowledge of if, when, or how their organizational expertise might be employed to bring about the end of communism. A similar group, Public Against Violence, simultaneously emerged in Slovakia and included within its ranks veteran activists from the environmental movement. Together with Civic Forum, it won most of the seats in the parliamentary elections of June 1990.

The events that followed the sudden break in the monopoly of power by the Communist Party in Czechoslovakia were no less dramatic than those in Poland. Veterans of the autonomous group movement left menial jobs (to which they had been "sentenced" precisely because of their activism) and prison cells to assume leading positions in the new government. Charter 77 had been the breeding ground for an alternative political leadership to whom citizens turned when the old guard was removed from power.

In November 1989 Todor Zhivkov's forced resignation precluded the mass mobilization of demonstrations in Bulgaria, although some public protests had already begun a month earlier.[57] Still, representatives of the newly formed autonomous groups were quick to put forth a set of demands calling for an end to the communist monopoly of power and for timely negotiations between the government and opposition forces in society. By December more than a dozen groups united under the common banner of the Union of Democratic Forces (UDF), constituting the major organization of political opposition in the country. Other former opposition groups provided the bases for additional independent political parties.

In June 1990 the old Communist Party, renamed the Socialist Party of Bulgaria, won a plurality of seats in the parliamentary elections. While amending the constitution to allow for a multiparty system and enacting various reform laws, the Communist Party retained the reigns of power and thus enjoyed a clear advantage in the elections. Major sources of information remained in the hands of the traditional rulers, and thus prevented opposition groups from launching a campaign forceful enough to topple the establishment.[58] Still, the combined efforts of Bulgarian autonomous groups, operating under the UDF banner, won clear victories in major Bulgarian cities and provided the country with its first viable political alternative in decades.

Finally, in Romania, where there was neither an established nor an emergent movement of autonomous groups, there was also no alternative leadership to whom Romanian citizens could turn following the downfall of Ceausescu. The National Salvation Front (NSF) was spontaneously formed immediately following Ceausescu's flight from Bucharest, assembling a largely mismatched collection of individuals—including former communist leaders who had fallen into disfavor with Ceausescu, academics, students, and individual dissidents representing no larger autonomous groups or well-defined constituencies within the society—who had the foresight to declare themselves the temporary leaders of the country. The controversial head of the NSF, Ion Iliescu, was himself a former Communist who had remained in Ceausescu's inner circle until being ousted in the early 1980s. Elected president in May 1990, he was often criticized for his authoritarian tendencies in dealing with those who opposed him. The sweeping NSF victory in those elections pointed not only to the weakness of newly emergent opposition groups and parties, which lacked the resources necessary to topple the remains of the communist (or former communist) order. It underscored as well that Romania lacked the autonomous group *tradition* and thus the period of gestation that might have allowed groups the time either to establish broader constituencies or to devise political platforms that better reflected the aspirations of fellow Romanians. Romania had no *organized* political culture of anticommunism. Had such an alternative political culture developed, a viable alternative leadership would undoubtedly have emerged as a principal player in the new political order.

## Conclusion

In any successful revolution, those who publicly once stood in opposition to the established order become the most likely candidates for an alternative political leadership. The focus here, however, has been on the role of *groups* as agents of change in Eastern Europe, first under communism and then under new, more democratic sociopolitical orders.

From the time, in the late 1970s, when autonomous groups began to emerge as more or less regular features of some East European societies, they played a very important role as agents of change. They provided forums for discussion and for checking programs of political strategy, and they established networks of support for the goals they were pursuing. They shook the foundations of communist rule by introducing elements into the sociopolitical order that were incompatible with a hegemonic structure of power. In some cases, they achieved their goals despite their seeming lack of power and the absence of institutionalized channels through which they could articulate their interests. They were the breeding ground for alternative political leaderships, skilled in strategy and organization. Initially, these autonomous groups were the *destabilizing agents* that helped to topple communist leaders.[59] Later, they emerged as the *stabilizing features* of the transition to new, more democratic orders.[60]

It is very clear how the precommunist political cultures of Eastern Europe found expression during the late 1970s and throughout the 1980s. In the northern tier countries—the German Democratic Republic, Poland, Czechoslovakia, and Hungary—civic mindedness was most advanced as was the ability to form civic organizations. These capabilities, of course, were tempered by the degree of repression in a given country, which, throughout the 1970s and 1980s, had its most consistent hold (within the northern tier) on Czechoslovakia and, to a lesser extent, on the GDR.

The southern tier countries—Romania and Bulgaria—had a far less developed sense of civil society and consequently produced far fewer autonomous groups as agents of change. As a result, they yielded a much smaller alternative political leadership, had a much less developed sense of possible alternative programs, and a much weaker demand nationally for a democratic system of government.

Yet it would be wrong to conclude that forty years of communism had no real impact on the political cultures of these societies. In fact, its effects can be seen in a number of contexts in the new political order. For example, communism left many East European citizens with an aversion to politics in general. In Poland, citizens are reluctant to join political parties because "party membership" as a concept remains distasteful. Moreover, political parties shy away from recruitment campaigns because such campaigns were a characteristic feature of Communist Party programs in the past.

Throughout the region, voter turnout has dropped precipitously following the first two major free elections. Western observers have been too quick to dismiss this phenomenon as irrelevant, pointing to the fact that voter turnout is very low in the United States as well. It may not be fair, however, to compare democracies that are two years old with one that is two hundred years old. In Eastern Europe, where literacy rates are very high and few citizens are without a political opinion, low voter turnout may well deserve more careful analytical attention. It may, for example, be a new dimension of political culture, resulting from decades of communist rule. Low voter turnout may reflect an aversion to formal politics in general, or a widespread belief in political inefficiency irrespective of the system. On the other hand, it may simply be the result of confusion in rapidly changing political circumstances. Another explanation may be that East Europeans, after decades of *mandatory* voting under communism, may view their decision *not* to vote as a newly won democratic freedom. It seems logical to assume that after forty years of being denied a free vote by secret ballot in competitive elections, East European citizens might be more eager to take an active part in determining the future course of their countries through large-scale voter participation.

Next, there seems to be an expectation among East European citizens— particularly workers and farmers—that "the government will provide." The exact equation for just how much the governments will provide in each of these societies has yet to be determined. It should come as no surprise, however, that the withdrawal of government subsidies from food, fuel, housing, transportation, communication, education, health care, and an entire host of other services adds dramatically to the economic uncertainty experienced by East Europeans and may undermine the legitimacy of their governments if economic reforms do not produce new growth soon.

Finally, there are democratic skills and traits that must be (re)taught or (re)introduced into the political cultures of these societies. They include tolerance, a willingness to compromise, trust in government, pragmatism and flexibility, and moderate rather than extremist partisanship. Today, the societies of Eastern Europe are at vastly different stages along this continuum of developed democratic skills and traits. The country with the strongest democratic characteristics is Hungary, where, during the last two decades of communist rule, citizens learned to coexist even with a government they viewed as basically illegitimate, having traded their own acquiescence for reduced government political and economic repression. This formula alone exemplifies some of the traits of democratic culture, such as tolerance, pragmatism, and flexibility.

Romanians are at the other end of this democratic continuum, having emerged from the last decade of communism as the most repressed society in Eastern Europe, with the exception of Albania. Romanians, today, are basically lacking in all of the skills and traits necessary for stable democracy. These will take generations to introduce and integrate into the larger society.

Today, East European societies, faced with the task of shaping their own political futures, will continue to provide a most interesting arena for the study of grassroots organization and political culture. Within a time span of four generations, these societies are experiencing their *fourth* major peacetime political reality: The first period came to an end with the World War I; the second was during the interwar period; the third was communism; and today, the fourth is a period of postcommunism and democracy. Each period left its mark on the political cultures of these societies, and today those political cultures will help to shape the future political systems in each of the countries.

## Notes

The Hoover Institution at Stanford University provided the exceptional context and stimulating environment in which this project was initiated. The National Council for Soviet and East European Research provided the funding for the research and writing of this chapter. Special thanks to Dr. Robert H. Randolph, the council's executive director, whose kindness at a time of need will not be forgotten.

1. The tens of thousands of autonomous groups that suddenly emerged in the Soviet Union in the late 1980s included many with social, cultural, and hobby-oriented purposes. See, for example, Vera Tolz, "Informal Groups in the USSR," *Washington Quarterly* (Spring 1988): 137-143; S. Frederick Starr, "Soviet Union: A Civil Society," *Foreign Policy*, Spring 1988, pp. 26-41; and Gail W. Lapidus, "State and Society: Toward the Emergence of Civil Society in the Soviet Union," in Seweryn Bialer, ed., *Politics, Society, and Nationality Inside Gorbachev's Russia* (Boulder: Westview Press, 1989), pp. 121-147.

2. Christine M. Sadowski, "Citizens, Voluntary Associations and the Policy Process," in Roger Kanet and Maurice D. Simon, eds., *Background to Crisis: Policy and Politics in Gierek's Poland* (Boulder: Westview Press, 1981).

3. Ibid.

4. The practice of burning down local Communist Party headquarters was the basis of Jacek Kuron's famous statement encouraging the creation of autonomous groups in Poland, "Instead of burning committees, build committees."

5. See, for example, Jedrzej Giertych, *Po wypadkach poznanskich: List otwarty do polskiej emigracji* (London: 16, Belmont Road, self-published, 1956); Vladimir Fomir and Iurii Shchekochikhin, "Togda, v Novocherkasske," *Literaturnaia gazeta*, 21 June 1989; Betsy Gidwitz, "Labor Unrest in the Soviet Union," *Problems of Communism* (November–December 1982): 32; Ewa Wacowska, ed., *Rewolta szczecinska i jej znaczenie* (Paris: Instytut Literacki, 1971), pp. 247-254; J. M. Montias, "Observations on Strikes, Riots and Other Disturbances," in Jan T. Triska and Charles Gati, eds., *Blue-Collar Workers in Eastern Europe* London: George Allen and Unwin, 1981), pp. 179-180; "Brasso Uprising: An Account by an Eyewitness," *East European Reporter* 3, no. 2 (1988): 61-63.

6. Jan B. de Weydenthal, "The Workers' Dilemma of Polish Politics: A Case Study," *East European Quarterly* 13, no. 1 (1979): 108.

7. Zbigniew Brzezinski, *The Soviet Bloc: Unity and Conflict* (Cambridge: Harvard University Press, 1967), p. 243.

8. Paul Kecskementi, *The Unexpected Revolution: Social Forces in the Hungarian Uprising* (Stanford: Stanford University Press, 1961), pp. 72-76.

9. Ibid., pp. 70-71.

10. Barbara Donovan, "Signs of Cultural Liberalization in the GDR?" Background Report/German Democratic Republic, *Radio Free Europe Research*, 21 June 1988.

11. Stephen Ashley, "Reformist Ferment in the Writers' Union," Situation Report/Bulgaria, *Radio Free Europe Research*, 14 April 1989, pp. 17-22.

12. Christine M. Sadowski, "Bread and Freedom: Workers' Self-Government Schemes in Post World War II Poland," in Jack Bielasiak and Maurice D. Simon,

eds., *Polish Politics: Edge of the Abyss* (New York: Praeger, 1984), p. 104.

13. Vaclav Havel, "The Power of the Powerless," in Jan Vladislav, ed., *Vaclav Havel or Living in Truth* (London: Faber and Faber, 1986).

14. Steven Sampson, "The Informal Sector in Eastern Europe," *Telos* 66 (Winter 1985-86): 50.

15. While it is true that the "Jazz Section" of the Czechoslovak Musicians' Union emerged as a hotbed of opposition in the 1970s, it was not technically an independent group, but rather part of the larger state-sponsored professional association. By the 1980s it functioned *as if it were* independent.

16. Personal interview with Wlodzimierz Zbiniewicz, in charge of printing for KOR and later head of Solidarity's propaganda needs in the Pulawy district of Poland, in Uppsala, Sweden, May 1987.

17. H. Gordon Skilling, "Independent Currents in Czechoslovakia," *Problems of Communism* (January–February 1985): 38-40.

18. The same was true of the civil rights movement in the United States in the 1960s, which used many of the resources of Southern Baptist Churches for purposes of mobilization.

19. The notion that fear was declining in Czechoslovakia in 1988 was repeatedly stressed by opposition representatives. See Lenka Prochazkova, "Fear No More!" *Uncaptive Minds* (November–December 1988): 32-33; "Not a Prophet But an Optimist: An Interview with Father Vaclav Maly," *Uncaptive Minds* (November–December 1988): 40; and "To Create Unsolvable Problems: An Interview with Jan Urban," *Uncaptive Minds* (July–August 1988): 33.

20. The striking similarities between Gorbachev's reform program and the program put forth during the 1968 Prague Spring must have profoundly raised expectations for change among Czechoslovak citizens.

21. Jan Jozef Lipski, *KOR: The History of the Workers' Defense Committee in Poland, 1976-1981* (Berkeley: University of California Press, 1985), pp. 198-200.

22. Solidarity was legally registered in November 1980, only to have its activities suspended in December 1981 and then banned altogether. It regained the right to legal registration again in April 1989, following the roundtable negotiations.

23. Alfred Reisch, "The Gabcikovo-Nagymaros Project: A Wasteland Awaiting the Fruits of Political Change," *Report on Eastern Europe*, 26 January 1990, pp. 25-29.

24. Vladimir Socor, "Romania Action Day" (Situation Report/Romania), *Radio Free Europe Research*, December 22, 1988. Also, from earlier in the year, see Vladimir Socor, "Independent Groups in Eastern Europe Urge Support for People of Romania" (Background Report/Eastern Europe), *Radio Free Europe Research*, 25 February 1988, pp. 1-6.

25. The Consultative Council included members from Poland's opposition who acted in this body as individual citizens rather than as representatives of a broader constituency. Solidarity, as a trade union or social movement, was not represented.

26. Jiri Pehe, "Human Rights vs. Communist Systems," *Freedom at Issue* (May–June 1989): 5-8.

27. Agnes Heller, "Can Communist Regimes be Reformed?" *Society*, May–June 1988, p. 23.

28. Fred Singleton, "Ecological Crisis in Eastern Europe: Do the Greens Threaten the Reds?" *Across Frontiers* (Summer 1985): 5-10.

29. Skilling, "Independent Currents," p. 49. Skilling is referring here specifically to Charter 77.

30. In some cases, the existence of autonomous structures radicalized their official counterpart organizations, as was the case with Solidarity and Poland's official communist-sponsored trade unions. During Solidarity's heyday in 1980-1881, during

the period of normalization in the mid-1980s, and again in 1989, following the rele-galization of Solidarity, the official trade union structures became more radical and outspoken in defense of workers' rights. The government-sponsored unions, after all, were now facing competition for the first time. See, for example, Andrzej Swidlicki, *Political Trials in Poland*, 1981-86 (London: Croom Helm, 1988), p. 163. The same was true of the official press in Poland. As underground publications became more and more available to a general public, at least some government-controlled periodi-cals felt the need to liberalize their censorship laws to counteract the "competition."

31. In the early issues, *Robotnik*, the clandestine publication of Poland's free trade union movement, was as much a "how to" manual as a forum for open discus-sion. In the late 1970s, articles included "How to Print" (on self-publishing tech-niques), "How to Confront Management," and "How to Construct an Antenna" (for better reception of Radio Free Europe broadcasts).

32. Christine M. Sadowski, "Resource Mobilization in a Marxist-Leninist Society: The Case of Poland's Solidarity Movement," *Journal of Communist Studies* (June 1988).

33. Vilem Precan, *Vyvoj Charty, Zaznam z konference ve Franken* (Cologne: Index, 1981), p. 27, cited in Skilling, "Independent Currents," p. 49.

34. Lipski, *KOR*, p. 450.

35. Vaclav Havel's essay "Living in Truth," in Jan Vladkslav, ed., *Vaclav Havel or Living in Truth* (London: Faber and Faber, 1986) best exemplifies this orientation. Of course, not all grassroots movements fighting oppression adopt this strategy, as evidenced by the disinformation campaigns launched by many wartime resistance movements. "Truth," however, proved a very powerful weapon against communism, having great appeal for both East European citizens and Western groups and political institutions.

36. For the entire decade between the late 1970s and the late 1980s, the autonomous groups of Eastern Europe did not conceive of their mission as being one aimed at toppling communism. Their goals, one might say, were more "modest," and their intentions were originally to initiate change within the existing structures. This strategy led to much debate in both East and West on whether communist systems could indeed be reformed.

37. Polish authorities were well aware of Michnik's strategy of using the court as a forum during his trials and thus did not allow him to speak at all in his own defense while being tried in 1985. See Jane Cave, ed., *On Trial in Gdansk: A Transcript of the Proceedings Against Adam Michnik, Bogdan Lis, Wladyslaw Frasyniuk* (Washington, DC: Poland Watch Center, 1986).

38. Zbigniew Romaszewski, "Radical Minimalism," *Uncaptive Minds* (March–April 1989): 14-16.

39. The Honecker regime reportedly appealed to the Soviet troops stationed in the GDR for assistance in quelling the mounting public unrest and huge demonstra-tions of October 1989. That assistance was denied.

40. Robert Sharlet argues correctly that "in the GDR . . . religious activism . . . serves as a patron and protector of a curious mix of mass political dissent and the youth counterculture. Similarly, in Czechoslovakia, both state-sanctioned religion and the religious underground are loosely confederated with Charter 77, the cynosure of political dissent in the CSSR." See "Human Rights and Wrongs: Dissent and Repression in Eastern Europe," in Nicholas N. Kittrie and Ivan Volgyes, eds., *The Uncertain Future: Gorbachev's Eastern Bloc* (New York: Paragon House, 1988), p. 95. Still, the point being made here, that Solidarity in Poland formed a unique protec-tive umbrella under which other autonomous groups could emerge and flourish, holds true. One need consider only that the independent trade union movement was a grass-roots organization claiming in 1981 some 30 percent of the population and the major-

ity of citizens in the labor force. Its popularity, even while it was officially banned during most of the 1980s, encouraged and inspired the creation of numerous other groups.

41. "Price of Dissent," *Eastern Europe Newsletter*, 15 July 1987.

42. Skilling, "Independent Currents," pp. 32-49.

43. Janusz Bugajski, *Czechoslovakia: Charter 77's Decade of Dissent* (New York: Praeger, 1987); and Vaclav Benda, "Can Charter 77 Influence Political Change in Czechoslovakia?" *Uncaptive Minds* (September–October 1988): 11-13.

44. Vladimir Tismaneanu, "Nascent Civil Society in the German Democratic Republic," *Problems of Communism* (March–June 1989): 93-99.

45. Pedro Ramet, "Church and Peace in the GDR," *Problems of Communism*, July–August 1984, pp. 48-57. Ramet suggests that the semiautonomous peace groups in the GDR began operating under the aegis of the church as early as the late 1970s.

46. Sharlet, "Human Rights and Wrongs," p. 100.

47. Stephen Ashley, "Dissident Movement Repressed" (Situation Report/Bulgaria), *Radio Free Europe Research*, 24 October 1988, p. 16.

48. Stephen Ashley, "Intellectuals Form an Independent Club for the Support of *Perestroika* and *Glasnost*" (Situation Report/Bulgaria), *Radio Free Europe Research*, 20 December 1988, pp. 11-13.

49. Vladimir Socor, "Romania Democratic Action" (Background Report/Romania), Radio Free Europe Research, 2 March 1988.

50. Zoltan D. Barany, "The Alliance of Free Democrats: From Underdog to Potential Victor," *Radio Free Europe: Report on Eastern Europe*, 6 April 1990, p. 14.

51. Fred Martin, "Politics at the Club Tomaj," *New York Times Magazine*, 20 May 1990.

52. This referendum, initiated by the Alliance of Free Democrats, was passed by only a fraction of a percentage (by about 6,000 votes out of 4.3 million). See Alfred Reisch, "Hungary in 1989: A Country in Transition," *Radio Free Europe: Report on Eastern Europe*, 5 January 1990, p. 20.

53. Sharlet, "Human Rights and Wrongs," p. 106.

54. The fact of so many expulsions created debate within the peace movement between those who wished to remain in the GDR and those who possibly viewed their activism as a guaranteed ticket to the West. See Vladimir Tismaneanu, "Nascent Civil Society," pp. 108-109. Also, for a discussion on the use of forced deportation as a countermeasure against dissent, see H. G. Huettich, "Dissent and Systemic Stability in East Germany," *Studies in Comparative Communism*, 12 (Summer–Autumn 1979): 254-262. Interestingly, Zhivkov and Ceausescu employed the same, largely effective policy of deporting "dissidents."

55. See Serge Schmemann, "Weekly Protests in Leipzig Draw 300,000 Marchers," *New York Times*, 31 October 1990.

56. David Binder, "East Germany's 'Utopian Socialist' Theology," *New York Times*, 5 May 1990.

57. Jeri Laber, "The Bulgarian Difference," *New York Review*, 17 May 1990.

58. Ibid.

59. Jacek Kuron writes, "By building independent organizations, society can erode totalitarianism from within." See "Overcoming Totalitarianism," *Journal of Democracy* (Winter 1990): 74.

60. Larry Diamond, "Beyond Authoritarianism and Totalitarianism: Strategies for Democratization," *Washington Quarterly* (Winter 1989): 141-163. Diamond argues that the existence of large numbers of diverse voluntary associations is a key element in the successful transition from authoritarianism to democratic systems in Asia, Africa, and Latin America.

# · 7 ·

# State Elites and Democratic Political Culture in Turkey

## Ergun Özbudun

Turkey is one of the more fortunate countries in the Third World in terms of the quantity and quality of data on its elites. Following the monumental work of Frederick W. Frey on Turkish parliamentary elites that covered the entire 1920-1957 period in great detail,[1] other researchers have continued the same line of work and brought the political elite data up to date.[2] There are also a number of studies on bureaucratic and, to a much lesser extent, military elites. Most of these studies, however, have concentrated on the social background characteristics of particular elite groups, not as a rule on their attitudes and values. Because this chapter intends to focus on the state elites' attitudes and values on democracy, it will be necessary to supplement whatever empirical data exists with historical and necessarily more impressionistic evidence.

It has been argued, correctly, that

> until quite recently, Turkish politics have been, for all major purposes, *elite* politics. As in most other developing societies, the political drama was limited to elite actors, elite institutions, and elite urban settings. Mass elements were excluded by the nature of the culture, the distribution of resources, and the design of the rulers. ... It ... is still possible to analyze much of the thrust of Turkish politics by focusing on the political elite—although this perspective will probably become increasingly inadequate in the future.[3]

## State Elites in the Ottoman-Turkish Political Tradition

The salience of elite politics in Turkey stems largely from its history and culture. It has been pointed out by virtually every observer of Turkish politics that the Ottoman Empire was almost a textbook example of a patrimonial state. Authority was concentrated in the hands of an absolute monarch (*sultan*) who wielded it with the aid of a vast bureaucratic-military apparatus. Members of the apparatus, namely, officers of the court and the army, civil servants, and *ulema* (Islamic scholars) constituted the ruling class; the rest of society, Muslim and non-Muslim subjects (*reaya*), had no part in the government. To this rigid dichotomy between the ruling class and the ruled were added other features which made the Sultan the undisputed master over the ruling class itself. One such feature was the recruitment (*devsirme*) system, which was a periodic levy of the male children of Christian subjects. They were reduced to the status of slaves and trained for the service of the state. Because these slaves legally became the sultan's property—as he could take their lives and confiscate their wealth without legal process—they were in no position to challenge his authority. Furthermore, their removal from their former social environments prevented the development of locally entrenched, semiautonomous elements in the provinces.

A second feature, also instrumental in maintaining a strong central authority over the large territories of the empire, was the Ottoman land tenure system. The system vested in the state the original ownership of all the land, and limited the rights of fief holders (*sipahi*) to the collection of taxes and the supervision of peasants under their jurisdiction. In return for the land grant, the fief holder was expected to recruit, train, and support a local contingent of soldiers to join the army in time of war. The fiefs were granted by the central government and, if necessary, could be taken away by it. Furthermore, the largest fiefs were the perquisites of office and consequently held only temporarily. Thus, fief holders were members of a state service class rather than of a hereditary aristocracy with independent bases of power in the provinces.

In short, with no feudalism comparable to that of Western Europe, no hereditary aristocracy, no autonomous church organization, no strong merchant class or artisan guilds, no self-governing cities, and with a ruling class staffed with slaves, the Ottoman Empire represented a close approximation of an Oriental despotism.[4] What kind of political culture did such a structure produce? Perhaps its most important element was the respect for and the exaltation of political authority. Since the Ottoman state was largely autonomous of societal forces in the sense that political power was divorced from economically defined class relations, a corollary of the respect for authority was that members of the ruling class were supposed to serve "the state" rather than any particular social group. A third element was that the social order was of divine origin and, hence, immutable. It was the sultan's duty to maintain this order by keeping people in their appropriate social positions. Finally, political power, absolute though it was, was to be exercised with justice and with the aim of promoting public welfare. This last notion gave the Ottoman-Turkish state its paternalistic character, if more in theory than in practice. Interestingly, not only the ruling class but also the subject masses seemed to share this belief in the paternalistic nature of the state, as evidenced by the popular expression of "father-state" (*devlet baba*).[5]

Given the highly centralized structure of the Ottoman state, the powerful socializing mechanisms provided by the palace schools that trained the recruited military and administrative officials, and the ever-present influence of Islam, it is not surprising that a remarkably high degree of unity in elite outlook was obtained. Indeed, this unity and the strong tradition of serving the state seem to have played a major role in the rapid rise of the Ottoman Empire. In the eighteenth century, concomitant with the gradual decay of the land tenure system and the weakening of the central government, some local notables were able to hold a measure of de facto autonomy in their areas. The influence of local notables seems to have reached its peak in the early nineteenth century, when they forced Sultan Mahmud II to sign a charter in 1808 that gave "formal recognition to feudal rights and autonomies in the Ottoman Empire."[6] However, the concept of power sharing between the central government and local forces was extremely alien to Ottoman political thought. Indeed, Mahmud II had signed the charter very reluctantly, and did not hesitate to suppress the autonomy of notables as soon as he restored central authority. From that time until the 1950s, local notables remained clearly subordinate in political influence to the central state elites.

More important for our purposes is the fracturing of the old elite unity, also starting from the early nineteenth century concomitant with the reform or modernization movement in the empire. Continued defeats at the hands of European powers convinced the sultans that the only way to save the state was to introduce modernizing reforms, first in the military field and later on in other fields as well. Reforming sultans were supported in this endeavor by a small number of officials who had been exposed to European ideas. This understandably caused a reaction by the more traditionalist elements of the state elites. Such opposition was motivated not only on religious grounds but also by the fear that reforms would undermine the bases of their power and status in the society. Indeed, much of nineteenth-century Ottoman history can be written in terms of the intraelite conflict between the reformist and conservative wings of the state elites. Gradually, the reforming bureaucrats and military officers established their domination over the state apparatus. While doing so, they also increasingly asserted their own authority vis-à-vis the sultans. In the Young Turk era (1908-1918) "they came to wield power themselves behind something of a smokescreen of constitutional reforms. The Young Turk revolution was in part a victory for the modern bureaucratic intelligentsia over the palace."[7]

Thus, politics was clearly elite politics during the last century of the Ottoman Empire, although the first signs of mass involvement in politics, such as political party activity, election campaigns, and mass rallies, could be observed in the Young Turk period. Elite domination was so strong, however, that Bernard Lewis succinctly states that the government of Turkey was still the accepted and recognized prerogative of an elite of professionals, who retained all the rights and duties of politics, including that of opposition. It was, therefore, among the servants of the state that the pioneers of revolutionary change emerged; it was in the schools—those nurseries of the civil and military elite, so carefully tended by the Sultan himself—that the seeds of a revolution were sown.[8]

In the second half of the nineteenth century and the early twentieth century, there appeared a new division within the official elite, in addition to the one between the reformers and the conservatives. This one pitted the liberals or the constitutionalists against the supporters of authoritarian reform from above. Although both sides were committed to modernization and thus differed from the traditionalists, the liberals soon found themselves with a dilemma that was to be faced by many generations of future modernizers: the liberals wanted to have a parliament as an alternative and modern source of legitimacy. They soon realized, however, than an alliance between the traditionalist elements within the old center and the local forces in the periphery could easily threaten the reform movement under a system of free, competitive elections. There lies one of the main sources of paradoxes and ambiguities in the Young Turks' views on democracy. Such ambiguities were inherited by the Kemalist Republic, as will be spelled out below.

## State Elites in the Kemalist Period (1920-1950)

Although the Kemalist Republic is often seen as a radical departure from the Ottoman past, a more careful examination reveals many important continuities. Rustow insightfully argues, for example, that

> a transformation in cultural content of such scope and speed was made possible through a remarkable degree of continuity in political leadership and political method. It has been characteristic of Turkey's gradualist pattern of political development that its political elite changed most drastically at times when political institutions underwent little change (e.g., 1908-18 and since 1950), and that its political institutions were extensively recast (in 1919-1925) when the composition of the elite remained essentially unchanged.[9]

Perhaps the most important element of continuity was the continued domination of the state elites. Rustow notes that fully 93 percent of the empire's general staff officers and 85 percent of its civil servants continued their service in Turkey after the breakup of the Ottoman Empire.[10] Just as the Young Turk movement was dominated by the officials (bureaucrats and the military officers), so were the single-party Assemblies of the Republic. Frey has shown that officials constituted about half of all members of Parliament in all single-party Assemblies from 1920 up to 1947 (Table 7.1)

Table 7.1 Occupations of Deputies and Deputies Born in Region of Constituency Represented, National Assembly, Turkey, 1920–1954 (in percentages)

| Occupation | Assembly | | | | | | | | | |
|---|---|---|---|---|---|---|---|---|---|---|
| | I 1920 | II 1923 | III 1927 | IV 1931 | V 1935 | VI 1939 | VII 1943 | VIII 1946 | IX 1950 | X 1954 |
| Officials[a] | 43 | 54 | 54 | 45 | 48 | 47 | 47 | 36 | 22 | 21 |
| Professionals | 18 | 20 | 22 | 22 | 24 | 27 | 31 | 35 | 45 | 44 |
| Economic[b] | 19 | 14 | 16 | 22 | 19 | 19 | 16 | 24 | 29 | 29 |
| Religion | 17 | 7 | 4 | 3 | 3 | 2 | 1 | 1 | 1 | 1 |
| Other[c] | 4 | 4 | 5 | 7 | 5 | 5 | 4 | 3 | 4 | 5 |
| Deputies born in region of constituency represented | 72 | 64 | 55 | 56 | 41 | 47 | 49 | 66 | 68 | 71 |

*Source:* Adapted from Frederick W. Frey, *The Turkish Political Elite* (Cambridge: MIT Press, 1965), pp. 181, 190.
[a]Includes government officials, military officers, and educators.
[b]Includes persons in trade, agriculture, and banking.
[c]Includes journalists.

The first Assembly elected in 1920 is a partial exception because the exigencies of the War of Liberation forced the Kemalists to co-opt a relatively large number of local notables and religious leaders. With the victory in the war, however, the Kemalists consolidated their position and the official representation in the Assembly reached its peak in the 1923 and 1927 elections, while the religious contingent dwindled rapidly.

The next major change was in 1946, when multiparty competition was introduced. Although the People's Republican Party (RPP) won the 1946 elections, there was a noticeable decline in the representation of officials and a corresponding increase in the percentage of deputies with a professional or economic background. This tendency became even more marked in the Ninth Assembly, when the opposition Democratic Party (DP) came to power with an electoral landslide in 1950 and the Republicans were turned out of office after almost three decades in power. Parallel to these changes in the occupational structure of the Assembly, one can also discern an interesting change in the degree of localism of parliamentarians (as measured by the percentage of deputies born in region of constituency represented). From a relatively high level in 1920, localism declines sharply in the single-party years and rises again with the introduction of multiparty politics. "Changes in the character of the People's Party itself in the last years of the single party era," Frey observes, "heralded further changes when the Democratic Party took over in the Ninth Assembly of 1950. One gains the impression from these data of mounting pressures gradually eroding a structure, which first shows relatively slight strains and cracks, is shored up, and then succumbs entirely with a startling and resounding crash."[11]

Going back to the single-party years, the elite background data cited above clearly demonstrate the ascendancy of the official elites in the period. In addition to the continuity of the social background characteristics of the political elites, the Republic also inherited from the Ottoman times an exceedingly elitist outlook. In this "bureaucratic ruling tradition," the official elites saw themselves as the true servants of a state above and autonomous from society, the sole guardians of public interest, and the chief agents of modernization. The Kemalist principle of revolutionism (inkilapcilik) means, among other things, that revolutionary cadres (in the Turkish case, the modernizing officials) had the right and duty to carry out a complete transformation of society. In Kemal Atatürk's view, "every society has a collective idea. If it is not always expressed or explained, it should not be concluded that it does not exist. In actuality, it always exists. ... True revolutionaries are those who know how to discover the real preferences in the spirits and consciences of people whom they want to lead into a revolution of progress and renovation."[12] Thus, the function of the revolutionary cadres was to discover this "collective idea" of the society, express it, and illuminate the people on the road to progress. In this perspective, politics was seen not as a process of accommodating and aggregating diverse demands and interests of social groups but of discovering what is right for the entire society.[13]

At this point, it can legitimately be asked how this elitist outlook can be reconciled with other Kemalist principles such as populism and national sovereignty. Indeed, populism was constantly emphasized throughout the Kemalist period, and the principle of national sovereignty was given a lofty place in the constitutions of 1921 and 1924. No easy answer is possible for this question. It will be argued here that such contradictions are inherent in the Kemalist views on democracy and that they go a long way in explaining many apparent paradoxes in Turkish politics, both in the Kemalist period and after.

Populism was used in three different senses by the Kemalists, often simultaneously. One was popular sovereignty or rule by the people. The second was equality before the law and a rejection of group and family privileges. The third was a solidarist view of society that held that the Turkish nation was "constituted not of classes but of solidary, closely interdependent occupational groups. It was a Turkish version of the solidarist ideas outlined by the French radical politician Leon Bourgeois and the sociologist Emile Durkheim."[14] Populism in this sense had strong antecedents in the Young Turk era, particularly in the thoughts of Ziya Gökalp, the leading ideologue of the Young Turks. Gökalp, a disciple of Durkheim's, defined populism as follows: "If a society comprises a certain number of strata or classes, this means that it is not egalitarian. The aim of populism is to suppress the class or strata differences and to replace them with a social structure composed of occupational groups solidary with each other. In other words, we can summarize populism by saying: there are no classes, there are occupations."[15] Similarly, Atatürk often expressed the view that Turkish society was not composed of antagonistic social classes with conflicting interests but of occupational groups that needed one another and whose interests were in harmony. He further argued that the Republican People's Party was the representative not of any particular social class but of the entire Turkish people.[16] The ambiguity of the notion of populism and its simultaneous use in different senses can perhaps be best seen in its definition provided by the RPP program adopted at the Fourth Party Congress in May 1935:

> The source of will and sovereignty is the nation. The Party considers it an important principle that this will and sovereignty be used to regulate the proper fulfillment of the mutual duties of the citizen to the State and of the State to the citizen. We consider the individuals who accept an absolute equality before the law, and who recognize no privileges for any individual family, class, or community to be ... populist. It is one of our main principles to consider the people of the Turkish Republic, not as composed of different classes, but as a community divided into various professions according to the requirements of the division of labor for the individual and social life of the Turkish people. The farmers, handcraftsmen, laborers and workmen, people exercising free professions, industrialists, merchants, and public servants are the main groups of work constituting the Turkish com-

munity. The aims of our Party ... are to secure social order and solidarity
instead of class conflict and to establish harmony of interests.[17]

Thus, populism in the sense of solidarism and corporatism was not compatible with liberal and pluralistic democracy, but populism in the sense of
popular sovereignty and popular rule provided a democratic impulse.
Although commitment to the principle of popular sovereignty did not prevent the establishment of a single-party regime, it remains a fact that no
component of the RPP doctrine provided a permanent justification for such a
regime. As Duverger points out, "The Turkish single-party system was never
based upon the doctrine of a single party. It gave no official recognition to
the monopoly, made no attempts to justify it by the existence of a classless
society or the desire to do away with parliamentary strife and liberal democracy. It was always embarrassed and almost ashamed of the monopoly. The
Turkish single party had a bad conscience."[18] The single-party system was
advocated as a temporary measure to protect the revolution, not as a permanent or ideal system befitting the Turkish nation. Two attempts were made
(in 1924 and 1930) to experiment with opposition parties. Although both
experiments were short-lived, that such attempts were made at all remains
highly significant.[19] Finally, it is impossible to understand the peaceful transition in 1945-1950 to a multi-party system without bearing in mind the
"democratic impulse" of the Kemalist regime.[20]

The Kemalist period was one not only of undisputed domination of the
state elites and of an elitist point of view but also of a very high degree of
elite unity. The intraelite conflict between the more radical and the more
conservative elements among the revolutionary officials, witnessed during
and immediately after the War of Liberation, was decisively resolved in
favor of the radicals by the mid-1920s.[21] Thereafter, various subgroups of
the official elites (the military, bureaucrats, intellectuals, parliamentary and
party elites) were effectively united under the leadership of Kemal Atatürk,
imbued with a sense of mission of transforming and modernizing Turkish
society. An elitist and bureaucratic outlook permeated the entire state apparatus. As one observer noted, "Until 1950, there existed a sort of closed corporation of professional public servants who, acting as politicians, passed
laws which they and their colleagues administered as bureaucrats."[22] Two
other students of Turkish bureaucracy argued similarly that "under the
Kemalists, the official elite grew accustomed to almost unchallenged power
and to the social prestige which accompanied such power. The Republican
People's Party was bureaucratized; bureaucratic and political power was
largely fused to create an apparatus to impose the officials' will on the public."[23]

However, the very success of the Kemalist efforts at modernization and
the consequent differentiation of society in time created an alternative or
counterelite. This elite was composed of businessmen, merchants, profes-

sionals, and local notables. Although they were also committed to modernization, they differed from the official Kemalist elites both in their social background characteristics and in their nonofficial, nontutelary view of state and society. With the introduction of free electoral competition in 1950, this new alternative political elite, organized in the Democratic Party (DP), came to power, easily mobilizing the peripheral forces such as peasants and urban lower classes. Thus, the 1950 elections can be described as a victory of the periphery over the center, that is, the world of officialdom. Frey succinctly summarized the meaning and implications of this change for Turkish politics:

> Much of the political history of the era is wrapped up in the decline of the officials and the rise of the professional and economic contingents in the Grand National Assembly. The new man in Turkish politics is the lawyer and the merchant, replacing the soldier and the bureaucrat at the pinnacle of formal power. . . . The deputies have changed from being primarily a national elite group, oriented toward the tutelary development of the country, to being primarily an assemblage of local politicians, oriented toward more immediate local and political advantages. . . . The key conflict of contemporary Turkish politics . . . is the conflict between the residual national elite, basically found within or in support of the People's Party (perhaps until recently), and the new breed of local politicians, basically found in the Democratic Party and its successor. The local politicos, however, now have obtained strong representation, even dominance, in all political parties. The nationalist politicians, with strong external support from some of the military, the bureaucracy and generally from intellectuals, want to continue intensive Turkish development under as strong central surveillance as seems politically feasible. They favor major sacrifices of present consumption and satisfaction so as to invest in creating a stronger industrialized nation in the future. They tend to be, like their Kemalist forebearers, intellectual and official in their approach to politics even if they are no longer so overwhelmingly official in vocation. The localists, on the contrary, are much more closely attuned to the immediate satisfaction of local expectations, both as a device for obtaining political power and from conviction. They tend to emphasize local initiative, free enterprise, a relaxation of religious restrictions, and an interpretation of democracy that caters to local interests.[24]

## Tension Between State Elites and Political Elites

One immediate outcome of the transition to a multiparty system in Turkey was the fracturing of the Kemalist unity within the elite and "the resurrection of severe intraelite conflict."[25] One could no longer speak of the unity between political elites, as represented by the DP, and the official elites with strong ideological and emotional ties to the RPP. The DP government attempted to "debureaucratize" the society consistent with its program, the official elites strongly resisted it. In the eyes of the DP leaders, this amounted to an unwarranted obstruction of the "national will." The bureaucrats, on the other hand, saw it as their duty to protect "public interest" against "incompetent and unprincipled" politicians elected by an "ignorant" majority. They viewed the use of state funds for political patronage purposes as an unforgivable squandering of the public treasury. They were also deeply troubled by the DP government's careless attitude toward the "rule of law," as well as by its more permissive policies toward religious activities, which they considered a betrayal of the Kemalist legacy of secularism. They resented political pressures by local party organizations, which they had not been accustomed to in the single-party period.

The DP era (1950-1960) can be described as one of the "debureaucratization" of Turkish society. Not only did official elites lose their once preeminent representation in parliament and their strong ties with political elites but their overall influence, status, prestige, security, and income declined sharply as well. The decline in prestige of bureaucratic careers is vividly demonstrated by a survey of high school students conducted in 1959. About half of the students ranked free professions as the vocation most respected, but only 12 percent thought so about the combined category of government and politics, and another 10 percent for the military. The percentage of those who expected to enter into a bureaucratic or military career was even lower: 7 percent each.[26] A 1956 survey found job satisfaction lowest in the Ministry of Interior (only 32 percent satisfied) compared with the Ministry of Finance (55 percent), the Ministry of Foreign Affairs (89 percent), and the new, non-central government organizations (91 percent). An obvious explanation is that officials in the Ministry of Interior (governors and district governors) are in closest contact with voters and therefore subject to much stronger political pressures than other bureaucrats. In fact, in the same survey, district governors were asked if they came across political interference that could be considered harmful to the conduct of public affairs. The distribution of answers was as follows: 14 percent replied "often;" 38 percent, "sometimes;" 40 percent, "seldom;" and 8 percent left the answer blank.[27] A similar decline could also be observed in the incomes of bureaucrats and army officers. A study showed that between 1952 and 1957, the purchasing power of civil servants fell by 43 to 69 percent.[28] Finally, the DP-dominated Assembly passed laws enabling the government to force higher civil servants (including judges) into early retirement and even precludied the judicial review of such acts, thus severely curtailing job security for the bureaucrats.

Against this background of constant tension, it is easy to understand the extent and intensity of negative feelings among bureaucrats towards the DP government. In fact, the 1960 military coup that toppled the Menderes government can be seen as a reaction of the official elites, military and civilian alike, against the decline of their power, status, and prestige in Turkish society. It is difficult to explain, without bearing in mind the intensity of such feelings, the ease with which a small group of relatively junior officers was

able to carry out the coup. A few quotations from interviews with the insti-
gators of the coup, who later organized themselves into the National Unity
Committee, suggest the political atmosphere that prevailed in 1960: "I am
convinced that the [Atatürk] reforms retrogressed during the period now
behind us. In fact this was the greatest evil" (General Gürsel). "The 27 May
Revolution was a rising-up of the present generation trained by the revolutionary spirit of Atatürk with a view to protecting and rescuing the revolution of the great Atatürk from those who, during the last ten years, wanted to
upset and destroy it out of a thirst for power" (Lieutenant Colonel Kabibay).
"After 1950 I saw with regret that they [the DP leaders] were leaving the
civilized road Atatürk had outlined for the improvement of the Turkish
nation, that the nation was being dragged backwards ... in every field"
(Colonel Yurdakuler). Atatürk's reforms "were betrayed" (Captain
Solmazer). The Democrats "dragged the country into disaster in the economic and social fields. ... An unreasonable consumption began. In 10 years we
became one of the poorest nations in the world" (Major Erkanli). "The corruption in the country and the social decay which was going on at great
speed were veiled and concealed by a policy of greed based on group domination under the guise of economic development" (Lieutenant Colonel M.
Kaplan).[29]

In the 1960 coup and its immediate aftermath, a very substantial degree
of unity could be observed among various sections of the state elites that had
been downgraded during the DP period. The coup was carried out, as was
pointed out above, by a small group of middle-ranking army officers, but it
found widespread and enthusiastic support within the military in general, the
civilian bureaucracy, and among intellectuals. It is symbolically significant
that in the wake of the coup, the task of drafting a new and democratic constitution was entrusted to a committee of university professors. Only when it
was perceived many months later that such a group would not be sufficiently
representative of public opinion did the National Unity Committee decide on
6 January 1961 to establish a Constituent Assembly for the task.

The Constituent Assembly was not, however, a popularly elected body.
The National Unity Committee acted as one of the chambers of this bicamer-
al assembly. The other chamber, the House of Representatives, was composed partly by members elected indirectly and partly by representatives of
various institutions such as the two existing political parties (the DP had
already been dissolved), the judiciary, universities, bar associations, labor
unions, chambers of commerce and industry, farmers' associations, the
press, and the like. The House of Representatives was effectively dominated
by the members and sympathizers of the RPP, while the DP supporters were
by and large excluded from the constitution-making process.

The product of the Constituent Assembly, the 1961 Constitution of
Turkey, ratified by popular vote on 9 July 1961, reflected the basic political
values and interests of the state elites. Thus, on the one hand, the constitu-

tion greatly expanded civil liberties and granted extensive social rights. On the other hand, it reflected a certain distrust of politicians and elected assemblies by creating an effective system of checks and balances to limit the power of such elected organs. These checks included the introduction of judicial review of the constitutionality of laws; the strengthening of the administrative courts with review powers over the acts of all executive agencies; independence for the judiciary; the creation of a second chamber of the legislative assembly; improvement of job security for civil servants and especially judges; and the granting of substantial administrative autonomy to certain public agencies such as the universities and the Radio and Television Corporation. It was hoped that the power of the elected assemblies would be effectively balanced by judicial and other bureaucratic agencies, and that the newly expanded civil liberties and social rights would ensure the gradual development of a genuinely pluralistic and democratic society.

## Toward an Accommodation

Tensions between state elites and elected politicians did not disappear with the making of the 1961 constitution. In fact, the 1961 elections gave a majority to the three parties (Justice Party, New Turkey Party, and the Republican Peasants Nation Party) that competed for the support of the former Democratic voters. The RPP, the party of the state elites, ended up with only 36.7 percent of the vote. Following a period of unstable coalition governments, the Justice Party (JP) gradually established itself as the principal heir to the DP. In the 1965 elections it gained about 53 percent of the popular vote and of the National Assembly seats. The JP repeated its success in 1969, when it won an absolute majority of the Assembly seats with a somewhat reduced percentage of the popular vote (46.5). Thus, Turkey appeared to have achieved, once again, a popularly elected and stable government.

Tensions continued to exist, however, on both sides in this period. The more radical elements in the armed forces were disappointed by the results of the 1961 elections. The two coup attempts in 1962 and 1963 led by Colonel Talat Aydemir, the commandant of the War College, were narrowly averted, mainly thanks to Ismet Inönü's presence at the head of the government, which was reassuring to most officers. Even after the failure of the Aydemir attempts, political activity by army leaders continued and eventually led to the "coup by memorandum" on 12 March 1971, as will be explained below.

The JP, in turn, was ambivalent in its attitude toward the 1961 constitution. It took care to operate clearly within the limits of the constitution, it criticized those aspects of it that, in its view, gave excessive powers to bureaucratic and judicial agencies. The JP also demanded a stronger executive. The views of Celal Bayar, the deposed president of the Republic under the DP regime, were both more systematic and more extreme on this matter. Bayar argued that the 1924 constitution was more in accordance with the Kemalist notion of unconditional sovereignty of the nation, because it concentrated all power in the National Assembly as the sole representative of the Turkish nation. The 1961 constitution, on the other hand, introduced new partners into the exercise of national sovereignty: the army and the intellectuals. Thus, it reflected a distrust of elected assemblies and represented a return to the Ottoman notion of tripartite (palace, army, and religious scholars) government.[30] No doubt, such negative views of the 1961 constitution were partly motivated by the fact that the old Democrats had been almost totally excluded from its making, and partly by their being the "natural" majority party in the 1950s and 1960s and therefore resentful of bureaucratic limitations upon the power of elected assemblies.

There are strong indications, however, that tensions between state elites and the JP as the majority party tended to decrease in the 1960s. The JP government treated the military with much greater care and respect than the DP government had. The National Security Council, an advisory body created by the 1961 constitution and composed of certain ministers and the highest commanders of the armed forces, gave the military a legitimate voice in the formulation of national security policies. The election of former military commanders as president of the Republic (General Gürsel in 1961 and General Sunay in 1966) was also a reassuring factor for most officers. Finally, salaries and other side benefits for officers were greatly improved in the 1960s. Although a strong radical faction within the armed forces was still quite unhappy with the JP government and its basically conservative policies, its conspiratorial activities failed to gain the support of the top military leadership. These radical officers, frustrated by the successive electoral victories of the JP, aimed at establishing a longer-term military regime to carry out radical social reforms. In fact, the military memorandum of 12 March 1971, which forced the JP government to resign, was a last-minute move by the top military commanders to forestall a radical coup. In the days following the memorandum, most of the radical officers were summarily retired or dismissed, thereby strengthening the position of the more conservative leadership of the military. The so-called 12 March Regime did not go as far as dissolving the parliament and assuming power directly. Instead, it urged the formation of an "above-party" or technocratic government under a veteran RPP politician, Professor Nihat Erim. The policies of the nonparty government, with strong behind-the-scenes support from the military, were more in line with the JP's conservative philosophy. The constitutional amendments adopted in 1971 and 1973 especially reflected the JP's desire to strengthen the executive authority and to restrict certain civil liberties that were seen as responsible for the emergence of political extremism and violence.

Signs of accommodation between political elites and bureaucratic elites were even clearer. Leslie Roos and Noralou Roos, who interviewed a sample

of Turkish administrative elites in 1956 and 1965, observed significant differences between the findings of the two surveys. Thus, as opposed to 40
percent of the 1949-1952 graduates of the Political Science Faculty who
reported satisfaction with their jobs in 1956, 60 percent of the same respondents reported satisfaction in 1965. Similarly, 61 percent of the younger officials (1958-1961 graduates who had not been interviewed in 1956) said that
they were satisfied with their jobs.

The Roos and Roos findings also indicated a marked decline in the perceived political interference. For example, of the district governors who
were dissatisfied with their jobs, 49 percent complained about too much
political interference in 1956 and only 34 percent in 1965. Among those who
were given major promotions in the meantime, the level of job satisfaction
was much higher (63 percent) and perceived political interference much
lower (22 percent) than described by those who remained in the job of district governor.

Significantly, the respondents in the 1965 survey also showed little hostility toward politicians and businessmen. Thus, the largest percentage (46
percent) thought that a citizen could best benefit his country by being a busi-
nessman and another 20 percent by holding political office. Roos and Roos
conclude that "businessmen and politicians—the groups which most successfully challenged the traditional power and prestige of the Turkish official
class—were the two groups seen as making the biggest contribution to the
development of the Turkish state. Government administrators were ranked a
poor third, and almost no one had a kind word to say for the military."[31]

Such change should not be attributed to an improvement in the status,
prestige, influence, or pay of civil servants in the 1960s. On the contrary,
more recent data show that government service remains, on the whole, a
poorly paid and low-prestige occupation to this day. In Ömer Bozkurt's 1978
survey of a representative sample of Turkey's civil servants, the largest
group (42 percent) cited unavailability of other jobs as the reason for their
choice of a government service career. Another 40.6 percent mentioned job
security, and only 6.2 percent job prestige. Satisfaction with authority or pay,
or the attractiveness of the job were hardly mentioned at all. Also, 52.8 percent had negative job evaluations; 28.8 percent had positive evaluations, and
18.4 percent were indifferent. Only 28.5 percent of the respondents thought
that a civil service career had greater respectability than other occupations;
however, 71 percent thought that civil servants ought to enjoy such a special
respectability.[32]

If there has been no improvement in the overall status of civil servants
since 1960, then lessening of the tensions between them and political elites
has to be explained by systemic factors. Roos and Roos have argued that

> several factors appear to have acted to diminish bureaucrat-politician con-
> flict between 1956 and 1965. The politicians' experience with military

> intervention might have been expected to lessen local interference in administrative matters. The psychological shock associated with the end of bureaucratic dominance would seem to have passed by 1965. Bureaucrats may have been more used to the ways of local leadership in 1965 than in 1956. ... An increase in mutual understanding between politician and bureaucrat may have occurred. A recognition of the importance of working together may have replaced some of the antagonism at the local level. ... Given the central role of bureaucrat-politician conflict in recent formulations of Turkish politics, this finding may have major significance for the political system."[33]

If one important trend in the post-1960 period was a gradual accommodation between political and bureaucratic elites, another was the decline in the unity of outlook of official elites. It must be remembered that the military, the bureaucrats, and the intellectuals retained such unity in the 1950s and collaborated closely in the 1960 coup. With the more liberal atmosphere provided by the 1961 constitution, however, intellectuals and bureaucrats have been increasingly exposed to and influenced by various political ideologies. Kemalism, although still a powerful intellectual legacy, ceased to be the unifying factor among official elites, particularly because it was open to various and conflicting interpretations. Furthermore, ties among the military, bureaucrats, and intellectuals seem to have been eroded by social change, as evidenced by the findings of the 1965 administrative elite survey mentioned above; when respondents were asked, "In which of the following ways can a citizen best benefit his country?" only one person noted serving in the military.[34] Similarly, the military's harsh treatment of intellectuals (professors, writers, journalists, and others) in the 1971 and 1980 interventions was a far cry from the cordial collaboration between the two groups in 1960.

Among sectors of the state elite, only the military seems to have retained its internal unity throughout the entire period, although some signs of factionalism and politicization were observed even within its own ranks in the 1960s and the 1970s.[35] The military's relative insulation from the political polarization and fragmentation of the period seems to be due to extraordinarily strong socializing influences within the Turkish military. Such socializing mechanisms and the resulting "military mind" have been aptly analyzed by a leading Turkish research journalist, Mehmet Ali Birand. Birand observes that for a majority of officers, politicians in general give precedence to personal or partisan-ideological interests over national interest. The armed forces should not get involved in partisan politics, but if the country or the Kemalist principles are endangered, it is their duty to intervene. Turkey owes its existence and independence to Atatürk and his revolution. It is the duty of the armed forces to protect Atatürk's principles. Turkey is located in a hostile international environment and, therefore, is constantly exposed to external and internal threats. A majority of the population is ignorant; they can be misguided or deceived by ambitious politicians.

Democracy, as Atatürk stated, is the best form of government for Turkey, provided that democratic competition does not endanger Atatürk's principles, in which case the army has not only the right but also the duty to intervene.[36] Certain corroborating evidence was provided by an officially conducted survey of the War College students. In this 1983 survey, 60.6 percent of the students thought that the most important reason for the failure of governmental institutions was the absence of "honest and hard working" ruling cadres, which indicated a certain distrust of politicians. For a majority of them (55 percent), the most important problem to be solved is education, and education must be based on Atatürk's principles.[37]

Thus, while Turkey went some way in bringing about an accommodation between political and state elites in the 1960s, this did not lead to a healthy balance between the expertise of an impartial and competent bureaucracy and the political control exercised by elected politicians. As of the mid-1970s, Heper observed, "the Turkish bureaucratic elite's longing for a tutelary bureaucracy" still continued, and it was still in a position to affect the parameters of the political stratification in Turkey.[38] The coalition governments of the mid and late 1970s, however, did much to destroy the professional competence, unity of outlook, and esprit de corps of civil bureaucracy. As one observer of the period succinctly summarizes,

> The coalition members were each heavily engaged in unrestrained patronage and nepotism. Never before in Turkish political development had the civil servants been reshuffled in such an arbitrary fashion. Governments, or rather political parties making up the coalition, did not confine themselves to bringing their own teams to the upper ranks of the civil service. The reshuffling involved all ranks. In addition, thousands of new civil service posts were created. Each ministry was brought under the complete jurisdiction of a political party as if each ministry had been "appropriated" by a political party. The more critical posts were usually filled by ideologically committed militants or by outright partisan roughnecks. Even the most sensitive agencies like the police and security services were not immune from this ideological and physical penetration of the civil bureaucracy by the political parties.[39]

Thus, when the military intervention of 12 September 1980 took place, the military was about the only bureaucratic institution that was by and large able to insulate itself from such fragmentation, infiltration, and colonization by political parties. With the military in power, tutelary bureaucratic values were again in ascendancy, and were strongly embodied in the 1982 constitution.

The 1982 constitution was even less trustful than its predecessor of the "national will," elected assemblies, political parties, politicians, and all other civil society institutions such as trade unions, professional organizations, and voluntary associations. If the 1982 constitution somewhat curbed the review powers of the judiciary and the autonomy of the universities, this was not intended as a measure to strengthen the hands of elected assemblies and responsible governments at the expense of bureaucratic agencies. Rather, the intention was to create a strong presidency, which the makers of the 1982 constitution (themselves almost all military officers and civilian bureaucrats) assumed would be controlled by the military for a long time to come (indeed, General Evren, the leader of the 1980 coup, served as the president of the Republic until November 1989). A major difference between the makings of the 1961 and the 1982 constitutions is that, in the latter case, the military no longer had much trust in civilian bureaucratic agencies, which it perceived as already highly fragmented and infiltrated by political parties and vulnerable to various kinds of radical political ideas. Therefore, the president of the Republic was given important substantive powers in the appointment of high-court judges and university administrators, the two areas considered particularly sensitive by the military. In short, the 1982 constitution was designed to maintain the military as the ultimate guardian and arbiter in the political system through a strengthened presidency and a strengthened National Security Council.[40]

## Post-1983 Developments

The Motherland Party (MP) government that came to power in the November 1983 elections, ending the three-year period of military government, continued essentially the anticenter, antibureaucratic line of its predecessors, the Democratic Party and the Justice Party. The MP's approach to the state bureaucracy, however, was simultaneously more ideological and more pragmatic compared to its predecessors'. More ideological in that for the first time in Turkish politics, smaller government, less governmental involvement in the economy, greater reliance on market forces, privatization of public economic enterprises, and an overall reduction of state activities became consciously articulated policy goals. More pragmatic in that the MP governments attempted to debureaucratize the political system through indirect methods (of which more to be said below) rather than by way of sweeping purges, as had been done in the 1970s, or by engaging in virulent anti-state rhetoric, as had been done by the Democratic Party leaders in the 1950s.

A reduction of bureaucratic red tape was one of the six major planks of the MP in its 1983 election platform, and it seems to have found a sympathetic response in public opinion. Prime Minister Özal, in the program of his first government emphasized this theme by saying that "public services should be saved from excessive formalities and the morass of details." He further argued that trust, instead of suspicion, should be the guiding principle in the relationships between individuals and state agencies.[41] Indeed, many such formalities were simplified or eliminated by the MP governments in the following years.[42]

Much more important than the reduction of bureaucratic red tape were the indirect ways in which the MP government reduced the overall level of influence of the state bureaucracy in Turkish politics. These methods can be summarized as follows:

• The ideological fragmentation of the civilian bureaucracy, which had started in the 1970s, was allowed to continue. Partly as a result of the coalitional character of the MP, certain ministries, especially those of Interior and National Education, became the strongholds of the religious, conservative, and/or ultranationalist wing of the MP. The unity of outlook within the bureaucratic elite; the reformist, secularist, and tutelary weltanschauung of the old bureaucratic center was further weakened and fragmented.

• The overall status and income of civil servants were allowed to decline even further, to such an extent that the prestige of a civil service job can no longer compete with that of a business or professional career.

• New public agencies were created, subject to more flexible rules and easier political manipulation (the typical examples are the Undersecretariat for Treasury and Foreign Trade, and the Board of Housing and Public Partnership Fund).

• A large number of "extra-budgetary funds" were established that are subject neither to the approval of the Parliament nor to the supervision of the Court of Accounts.

• Many bureaucratic posts were filled on a contractual basis, which offered much less job security but higher salaries.

• Instead of relying on the seniority rule, the MP governments appointed a large number of young, bright, U.S.-educated managers with no previous public bureaucratic experience (jokingly referred to as Özal's princes) as the heads of some of the most important governmental agencies (including the Central Bank) and public economic enterprises.

• The reduction of government controls over economic affairs led to a decline in the overall influence of public bureaucracy.

• In the same vein, the devolution of some powers to elected local governments meant a decline in the influence of the central bureaucracy.[43]

Furthermore, the general political atmosphere in the country in the post-1983 period has not been conductive to a tutelary bureaucratic mentality. With the transition back to democratic politics in 1983, there has been a sudden surge of interest in liberal values and an increasing emphasis on civil society institutions. There seems to be a much stronger consensus now among political parties and in the society at large on the preservation and consolidation of the newly reestablished democratic regime. Consequently, the tendency to see the state bureaucracy as the sole guardian of public interest is much less evident today compared to earlier periods. A parallel and related development is the greater legitimation of a free market economy and private sector activities. This is in marked contrast tothe earlier negative attitude toward business groups, as summarized by a student of these groups as late as the mid-1960s:

> In Turkey, the notion of business is misunderstood. Often, the businessman is viewed as a speculator, if not a thief. Business in general and retailing and wholesaling in particular, were for a long time downgraded and looked upon as occupations which no respectable Turk would enter. ... No great business heroes have emerged in Turkey, no entrepreneur has gained social recognition, and no business leader has ever held public office.[44]

These developments, helpful though they are in a broad sense to the consolidation of democracy in Turkey, have not resulted in a clear delineation of roles between elected politicians and a stable, competent bureaucracy with a procedural (not substantive) rationality and an instrumental attitude. Rather, the result has been a chaotic situation characterized by the personalistic style of government of Özal and his entourage, frequent disregard for the rules and regulations, conflicts of jurisdiction among various public agencies, and a general decline in the quality and effectiveness of the state bureaucracy. Such a combination of a still high degree of "stateness" and a virtually complete debureaucratization of government is a potentially unstable mixture and "may portend an even more volatile political institutionalization pattern in future."[45]

## Notes

1. Frederick W. Frey, *The Turkish Political Elite* (Cambridge: MIT Press, 1965).
2. For the National Assemblies of 1961, 1965, 1969, and 1973, see Frank Tachau, "Parliamentary Elites: Turkey," in Jacob M. Landau, Ergun Özbudun and Frank Tachau, eds., *Electoral Politics in the Middle East: Issues, Voters and Elites* (London: Croom Helm; Stanford: Hoover Institution Press, 1980), pp. 205-242. Tachau also gives the occupational breakdown for the 1977 legislature, although he does not include it in his more detailed analyses. For the 1983 legislature, see Ersin Kalaycioglu, "Elites, Political Culture and the Political Regime in Turkey" (Paper presented at the annual meeting of the Middle Eastern Studies Association, San Francisco, 28 November–1 December, 1984), p. 6.
3. Frederick W. Frey, "Patterns of Elite Politics in Turkey," in George Lenczowski, ed., *Political Elites in the Middle East* (Washington, DC: American Enterprise Institute, 1975), p. 42.
4. The last two paragraphs draw from Ergun Özbudun, "Turkey: Crises, Interruptions and Reequilibrations," in Larry Diamond, Juan Linz, and Seymour Martin Lipset, eds., *Democracy in Developing Countries*, vol. 3, *Asia* (Boulder: Lynne Rienner Publishers, 1988); and Özbudun, *Social Change and Political Participation in Turkey* (Princeton: Princeton University Press, 1976), pp. 25-29. See also the sources cited therein.

5. Andrew Mango observes that "experience in statecraft, respect for the state, the importance of the state in Turkish culture, have all been specific steadying factors in the history of the Turkish Republic, endowing it with a degree of political gravitas, absent from most new countries." "The State of Turkey," *Middle Eastern Studies* 13 (May 1977): 265. On the traditional Ottoman political culture, see also Frank Tachau, "The Political Culture of Kemalist Turkey," in Jacob Landau, ed., *Atatürk and the Modernization of Turkey* (Boulder: Westview Press, 1984), pp. 58-62; C. H. Dodd, *Democracy and Development in Turkey* (North Humberside, U.K.: Eothen Press, 1979), pp. 34-40.

6. Bernard Lewis, *The Emergence of Modern Turkey* (London: Oxford University Press, 1968), p. 448.

7. Dodd, *Democracy and Development*, p. 43.

8. Lewis, *The Emergence*, pp. 194-195.

9. Dankwart A. Rustow, "Atatürk as Founder of a State," in *Professor Dr. Yavuz Abadan'a Armagan* (Ankara: A. U. Siyasal Bilgiler Fakultesi Yayinlari, 1969), pp. 567-568. See also Rustow, "Turkey: The Modernity of Tradition," in Lucian W. Pye and Sidney Verba, eds., *Political Culture and Political Development* (Princeton: Princeton University Press, 1965), pp. 197-198. An excellent article that stresses the elements of continuity with the late Ottoman period is Paul Dumont, "The Origins of Kemalist Ideology," in Landau, ed., *Atatürk and the Modernization of Turkey*, pp. 25-44. On the continuity between the late Ottoman and early Republican elites, see also Joseph S. Syliowicz, "Elites and Modernization in Turkey," in Frank Tachau, ed., *Political Elites and Political Development in the Middle East* (New York: Schenkman, 1975), pp. 30-31. He observes, however, that there was an evolutionary broadening of the pool of recruitment to bureaucratic elites, as measured by the increase in the number of students of nonelite and nonofficial backgrounds attending the Civil Service School (Mulkiye, the main source of bureaucratic elites) during the Atatürk era (pp. 31-32).

10. Dankwart A. Rustow, "The Military: Turkey," in Robert E. Ward and Dankwart A. Rustow, eds., *Political Modernization in Japan and Turkey* (Princeton: Princeton University Press, 1964), p. 388.

11. Frey, *The Turkish Political Elite*, pp. 180-182.

12. *Atatürk'un Söylev ve Demecleri*, vol. 2 (Ankara: Turk Inkilap Tarihi Enstitusu Yayinlari, 1959), pp. 197, 214.

13. Metin Heper, "Atatürk'te Devlet Düsüncesi," in *Cagdas Düsüncenin isiginda Atatürk* (Istanbul: Dr. Nejat F. Eczacibasi Vakfi Yayinlari, 1983), pp. 221-227. See also Heper, *Bürokratik Yönetim Gelenegi* (Ankara: O.D.T.U. Yayinlari, 1974); also Ilter Turan, "Continuity and Change in Turkish Bureaucracy: The Kemalist Period and After," in Landau, ed., *Atatürk and the Modernization of Turkey*, pp. 103-112.

14. Dumont, "The Origins," p. 31.

15. Ibid., p. 32.

16. Ibid., pp. 32-33; Ergun Özbudun, "Atatürk ve Devlet Hayati," in *Atatürk Ilkeleri ve Inkilap Tarihi II, Atatürkculuk: Atatürkcu Dusunce Sisteminin Temelleri* (Ankara: Yuksekogretim Kurulu Yayinlari, 1986), pp. 66-68.

17. Official translation quoted by Suna Kili, *Kemalism* (Istanbul: Robert College Publications, 1969), p. 78.

18. Maurice Duverger, *Political Parties* (New York: Wiley, 1959), p. 277. See also Ergun Ozbudun, "The Nature of the Kemalist Political Regime," in Ali Kazancigil and Ergun Özbudun, eds., *Atatürk: Founder of a Modern State* (London: C. Hurst, 1981), pp. 79-102.

19. For the Free Party episode of 1930, see Walter F. Weiker, *Political Tutelage and Democracy in Turkey: The Free Party and its Aftermath* (Leiden: E. J. Brill, 1973).

20. For details, see Özbudun, "Transition from Authoritarianism to Democracy in Turkey, 1945-1950" (Paper presented at the International Political Science Association World Congress, Paris, 15-20 July 1985).

21. For interesting comparative insights, see Frey, *The Turkish Political Elite*, pp. 410-413.

22. Richard L. Chambers, "Bureaucracy: Turkey," in Ward and Rustow, eds., *Political Modernization*, p. 326.

23. Leslie L. Roos, Jr., and Noralou P. Roos, *Managers of Modernization: Organizations and Elites in Turkey (1950-1969)* (Cambridge: Harvard University Press, 1971), pp. 31-32.

24. Frey, *The Turkish Political Elite*, pp. 195-197.

25. Ibid., p. 391.

26. Quoted by Roos and Roos, *Managers of Modernization*, pp. 83-84.

27. Ibid., pp. 45, 89.

28. C. H. Dodd, *Politics and Government in Turkey* (Berkeley and Los Angeles: University of California Press, 1969), p. 53.

29. These interviews were published by the Turkish daily, *Cumhuriyet*, between 16 July and 23 August 1960. An English translation is also available: Cevat F. Baskut, Yasar Kemal, and Ecvet Guresın, *Interviews with Members of Turkey's National Unity Committee* (Washington, DC, U.S. Joint Publications Research Service, 1960). See also Ergun Ozbudun, *The Role of the Military in Recent Turkish Politics*, Occasional Papers in International Affairs, No. 14, (Cambridge: Harvard University Center for International Affairs, 1966), pp. 15-21.

30. Quoted by Bulent Tanor, *Iki Anayasa, 1961-1982* (Istanbul: Beta, 1986), pp. 29-37, 61-67.

31. Roos and Roos, *Managers of Modernization*, pp. 95-98, 131-134, 160-165; the quotation is from p. 161.

32. Ömer Bozkurt, *Memurlar: Turkiye'de Kamu Burokrasisinin Sosyolojik Gorunumu* (Ankara: TODAIE, 1980), pp. 100-153.

33. Roos and Roos, *Managers of Modernization*, pp. 95, 221.

34. Ibid., p. 161.

35. For some useful insights on the recent role of the military in Turkey, see Kemal H. Karpat, "Military Interventions: Army-Civilian Relations in Turkey Before and After 1980," in Metin Heper and Ahmet Evin, eds., *State, Democracy and the Military: Turkey in the 1980s* (Berlin and New York: Walter de Gruyter, 1988), pp. 137-158; William Hale, "Transition to Civilian Governments in Turkey: The Military Perspective," ibid., pp. 159-175; George S. Harris, "The Role of the Military in Turkey in the 1980s: Guardians or Decision-Makers?" ibid., pp. 177-200.

36. Mehmet Ali Birand, *Emret Komutanim* (Istanbul: Milliyet, 1986), esp. pp. 114-154.

37. Osman Metin Ozturk, "Turkye'de Silahli Kuvvetler ve Siyaset" (Ph.D. diss., Ankara University, 1987), pp. 126-130.

38. Metin Heper, "The Recalcitrance of the Turkish Public Bureaucracy to 'Bourgeois Politics': A Multi-Factor Political Stratification Analysis," *Middle East Journal* 30 (Autumn 1976): 499-500.

39. Metin Heper, *The State Tradition in Turkey* (Walkington, U.K.: Eothen Press, 1985), pp. 114.

40. For a radically different interpretation of the 1980 military intervention and the 1982 constitution, see ibid., especially chap. 6. Heper, in fact, argues that now the state elites (including the military) do not presume that they are the sole possessors of truth, that they use Atatürkist thought as a technique and not as a source of substantive public policies, and that they aim at the creation of a political environment in which, through multiple confrontations of civil societal groups, a dynamic consensus

may be possible.

41. Nuran Dagli-Belma Aktürk, *Hükümetler ve Programlari, vol. 3, 1980-1987* (Ankara: TBMM Kütüphane-Dökümantasyon ve Tercüme Müdürlügü, 1988), p. 64.

42. Ibid., p. 104, as stated in the program of the second government of Özal read in the National Assembly on 25 December 1987.

43. For these trends, see Metin Heper, "The State and Debureaucratization: The Turkish Case," *International Social Science Journal* (forthcoming); and Heper, "The State, Political Party and Society in Post-1983 Turkey," *Government and Opposition* 25 (1990): 1-13.

44. Quoted by Heper, "The Recalcitrance," p. 491. Also interestingly, in the 1950s the Chamber of Commerce in Istanbul demanded that the bureaucrats be respectful to businessmen, and not to see them as "thieves with ties" (Heper, *The State Tradition*, p. 103).

45. Heper, "The State and Debureaucratization."

# • 8 •

# Christian Democracy, Liberation Theology, and Political Culture in Latin America

## Paul E. Sigmund

Twenty years ago the most influential book on religion and social change in the English-speaking world was Harvey Cox's *The Secular City*[1] which argued for acceptance by theologians of the inevitability of the process of secularization and called for the involvement by religious people in secular movements of social change. In Latin America, at least until the emergence of liberation theology, church-influenced reform movements seemed to be on the defensive, and some of them, for example, adopted in a wholly uncritical fashion the Marxism that dominated the universities, intellectual discourse, and nearly all protest movements in the continent. Only one important book, Ivan Vallier's *Catholicism, Social Control, and Modernization in Latin America*[2] was devoted to the possibilities of religiously based political movements, and it did so in a schematic and sociological way.

Now writings on the Roman Catholic Church and social change are a major sector in the area of Latin American studies in the United States. Besides general collections, including two published by Daniel Levine, we have country studies on Chile (Brian Smith), Brazil (Thomas Bruneau, Scott Mainwaring), Cuba (John M. Kirk), Central America (Phillip Berryman), Venezuela and Colombia (Daniel Levine), and Bolivia (Susan Nelson in the 1986 Levine collection).[3] In addition there is an immense bibliography on the Catholic left. A bibliography of works in English published in 1981 contains 3,966 entries; a similar list in Spanish published in Buenos Aires in the same year contains 6,000 entries; and Orbis Press has published more than 500 titles on related subjects.

Why is there so much interest in the subject? We can refer to the worldwide revival of interest in religion and to the politicization of what had been thitherto uninvolved religious groups from Iran to the American fundamentalists. However, in the Latin American case the explosion of scholarship and attention to the relation of religion to social change is a result of the continuing importance of Christianity—especially Roman Catholicism—as a source of legitimation and inspiration for political ideas, and of the rapid development over the past twenty-five years of a variety of competing politi-

cal ideas, ideologies, and political movements that are explicitly based on
the Christian message. In Latin American Catholicism, alternatives have
emerged to the traditional authoritarian conservatism that dominated the
continent for so many centuries. In this chapter I would like to trace the
"opening to the left" of Latin Catholicism, beginning first with the emergence of Christian reformist movements—mainly, but not only, the Christian
Democratic parties and related trade union and peasant movements—and
then moving to an analysis and evaluation of the set of writers and movements that are customarily referred to as the liberation theologians. In both
cases, as well, I would like to evaluate the content of their political thinking
as it relates to political democracy and their impact on Latin American political culture. The overall thesis of the chapter is that mainstream Catholicism
in Latin America now supports democracy and that the extremes of left (revolutionary liberationists) and right (integralist authoritarians) are now much
weaker than they have been in the past.

## The Opening to Liberal Democracy

To understand why it took so long for the Roman Catholic Church to relate
its spiritual message to the ideals of democracy and freedom, not only in
Latin America but also in France, Italy, and Spain, it is necessary to know
something of the history of liberalism and democracy in those areas. That
history had as its initial point of reference the French Revolution, which
included in its program a militant anticlericalism that attacked not only the
privileges that the Church had enjoyed under the *ancien régime* but the very
foundations of its religious and educational mission. In Latin Europe, liberalism was identified with militant anticlericalism, with agnosticism and athe-
ism, and in the Italian case with the annexation of the Papal States as part of
the process of Italian unification. Similarly in Latin America, when political
parties were formed in the nineteenth century in many countries, they tended
to divide into conservatives who were closely identified with the interests of
the Church, and liberals who were more or less anticlerical in their attitudes
and programs. Liberalism was also identified—indeed, it still is in many
parts of Latin America—with laissez-faire capitalism, which was materialist
in character and exploitative in its social effects.

The nineteenth-century papal encyclicals are full of attacks on liberalism, and even when a more open pope, Leo XIII (1878-1903), succeeded the
conservative Pius IX (1846-1878) and wrote a famous encyclical on social
concerns, *Rerum Novarum* in 1891, he combined the defense of the right of
workers to organize trade unions and to receive a living wage with attacks
on both liberalism and socialism as opposed to justice and Christian principles. As a result of that encyclical, and even more after a later encyclical by
Pius XI, *Quadragesimo Anno* was published in 1931, the Church took the

lead in organizing Christian trade unions, but its political attitudes in most Latin American countries tended to be conservative, corporatist, and hostile to liberal democracy. This was combined with a Hispanist attitude that tended to look to monarchist Spain and then, during and following the Civil War (1936-1938), to the Franco regime for political inspiration.

This began to change only in the 1940s and 1950s with the beginnings of Christian Democracy in Latin America. In twentieth-century Europe a number of Christian Democratic parties of Catholic (or in the case of Germany both Catholic and Protestant) inspiration had emerged that combined the earlier "social Catholicism" with a commitment to political democracy, religious pluralism, and human rights. They differed from the corresponding secular parties both in the ultimately religious basis of their political programs, and in the more social—although not socialist—orientation of their philosophies and programs. Arguing that they represented a middle way between liberal individualism and collectivist socialism, they drew on the writings of the French Catholic philosopher Jacques Maritain to develop party ideologies and programs that favored a pluralist welfare state democracy as the form of government most faithful to the principles of the Christian gospels.[4] Following World War II these parties, either alone or in coalition, were in power in France, Italy, and Germany and made important contributions to the political and economic stabilization of Europe.

One can trace the beginnings of Christian Democracy in Latin America to the influence of European Christian Democratic thinkers and political leaders on the young Catholic student leaders of Latin America beginning in the 1930s. In the case of Chile, a split-off of the youth section of the Conservative Party, which first called itself the Falange and later combined with another reform-oriented Conservative group to form the Christian Democratic Party, was led by future president Eduardo Frei, who had first come in contact with Maritain's thought during a visit to Europe in 1934 when he heard Maritain's lectures on what was to be published later as *Integral Humanism*. In 1938 Maritain himself went to Latin America to lecture in Brazil and Argentina, and a reprint of one of his lectures in a Chilean newspaper formed an important part of the continuing argument between the former Conservative youth leaders and the party that had expelled them for their socially advanced ideas. In Venezuela, the leaders of the future COPEI (Comité de Organización Política Electoral Independiente), the Social Christian Party, also came out of the Catholic student movement. They formed the principal opposition to the social democratic party, *Acción Democrática* (AD), when it was in power from 1946 to 1948, and later worked with it in the reestablishment of democracy in that country after 1958. Similar parties were also founded in the post–World War II period in many other countries in Latin America. Most have remained small, exercising influence mainly on intellectuals and students. In Central America, however, they have had significant electoral success. El Salvador's Christian

Democratic president from 1984 to 1989, José Napoleon Duarte, was repeatedly elected mayor of San Salvador long before he became president of that country, and in Guatemala a Christian Democrat, Vinicio Cerezo, was elected President in December 1985 with 68 percent of the vote. In Panama the Christian Democrats were a mainstay of the opposition to General Noriega, and in Costa Rica, they form the principal alternative to the social democratic National Liberation Party (PLN).

The emergence of Christian Democratic parties in a number of countries in Latin America signified a break with the old integralist hierarchical model that had predominated for so long in Latin America. Particularly when combined with Christian-inspired trade unions, they provided a mass base for social reform and democracy. Along with the populist or social democratic parties of a more secular orientation, they constituted the central political support for the development and maintenance of constitutional democracy and redistributive social politics in Latin America as a democratic alternative to the Cuban Revolution. Although the Christian Democrats continued to talk of their programs as located in a "third position" (*tercerismo*) distinct from liberal individualism and collectivist socialism, in fact they represented a populist welfare-state liberalism not significantly different from that of reformist liberal and social democratic parties and governments in Europe, the United States, and the British Commonwealth. The difference was in the philosophical base and the broad electoral appeal of a party that, while secular in its programs and policies, was Christian in its inspiration, mystique, and in the educational background and formation of its leaders. The religious connection, although not direct, clearly aided in recruitment and voting support, and it motivated its members to spend time and energy in combating Marxist elements in trade union, youth, student, and shantytown organizations. At the same time it alienated some of the more militantly secular politicians and voters, especially those who supported social democratic or radical party organizations.

The emergence of important Christian Democratic parties in Chile and Venezuela began in 1958. In that year the dictatorship of Marcos Pérez Jiménez was overthrown in Venezuela, and the Christian Democratic COPEI, in pursuance of an agreement made earlier with the social democratic Acción Democrática, agreed to enter the government of the AD candidate, Rómulo Betancourt, taking particular responsibility for the drafting and implementation of an agrarian reform law. In that year as well, Eduardo Frei ran for president of Chile for the first time, and although he did not win, his party began a meteoric rise that culminated six years later in his election by an absolute majority, a very rare occurrence in Chile's multiparty system. Nineteen fifty-eight was also the year of Pope John XXIII's election as successor to the austere and authoritarian Pope Pius XII, who had been pope since 1939. John was supposed to act as an interim compromise pope but he began almost immediately to carry out what he called the *aggiornamento*, or updating, of the Church, publishing a number of encyclicals concerned with social and international questions, notably *Mater et Magistra* (1961) and *Pacem in Terris* (1963), that officially committed the Church to human rights, religious ecumenism, and domestic and international social justice. Most important of all, he convened the Second Vatican Council, which met from 1962 until 1965 and carried forward the task he outlined for it in ways that had an enormous impact on the relation of the Roman Catholic Church to the modern world, especially in Latin America.

Nineteen fifty-eight was also the final year of the Cuban Revolution, culminating in the triumphal entry of Fidel Castro into Havana on New Year's Day of 1959. This is not the place to trace the radicalization of the Cuban Revolution, which I have examined elsewhere,[5] but it is sufficient to note that by late 1961 Castro had formally committed himself and his country to Marxism-Leninism ("I am a Marxist-Leninist, and I will be one until the last day of my life") and had begun to attempt to export his revolution to the rest of the continent ("the Andes as the Sierra Maestra of Latin America"). In response, the newly elected U.S. president, John Kennedy, announced the establishment of a ten-year program of assistance to Latin America, the Alliance for Progress, which was to demonstrate that reform and development could best be carried out under democratic auspices. His natural allies in that effort were the Social Democratic and the Christian Democratic parties of the center-left in Latin America.

The Catholic Church also saw the Cuban Revolution as a challenge that required a response, after the relatively weak influence it had enjoyed in Cuba had been almost totally eliminated by Castro's shutdown of the entire system of private education and by the combined expulsion and withdrawal of the foreign clergy, who constituted the bulk of the priests and nuns in Cuba. The response of the Church included the establishment of a large number of socially oriented research institutes, mainly but not only by the Jesuit order, the best known of which was the Centro Bellarmino in Chile, a spin-off of which, DESAL (Desarrollo Económico Social de América Latina), run by the Belgian Jesuit Roger Vekemans, became the major think tank to develop the program of Eduardo Frei's "Revolution in Liberty" for the 1964 presidential elections. In the United States as well, a major effort was made to recruit missionaries to go to Latin America. The Maryknoll order, for example, which had originally been concerned mainly with missionary work in China, reoriented its programs to Latin America. There were critics of these programs,[6] but large numbers of young, committed missionaries from the United States and Europe began to work among the rural and urban poor; the Church hierarchy in countries such as Chile, Brazil, and Venezuela began to take a greater interest in social and agrarian reform, and turned its attention to what were now beginning to be described as the "marginalized" sectors of Latin American society—the peasantry, the slum dwellers, and the poor.

## Vatican II and Democracy

The interest of the Church was intensified by the common experience of the six hundred or more Latin American bishops who participated in the Second Vatican Council (1962-1965). The bishops of Latin America had formed a regional organization, the Conference of Latin American Bishops (CELAM), in 1955, but they had not met as a group since that time. Now they were in continuous day-to-day contact during the meetings of the council and were discussing common experiences and problems as well as the major theological decisions of the council. Those decisions included important changes in the official Church position on religious freedom, democracy, relations with other faiths as well as with atheists, and more generally the relation of the Church to the modern world. The last topic, summed up in *Gaudium et Spes* one of the last conciliar decrees, called for continuing dialogue between the Church and the world, denounced economic inequality and the disparity between rich and poor nations, and endorsed agrarian reform. Most important, it committed the Church fully to political democracy, declaring, "It is in full accord with human nature" that all should "participate freely and actively in establishing the constitutional bases of a political community, governing the state, determining the scope and purpose of various institutions, and choosing leaders."[7]

The council also redefined the constitution of the Church itself, modifying the highly centralized, defensive structure that had been adopted in the sixteenth century at the time of the Counter-Reformation and Council of Trent and reinforced by the decrees of the First Vatican Council in 1870-1871. It endorsed the "collegiality of the bishops" (under the pope) through national bishop synods and regular worldwide synods of bishops (in Rome), and it defined the Church as "the People of God" in which the laity was to have a significant role.

Thus, by the middle of the 1960s the Roman Catholic Church and Church-influenced institutions in Latin America had undergone a significant opening toward democracy and what we—but not they—would call welfare state liberalism. Conservative bishops and lay groups remained, and in Brazil a new organization, *Tradição Familia e Propiedade* (TFP), was founded to fight the new liberalizing tendencies. But a clear commitment had been made to democracy and social reform, both by the majority of the hierarchy and by significant Church-influenced parties and student, youth, labor, and peasant organizations. What had been a bastion of conservatism, hierarchy, fatalism, and opposition to modernization and often to democracy had gone a long way toward embracing democracy, equality, social justice, and modern pluralist politics. An institution that through its supreme pontiff, in *The Syllabus of Errors* in 1864, had described as the last (and by implication the most serious) error the belief that the Church through its leader "can or should reconcile itself to ... progress, liberalism, and modern civilization" had done all three.

From the point of view of those sympathetic to democracy and social reform in Latin America, this was certainly a positive development. Indeed, the author of a book on Chilean Christian Democracy called it "the last best hope" of Latin America.[8] Church-inspired groups and parties alerted the middle classes to the social problems of the peasants and shantytown dwellers; they broadened support for agrarian reform laws in Chile, Peru, and Venezuela; and they showed that democratic governments could respond to the problem of social justice and political participation. On the other hand, the existence of these groups also divided the democratic center because, as Americans often are not aware, there is a substantial legacy of anticlericalism or at least apathy toward the Roman Catholic Church and its teachings in what appears to foreigners to be an overwhelmingly Catholic region. There were also Catholics on the right who resented and opposed what appeared to them to be an attempt by one party to monopolize the legitimacy derived from the Church's social teachings, which they too felt they were applying in their own programs. In some countries—Venezuela for example, and in a slightly different way, Costa Rica—the emergence of Christian Democracy and Church-influenced labor and peasant groups produced a healthy alternation between Social Democratic and Christian Democratic parties in which both parties would take a left-of-center position in opposition and a more centrist position in power, while despite the differences in ideological base, both party programs were similar. In a country such as Chile before the 1973 coup, with a strong Marxist left and a resurgent neoconservative right, however, the existence of the Christian Democrats meant that the beleaguered center was weakened by the divisions between Christian and lay parties, with both groups themselves torn by internal debates over whether to make appeals to the left or the right in their electoral competition. This became less of a problem during the late 1980s as opposition to President Pinochet produced a multiparty coalition from the moderate right to the democratic socialist left, with the Christian Democrats as the largest and best-organized party in the coalition.

## From Liberalization to Radicalization: The Emergence of Liberation Theology

Those who argued that the Christian Democrats should move to the left did so not only on electoral grounds. Important doctrinal and attitudinal shifts in the direction of radicalization had begun to occur in Church-influenced circles in Latin America—now legitimized by the opening that had taken place in the Second Vatican Council. The first indication of this impending radicalization was an important symbolic act, the decision in 1966 by Camilo Torres, chaplain at the National University in Bogotá and representative of one of Colombia's oldest families (a Camilo Torres was among the country's founding fathers), to join the guerrillas, and his subsequent death in a confrontation with the military. More important, however, were certain not too subtle shifts in the official position of the Church as expressed in the documents of the Second Meeting of CELAM at Medellín, Colombia, in 1968. The two-week meeting in August and September was timed to coincide with the visit of Pope Paul VI to the Eucharistic Congress in Bogotá, but its declarations went far beyond the traditional sacramentalism of the earlier Church. The bishops' Medellín documents described contemporary attitudes toward social problems as "traditionalist," "developmentalist," and "revolutionary"—and seemed at times to be favorable to the third group because of their critical comments concerning the excessively "economistic" orientation of the developmentalists and their identification of the revolutionary position as support for popular participation in social decisions. The bishops specifically criticized the international system of "dependence" in accordance with which "our nations are frequently not owners of their goods nor masters of their economic decisions." They condemned both Marxism and liberal capitalism and in an important terminological development spoke of the need to offer man "the possibilities of a full liberation" and to relate evangelization to the "lived experiences of the People of Israel ... the ecclesial community in which the Spirit of the risen Christ lives and operates continually." Most significant of all for the future, the bishops concluded,

> Latin America finds itself in many places in a situation that can be called *institutionalized violence* whereby for lack of structures in industry and farming, in the national and international economy, and in cultural and political life, whole populations lacking basic necessities live in such a dependence that it impedes all initiative and responsibility, as well as all the possibility of cultural promotion and participation in social and political life.[9]

The Medellín declarations were very important in giving theoretical legitimation to the radicalizing tendencies that were developing in certain circles of the Latin American Church. Those included, not surprisingly, labor and students and those who worked with them—as well as the aforementioned missionaries working with the poor in the burgeoning shantytowns that surrounded most Latin American cities. Now groups like the Third World Priests in Buenos Aires, ONIS (Oficina Nacional de Informacisn Social) in Peru, the Golconda Group in Colombia, and a sector of the Jesuits led by Gonzalo Arroyo, S. J. working with the influential magazine *Mensaje* in Chile, cited the bishops of Latin America in their attacks on *dependencia*—a word that was just beginning to receive widespread currency—and in their criticisms of the inadequacy of the "developmentalist" assumptions underlying the approach of the Alliance for Progress to the resolution of Latin American problems. It had been only a year since the death of Ché Guevara in Bolivia, right-wing military coups had taken over in Brazil and Argentina in 1964 and 1966, while in Peru a more progressively oriented military took power in October 1968. Students were demonstrating in the streets of Paris and Chicago, had seized Columbia University in New York, and had been gunned down by the hundreds in Mexico City after six weeks of antigovernment demonstrations. This was the context in which the movement known as liberation theology was born.

## Liberation Theology

The book by Gustavo Gutierrez which gave the liberation theology movement its name was published in Spanish in 1971 and in English in 1973. However, it is based on lectures originally delivered in Peru in 1968, published by the International Movement of Catholic Students in Montevideo in 1969, revised for presentation as lectures in Switzerland in 1969, and published in the United States in *Theological Studies* in 1970.[10] In its original form, then, it is very much a product of the ferment of the late 1960s. Yet in its theological roots it goes back to Europe of the 1950s and consciously relates to, and distinguishes itself from, certain movements in German theology of the period when the Latin American theologians were studying in Europe. There is no space here to describe these movements in detail but they include the "political theology" of J. B. Metz and Jürgen Moltmann, which argues against the separation of theology from critical application to, and judgment of, contemporary political and social movements, and various efforts at Christian-Marxist dialogue involving the use of Marxist modes of analysis for theological purposes. The Latin Americans, however, made a conscious effort to distinguish their theological thinking from that of the Europeans, due to its more specifically political application to the needs of the poor and the oppressed in the Third World and especially in Latin America. Liberation theology, then, is an effort to apply the Christian message to the needs of the poor through new methods of theological and sociological analysis.

What are the methods? In theology the liberation theologians talk of a new "hermeneutic," that is, amethod of interpretation of the Scripture, which relies on "praxis," a dialectic between the lived experience of the poor and the Word of God in the scripture. They even speak of the need to replace orthodoxy with "orthopraxis"—a commitment to action on behalf of the poor.

Second, they criticize the theology of the two planes—the natural and the supernatural—arguing that people live and God acts in a world in which the two planes are not separated but united. Third, they call on theology to draw on "the tools of social analysis" to understand the world in which man lives—and the methods that were current, if not universal, among Latin American social scientists at the time that the principal works of liberation theology were written tended to be Marxist or Marxist-influenced.

Uncritically adopting the arguments of the proponents of the *dependencia* school that blamed Latin America's ills on domination by the "center" over the "periphery," the liberation theologians rejected the developmentalist model in favor of one that stressed "liberation" from oppressive structures. In some of the liberation theologians' writings, liberation could come only through revolution against "the institutionalized violence" of the capitalist system.

A fourth element that runs through much of the liberation theologians' writings (especially those of Juan Luis Segundo, Hugo Assmann, and Enrique Dussell[11]) is an emphasis upon the ideological character of most theology and social science ("the concept of development has been shown up for the lie that it is"—Assmann) and a call for new theoretical break-throughs that can overcome these ideological conditionings in the interests of the newly emerging groups—in Latin America the poor, in the United States women and blacks.

A fifth theme is educational and psychological in character, the need for *concientización* ("consciousness-raising") of the poor and the oppressed, a concept developed earlier by Paulo Freire[12] encouraging the poor to engage in a critical analysis of how oppressive structures affect their own lives and how collective action can change those structures.

Finally and most significant in the view of the present writer, the liberation theologians emphasized the importance of the emerging movement of Basic Christian Communities (CEBs) that were in the process of being created in many Latin American countries, especially Brazil, Chile, and Peru, as a way to involve the poor in relating the biblical message to their day-to-day problems in situations of oppression and exploitation. Implicit in this emphasis (and it became explicit in the writings of the Brazilian Franciscan theologian Leonardo Boff) was a new model of the Church that deemphasized its hierarchical character, gave special priority to the theological insights of the grassroots community, and promoted social and political involvement of the poor.[13]

## Democracy or Revolution?

As this summary of what is an enormous and growing literature indicates, there are two major thrusts to the writings of the liberation theologians that are of interest to social scientists: (1) the use of—mainly Marxist—tools of social analysis to argue that only through the overthrow of capitalism could the poor be liberated, and (2) the emphasis on the participation of communities of the faithful, especially of the poor, in the life of the Church and of society. Both provoked controversy and criticism within and outside the Church. The use of praxis, the dialectic, the ideological "demystification" of theology, the discussion of violence and revolution, a class struggle analysis involving glorification of the poor and vilification of the rich—all seemed to call in question traditional ways of doing theology and to possess Marxist overtones that were reinforced by the mention by some liberation theologists of the need for a "strategic alliance" with the Marxist left to bring about social transformation. The decentralized model of base communities, especially when it was described as "the people's church" (*iglesia popular*), seemed to call into question the *magisterium* or teaching message of the hierarchy and to verge upon a congregational model of ecclesiastical organization. The mainstream Church had long criticized many aspects of modern capitalism, in particular its materialist and exploitative character, but when liberation theologians spoke of the need to replace capitalism by a socialist revoution that would produce a "new man," Church leaders began to worry.

The issue of the relation of the Catholic left with Marxism was focused most dramatically in Chile after the election of Salvador Allende in 1970, at the head of a Marxist-dominated coalition that included the MAPU (Movimiento de Acción Popular Unitaria) that had split off from the ruling Christian Democratic party in 1969 and was soon to be joined by another splinter group, the Izquierda Cristiana, or Christian Left, in 1971. The Chilean bishops wrote a document on the problem, *Gospel, Politics, and Socialisms*, which argued that it was legitimate for Christians to support certain types of socialism but warned that other forms (referring presumably to Marxism-Leninism) were opposed to Christian doctrine. When a group of eighty priests organized a continent-wide meeting in Santiago of Christians for Socialism in 1972, which adopted resolutions that were indistinguishable from those of any Marxist party, this led to a specific condemnation of the movement by the Chilean hierarchy in the following year.[14]

Action also took place on a broader basis. Bishop (later Cardinal) Alfredo Lopez Trujillo of Medellín, Colombia, wrote a book against liberation theology, and used his position as newly elected secretary of CELAM to limit the movement's influence. Roger Vekemans, S.J., who had left Chile for Colombia at the time of the election of Allende, founded a journal, *Tierra Nueva*, in Bogotá, that gave major attention to combating it. On the other side, the *National Catholic Reporter* in the United States and articles in *The Nation* by Penny Lernoux gave favorable publicity to the new theological movements. In 1975 a meeting was held in Detroit with somewhat mixed results; it attempted to link the Latin American and North American liberationists in a continent-wide dialogue that would include feminist and black theologians as well as those who were working for the poor in North and South America.[15]

## The Puebla Meeting, 1979

The controversy between the pro- and antiliberationists came to a head in connection with the Third Meeting of CELAM at Puebla, Mexico, in 1979. Pope John Paul II had been elected in 1978 and already had given some indication that he favored more conservative theological currents in the Church. A draft document was circulated by the CELAM secretariat before the meeting that also was reported to be critical of the new currents.

To summarize a complicated process, the Puebla CELAM meeting ended in a theological draw. On the one hand, it insisted that "party politics is the realm of lay people" and that although the Church is concerned with politics when it involves fundamental moral values, "the priest as priest should not directly concern himself with decisions or leadership nor with the structuring of solutions" (a quotation from the 1968 Medellín conference). It repeated earlier Church condemnations of "capitalist liberalism, the idolatrous worship of wealth in individualistic terms" and of "Marxist collectivism," but added a warning against "the risk of ideologization run by theological reflection when it is based on a praxis that has recourse to Marxist analysis." On the other hand, it also condemned "the Doctrine of National Security" understood as an absolute ideology that is "not compatible with the Christian vision of the human being"; it supported the organization of Basic Christian Communities; and, most important, it strongly endorsed a "preferential option for the poor" as a primary goal of evangelization in Latin America.[16] Each side could thus cite the Puebla meeting in support of its point of view, and argue that the pope and the Latin American bishops favored its position.

The debate continued, however. As the neoconservative movement became stronger in the United States and the Central American conflict heated up, more attention was paid to what were seen as the theoretical bases of the participation by the clergy in support of the Sandinistas in Nicaragua. Michael Novak at the American Enterprise Institute, James Schall, S. J., in San Francisco, and Quentin Quade at the Ethics and Public Policy Center in Washington published books critical of the liberation theologians, in the first case because of their excessive reliance on a discredited theory of *dependencia* that ignores the need for promotion of the domestic sources of productivity and entrepreneurship; in the second, because of their endorsement of revolutionary Marxism; and in the third, because of the politicization of the Christian message.

The Vatican itself became formally involved in 1984 when the Congregation for the Doctrine of the Faith issued *Instruction on Certain Aspects of "The Theology of Liberation" (Libertatis Nuntius),* a carefully worded warning that attacked some (unspecified) versions of liberation theology ("that current of thought which, under the name 'theology of liberation' proposes a novel interpretation ... which seriously departs from the faith of the Church and, in fact, actually constitutes a practical negation [using] concepts uncritically borrowed from Marxist ideology and theses of a biblical hermeneutic marked by rationalism ... corrupting whatever was authentic in the general initial commitment in behalf of the poor," nos. 9-10).

The *Instruction* argued that "some theologians" tended to identify the poor with the Marxist proletariat and truth with the class struggle, and that they were inadequately concerned about the danger of replacing one form of domination with another more dangerous one. The Vatican statement was a considerably toned-down version of an earlier draft critique by the prefect of the Congregation, Cardinal Joseph Ratzinger, that had been leaked to the Italian press and was later published in a book of interviews with the cardinal. Shortly after publication of the *Instruction,* Leonardo Boff was summoned to Rome to explain certain statements in his book *Church, Charism and Power* including one that referred to an ecclesiastical "division of labor" through which the hierarchy had engaged in "the expropriation of the means of religious production from the Christian people."[17] Boff was accompanied by two Brazilian cardinals for the interrogation, indicating the extent of support for his writings in Brazil, but the congregation later issued a judgment that certain statements in his book were "theologically unacceptable."

Boff accepted the Vatican decision, saying, "I prefer to walk with the Church rather than go it alone with my theology." Gutierrez and others denied that they were interested in a synthesis of Marxism and Christianity, and emphasized that the incorporation of the insights of "social science" into their theology was always provisional and subject to revision in the light of new evidence. The Peruvian bishops met to consider Gutierrez's works and endorsed the *Instruction* but refused to censure him. The Brazilians lobbied in Rome repeatedly, emphasizing the important work that the base communities inspired by liberation theology were carrying out in that country. (The Brazilian Church carries a good deal of clout because next to Italy it has the largest number of bishops in the world.)

A second Instruction had been promised when *Libertatis Nuntius* was issued. After some delay (reportedly because the pope wished to give it a more positive tone) it was published in March 1986 under the title *On Christian Freedom and Liberation (Libertatis Conscientia).* It endorsed Christian Base Communities "if they really live in unity with the local and universal church" and it encouraged theological reflection based on practical experience "in the light of the experience of the church itself." It also supported a special concern for the poor, but it reworded the Puebla description of that concern—"the preferential option for the poor"—to "preferential love for the poor," apparently in order to remove any implications of the acceptance of a rich-poor, class-struggle approach. The incorporation of a defanged notion of liberation in Catholic theology culminated in April 1986 with a widely publicized letter from the pope to the Brazilian bishops endorsing liberation theology as "not only timely but useful and necessary [provided that it is] coherent and consistent with the Gospel, the living tradition, and the ongoing *Magisterium* [teaching] *of the Church.*"[18]

Why did the attack on liberation theology by the Vatican take place, and what were its effects? It seems to have resulted partly from Cardinal Ratzinger's concern as a theologian about the heavy admixture of Marxism in the early writings of the liberationists and partly from Pope John Paul II's belief that it was legitimizing close cooperation between Christians and Marxists in Nicaragua and El Salvador and the promotion of a "popular church" opposed to the hierarchy. When the liberation theologians hastened to reassure him both on their differences from Marxism and their willingness to obey the Vatican, the next step was to recognize the validity of many aspects of the new theology, especially the base communities and the application of the Bible to the experience of the poor.

What has all this to do with democracy? In the period of revolutionary lyricism of the 1970s, the liberation theologians along with others on the left denounced "bourgeois democracy" as a "fraud" and a "lie," and argued for "people's power" to replace the outmoded representative institutions. In Chile and Bolivia, the Catholic leftists joined the more radical Marxist groups in calling for the immediate overthrow of capitalism. In Brazil, Dominican priests aided and supported the urban guerrilla movement led by Carlos Marighela. In Central America, the Jesuits in Guatemala conducted Marxist study groups, and in Nicaragua priests at the Jesuit-run secondary school and university in Managua put Catholic students in touch with the Marxist Sandinista revolutionaries. In El Salvador, Catholic intellectuals left the Christian Democratic Party to form the Popular Social Christian Movement (MPSC), which allied itself with the Marxist guerrillas. For a time, it seemed that the strategic alliance between Christians and Marxists that Fidel Castro had begun to advocate was actually taking place.

Yet in Chile and Bolivia rightist military governments soon seized power, and in Brazil the military rulers brutally repressed the revolutionaries and ambushed and killed Marighela. In Guatemala many of those connected with Church-sponsored reform movements in the countryside, including a number of priests, were gunned down by government-sponsored terrorists. In El Salvador, death squads linked to the military government murdered churchmen and -women, including the archbishop of San Salvador, Oscar Romero. And in Nicaragua, after the July 1979 triumph of a national uprising against Somoza that included both Christians and Marxists, the relations between the Sandinistas and the Church began to turn sour in the early 1980s as the Sandinista-sponsored "popular church" movement attacked the hierarchy and demanded unconditional loyalty to the Sandinistas. Later in the decade as living standards deteriorated by an estimated 70 percent, it was not at all clear that a Christian-Marxist alliance in support of the Sandinistas was the appropriate application of the "preferential option for the poor."

By the mid-1980s the military governments of Latin America were being replaced in one country after another by elected civilian democracies, and the likelihood of revolutionary transformation seemed increasingly remote. By that time the experience of repression and torture under brutal dictatorship had given the Catholic left a renewed appreciation of the virtues of representative government, however flawed. In Brazil, the new Workers Party (PT) with roots in the liberationist Christian Base Communities began to elect mayors in a number of cities, notably São Paulo. In Chile, following the defeat of the dictator, Augusto Pinochet, in the October 1988 plebiscite, the reemergent MAPU and Christian Left joined the other parties of the left in support of a centrist, Patricio Aylwin of the Christian Democrats, against the pro-Pinochet presidential candidate in the December 1989 presidential elections. In El Salvador, Rubén Zamora of the Popular Social Christian Movement (MPSC) returned from exile to participate in the 1989 presidential elections.

The changes in practice were accompanied by shifts in theory on the part of the leading writers on liberation theology. In 1986 Hugo Assmann, once the most radical of all the liberation theologians, wrote that the members of the Latin American left recognized that they "must now reestablish their organic relation to the popular majorities which never understood their abstract revolutionism." Arguing that "democratic values are revolutionary values," he asserted that "revolutionaries have learned to value democratic participation and the authentically popular movements [and] are no longer interested in chaotic social explosions." Similarly in a book published in the same year, *La Verdad Los Hara Libres* (*The Truth Shall Make You Free*), Gustavo Gutierrez called for a new socioeconomic order oriented toward the poor that, however, must be characterized by "liberty for all" because "personal liberty is the necessary condition for an authentic political liberation." In addition, the emergence of the Sendero Luminoso guerrilla group in Peru led him to change his tune on violence. Where twenty years ago he accepted the inevitability of "counter violence" to the "institutionalized violence" of contemporary Latin America, now he denounces both "terrorist violence" and the "repressive violence" of the military response.[19]

It is true that some of the liberation theologians did not end their love affair with Marxism. Leonardo Boff returned from a trip to the Soviet Union in July 1987 to argue that despite its repression and its restriction of religion, the Soviet system offers "the objective possibility of living more easily in the spirit of the Gospels and of observing the Commandments" than does the "eroticization and commercialization" of the West. In El Salvador another well-known liberationist, the Basque Jesuit Ignacio Ellacuria, continued to insist that "the difference between the social doctrine of the Church and liberation theology is that the social doctrine believes that capitalism is reformable and Marxism is irreformable, while liberation theology believes that Marxism is reformable and capitalism is irreformable."[20]

By the late 1980s, however, there had emerged in Latin America a radical left drawing its legitimation from Catholicism and committed to a deep-

ening of the democratic process to produce, in the words of the Third World
Theologians meeting in Mexico in December 1986, "a new democracy with
the participation of the majorities."[21] This new Catholic left is still critical of
capitalism, but its commitment to revolution has given way to a belief in the
central importance of the values of democracy and personal freedom.


## The New Right in Latin America

One can also perceive a number of shifts in the position of the Catholic-
influenced right in Latin America. If one wanted to demonstrate the flexibility of the interpretation of Catholic social thought, a prime example would be
the Pinochet government's *Declaration of Basic Principles* published in
March 1974 in order to justify the coup. It appealed to "the Christian conception of man and society" shared by "the immense majority of our people"
to justify the overthrow of Marxism in September 1973, and it performed an
extraordinary act of intellectual legerdemain by arguing that a free enterprise
economy—which the popes have always criticized—was an example of "the
principle of subsidiarity"—that the state should not carry out what lower
associations and groups can perform—enunciated by Pius XI in
Quadragesimo Anno in 1931.[22] In many countries of Latin America the
Spanish-based conservative lay religious group, Opus Dei, expanded its
influence in the 1970s and 1980s among businessmen, professionals, and
university students and professors. Although traditionalist in its theology,
Opus is modern in its commitments to a market economy. Less clear is its
commitment to democracy, but Vatican II's endorsement of democracy and
the Spanish example of a peaceful transition from an authoritarian government have not been lost on it. Similarly, the adverse economic consequences
of the military governments in many Latin American countries in the late
1970s and early 1980s began to alienate conservatives and business groups.
In Brazil, they pressed for a return to democracy beginning in the late 1970s.
In Chile, conservatives began to oppose Pinochet in the protests of 1983—
and the National Party, the traditional expression of conservatism, participated in most of the anti-Pinochet party coalitions. Many of the conservatives
have attended Catholic schools, and the process of *aggiornamento* has also
affected them. Instead of continuing to embrace an integralist hierarchical
authoritarian Catholicism, many of them now see a socially concerned and
democratically oriented approach as more in keeping with their faith. This
process has been encouraged by U.S. and European governments and conservative think tanks and foundations such as the Adenauer and Seidel gov-
ernment-financed political foundations, which are sponsored by the German
Christian Democratic Party (CDU/CSU) and spend millions in Latin
America on "educational" work.

## Conclusion

I have described what amounts to a fundamental change in the political role of Catholicism in Latin America. Rather than acting as a bulwark of a traditionalist authoritarianism that assumes that "the poor you have always with you" (Matthew 26:11) and "the powers that be are ordained of God" (Romans 13:1), it has provided religious justifications for a range of political approaches from conservative to liberal to radical. The combination of the opening to the world associated with the Second Vatican Council and unhappy experiences with governments of the extreme left and right has produced a situation in which democracy is accepted by a broad spectrum of ideological groups—all of which claim legitimation from Christianity. Thus, what this paper has described is a reproduction on the level of "political theology" in Latin America of the range of approaches from radical to liberal to conservative that one finds in political philosophy—combined with a process of education and experience that has made the antidemocratic extremes of left and right less and less attractive.

In a continent that is overwhelmingly Catholic in culture—although much less so in practice—this is a positive development for liberal pluralist democracy. The Church-influenced left is promoting communitarian grassroots democracy; the center, participation and human rights; and the right, free market economies and civilian consensual government. There are pessimists who say that this is only temporary and that the dictators will return. I would argue, however, that despite all of Latin America's terrible problems, there has been a perceptible shift toward a democratic consensus, and the changes in Latin American Catholicism have made a significant contribution to that shift.

## Notes

Research for this paper was conducted while the author was a fellow in the Latin America Program of the Woodrow Wilson Center in Washington, DC.

1. Harvey Cox, *The Secular City* (New York: Macmillan, 1965).

2. Ivan Vallier, *Catholicism, Social Control, and Modernization in Latin America* (Englewood Cliffs, NJ: Prentice-Hall, 1970).

3. See Daniel H. Levine, ed., *Churches and Politics in Latin America* (Beverly Hills: Sage, 1980), and *Religion and Political Conflict in Latin America* (Chapel Hill: University of North Carolina Press, 1986); Brian H. Smith, *The Church and Politics in Chile* (Princeton: Princeton University Press, 1982); Thomas C. Bruneau, *The Church in Brazil* (Austin: University of Texas Press, 1982); Scott Mainwaring, *The Brazilian Catholic Church and Politics, 1916-1985* (Stanford: Stanford University Press, 1986); John M. Kirk, *Between God and Party: Religion and Politics in Revolutionary Cuba* (Tampa: University of South Florida Press, 1989); Phillip Berryman, *The Religious Roots of Rebellion: Christians in Central American Revolutions* (Maryknoll: Orbis Books, 1984); and Daniel H. Levine, *Religion and*

228                                    POLITICAL CULTURE AND DEMOCRACY

*Politics in Latin America: The Catholic Church in Venezuela and Colombia* (Princeton: Princeton University Press, 1981). See also Scott Mainwaring and Alexander Wilde, eds., *The Progressive Church in Latin America* (Notre Dame: University of Notre Dame Press, 1988).

4. Maritain described the central concepts of his political philosophy as *personalism, pluralism,* and *communitarianism* occupying a middle position between the egotistic individualism of liberalism and the collectivist statism of socialism. He endorsed democracy, human rights, the religiously neutral (although not secular) state, and encouragement of intermediate associations as best from a Christian point of view. See also Paul E. Sigmund, "Maritain on Politics," in Deal W. Hudson and Matthew J. Mancini, eds., *Understanding Maritain* (Macon: Mercer University Press, 1987), pp. 153-170.

5. Paul E. Sigmund, *Multinationals in Latin America* (Madison: University of Wisconsin Press, 1980), chap. 4.

6. Ivan Illich, "The Seamy Side of Charity," *America* (21 January 1967).

7. "Gaudium et Spes, The Pastoral Constitution on the Church in the Modern World," in Joseph Gremillion, ed., *The Gospel of Peace and Justice: Catholic Social Teaching Since Pope John* (Maryknoll: Orbis Books, 1976), p. 310. See also Paul E. Sigmund, "The Catholic Tradition and Democracy," *Review of Politics* 49 (Fall 1987): 530-548.

8. Leonard Gross, *The Last Best Hope* (New York: Grosset and Dunlap, 1967).

9. Medellín Conference "Conclusions," quoted in Sergio Torres and John Eagleson, eds., *Theology in the Americas* (Maryknoll: Orbis Books, 1976), pp. 222-224.

10. Gustavo Gutierrez, "Notes for a Theology of Liberation," *Theological Studies* 31 (June 1970): 243-261.

11. See, for example, Juan Luis Segundo, *The Liberation of Theology* (Maryknoll: Orbis Books, 1976); Hugo Assmann, *Theology for a Nomad Church* (Maryknoll: Orbis Books, 1976); and Enrique Dussel, *History and the Theology of Liberation* (Maryknoll: Orbis Books, 1976).

12. Paulo Freire, *The Pedagogy of the Oppressed* (English translation; New York: Herder, 1970).

13. See Leonardo Boff, *Church, Charism, and Power* (New York: Crossroad, 1985).

14. The documents of the meeting, but not the bishops' statement, are translated in John Eagleson, ed., *Christians and Socialism* (Maryknoll: Orbis Books, 1975). See also Smith, *The Church and Politics in Chile.*

15. The Detroit documents and discussions are published in Torres and Eagleson, *Theology in the Americas.*

16. See the documents in John Eagleson and Philip Sharper, eds., *Puebla and Beyond* (Maryknoll: Orbis Books, 1979).

17. Boff, *Church, Charism, and Power,* p. 112.

18. *Origins* (Washington, DC), May 1986, p. 14.

19. Gustavo Gutierrez, "Aún Es Tiempo," *Páginas* 11 (July 1986): 4-5; Gustavo Gutierrez, *La Verdad Los Hara Libres* (Lima: Centro de Estudios y Publicaciones, 1986), pp. 191-192. Hugo Assmann's statements appear in "Democracy and the Debt Crisis," *This World* 14 (Spring/Summer 1986): 92-94.

20. Personal interview, 19 August 1987. Ellacuria was murdered by the Salvadoran army in November 1989. For the Boff statements, see "O Socialismo Como Desafio Teológico," *Vozes* (Petropolis) 81 (November–December 1987): 692. In July 1992 Boff announced that he was leaving the priesthood.

21. *Revista Latinoamericana de Teología* (San Salvador) September/December 1986, p. 305.

22. *Declaración de Principios del Gobierno de Chile* (Santiago), March 1974, pp. 4-7.

# · 9 ·

# Causes and Effects

## *Larry Diamond*

No one volume can fill the many gaps in our understanding of how political culture relates to democratic development and decay dynamically over time. Systematic survey research of the kind now being undertaken in Eastern Europe and Latin America should tell us much about how political (and economic) attitudes and values persist and change in the course of regime change, and how shifts in political culture interact with other factors to shape the prospects for democracy. This volume has not sought to offer such quantitative cross-national comparisons. Rather, in more synthetic fashion, it has brought together different disciplinary, methodological, and regional perspectives in an effort to generate new and strengthened insights into the relationship between political culture and democracy. Comprehending this relationship involves addressing several questions: What are the sources of political culture and political culture change? What are the direct effects of political culture (change) on democracy? What features of political culture are most important for democratic development, and does this vary by stages of development? Can we speak of cultural conditions or "preconditions" for democracy? To what extent does political culture serve as intervening variable in a wider context of causality?

## Sources of Political Culture

### *Historical Influences*

The most basic question one can ask about political culture is, where does it come from? To a considerable extent, political culture is a legacy of the historical past, and elements of the political culture may be traced well back in time. However, the essays in this volume suggest that it is quite misleading to conceive of political culture as a body of changeless values and orientations dating back to the formation of the community (or the myths about it) many centuries ago. In many of our cases, historical legacies and traditions visibly resonate in contemporary beliefs and values, but they coexist with other, more recent, influences. Political culture is better conceived not purely as the legacy of the communal past but as a geological structure with sedimentary deposits from many historical ages and events.[1]

Virtually every one of our cases could be understood from this geological perspective. Some historical legacies have proven especially resilient. The "geological" structuring of political culture through historical time is quite evident in the case of Turkey, for example. Özbudun shows how the long-standing legacy of the Ottoman Empire—a centralized, despotic, paternalistic state—remains visible in the political values of many Turkish elites, particularly in the military and bureaucracy. But new geological strata of cultural influence have been deposited from later historical periods: the egalitarian, populist, unifying currents of Kemalist ideology; the post–World War II emergence of a more liberal, pluralist, democratic value orientation; and the post-1983 emergence of more powerful free-market orientations, as well as a stronger consensus on consolidating and preserving democracy. In each new historical period, new value orientations have partially displaced but not completely erased preexisting ones. The result is a mixed political culture, or more properly, a mix of political subcultures with different combinations of emphases from different periods. Political party elites and many social actors manifest stronger democratic, pluralist value orientations than the typical military officer or bureaucrat, but a key point of Özbudun's essay is that the (political cultural) unity of state elites has eroded over time, and Turkish society as a whole has moved in the direction of more democratic values and beliefs.

Naomi Chazan shows how the political cultures of Africa have been shaped by three distinct historical legacies: precolonial traditions and institutions; colonial administrative, social, and economic structures; and the experience of the anticolonial struggle and the postcolonial frameworks it constructed. Precolonial traditions exhibited great variety across sub-Saharan Africa, but many had significant democratic features. Where these existed, they tended to be undermined, and where hierarchical traditions existed, they tended to be reinforced, by the highly authoritarian structures of colonial rule. Democratic ideals diffused to many Western-educated elites, but the geological deposit of the colonial experience on political culture was, universally throughout Africa, "hegemonic rather than incorporating and imposed rather than integrating." The institutional legacy was centralized and authoritarian. The anticolonial struggle featured norms of resistance to colonial authority, national liberation, and self-rule, yet these never assumed a positively prodemocratic value orientation. Thus, through the 1980s, an elite culture of statism and authoritarianism coexisted with relatively weak and inchoate democratic norms, which manifested themselves mainly as a culture of resistance and then subsequently withdrawal at the mass level. Only in the past few years has there emerged what could be termed a fourth historical phase, more fundamentally conducive to democracy, as a result of grassroots democratic mobilization from below and the utter failure and discrediting of postindependence authoritarian models.

The geological strata of history are similarly evident in the contemporary political cultures of Eastern Europe, as Christine Sadowski shows. The autonomous organizational skills and civic-mindedness that emerged during pre–World War II democratic experiences aided democratic mobilization against communist domination in Poland, Hungary, and Czechoslovakia and bolster democratic prospects there today. Although communist regimes failed to obliterate these democratic cultural strands, or to create a sincerely allegiant communist citizen, a communist cultural legacy is nevertheless evident in the cynical aversion to politics and organized political parties, the lack of trust, and the expectation that government should provide. Finally, the experience of resisting communism through autonomous organizational activity, especially during the 1980s, has left its own impact on East European political cultures, generating (especially in the three countries above) increased efficacy and participation and greater appreciation for the values of truth, accountability, lawfulness, and free discourse.

Implicit in this conception of political culture as a geological layering of historical episodes and influences are the notions of institutional experience and political learning. Both have had significant impacts in shaping the political cultures examined in this volume. We have already noted in the introduction how the relatively lengthy experience with evolving democratic institutions before independence gave Indian political elites a chance to develop norms of tolerance, bargaining, accommodation, and incorporation, within a limited but gradually expanding framework of electoral competition and self-rule. The most important popular institution for political incorporation and mobilization, the Indian National Congress, was formed a full six decades before independence, and half a century of preindependence reforms widened the basis and deepened the significance of elections, while power was devolved away from the center.

Some parallels can be drawn with Taiwan's political development, in which the transition away from authoritarian rule was also gradual and tutelary, featuring more than three decades of electoral competition and self-rule at provincial and local levels before power began to be democratized at the center in the mid-1980s. While stability was ensured through the central dictatorship of the Kuomintang, beginning in 1950 local elections (and after 1969, limited national elections) did allow for and stimulate genuine political participation and competition. This partial democratic experience gradually socialized, or "habituated," Taiwanese to democratic norms, values, and attitudes, so that by the late 1980s full democratization appeared to the political elite much less destabilizing than it had seemed previously.[2] By contrast, the greater turbulence and conflict in South Korean politics since the democratic transition may owe in part to the more spasmodic nature of regime change there and the less institutional practice the country enjoyed previously with electoral competition. Further comparative analysis, and the passage of time in the current Korean democratic experiment, may help explain whether the more confrontational, uncompromising style of Korean politics derives not simply from the deep-rooted elements of national history and culture discussed by Pye but also from the long periods of interruption of electoral competition, even at the local level, denying Koreans a chance to become habituated to the give-and-take of political contestation.[3]

Many factors interact to explain the trajectory of a country's political development, but Chazan certainly seems justified in attributing much of the explanation for Africa's postindependence democratic failures to the lack of experience with the institutional practice of democracy prior to independence. She writes, "The structures of democratic government were implanted in Africa with very little prior preparation by external elements. By independence, Africans had barely had a chance to familiarize themselves with competitive institutions and the franchise, let alone acquire any experience with their operation." The contrast between India and Nigeria (Britain's largest African colony) is particularly salient: Whereas preindependence India experienced several decades of electoral competition and incrementally increasing self-rule throughout the country, in Nigeria this practice was compressed into a single decade.[4]

Just as positive experiences with democracy can develop democratic norms, so negative regime experiences can also leave their mark on the beliefs and values of elites and citizens. Democratic developments in Eastern Europe, Latin America, and Africa in recent years have all been stimulated by reactions against the abuses and failures of previous authoritarian regimes. In Eastern Europe, the long, hated experience with communism produced an intense revulsion against the party-state. As we have just seen, this has been reflected positively in strong cultural commitments to free discourse, open information, and popular control of government, but also negatively in a general suspicion of parties and politicians. The result has been a contradictory political culture, demanding open, democratic, and accountable governance but undermining the political institutions for achieving it. This cynical hangover from communist misrule has left the subject orientation weak, along with cultural orientations toward compromise and trust. These factors further undermine governability in the postcommunist states.

The situation is similar in many African states, where democracy to date has manifested itself mainly as a culture of resistance to authoritarian encroachments and abuse. As in Eastern Europe, many African citizenries are suspicious of state authority and increasingly inclined to mobilize, criticize, and protest openly. These are important cultural building blocks for democracy. But in Africa, the positive dimensions of democratic citizenship—allegiance to democratic state authority, accommodation, and compromise among contending interests—are weakly developed. Thus, in both regions the experience of living in and resisting authoritarian regimes has bred in reaction some strong democratic norms, but not yet anything approaching a civic culture.

The impact of historical experience on political culture is also manifested through formative changes in the perceptions, tactics, and beliefs of political elites and their followers. This process of "political learning" appears most important during the creation or reconstruction of a democracy, "at the critical moment between the crisis of the old order and the consolidation of the new one."[5] I have mentioned in the Introduction a number of scholars who recognize how the experience of authoritarian repression in Southern Europe and Latin America caused civilian political leaders and thinkers, particularly on the left, to reappraise the value of democracy. As Paul Sigmund observes, this revaluing of democracy was particularly prominent within the ranks of the liberation theology movement throughout Central and South America. By the mid-1980s, "the experience of repression and torture under brutal dictatorship had given the Catholic left a renewed appreciation of the virtues of representative government, however flawed." Repressive military rule has had something of this same effect on intellectuals and other professionals, again especially on the left, in Nigeria. Around the world—from Spain and Brazil to Korea and the Philippines, and including much of Africa—the church and professional associations have been pivotal arenas of political learning and democratic value diffusion.[6]

Of course, it would be simplistic to argue that the failure or harshness of an authoritarian regime results reflexively in the strengthening of democratic preferences. Again, a number of factors interact in complex ways to shape changes in political culture. Delegitimation of an existing regime type may open several possible directions for cultural and institutional change. Which one predominates depends on the social structure, the balance of domestic political forces, economic changes, and the influence of global culture, among other factors. In Thailand, the long experience of unsuccessful struggle with communist insurgency eventually persuaded military leaders that a purely military victory was impossible, and that socioeconomic development and active political engagement in the countryside were essential. Although this produced a strong developmental response, it did not generate more democratic values and norms among military officers. Quite to the contrary, it bred during the 1970s a new military ideology quite hostile to the divisiveness of liberal democracy, legitimating a greatly expanded role for the military in economic development, rural administration, mass media, and national politics. In Egypt, the failure of the secular authoritarian state to legitimate itself has given rise to a growing cultural preference not for democracy but for an Islamic authoritarian state.

## Institutional Socialization

Culture springs from history, tradition, and collective myths, and is also forged and reproduced through a variety of institutional settings in which norms are learned, beliefs generated, and values internalized. Prominent among these settings are, of course, the family and the school; these are generally not the sites where culture is created, although innovation in the school curriculum, and in the ideas and knowledge generated in the universities, can contribute to significant change in political culture over time.

The tighter the solidarity of particular institutions, the more effective their socialization processes are likely to be. The military is a particular case in point here, as we see in the case study of Turkey, where the military institutions have been able to perpetuate (especially among the officer corps) a strong political subculture emphasizing national unity and order and suspicion of democratic mass mobilization.

This volume has bypassed completely the process and agents of childhood socialization. This is not to diminish their importance for reproducing political culture but, rather, to convey two points. First, socialization—including political socialization—is a lifelong process, and the literature on political learning certainly explodes the myth that new values and beliefs cannot be internalized well into adulthood. Second, the agents of cultural *change* are not to be found in the early socializing agents of family and school but in distinctive carriers of new political ideas and norms: individual leaders, intellectual and artistic innovators, autonomous groups, new class forces, and domestic and international media.

## Political Leadership and Interests

We tend to think of culture as the product of great historical and social forces. But values, beliefs, and orientations can also be reshaped by the deliberate actions, doctrines, and teachings of political leaders. Inevitably, scholars will debate to what extent great leaders shape or instead reflect their national political cultures. But it is difficult to deny that the great revolutionary leaders of this century—Lenin, Stalin, Hitler, Mao, Castro—had a measurable impact on the political ideas, values, norms, and feelings of their people and their time. And it is not just tyrants who have had such an effect. Sun Yat-sen, Kemal Atatürk, and Mahatma Gandhi all had at least partially democratic effects on the political cultures of their countries, through their leadership styles and political doctrines.[7] Moreover, as we see here in the case studies of Taiwan, Turkey, and India, their ideas continued to shape political thought and structures long after their deaths. It appears that the more charismatic the leader—in the Weberian sense of possessing extraordinary qualities that legitimate his or her authority—the greater the impact he or she may have not just on the behavior of political followers but on their deeper political orientations and beliefs. However, the impact of leadership on political culture may come not only through changes in political ideology, values, and styles but also indirectly through experience with the institutions leaders create. This was an especially significant effect of Kemal's revolution in Turkey.

The clearest case in this volume of a leadership effect on political culture is the influence of Mahatma Gandhi in India. Sisson shows how Gandhi built on reformist and activist traditions in recent Indian political history but shaped the anticolonial movement in a personal way by systematically resisting violence, "to the dismay of many activists," and emphasizing the consensual resolution of conflict. Gandhi also shaped the political culture of the independence movement by crafting a highly inclusive political strategy, "raising mass society to new levels of consciousness" while stressing values of political incorporation, social equality, and responsive, accountable government. The political norms and methods of the movement significantly reflected Gandhi's personal values, and Indian politics was never quite the same after his assassination. In particular, many students of Indian politics have discerned a marked deterioration in India's democratic culture, particularly at the elite level, with the departure of Nehru and the rise to power of his daughter, Indira Gandhi, whose relentless centralization and personalization of political power not only caused serious institutional decay but diminished the tolerant, consensual, accommodating, nonviolent attributes of (elite) political culture in India.[8]

Politics in a different sense may also bring about changes in political culture. In trying to account for the anomalously high support for democratic liberties in Nicaragua, and the anomaly of greater support for liberties on the political right in Nicaragua, Booth and Seligson make an intriguing and provocative case for the role of utilitarian considerations. People, they maintain, are more inclined to support greater liberty when it is needed to protect their own relatively weak power position. Even political beliefs that appear to tap a strong value dimension may be heavily (if not entirely consciously) motivated by instrumental factors. Their preliminary finding of a reversed "positional" effect (with the left now more supportive of liberty) after the transition from a left-wing to center-right regime adds to the plausibility of their argument and raises important issues for future research about the origins and lifespans of political "values." An important methodological issue for future research will be how to differentiate between value positions taken for short-term instrumental reasons and those embraced from a deeper and more coherent belief system.

## Social and Economic Change

Although this volume was in no way designed to "test" modernization theory, the historical cases do lend support to some of the central assumptions of the modernization literature. To be sure, there is no certain and continuous relationship between economic development and democratic culture change. It was amid the stresses and turbulence of socioeconomic development that liberation theologians and other Latin American left intellectuals rejected "bourgeois democracy" in the early 1970s in favor of militant, revolutionary, and Marxist options. The rapid expansion of higher education in South Korea brought not a steady increase in democratic values and practices but surges of militant student radicalism that played into the hands of military hard-liners. Again, many factors affect the evolution of political culture. One does not need to accept modernization theory in all of its linear and sometimes teleological assumptions of progress in order to argue that there is a broad causal relationship between socioeconomic development and democracy, and that political culture is a crucial intervening variable in that relationship.[9]

As Lucian Pye observes, "Taiwan is possibly the best working example of the theory that economic progress should bring in its wake democratic inclinations and a healthy surge of pluralism, which in time will undercut the foundations of the authoritarian rule common to developing countries."[10] With Pye, Ambrose King sees substantial modification of traditional Confucian attitudes toward power and authority as a result of Taiwan's four decades of rapid development. In particular, the demand for democratic change (albeit gradual) has been closely linked to growth in the middle class and "the dramatic expansion of higher education," where liberal democratic values were more in evidence because of the predominance of Western-trained teachers. A similar process has been under way in Thailand, where the new middle class formed the backbone of the movement that brought down the military-dominated, pseudodemocratic regime in 1992 through unprecedented popular protests. And in Turkey, Özbudun finds that modernization under the Kemalist regime "in time created an alternative or counter elite . . . of businessmen, merchants, professionals, and local notables" who rejected the tutelary dominance of a centralized, bureaucratic state in favor of a more open, competitive, and decentralized system.

Changes in political culture are also stimulated by the mobilization of autonomous social groups. This is the central point of Sadowski's chapter on Eastern Europe: The mobilization of these independent groups in civil society not only revived earlier, long suppressed, elements of democratic culture but reduced the fear, fatalism, and demoralization that characterized the mass political culture of communism, while giving citizens precious experience with free discussion and political organization. The resulting increases in protest and other autonomous political activity would not have been possible without the changes in political culture brought about by emergent autonomous groups. These groups and movements began as tiny bands of courageous dissidents opposing and resisting the totalitarian state. We should therefore not lose sight of the contribution of charismatic and heroic dissident leaders, such as Lech Walesa, Jacek Kurón, Adam Michnik, and Vaclav Havel, in inspiring many others to shed their cynicism and passivity. Here again, we see how political culture is affected not just by impersonal historical forces but by the initiatives and examples of individual leaders.

## International Diffusion

We have seen that culture springs from the deep wells and recent currents of history. It is forged through practice and experience, reproduced through socialization in various institutions, and shaped and reshaped by the examples, ideas, doctrines, strategies, and institution building of political leaders. Culture can be modified, gradually but profoundly, by long-term changes in social structure wrought by economic development. More rapidly, it may reflect the impact of mobilization by autonomous organizations. A final source of cultural change prominent in this volume is the impact of the international environment.

We see in a number of our cases how political culture may be changed by the international diffusion of values and beliefs. Although it was contradicted by the reality of authoritarian domination, appreciation of the political and civil liberties intrinsic to liberal democracy (particularly among political and intellectual elites) was encouraged by French and especially British colonial rule. This value diffusion occurred in part through practice within the democratizing institutions constructed by British colonial regimes, especially over long periods of time (as in India, Sri Lanka, and Jamaica). But it also happened through colonial education (including the important influence of missionary education), the spread of international mass media, and through direct experience with the educational and other institutions of the metropole.[11]

In the current wave of democratic expansion, international cultural influences have been significant. The dramatic growth in university education in both Taiwan and South Korea has corresponded with a huge increase in the number and proportion of Western-trained professors, the largest number of whom were trained in the United States. This intellectual influence from democratic countries gradually imparted to higher education in South Korea and Taiwan a liberal and democratic value orientation. Western-trained professionals and intellectuals formed the bulk of the democratic opposition in Taiwan and also emerged as a major constituency within the younger KMT leadership pressing for political liberalization in the 1970s and 80s. These new political leaders returned from their higher education abroad "ready to apply at home" the "ideas and institutions of a reference society" in the West.[12]

In a different but perhaps even more significant way, the Western democracies nurtured and fostered democratic changes in the political cultures of Eastern Europe. For many years, Western media, particularly via shortwave radio, were one of the few reliable sources of information about politics in the communist regimes and abroad. Among other things, these foreign radio broadcasts helped to publicize and generate support for the activities of opposition groups. The provision of this more truthful news and information was, Sadowski shows, an important aid in reconstructing a culture of criticism, independent thinking, and free discourse. Of course, Western organizations and governments also provided essential material, moral, and political support that helped pioneering human rights and other autonomous organizations press out the boundaries of political opposition and resistance to communist rule. Finally, Western countries strengthened the aspiration for democracy by providing a model of a successful, democratic alternative to the failed communist system.

International value diffusion has been a profound and pervasive, if subtle, factor in the globalization of democracy during the past two decades. Since 1990 in particular, many democratic transitions have been advanced by what Samuel P. Huntington calls the "snowballing" effect of some earlier transitions "stimulating and providing models for subsequent efforts at democratization."[13] It has not only helped to establish democracy as the most legitimate form of government internationally but has raised expectations in many parts of the world that democracy is *possible* to achieve. The example of people power toppling Ferdinand Marcos in the Philippines in early 1986 had an energizing impact on democratic forces in South Korea, and to some extent throughout Southeast Asia. The sudden crumbling of communism in Eastern Europe and then in the Soviet Union electrified democratic forces in Africa and helped to destroy many lingering beliefs in the efficacy and human potential of communist or socialist regimes.[14] All of this points to the important elements of strategic thinking and cross-country comparisons in political learning and culture change.[15]

## Effects of Political Culture

We are still a long way in political science from comprehensively modeling the complex (and variant) causal paths by which democracy emerges, consolidates, erodes, aborts, dies, reequilibrates, and endures. Many models have been offered; the more parsimonious, the more popular. Parsimony has its theoretical seductions and contributions, but it cannot suffice to explain an outcome as complex in its causation as the nature of a political regime. History, social structure, economic change, political institutions, and the international environment may all affect the possibility, form, and pace of democratic emergence and consolidation. The analyses in this volume have shown, however, that political culture is often an intervening variable in that relationship, and that cultural change may ultimately feed back into institutional change, social change, economic change (in part through new policies and institutions as well as new values), and international diffusion or demonstration effects elsewhere in the world.

Democratic culture is certainly not a precondition for the initiation of democracy, but that process inevitably begins with shifts in the outlook, beliefs, and strategies of key elites, and eventually spreads to encompass the thinking of a wider circle of elites and ultimately the values and perceptions of the citizenry at large. It would be foolish to offer as anything more than heuristic a neat, parsimonious model of causal arrows running, say, from elite negotiations to institutional democratization to democratic habituation. In fact, democratization seems to involve an iterative process of constantly resonating reciprocal influences between new actions, new institutions, new social forces or configurations, new environmental constraints and opportunities, and new perceptions, beliefs, and values. Clearly, political culture is both effect and cause, and its significance in both these respects varies across countries, across historical epochs, and across phases within a single process of regime change.

Without repeating all the evidence already discussed here, we can summarize here in conclusion some of the ways that political culture acts as independent or intervening variable to influence the creation, performance, and viability of democratic regimes.

## Democratic Transition and Emergence

We have seen three principal ways in which political culture contributes to democratization or redemocratization: by changing beliefs and perceptions of key elites, by effecting broader changes in mass political culture, and by reviving established but dormant democratic norms and preferences. At the elite level, contending political leaders come to conclude that democratic change is a good thing in and of itself, or that it is necessary to achieve other ends they value (such as domestic stability and peace, or international acceptance). The first change is less common—in politics there are not many conversions on the road to Damascus. But we learn from the literature on political learning that leaders do weigh historical experience (not only their own but that of other countries) and sometimes truly internalize its lessons.

On the other hand, some political leaders may always have had some appreciation for democracy as one among several long-term goals. When other goals are reached, democracy may come into play as a sincere aspiration (if only to be realized gradually). It appears that this type of normative and strategic calculation heavily motivated Chiang Ching-kuo to initiate fundamental democratizing reforms during 1986. Democratization had always been one of the long-range objectives of the KMT's ideology, derived from the principles of Sun Yat-sen, and by 1986 economic development was already substantially achieved and democratic change was sweeping East Asia.[16] Similarly, when the Turkish military seized power in 1980, it never intended to remain indefinitely but only long enough to "correct" the system. Acceptance of the idea that civilian, democratic rule should be the norm was an important factor in the relatively brief stay in power by the military in Turkey, in contrast to Thailand, where the norm of civilian democratic rule has never been internalized by the military. Nigeria has been in something of the middle ground, with the military professing a commitment to civilian democracy but ruling in an abusive and self-serving manner that betrays a lust for power and ill-gotten wealth.[17]

At the mass level, democratization can be stimulated both by cultural change and by the resurgence of long submerged cultural beliefs and styles. In Eastern Europe, the revival of precommunist democratic methods, values, and beliefs through autonomous groups and information networks, initially within small circles of opposition, was a key factor in undermining the authority and legitimacy of communist regimes and paving the way for their toppling when international circumstances became ripe. In parts of Latin America, democratic cultural traditions made it more difficult to perpetuate and institutionalize authoritarian rule. In Uruguay, the military regime's lack of legitimacy hampered its effectiveness, while its need "to justify every action as necessary for the promotion of democracy" showed "the resilience of the democratic political culture permeating even the armed forces, and the inhospitable climate for authoritarian discourse."[18] In both Uruguay and Chile, the self-perceived need for legitimation compelled the authoritarian regimes to resort to popular plebiscites that ultimately backfired, advancing the transition to democracy and demonstrating the continuing and renewed vitality of democratic culture.

The most common factor here is the development of a diffuse reaction against authoritarian rule that generates legitimacy for democracy, at least by "default." This has certainly been the case, as Chazan shows, in much of Africa, with Nigeria being a particularly striking example. However, mass-level cultural change often exhibits signs of deep normative shifts that change the national political context. Throughout Latin America, the abandonment of revolutionary fantasies and democratic contempt by the left — both religious and secular—was an important factor not only in expanding the civic base of pressure for democracy but in reducing the sense of threat by powerful state and economic elites that might have inhibited their commitment to or acceptance of democratization. The corresponding rise in values of tolerance and support for democratic liberties, as documented by Booth and Seligson, also seems to make the transition to democracy more plausible and less threatening in countries like Nicaragua and Mexico. Most clearly in the case of India, the unique cultural blend of the Gandhian movement—tenacious public mobilization and resistance, combined with readiness for accommodation and negotiation—was a major factor in its successful achievement of national independence with democracy.

## Consolidation and Persistence

In Turkey, Özbudun suggests, the process of consolidation has been advanced by the greater emphasis on liberal values and the stronger consensus among political parties on the need to preserve the democratic system, after three military interventions in twenty years. But few political scientists would rank Turkey's democracy as fully consolidated, and old habits die hard. Continued "personalistic style of government" and "frequent disregard for the rules and regulations" have made for continued tension and volatility in politics (and between politicians and bureaucrats).

In the two cases in our study (India and Costa Rica) of surprising democratic persistence despite low or moderate economic development, political culture at both the elite and mass levels clearly plays a strong supporting role. Sisson observes: "Political elites brought with them to independent India a strong commitment to liberal democracy." In distinct contrast to so many African cases, the leaders of the Congress party responded to political competition and opposition with substantive reforms (such as the linguistic reorganization of states) and incorporative policies, appointments, and political strategies. Ruling party elites reached out democratically to new and disaffected groups, offering them tangible incentives, while seeking to deepen democracy at the grassroots. Furthermore, democracy became buttressed from the ground up through the regular participation of a relatively knowledgeable, interested, opinionated, efficacious, and increasingly independent-minded electorate. This history, particularly during the first two decades of independence (to 1967), provides a classic account of the role of political culture—interacting with political leadership, institutionalization, and social change—in helping to consolidate democracy.

A similar story is visible in the post-1948 democratic history of Costa Rica, where, Booth and Seligson suggest, "reciprocal influence" between "elite culture, mass culture, and institutional development contributed to both the stabilization of democratic institutions and widespread allegiance to democratic norms." John Booth has noted a number of features of contemporary Costa Rican political culture that have helped to consolidate and sustain democracy, and these are strikingly reminiscent of the postindependence Indian experience: an elite striving for compromise and consensus, which has diffused to the rank and file; widespread support for the political system and the legitimacy of democracy; and extensive political knowledge, discussion, opinions, voting, electioneering, and organizational participation.[19] As in India, these orientations developed in part gradually from earlier (though partial and discontinuous) democratic experience, and were encouraged by a rather unique social structure that mitigated class divisions. Booth summarizes the contribution of a conciliatory political culture to democratic persistence in Costa Rica as follows:

> Costa Rica's political culture has contributed significantly to the maintenance of democracy. Costa Ricans and their organizations generally engage in pacific demand-making, and the state has had a tradition of acquiescing to such demands. Political elites and masses share considerable commitment to the liberal system of parties and clean elections. There exists a strong tendency toward popular loyalty to the political system, regardless of disapproval of momentary incumbents. Though present, political confrontation and violence are very mild by regional standards, and the state reacts to them with moderation and conciliation.[20]

Precisely because of the diffuse and deeply internalized belief in democratic regime legitimacy, Costa Rica was able to weather sustained economic crisis in the 1980s with relatively little political instability.[21]

Similar arguments about the democratically sustaining effect of a moderate, accommodating, and participant political culture have been made about Venezuela.[22] However, statism, political corruption, and the prolonged political monopoly of two centralized, clientelistic, and increasingly unresponsive parties have diminished the capacity of an otherwise democratic culture to buffer the destabilizing effects of economic downturn and structural adjustment, as evidenced in the nearly successful military coup attempt of February 1992.[23] The recent turbulence in Venezuela illustrates well the dynamic and multidimensional character of political culture, and the complex ways it may interact with political institutions and emergent social forces that fail to achieve incorporation into and responsiveness from existing political structures.

## Erosion of Democracy

As I argued in the Introduction, it is not enough to achieve a democratic culture and democratic patterns of elite interaction. Democratic values, modes, beliefs, and sensitivities grow from but also sustain democratic institutions. Where these properties of democratic culture erode or fail to renew themselves across generations, democratic institutions themselves become endangered.

Erosion may occur in many guises, for many different reasons. Certainly one of the most common origins is social and generational change, which produces new interests, movements, and elites seeking entrance into the system and benefits from it. Elite bargains, pacts, settlements, and understandings must then be reproduced, and sometimes modified through institutional change, to incorporate these new groups and adapt to new circumstances, or new demands are likely to find expression through violent, semiloyal, and disloyal actions and movements. Elite responses in the face of these pressures are driven by strategic power considerations, but they are also heavily shaped by political values and goals.

A common problem for democracy, evident in the experience of Venezuela above, of neighboring Colombia, and quite prominently of India since 1967, is that elite democratic commitments may themselves weaken, erode, or become hollowed out by the temptations of power and the proliferation of demands that become difficult to satisfy or reconcile through existing institutional arrangements. As in Venezuela, semiconsociational arrangements in Colombia became outdated and yet difficult to restructure because they served so well the interests of the existing elite.[24] In India, proliferating demands by increasingly mobilized class, caste, ethnic, and religious groups have seriously strained decaying political institutions, and the post-1967 generation of less skillful, cohesive, and democratically committed leaders has failed to produce new, democratically incorporating policies and institutions.[25] This deterioration in the culture and institutions of Indian democracy has in turn produced decay in its performance (as indicated by rising levels of corruption, violence, human rights violations, and extra-legal conflict) and in its democraticness: India at the end of 1991 was rated by Freedom House as only "partially free" for the first time since Indira Gandhi's emergency rule in the late 1970s.[26] Yet leading scholars, including Sisson in this volume and Atul Kohli, continue to regard India as essentially still a democracy, and attribute its persistence amid adversity in good measure to the resilience and deep entrenchment of its democratic culture.[27]

In these circumstances of inexorable social and political change, the challenge for democracy is institutional reform: "reinventing" or reinvigorating democracy. However, second and third (and subsequent) generations of democrats, grown comfortable (if not avaricious) with the perquisites of power and the predictability of the current system, are often not up to the task. The erosion of democracy then becomes a matter not just of socioeconomic change producing social mobilization in the context of stagnant and inadequate political institutions. It may also involve subtle and not-so-subtle cultural decay, in which politicians' commitments to democracy revert to an instrumental form and democrats lose the energizing force of deep conviction in the innate value of democracy itself.

## Abortion and Breakdown

There is no shortage of evidence documenting the prominent role of political culture and culture change in the failure and breakdown of democracy. Chazan shows in this volume how the superficial and expedient commitments to democracy by rising African elites easily gave way to authoritarian impulses, under the immense pressures faced by struggling new regimes after independence. Low levels of civic competence and democratic under-standing on the part of mass constituencies, and high levels of corruption, intolerance, mistrust, and abuse of power on the part of competing politi-cians, further contributed to the chaotic, violent, and ruleless politics that brought down fledgling or potential democratic regimes throughout the con-tinent. Although the structural problems were daunting and the colonial lega-cy (both culturally and institutionally) largely inauspicious, political culture must be identified at least as a crucial intervening variable in Africa's many aborted and failed attempts at democracy.[28]

One can point to countless instances where political culture undermines democracy or inhibits transition to it. In Egypt, the maximalist, authoritarian character of the principal regime opposition, the Islamic movement, inhibits regime leaders from moving beyond their current very partial and tentative liberalizing steps to respond to international pressures and their own impuls-es for democratic change. In the face of a movement that seeks a total politi-cal, economic, and social transformation, the costs and risks of political toleration appear to elites to outweigh considerably the costs of suppression. This assessment has sharpened in favor of still greater caution with the huge victory of the leading Islamist party (the FIS) in the first round of Algeria's December 1991 elections, and the subsequent military intervention and vio-lent polarization of that country's politics.

The abortion or failure of democracy rarely results from the uniform and equal contributions of all subcultures and societal elements. Frequently, one or a few groups exert a disproportionate impact. The radical mobilization of leftist groups in the unions, churches, and universities provided an intense stimulus to reactionary military intervention in Latin America, and con-tributed for many years to a risk assessment by strategic groups (economic as well as military) that rejected democracy as too threatening to their values and interests. In most cases, ruling groups hold the trump cards for determin-ing the character and pace of democratization, and in such cases (as in Taiwan) their values and perceptions have a disproportionate impact on the outcome.

## Conclusion

This volume has depicted political culture as a complex, multifaceted, and dynamic phenomenon, open to change (including dramatic change well into the lives of people and regimes) and yet potent in its effects on democracy, both immediate and long-term. In keeping with our theoretically cautious approach, I will not attempt to synthesize what we have learned into any kind of grand model. Nevertheless, some of our insights merit special emphasis in conclusion.

It is apparent from all we have learned and presented here that a democratic culture is not a precondition for the emergence of democracy, that in fact there is no purely democratic culture, and that as both Gabriel Almond and Richard Sklar have recognized, all democracies (if they are not stagnant or dying) are in a continuous state of becoming.[29] Democracies can persist with important subcultures being hostile to or suspicious of them, but their stability will increase to the extent that either the power of these groups or their hostility to democracy erodes over time. Democracies do persist, always, with mixed political cultures—in fact, as Almond and Verba and others insist, they precisely require some kind of mix or balance of cultural attributes. However, some features of political culture are more important to democracy than others, and it is more important to democracy that some groups manifest them than that others do so.

Most theoretical treatments of democratic transition and consolidation in the past two decades have erred in virtually ignoring mass culture, but it is undeniable that the political beliefs, values, and styles of elites have a disproportionate effect on democracy, especially in its early formative years. There is little reason, then, to revise Dahl's argument of more than two decades ago that the beliefs of political leaders and activists are particularly important for three reasons: they have more power than other actors and so "more influence on political events, including events that affect the stability or transformation of regimes"; they are more likely to have "moderately elaborate systems of political beliefs"; and their actions are more likely to be guided by those belief systems.[30]

Nor can one quarrel with Dahl's identification of democratic legitimacy as the first and most important type of political belief for democracy. The only real precondition for democracy is that a politically powerful set of elites becomes committed to it. The broader this commitment becomes, and the sooner it assumes intrinsic and deep valuation, the better the prospect for the installation and consolidation of democracy. Democracy can persist for a long time with equivocal or conditional commitments to it on the part of political leaders and followers alike. But it will always be vulnerable in those circumstances. As Seligson and Muller showed for Costa Rica and Lipset argued long ago in *Political Man*, democracy becomes truly stable only when people come to value it widely not solely for its economic and social performance but intrinsically for its political attributes.[31]

Beyond this, the preeminent lesson for democracy from this and much other work is the importance of accommodation. It has many synonyms and implications: compromise, moderation, flexibility, pragmatism, trust, cooperation, toleration. However one wishes to formulate the proposition, the essence is that contending interests and groups must find a way to work and live with one another, whether at the apex through the interactions of elites in a consociational system or in a much more comprehensive field of interaction. Consociational arrangements hold distinct attractions as a mechanism (some would say a crutch) facilitating such cooperation and bargaining between deeply divided groups in the early stages of democracy when hostility is intense and trust low. The problem is that they inevitably become out-dated with time, requiring revision or complete abandonment that may prove painful to elites who have come to benefit from them in predictable ways.

This returns us to the issue of the relative importance of elite versus mass culture. It is fine to specify political leaders and activists as the most important arena of culture for democracy, particularly in the short term. But to ignore the beliefs of the wider society is to fail to appreciate the consider-able degree to which influence and pressure for action may flow from the bottom up, constraining elites and perhaps vitiating or undermining even their sincerely democratic inclinations. This is one reason why stable democ-racy requires mass habituation to democratic values and orientations, and thus why a vigorous civil society is important, alongside a well-articulated party system, to provide arenas in which citizens can practice democracy, internalize its values and limits, and hold elites accountable.

Another reason why attention to mass political culture is important is that the composition of the political elite does not remain stable over time. This reality has not been adequately appreciated in the literature on consoci-ationalism, transitions, and consolidation. Social, economic, and genera-tional change give rise to new interest groups and leaders out of old mass constituencies. It helps if these new interests and elites have already internal-ized democratic values and styles. And it is essential that these rising inter-ests be given a place at the democratic table, if they are not to turn it over.

Democracy requires flexibility not only in dealing with adversaries but in adapting to change over time. One of the most common sources of democ-ratic crisis, decay, and destruction is the rigidity of democratic arrangements that have outlived their usefulness, excluding important new social groups and precluding democratic efficacy and responsiveness. It is difficult to find a long-established democracy that has not found the need repeatedly to renew and revise its institutions, to incorporate new groups and restrain old practices that have become corrupt and corrosive of democratic confidence. One need only mention Watergate and PACs (political action committees) in the United States, or the rising scandal of political campaign financing in Japan, to appreciate the point. Israel's democracy has been under serious and costly stress, and India's even more so, because elites have not proved adapt-able and flexible but, rather, have become locked (as are American politi-cians in pursuit of PAC contributions and Italian and Japanese politicians in their ties to corporate and criminal networks) in the narrow pursuit of imme-diate political self-interest.

One can point to a welter of structural constraints and inducements that block reform, but to stop there is to surrender individual choice and initiative as causal forces in history. All democracies require periodic institutional ren-ovation and renewal. Social movements can press for them, on the wings of an efficacious and mobilized citizenry. This is a crucial dimension of politi-cal culture, and the more developed it is, the more likely democratic renewal will be. But in the end, political elites must respond, even if they do not always lead. Only political elites—presidents, prime ministers, parties, and parliaments—can enact reforms. The persistence of democracy through long periods of time entails many small transitions and adjustments, in which elites—valuing democracy and responding to and incorporating diverse interests—continually reform and reinvent democracy. In this never-ending quest for renewal and improvement, political culture plays no small role.

## Notes

1. As a blend of values and attitudes, of relatively stable orientations to action and relatively fleeting opinions and assessments, political culture is, almost by definition, shaped by factors from different historical moments. But even basic value preferences are likely to have this complex, sedimentary structure.

2. The Taiwanese experience suggests a revision of Dahl's thesis about favorable paths for the emergence of polyarchy. It tends to confirm his arguments about the values of gradualism and prior historical experience with limited democratization. However, it indicates that limited (nonparty) political competition, with mass suffrage, may be a functional substitute in the contemporary world for the nineteenth and early twentieth century model of democratic (multiparty) competition with limited suffrage. In each case, the dominant social and political forces sanction limited competition that does not threaten their basic interests. As emergent elites and the public at large become socialized into the norms and requirements of democracy (including moderation and compromise), political competition can be expanded with a minimum of risk to essential interests of dominant groups.

3. On the confrontational features of Korean political culture, see Lucian Pye, *Asian Power and Politics: The Cultural Dimensions of Authority* (Cambridge: Harvard University Press, 1985), pp. 226-228. Pye appreciates the importance of gradual political accommodation between the KMT and the *dang-wai* (independent opposition candidates) as electoral politics evolved during the 1970s and early 1980s. However, he attributes the greater modification of Confucian political culture in Taiwan (as opposed to China or Korea) to other factors (ethnic and generational cleavages, the trauma of defeat, and distinctive features of political economy) (pp. 228-236). It should be noted that Pye's analysis was written before the dramatic democratizing reforms in both Korea and Taiwan in the latter half of the 1980s.

4. James S. Coleman, *Nigeria: Background to Nationalism* (Berkeley: University of California Press, 1958); Richard L. Sklar, *Nigerian Political Parties: Power in an Emergent African Nation* (Princeton: Princeton University Press, 1963); and Larry Diamond, *Class, Ethnicity, and Democracy in Nigeria: The Failure of the First Republic* (London: Macmillan, and Syracuse: Syracuse University Press, 1988).

5. Nancy Bermeo, "Democracy and the Lessons of Dictatorship," *Comparative Politics* 24 (April 1992): 273.

6. Bermeo, "Democracy and the Lessons of Dictatorship," pp. 286-287; Larry Diamond, "The Globalization of Democracy: Trends, Types, Causes, and Prospects," in Robert O. Slater, Barry M. Schutz, and Steven R. Dorr, eds., *Global Transformation and the Third World* (Boulder: Lynne Rienner Publishers, 1993).

7. There are interesting similarities in the doctrines of Sun Yat-sen and Kemal Atatürk, both of whom favored some kind of strong-handed, tutelary, "guided" democracy during the early phases of political development but envisioned at some

point down the historical road evolution toward a fuller and more open democracy.

8. See, for example, Robert L. Hardgrave, Jr., and Stanley Kochanek, *India: Government and Politics in a Developing Nation*, 4th ed. (New York: Harcourt Brace Jovanovich, 1986), pp. 121-122; James Manor, "Parties and the Party System," and Atuhl Kohli, "State-Society Relations in India's Changing Democracy," in Atul Kohli, ed., *India's Democracy: An Analysis of Changing State-Society Relations* (Princeton: Princeton University Press, 1988), pp. 62-98, 305-318; and Paul Brass, *The Politics of India Since Independence* (Cambridge: Cambridge University Press, 1990), pp. 321-323. For a view that acknowledges the "deinstitutionalizing role of national and regional leaders" (p. 387) but gives more weight to structural factors and constraints, see Atul Kohli, *Democracy and Discontent: India's Growing Crisis of Governability* (Cambridge: Cambridge University Press, 1990).

9. For a comprehensive review of the theoretical and empirical literature on the relationship between socioeconomic development and democracy, which arrives at this conclusion, see Larry Diamond, "Economic Development and Democracy Reconsidered," *American Behavioral Scientist* 35 (March/June 1992): 450-499, reprinted in Gary Marks and Larry Diamond, eds., *Reexamining Democracy: Essays in Honor of Seymour Martin Lipset* (Newbury Park, CA: Sage, 1992), pp. 93-139.

10. Pye, *Asian Power and Politics*, p. 233.

11. Larry Diamond, Juan J. Linz, and Seymour Martin Lipset, *Democracy and Developing Countries: Persistence, Failure, and Renewal* (Boulder: Lynne Rienner Publishers, forthcoming), chap. 4, "The Legacy of the Colonial Past."

12. Tun-jun Cheng, "Democratizing the Quasi-Leninist Regime in Taiwan," *World Politics* 41 (July 1989): 483.

13. Samuel P. Huntington, "Democracy's Third Wave," *Journal of Democracy* 2 (Spring 1991): 13; see also Huntington, *The Third Wave: Democratization in the Late Twentieth Century* (Norman: University of Oklahoma Press, 1991).

14. Diamond, "The Globalization of Democracy."

15. Bermeo, "Democracy and the Lessons of Dictatorship," pp. 274, 283.

16. Ramon Myers, "The Republic of China on Taiwan: The Political Center, Economic Development, and Democracy" (Paper presented at conference, Economy, Society, and Democracy, sponsored by the Agency for International Development and the Hoover Institution, Washington, DC, 7-9 May 1992), pp. 25–26. Myers also notes that Chiang was motivated to act by the knowledge that he was dying and that whatever legacy he wanted to impart would need to be effected relatively quickly.

17. Larry Diamond, "Nigeria's Search for a New Political Order," *Journal of Democracy* 2 (Spring 1991): 54-69, and "Political Corruption: Nigeria's Perennial Struggle," *Journal of Democracy* 2 (Fall 1991): 73–85; Larry Diamond and Oyeleye Oyediran, "Military Authoritarianism and Democratic Transition in Nigeria," *National Political Science Review* 1 (forthcoming).

18. Charles Guy Gillespie and Luis Eduardo Gonzalez, "Uruguay: The Survival of Old and Autonomous Institutions," in Larry Diamond, Juan J. Linz, and Seymour Martin Lipset, eds., *Democracy in Developing Countries: Latin America* (Boulder: Lynne Rienner Publishers, 1989), p. 223.

19. John A. Booth, "Costa Rica: The Roots of Democratic Stability," in Diamond, Linz, and Lipset, *Democracy in Developing Countries: Latin America*, pp. 402-404.

20. Ibid., p. 416.

21. Mitchell A. Seligson and Edward Muller, "Democratic Stability and Economic Crisis: Costa Rica, 1978-83," *International Studies Quarterly* 31 (1987): 301-326.

22. Daniel H. Levine, "Venezuela: The Nature, Sources and Future Prospects of Democracy," in Diamond, Linz, and Lipset, *Democracy in Developing Countries:*

*Latin America*, pp. 278-280. Levine here attaches particular importance to the democratically enculturating impact of widespread citizen participation in autonomous organizations.

23. Michael Coppedge, "Venezuela's Vulnerable Democracy," *Journal of Democracy* 3 (October 1992): 32-44.

24. Jonathan Hartlyn, "Colombia: The Politics of Violence and Accommodation," in Diamond, Linz, and Lipset, *Democracy in Developing Countries: Latin America*, pp. 329-330. For this reason, Hartlyn questions the suitability of consociational practices for developing countries: "Their inevitable requirement of considerable elite autonomy and their fear of mass mobilization may inhibit development of broader democratic practices" (p. 330). This problem underscores the intricate reciprocal relationship between values and institutions.

25. Atul Kohli, *Democracy and Discontent*, and "Indian Democracy: Stress and Resilience," *Journal of Democracy* 3 (January 1992): 52-64.

26. Freedom House, *Freedom in the World: Political Rights and Civil Liberties, 1991-1992* (New York: Freedom House, 1992).

27. For Kohli's view on this, see "Indian Democracy," p. 63.

28. See also Larry Diamond, "Introduction: Roots of Failure, Seeds of Hope," in Larry Diamond, Juan J. Linz, and Seymour Martin Lipset, eds., *Democracy in Developing Countries: Africa* (Boulder: Lynne Rienner Publishers, 1988): 13-15, 18.

29. Gabriel A. Almond, "Democracy and 'Crisis, Choice, and Change'" (Paper presented to the annual meeting of the American Political Science Association, Chicago, 4 September 1992), p. 6; Richard L. Sklar, "Developmental Democracy," *Comparative Studies in Society and History* 29 (October 1987): 687-714.

30. Robert A. Dahl, *Polyarchy: Participation and Opposition* (New Haven: Yale University Press, 1971), p. 128.

31. Seymour Martin Lipset, *Political Man* (Baltimore: Johns Hopkins University Press, 1981), pp. 68-70; Seligson and Muller, "Democratic Stability and Economic Crisis."

# About the Contributors

**JOHN A. BOOTH** is Regents' Professor of Political Science at the University of North Texas. He is the author of *The End and the Beginning: The Nicaraguan Revolution*, coauthor of *Understanding Central America*, and coeditor of *Political Participation in Latin America, vols. 1 and 2* and *Elections and Democracy in Central America*. He also has written numerous journal articles and anthology chapters on political participation, political culture, violence, revolution, and democratization in Central America, Mexico, and Colombia.

**NAOMI CHAZAN** is professor of political science at the Hebrew University of Jerusalem. She is the author of numerous articles on politics, the state, civil society, and democracy in Africa. Her books include *An Anatomy of Ghanaian Politics: Managing Political Recession, 1969-82*, *Ghana: Coping with Uncertainty* (with Deborah Pellow), *The Precarious Balance: State and Society in Africa* (edited with Donald Rothchild), *The Early State in Africa* (with S. N. Eisenstadt and M. Abitol), and *Politics and Society in Contemporary Africa* (with Robert Mortimer, John Ravenhill, and Donald Rothchild). She was elected in 1992 to the Israeli *Knesset.*

**LARRY DIAMOND** is senior research fellow at the Hoover Institution and coeditor of the *Journal of Democracy*. He is the author of *Class, Ethnicity and Democracy in Nigeria*, and of numerous articles and book chapters on democracy and democratization in Nigeria, Africa, and comparatively throughout the world. His edited books include *Democracy in Developing Countries* (with Juan J. Linz and Seymour Martin Lipset), *The Democratic Revolution: Struggles for Freedom and Pluralism in the Developing World*, *Reexamining Democracy* (with Gary Marks), *Israeli Democracy Under Stress* (with Ehud Sprinzak), and *The Global Resurgence of Democracy* (with Marc F. Plattner).

**AMBROSE Y. C. KING** is professor of sociology and pro-vice-chancellor (1989-present) at the Chinese University of Hong Kong. Among his many authored and coedited books are *From Tradition to Modernity, The Predicament and Development of Democracy in China, The Modernization of China and Intellectuals, The Developmental Experience of Hong Kong* (edited with H. M. Hsing), *Social Life and Development in Hong Kong* (all in English), and *The Idea of the University, The Politics of the Three Chinese Societies*, and *The Historical Development of Chinese Democratic Thought* (all in Chinese). He has also published numerous articles on development, Chinese bureaucracy, Chinese culture, Confucianism, politics, and development in China and Hong Kong. He is a member of the editorial board of *The China Quarterly.*

**ERGUN ÖZBUDUN** is professor of constitutional law and comparative politics at Ankara University Law School, president of the Turkish Political Science Association and vice-president of the Turkish Democracy Foundation. Among his extensive writings on democratic politics both in Turkey and in comparative perspective are three books, including *Social Change and Political Participation in Turkey.* Among his edited works are *The Political Economy of Income Distribution in Turkey* (with Aydin Ulusan), *Atatürk: Founder of a Modern State* (with Ali Kazancigil) and *Competitive Elections in Developing Countries* (with Myron Weiner).

**CHRISTINE M. SADOWSKI** is the director of special projects at the AFL-CIO's Free Trade Union Institute, which conducts programs to promote free trade unions in the former Soviet Union and Eastern Europe. Prior to taking this position, she was a private contractor for the U.S. government, working as an evaluation research specialist for USAID democracy programs in Eastern Europe and trade union programs internationally. At the Hoover Institution as a national fellow and visiting scholar, she conducted research on voluntary associations, autonomous groups, and worker organizations in Eastern Europe, particularly Poland.

**MITCHELL A. SELIGSON** is professor of political science and director of the Center for Latin American Studies of the University of Pittsburgh. His books include *Peasants of Costa Rica and the Development of Agrarian Capitalism, Political Participation in Latin America* (with John Booth), *The Gap Between Rich and Poor: Contending Perspectives on the Political Economy of Development, Authoritarians and Democrats: Regime Transition in Latin America, and Elections* and *Democracy in Central America* (with John A. Booth). Along with John Booth, he has won the Hoover Institution Prize for the best article published on Latin America.

**PAUL E. SIGMUND** is professor of politics at Princeton University. His fourteen books and more than one hundred articles have focused on Latin

American politics and political economy, Chilean politics in particular, political thought, natural law, democracy, and liberation theology. Among his books are *The Democratic Experience* (with Reinhold Niebuhr), *Natural Law in Political Thought*, *The Overthrow of Allende and the Politics of Chile, 1964-76*, *The Military Institution in Latin America* (with Robert Wesson et al.), and *Liberation Theology at the Crossroads: Democracy or Revolution?*

**RICHARD SISSON** is professor of political science and senior vice chancellor at the University of California, Los Angeles. His many published works include *Elections and Party Politics in India* (coedited with Dwaine Marvick), *The Congress Party in Rajasthan, Representative Institutions and the Democratic Polity: Some Socioeconomic Explanations, Comparative Politics: Institutions, Behavior and Development* (with David T. Cattell), *Congress and Indian Nationalism* (coedited with Stanley A. Wolpert), and *War and Secession: Crisis and Decision in South Asia, 1971* (with Leo Rose). He serves on the editorial boards of *Asian Survey* and *Asian Affairs*.

# Index

participation in, 107, 128 (n43); political
rights in, 111-112, 113-114, 115, 117-119
(tables)
Côte d'Ivoire, 72, 75, 76, 82, 86, 87
Coups, 20, 219; in Turkey, 198-199, 201, 205
Cox, Harvey: *The Secular City*, 211
Crime networks, 79-80
Crooked Circle Clubs, 158
Cuban Revolution, 215
Culture, 60, 77, 237; changes in, 144-145;
democratic, 238-239; and regime type, 127-
128 (n33); preservation of, 143-144; role, 3,
127 (n32). *See also* Mass culture
Czechoslovakia, 19, 164, 165, 170, 172, 180,
231; autonomous groups in, 156, 160, 161,
175-176, 179, 182, 186 (n40); writers'
unions in, 158-159

Dang Wai (DW), 140, 141, 143, 247 (n3)
Death squads, 224
Declaration of Basic Principles, 226
Decolonization, 66, 67, 68
Democracy, 88, 134, 184, 224, 228 (n4), 246-
249; in Africa, 67-68, 88-89; breakdown of,
243-244; and Catholicism, 213, 226, 227;
consolidation of, 5-7, 11, 241-242;
development of, 231-233 elites and, 2-4;
emergence of, 1, 123-124, 239-241; erosion
of, 242-243; independence and, 71-72;
monistic, 99-100; representative, 101
Democratic Party (DP), 194, 197-198
Democratic Progressive Party, 143
Democratization, 239-240; in Bulgaria, 180-
181; and education, 210-211; in Latin
America, 99, 126 (n13); in Poland, 177-178;
in Republic of China, 134, 142-143
Demonstrations, 111, 141, 164
Dependencia, 220, 222
Dependency theory, 2, 133
DESAL. *See* Desarrollo Económico Social de
América Latina
Desarrollo Económico Social de América
Latina (DESAL), 215
Determinism, 8-9
Díaz, Porfirio, 103
Dissent, 17; right to, 109, 110-119, 113, 114,
115, 117 (table), 119 (table)
Doctrine of National Security, 222
Doe, Samuel, 77, 85
DP. *See* Democratic Party
Duarte, José Napoleon, 214
Dubcek, Alexander, 164
Dussell, Enrique, 220
DW. *See* Dang Wai

Eastern Europe, 18-19, 155, 163, 206, 231,
233, 236-237; human rights issues in, 170-
171; informal networks in, 159-160; politics
of, 183-184; strikes in, 157-158; voter
turnout in, 182-183; Western media in, 237-

238. *See also various countries*
East German Writers' Union, 159
East Germany. *See* German Democratic
Republic
Economic development, 1, 2, 21, 68, 237; in
Republic of China, 131-133, 138-139, 149
Economy, 64, 81-82, 105
Education, 1, 7, 215, 220; and political values,
103, 112, 113-114, 145; and social change,
236
Elections, 107; in Africa, 70-71, 72; in Costa
Rica, 128-129 (n44); in Hungary, 178-179;
in India, 29-30, 31, 42, 43-45, 56 (n35); in
Poland, 177-178; in Republic of China, 138,
140-141, 145-147; in Turkey, 194, 200, 201,
205; voting patterns in, 46-47, 182-183
Elites, 5, 10, 15, 17, 23 (n23), 35, 81, 138,
165, 169, 172, 189, 249 (n24);
accommodation among, 2-3, 5, 6, 200-205;
African, 68-69, 72, 74, 78-79, 243-244;
colonially dependent, 64-65; and
democracy, 2-5, 7, 16, 51, 125, 239, 241,
243, 245-246; domination of, 191-194;
information access by, 167-168; and
liberalism, 69-73; and mass participation, 5-
6, 46; and modernization, 191, 196-197;
nationalist, 31, 32, 37-38, 51, 52; political,
197-198, 241; state, 75-76, 77, 207, 213,
208 (n9), 209-210 (n40)
Ellacuria, Ignacio, 225, 228 (n20)
El Salvador, 214, 224, 225
EP. *See* Participation, extensive
Equatorial Guinea, 77, 85
Ethiopia, 76
Ethnic groups, 8, 39, 49-50, 70
Ethnicity, 64
Evangelical Church, 179-180
Evren, General Kenan, 205

Falange, 213
Four Little Dragons, 131
France, 64, 65, 69, 212, 213, 237
*Free China* (journal), 137
Freedom and Peace Movement (WiP), 163
Freedoms: political, 137-138
Free Trade Union Movement, 167
Frei, Eduardo, 213, 215
Freire, Paulo, 220
French Revolution, 212
FSLN. *See* Sandinista National Liberation
Front
Fundamentalism, 50-51
Fundamental Rights of the Citizen (India), 39
Fund-raising, 171-172

Gambia, 59, 71
Gandhi, Indira, 44, 45, 235, 243
Gandhi, Mohandas K. (Mahatma), 16, 38, 40,
234
Gandhi, Rajiv, 45

Tolerance, 102, 115, 129 (n49)
Torres, Camilo, 217-218
Tradiçao Familia e Propriedade (TFP), 216
Tswana, 62
Tukulur, 63
Turkey, 19-20, 189, 230, 234, 240, 241;
  constitutions, 199-200, 204-205; coups in,
  198-199; debureaucratization in, 197-198;
  elite accommodation in, 200-205; elite
  domination in, 191-194; modernization in,
  196-197, 236; populism in, 195-196;
  revolutionism in, 194-195, 235
12 March Regime, 201

UDF. *See* Union of Democratic Forces
Uganda, 74, 76, 77, 85
Underdevelopment, 133
Union of Democratic Forces (UDF), 180-181
Unions, 166; Catholicism and, 212, 213; in
  Eastern Europe, 158, 185-186 (nn30, 40);
  free trade, 159, 171, 186 (n31)
United Nicaraguan Opposition (UNO), 115,
  116, 120, 124, 129 (n55), 130 (n58)
United States, 136, 170, 171, 185 (n18), 246;
  Catholic Church in, 215, 222; influence of,
  6, 123, 124
Universities, 200, 237
UNO. *See* United Nicaraguan Opposition
Uruguay, 6, 240

Values, 1, 8, 10, 62, 102; democratic, 47-50
Vatican II. *See* Second Vatican Council

Vekemans, Roger, 215, 221
Venezuela, 213, 214, 215, 217, 242, 243
*Verdad Los Hara Libres, La* (Gutierrez), 225
Violence, 17, 38, 49, 50, 179, 225; in political
  movements, 66-67
VONS, 160, 175
Voting, 33 (n81); and government, 46-47;
  patterns of, 145-147, 182-183
Voting rights, 111

Walesa, Lech, 165, 237
WiP. *See* Freedom and Peace Movement
Workers' Defense Committee (KOR), 163,
  167
Workers Party (PT), 225
Working class, 157-158, 159
World Bank: structural adjustment programs,
  86-87
World War II, 65
Writers' unions, 158-159

Yoruba, 62
Young Poland, 167
Young Turks, 191, 192, 195

Zaire, 69, 77, 82, 85, 87
Zambia, 76, 86
Zamora, Rubén, 225
Zhivkov, Todor, 172, 177, 180
Zimbabwe, 67
Zulu, 63

# About the Book

Part of an emerging intellectual trend that Gabriel Almond identifies as "the return to political culture," this book explores the complex and reciprocal interactions between a society's dominant beliefs, values, and attitudes about politics and the nature of its political system. The authors examine how political beliefs and values have affected the nature and limits of democracy in specific cases, and how these elements of political culture respond over time to social, political, and institutional changes. Among the issues they address are: to what extent is political culture cause or effect; how does one weigh its causal importance for democracy; what are the most important elements of a democratic political culture; and how are these developed over time?

263